MODELS OF POLITICAL ECONOMY

MODELS OF POLITICAL ECONOMY

Edited by
Paul Whiteley

SAGE Modern Politics Series   Volume 4
sponsored by the European Consortium for Political Research / ECPR

 SAGE Publications · London and Beverly Hills

Copyright © 1980 by
SAGE Publications Ltd.

For information address:

 SAGE Publications Ltd, 28 Banner Street London EC1Y 8QE
SAGE Publications Inc, 275 South Beverly Drive Beverly Hills
California 90212

British Library Cataloguing in Publication Data
Models of political economy. — (SAGE modern
politics series; vol. 4).
1. Economic history — 1945-
2. Economic policy
I. Whiteley, Paul   II. European Consortium
for Political Research
330.9   HC59   79-63823

ISBN 0-8039-9834-1
ISBN 0-8039-9835-X Pbk

First Printing

Contents

Foreword
Richard E. Wagner   1

Introduction
Paul Whiteley   7

**I   Modelling Politico-Economic
Interrelationships**

1   Electoral Outcomes and Macro-Economic Policies:
The Scandinavian Cases
Henrik J. Madsen   15

2   Popularity Functions:
The Case of the US and West Germany
Bruno Frey and Friedrich Schneider   47

3   Politico-Econometric Estimation in Britain:
An Alternative Interpretation
Paul Whiteley   85

4   Economic Conditions and Elections in France
Jean Jacques Rosa   101

5   Economic Conditions and Mass Support in Japan,
1960-1976
Takashi Inoguchi   121

II   The Political Business Cycle

6   Political Business Cycles in Britain
James Alt   155

7   The Political Business Cycle:
Alternative Interpretations
Gareth Locksley   177

III   Politics, Inflation and Economic Policy

8   Public Choice, Monetary Control and
Economic Disruption
Richard E. Wagner   201

9   The Demand for Inflation in
Liberal-Democratic Societies
John Burton   221

**IV   Formal Approaches to the Analysis
of Political Systems**

10   Equilibrium in a Political Economy
Norman Schofield   251

11   A Note on the Political Economy of Pure Space
Hans Schadee   277

12   Modelling Uncertainty in
Political Decision-Making
Hannu Nurmi   291

**V   Strategic Behaviour at the National
and International Levels**

13   Strategic Voting:
An Empirical Analysis with Dutch Roll Call Data
Menno Wolters   319

14   Economic Conditions and Conflict Processes
Dennis J. D. Sandole   343

Notes on Contributors   385

Foreword
Richard E. Wagner
Auburn University, USA

One of the noteworthy developments of this century has been the growing interdependence between the economy and the polity. A generally large and growing public sector in Western democracies is one frequently cited indication of this interdependence. Decisions about legislation and regulation can also influence significantly the profitability of business firms, leading to a complex network of reciprocal relations between the economy and the polity. In the division of academic labor, politics has been typically regarded as exogenous in the study of economics, while economic conditions have typically been regarded as exogenous in the study of politics. Only recently has there arisen a strong interest in treating the economy and the polity as endogenous to one another in democratic societies. The papers in this volume represent a part of the intensifying interest in the integrated treatment of politics and economics — the new political economy.

WELFARE ECONOMICS, ECONOMIC POLICY, AND THE PROBLEM OF POLITICS

A considerable part of economics, theoretical as well as applied, developed out of efforts to give advice on particular aspects of economic policy. David Ricardo's *Principles of Political Economy and Taxation*, for instance, was unified by its effort to explain the harmful properties of the Corn Laws in England at the time he wrote. While the concern over economic policy has been present since there has been any thinking on matters economic, welfare economics imposed a more formal structure on the develoment of policy advice. With respect to the allocation of resources, the state was assigned two primary tasks. One task was to ensure that the conditions of industrial production corresponded to those described by the model of a competitive economy. In some cases this would require state regulation of industry, while in other cases it might require state ownership of enterprise. The other task was to provide those services, called public goods, which it was felt could not be supplied efficiently within a market process because of the difficulty of excluding those who do not pay from consuming the service anyway.

Welfare economics was developed as a vehicle for offering normative advice on economic policy. The thrust of the analysis was to rationalize various types of public policy. The state subsidization of schooling, or the state operation of schools, was one type of policy rationalized by welfare economics. The purchase of education by one person was presumed to provide external benefits for others. From this presumption, the inference was drawn that too little education would be provided in a regime of private choice. Equilibrium in private choice will result when each person equates his marginal benefit from education with his marginal cost. By presumption, however, other people also receive benefits from the education received by any one person. The sum of the marginal benefits received from any person's education will therefore exceed the marginal cost. Each person acting individually will choose a lesser quantity of education than would be chosen if somehow the benefits received by external parties could also be incorporated into the choice.

It would be exceedingly difficult or prohibitively costly to attempt actually to organize the complicated pattern of individual contracts that would be necessary to achieve efficient provision within a market setting. This inability to achieve efficiency through individual choice leads to a rationalization for state support of education. State support in this instance is regarded as a lower cost method of accomplishing essentially the same thing as could be accomplished by the set of individual contracts, if only the cost of contracting were not prohibitive.

We have here a normative argument used as intellectual support for state subsidization or provision of education. This type of argument is, of course, of no value in developing an understanding of political-economic reality, for it offers no conceptually falsifiable statements. A critical problem of inference arises when the analytical focus is shifted to a positive understanding of actual processes of policy formation. While welfare economics may be used to rationalize a certain class of practice, the presence of that class of practice does not imply that the conditions postulated by the welfare analysis are present. Therefore, there is no necessary implication to the effect that the observed policy is producing the type of beneficial effects envisaged by the welfare rationalization. It is one thing to state that condition X implies the normative desirability of policy A. It is invalid, however, to infer that the presence of policy A implies the prior existence of condition X, a condition altered by policy A, if it is possible for policy A to have been created even in the absence of condition X.

Rather than developing a rationalization for subsidized education, an effort could be made to provide an explanation for the existence of subsidized education, or at least to show the inapplicability of some explanations. Did subsidized education develop as an effort to internalize external benefits that were sensed by the population? How does this explanation compare with such other possible explanations as that subsidized education represents the use of a public expenditure program to transfer income? Rather than being the outcome of a consensus about the desirability of more education, subsidization would be the outcome of a political contest in which some people were able to enrich themselves at the expense of others. In particular, people who could get more favorable terms of trde in the public sector would gain from those for whom the terms of trade would be unfavourable. With progressive taxation, the gainers would encompass, among others, a set of people with lower incomes and with larger families.

Alternatively, public subsidization could have been the outcome of a process of cultural imperialism, in which one dominant set of people in society wanted to shape or mould other people. Indeed, the arguments based on external benefits could easily be interpreted as a disguised form of cultural imperialism. The external benefit arguments for subsidized education argue for a greater degree of homogeneity than the articulators believe would exist if people possessed freedom of choice. If this is so, a choice must be made about which set of values and characteristics is to be reinforced, and which are to be erased. This choice is inherent in and implied by the external benefit argument that subsidization is necessary to promote greater commonality. The external benefit argument becomes a tool in the service of a ruling elite, and it is used to justify the imposition of their values on others, under the guise of promoting the common good.

My purpose here is not to try to determine the falsity of these different possible explanations for subsidized education. Rather, my purpose is only to show that there is no necessary relation between reality and the presuppositions of the normative argument that can be inferred from the presence or the absence of a particular policy. There is a missing link, namely a theory of the formation of economic policy in a democracy. The normative arguments proceed from the mind of the articulator to the development of policy. An economist with the ear of an enlightened despot might possibly be able to reach some inference from the presence of policy, but inference about policy is not so simple in a democracy.

A CLASH BETWEEN DEMOCRACY AND PROSPERITY?

In the normative theory of democracy, the purpose of state action is to enhance prosperity. Recent work in political economy has tended to suggest that there may be no necessary congruence between democracy and prosperity. Incongruity means that democratic politics contains negative sum features. In politics as in the market, the extent to which self-interest promotes positive-sum or negative-sum outcomes depends importantly on the incentives provided by and the knowledge produced within a particular institutional order. If, in a particular institutional order, the interests of politicians are promoted more effectively through actions and policies that are negative sum, we should expect such actions and policies to result. Several suggestions have arisen in recent years to suggest that there are important areas of economic life where state policies conflict with prosperity. Yet such policies are undertaken because within the existing institutional order they seem to be in the interest of those in charge of the political establishment.

The papers in this volume represent, from a variety of perspectives, an examination of the relation between democracy and prosperity, and an effort to integrate aspects of economics and politics. The first five papers contain studies of the relation between economic circumstances and political success in democracies. The main interest in this line of research is in whether economic circumstances can influence political success, an interest that in turn leads to a consideration of the use of political authority to enhance the incumbent party's chance of continued political control. Considerable disparity exists among the authors as to their findings about the relation between economic conditions and political success, indicating that considerable scope exists for future research, including possible reformulations of the research agenda.

The second section contains two papers on what has come to be called the political business cycle, while the third section contains two papers on politics and inflation. While the subjects of these two sections are somewhat different, they both deal with the conduct of macroeconomic policy in a democracy. The literature on the political business cycle suggests that democratic governments may be able to enhance their prospects of re-election by deliberately creating economic fluctuations, pursuing expansionary policies shortly before an election, followed by contractionary policies soon after the election. The literature on politics and inflation is related to that on political business cycles because there is a relation between inflation and fluctuations in economic activity. In this literature, an effort is made to understand the existence and the pattern of inflation as a natural outcome of a particular institutional order rather than being simply an accident.

The five papers in the fourth and fifth sections are not so directly concerned with the relation between democracy and prosperity as are the nine papers in the preceeding three sections. Section 4 contains three formal analyses of aspects of the theory of political economy, while Section 5 contains two empirical studies of political behaviour. While these five papers are less directly concerned with the relation between prosperity and democracy, such conceptual and empirical work of a more general nature is essential for the ultimate development of a better understanding of the relation between the economy and the polity.

Scholars interested in the development of a better understanding of the relation between the polity and the economy will find in this volume much that will be of use to them. This area of research is, of course, fairly recent, for it represents various attempts to explore topics that have long been felt to lie outside the boundaries of economics and politics, consequently tending to be ignored by practictioners of both disciplines. No doubt the research agenda will come to be clarified and reformulated in the years ahead. To date, there is not yet even a consensus as to the strength, or even the existence, of a possible conflict between prosperity and democracy. And even among those who see a conflict present, there is considerable difference as to the source of the fundamental points of conflict. And then there is the further matter of suggestions of what might be done to ameliorate this conflict, if it exists and if it can be understood.

Introduction

Paul Whiteley

University of Bristol, UK

Political Economy is simultaneously an old and a new discipline. It is a term which was originally used to describe the subject matter of contemporary economics, much of political science and an important element of present day sociology. Several academic chairs in the older universities, particularly in Scotland, are referred to as Chairs of Political Economy, although in practice this refers to economics. It is a new discipline in that a number of contemporary scholars with different subject backgrounds are developing a literature which is neither economics nor politics, but is both. The central concern of this hybrid subject is collective action, and how individual preferences are moulded and channelled by various institutions to produce a collective policy outcome. This development represents a new departure in the intellectual traditions of both economics and political science and has come about for a number of different reasons.

One reason relates to the contemporary stature of economics vis-à-vis the other social sciences. An academic generation ago economics was flushed with the success of post-war Keynesianism. Economic theory seemed to be able to approach the theoretical sophistication of the natural sciences. The doctrine that the economy could be 'fine tuned' to suit the preferences of decision makers was all the rage. Such certainties have collapsed, and the problem of adequately modelling the macro behaviour of the economy looks considerably more daunting than it did in the early sixties. This has led to a recognition of the importance of political concepts such as power, influence and social class. It is no longer true that political factors can be regarded as troublesome exogenous influences, or even irrational residual factors which interfere with the aesthetics of the neo-classical model. Anyone seriously trying to understand the aggregate behaviour of the international economy must incorporate political variables as being central to the operation of the system.

Such considerations also operate of course at the microeconomic level. Production and investment in the multi national corporation cannot be understood by the traditional framework of the analysis of perfect and imperfect competition, without regard to the political framework in which firms operate. In the traditional theory of the firm, the state is a corporate nightwatchman. The contrast between this and the reality of state subsidies, industrial pressure groups and state intervention in microeconomic decisions is too great to ignore. Another fundamentally important development at the micro level is the retreat of the market as a mechanism for resource allocation. In education, housing, health and social welfare wherever one looks in the western world the market is on the retreat as a mechanism for resource allocation. Traditionally microeconomics is essentially about market decision-making. This decline in the importance of the market has led to the development of the public choice literature which is an important component of the new political economy. For a period the public choice literature was almost wholly concerned with the impossibility of obtaining a collective decision which fairly represented individual preferences in a society. This followed the celebrated work by Kenneth Arrow. But it has now developed into a much wider field, while retaining the distinctive methodological approach of economics.

Even now though, the public choice tradition retains the ideological bias of its intellectual origins. Non-market collective action is often seen at best as problematic, and at worst as illiberal. On the other hand, market allocation is seen for the most part as an ideal type system which provides for the greatest happiness of the greatest number. The fact that the retreat of the market has been caused by mass collective action through the ballot box or through revolution does not seem to disturb this ideological perspective for most of its adherents. If the market provides the greatest good for the greatest number why has the arrival of democratic politics led to its demise in large areas of policy? Such a fundamental question is bound to lead to a crisis in the traditional paradigm, which will further divorce the public choice approach from the traditional concerns of economics.

Up to this point I have stressed developments in economics which have brought about a movement towards a new political economy. But there have been important developments in political science which have also done this. A generation ago the behavioural revolution swept American political science, and now after considerable modification it is the dominant paradigm in western political science. It was originally a reaction against the descriptive, insitutionalist and normative preoccupations of the traditional subject. In essence it advocates a model building and testing approach to political analysis, and in this respect the mainstream of political science has come closer to the mainstream of economics. Of course important differences between the disciplines still exist, but the subjects are closer to each other in the methodological approach than ever before in the twentieth century. Clearly this makes the climate for inter-disciplinary cooperation more congenial.

On the general point of the climate of inter-disciplinary cooperation, there have been a number of developments in recent years which have fostered cross-disciplinary work. One important factor is the re-emergence of Marxism in economics. Though not central to the new political economy, Marxism has made a vital contribution, because it recognizes no subject demarcations. Social analysis is approached simultaneously from a philosophical, sociological, political and economic perspective. Thus the revival of Marxism has re-introduced concepts to economics which have been neglected for decades. There are other influences on the intellectual climate which have fostered interdisciplinary work. Systems theory through the work of writers like Easton and Deutsch has brought a common core of concepts to bear on diverse problems in politics. Structuralism has also, to a lesser extent, generated a cross-disciplinary intellectual climate.

It is perhaps appropriate at this point to be rather more specific about the subject matter of the new political economy. It has been variously described as 'positive political theory', 'formal political

theory', 'economic approaches to politics', and so on. To clarify
the discussion it is useful to adopt the definition applied by Riker
and Ordeshook, which provides a research agenda:

> We have thus at least three central processes of politics: the selection of societies'
> preferences, the enforcement of choices that revealed them, and, finally, the pro-
> duction of goals or outputs that embody the choices.

This is comprehensive enough to incorporate the recent
developments of the subject. It incorporates the Public Choice
literature which grew out of Welfare Economics and Public
Finance. It incorporates the work on spatial modelling of party
competition and voter preferences, and also the work on conflict
processes arising out of game theory. It would involve structural
equation modelling of the economy which incorporate political
variables, and various departures in political theory which use a rational choice framework.

The present volume grew out of the European Consortium for
Political Research Workshop on formal political analysis at the
University of Grenoble, at Easter 1978. The original call for papers
asked for contributions which particularly emphasized the importance of empirical analysis in political economy. In the event, a
core of papers emerged around the theme of politico-economic interactions, and the relationship between the political and economic
systems. The papers are divided into five sections which serve to
emphasize the diversity of modern political economy, but a diversity which operates within a common methodological approach.

The largest section is concerned with the politico-econometric
estimation of the relationship between the economy and the polity.
This has caused a number of methodological, statistical and
theoretical problems, but the five papers bring together evidence
from a number of western countries concerning the electoral impact of government economic policy, and also the influence of electoral considerations on economic policy-making. The section on
political business cycles serves to examine the literature on this
topic, and the empirical validity of the concept of a political cycle
in the case of Britain. The papers in the section on politics, inflation and economic policy focus on the key problems of inflation in
western democracies and the role particularly of political factors in
influencing the rate of inflation. The fourth section develops some

formal theses in the literature on collective action, but themes which have significant empirical implications. Finally, the section on strategic behaviour is concerned with the relationship between individual behaviour and the collective policy outcome, at the national and cross-national levels.

I would like to thank the contributors for their time and effort, particularly Professor Richard Wagner for providing the foreword. They should also be thanked for adhering to a pretty tight publication schedule. I would also like to thank the ECPR, particularly Professor Jean Blondel, the former Executive Director, for providing the institutional framework for bringing together contributors. The primary aim of this reader is to stimulate ideas and research in political economy. The workshop from which it arose was an enjoyable and stimulating experience. I hope that some of the enthusiasm which was generated communicates itself to the reader.

Paul Whiteley
Bristol, February 1979

1 Modelling Politico-Economic Interrelationships

1 Electoral Outcomes and Macro-Economic Policies: The Scandinavian Cases

Henrik J. Madsen

Harvard University, USA, and
University of Aarhus, Denmark

THE QUESTION

> When you are together with politicians they always ask you what the economy is
> going to be like at the next election.
>
> A. Lindbeck, lecture, Yale 1977.

Several studies of short-term fluctuations in US voting behaviour
have confirmed the sensitivity of electoral outcomes to changing
economic conditions. Generally, incumbent parties benefit from
favourable ones and experience net vote loss when times are less
prosperous.[1]

This paper addresses the possible generalizability of these findings to the Scandinavian countries, a subsample of a larger set of
Western democracies which eventually shall be included in this inquiry. Several considerations make such generalizability less obvious. Non-Americal electorates are generally considered more prone to class-voting or seem more ideologically bent. Even though the

macro-findings of Kramer and others clearly do not imply a pervasive rationality of some sort in the electorate at large, the existence of firm partisan allegiances may very well destroy the relation between economic conditions and net vote change at the aggregate level.

Most non-US countries are heavily trade-dependent. Hence, fluctuations in the world economy seem as important for domestic economic conditions as national governmental policies.

The Model

An appropriate model specification for vote fluctuations is particularly difficult in the case of multiparty systems with possible coalition governments as opposed to a two-party system with only one party incumbent. This can perhaps best be illustrated if we take as our starting point the model which Kramer[2] introduced and which is a special case of the general two-party model entertained by Fair

$$z_t = V_t + \delta(\alpha + \beta\Delta_t) + \epsilon_t \tag{1}$$

The net gain for party zl at an election, l, in which it is incumbent is

$$zl_l = V_l + \alpha + \beta\Delta_l \tag{2}$$

z_t is the vote share for one of the 2 parties in the system, in the following denoted Z.1 and Z.2, say Z.1. 't' indexes the election.
V is a long term normal vote, possibly constant.
δ is equal to $+1$ if Z.1 is incumbent
           -1 otherwise.
α is a constant denoting the net effect of incumbency.
Δ is some measure of the difference between the actual and expected performance of the economy as assessed by the electorate.
β is a parameter representing the effect of such difference.
ϵ is an error term with zero mean, constant variance and zero covariance.

The model captures in a parsimonious way the basic choice for a voter in a two-party or two-bloc system. If dissatisfied with the incumbent — and only economic conditions are assumed to be a systematic source of such dissatisfaction — he can only vote for the non-incumbent to bring about a change in government.[3]

If, however, we allow for more than two parties, the choice of any voter is hardly adequately presented in (1). Dissatisfaction with the incumbent party may benefit any one of a number of parties. Party zl can, when incumbent, experience net loss of votes as a result of less favourable economic conditions, yet need not experience net gain when another incumbent party faces a dissatisfied electorate.

Being incumbent at election t, (1) then reduces to

$$z_{t,i} = V_{t,i} + \alpha + \beta \Delta_t + \epsilon_t \tag{3}$$

where i indexes the incumbent parties. The vote for the incumbent party at time 't' is a linear combination of its normal vote share, V_i, an incumbency advantage plus a net gain depending upon the extent to which voters' expectations have been fulfilled. Equation (2) is not estimable containing as it does two constant terms.

As our interest centres on estimation of short-term fluctuations rather than long-term trends, the V- terms are of less interest. A convenient and not too implausible assumption which will dispense with them is to regard the normal vote for any one party as a simple arithmetic average of vote shares received in previous k elections.

$$\hat{V}_i(t) = \sum_{j=i}^{j} V_i(t-j)/k \tag{4}$$

Rewriting (3) and changing notation then yields

$$Y_t = z_{t,i} - V_{i,t} = \alpha + \beta \Delta_t + \mu_t \tag{5}$$

Net vote deviation is a sum of some typical change α, an effect arising from the state of the economy and some factors unique to each election, μ_t (particular events such as scandals, media gimmick etc.) whose net effect on average is nil and which is uncorrelated through time.

The simple model in (5) ignores macroscopic changes (mobilization of the social and regional peripheries, the changing economic role of the state etc.) to the extent that they are not adequately represented by the assumptions about μ .

Before embarking upon less parsimonious specifications, however, it does seem worthwhile to explore how far simple models will bring us.

The Estimation

The period considered is 1920-73. Specification of the dependent variable met certain difficulties. In applying (5), a complication arises from the fact that coalition governments have been rather frequent in Denmark. It seems dubious that coalition parties will experience proportionately identical deviations from their respective normal vote, particularly if they are of vastly different size, making them — in the minds of voters — unequally responsible for past policies.

I shall assume that the party supplying the Prime Minister gets both the blame and the benefit. Accordingly, in the case of Denmark, $y(t)$ denotes the deviation from the normal vote share of the coalition dominant party as defined above. As the model in (5) does not allow the disentanglement of a prime ministerial personality effect (cf. Presidential coat-tails in the US context) we assume such net effect to be nil. The average of three previous elections was chosen as the normal vote.

Various indicators of economic conditions were included as independent variables. The most frequently used indicators of the general state of the economy are change in real GDP per capita, rate of inflation, level of and net change in unemployment, all in the year of election. This specification in effect amounts to a particularly simple assumption about voters' expectations being formed from the experience of the preceding year only. This assumption has been empirically justified within the US context by Fair.

During the period we are considering — i.e. 1920 to 1975 — all three countries have experienced a secular growth of the public sector. We should therefore allow for the importance of taxation, both in the sense that it would seem appropriate to control for the typically increasing taxation when estimating the effect of other variables, and in the sense that changes in tax revenue in itself may be a source of electoral response. However, in case of fully tax-financed public outlay, the change in taxation is a proxy variable (as transfers cannot be separated) for increase in public provision of goods and services. The plausible assumption that voters are both tax-averse and positively value such provision leaves the sign of the tax parameter ambiguous.

We expect that rise in real GDP per capita, controlling for taxation, leads to net gains for incumbents, whereas high or net increase in unemployment as well as inflation causes net loss. Table 1 summarizes our a priori expectations and presents the abbreviations for the variables.

Equation (5) with Δ_t appropriately specified was estimated for Denmark, Norway, and Sweden from the end of World War I — i.e. after full franchise, parliamentarism, and proportional representation were institutionalized — to 1975, excluding war-time elections in Denmark and Sweden as well as the Danish and the Norwegian 1945-elections were virtually all-encompassing coalitions faced the electorate.

TABLE 1

Variable	Abbreviation	Expected sign of parameter
Per cent increase in real GDP per capita	REALGD	+
Level of unemployment	U	—
Net change of unemployment	UCHG	—
Inflation	CPI	—
Per cent increase in tax revenue	TAX	?

The results are reported in Tables 2-4. The fit varies across countries and between spefications. No single specification shows the best performance for all three countries.

Inflation has played some role in influencing electoral outcomes.

The sign of the inflation parameter is consistently negative, it often has a plausible magnitude, but is precise only in the case of Denmark. In fact, among the economic variables included, only inflation seems systematically related to Danish election results. The effect of unemployment — both in the 'level' and 'change-of-levels' form — shows anomalous sign a few times but is in any case very imprecise. Sometimes, however, the estimate of the effect of net change in unemployment suggests a non-negligible, although uncertain effect. A non-significant or even anomalous effect of unemployment has been found in other studies as well.[4]

The argument that the actual or potentially unemployed are less politically mobilized can only be part of an explanation, first because turnout levels generally have been high, second because people other than the unemployed and their families are affected by slack in the economy. The negligible effect is hardly due to the fact

TABLE 2

Denmark. Dependent Variable: Deviation from Normal Vote of Coalition Dominant Party (in per cent)

Coefficient of	(1)	(2)	(3)
α	0.59	1.3	0.86
	(2.7)	(1.3)	(1.7)
CPI	-0.42	-0.43	
	(0.28)	(0.23)	
U	0.07		
	(0.16)		
UCHG		0.19	
		(0.26)	
REALGH			0.25
			(0.38)
TAX			0.10
			(0.23)
R^2	0.26	0.28	0.11
Durbin-Watson Statistics = D.W.	2.2	2.2	2.0
Number of Observations = Numobs.	16	16	16

Standard error of the estimates in parentheses.

TABLE 3
Norway. Dependent Variable: Deviation from Normal Vote
of Incumbent Parties (in per cent)

Coefficient of	(1)	(2)	(3)	(4)
α	0.98	0.27	0.37	0.29
	(2.5)	(1.5)	(1.4)	(1.5)
CPI	-0.36	-0.15		
	(0.48)	(0.41)		
U	-0.10			
	(0.17)			
UCHG		0.05		
		(0.38)		
REALGD			-0.22	-0.22
			(0.28)	(0.3)
TAX				0.03
				(0.16)
R^2	0.07	0.04	0.05	0.05
D.W.	1.2	1.2	1.4	1.4
Numobs.	13	13	13	13

that lower levels of activity were politically more acceptable in the prewar period when employees had no peace-time experience of anything approaching full employment. The minimum rate of unemployment in the pre-war period was close to identical to the post-war maximum. The change in levels of unemployment which can be perceived as one simple way of taking such shifting expectations into account does not generally perform better. Only in the case of Sweden does change of unemployment seem to exert a considerable influence upon the fate of the incumbent. The accuracy with which the unemployed are counted as well as changing definitions of unemployment may play a role, and post-war unemployment compensation close to normal earnings — making unemployment less of a social hardship (and a less effective instrument in aggregate demand management) — would seem important.

The truly puzzling finding is the negative, but entirely insignificant effect of an increase in real GDP per capita, perhaps the best single indicator of overall economic well-being. With taxes held

TABLE 4
Sweden. Dependent Variable: Deviation from Normal Vote of Incumbent Parties (in per cent)

Coefficient of	(1)	(2)	(3)	(4)
α	2.2	0.18	1.3	-3.0
	(3.5)	(1.0)	(1.2)	(1.0)
CPI	-0.45	-0.29	-0.22	
	(0.56)	(0.26)	(0.26)	
Log U*	-1.3			
	(1.6)			
UCHG		-1.0	-2.4	
		(0.26)	(1.0)	
REALGD				0.73
				(0.26)
R^2	0.07	0.37	0.47	0.4
D.W.	2.6	1.7	2.4	1.9
Numobs.	12	13	13	13

*The natural logarithm of the rates of unemployment, suggested by scatterplots. In substantive terms, the net vote loss was proportionally less at high rates of unemployment. As high rates were prevailing before World War II. The estimates in effect imply that high unemployment was marginally more costly in terms of vote shares after the war.

constant, the Danish and Norwegian estimates indicate a negative effect upon the net deviation from the normal vote. We shall return to possible explanations for this later on. Sweden, on the other hand, shows a very strong positive effect.

We can conclude then that fluctuations in the vote share for Swedish incumbent parties are consistent with the proposition that the electorate in the aggregate responds to changing economic conditions. Figure 1 shows a plot of the dependent variable against percent change in real GDP per capita. Inspection of the residuals did not suggest additional variables. The sign of the net vote share deviation was correctly predicted in 9 out of 13 cases. The predictions with incorrect sign — occurring in 1924, 1958, 1960, and 1968 — do not appear to show any systematic trait. The two most recent elections included in this study are overpredicted which may be suggestive of rising, but unfulfilled expectations. The results for Sweden match the findings by Lewin and his associates.[5] Their principal components — used to account for interregional vote variations at each election — consistently include one or more dimensions of close relevance to economic conditions if not identical with them, e.g. unemployment, income, wealth and mobility.

FIGURE 1
Sweden. Scatterplot of Per Cent Change in Real GDP
per Capita against Net Vote Deviation

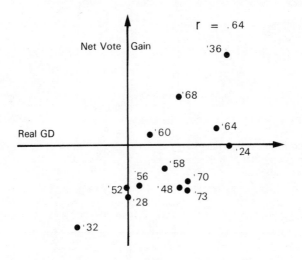

The Danish and Norwegian electorates — the latter in particular — have shown little or no systematic response to change in economic conditions as measured by our aggregate indices. Alternative specifications of the dependent variable both in terms of specifying the normal vote and in terms of including and deleting parties for Denmark and Norway, respectively, did not produce more satisfactory fits.

FIGURE 2
Denmark: Net Deviation of Normal Vote

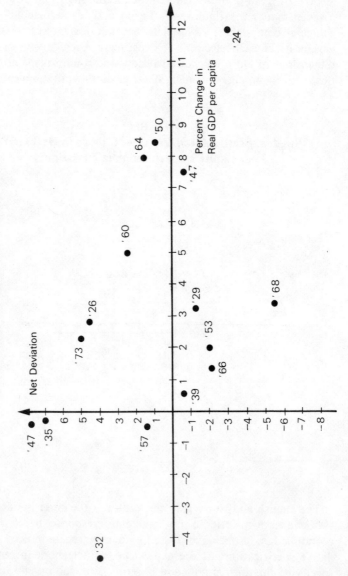

Figures 2 and 3 show the relationship between the dependent variable and percent change in real GDP per capita for Denmark and Norway respectively. They both reveal the simple fact that no apparent link exists between electoral outcomes and the state of economy as measured in this paper, although one may argue that, generally, one should perhaps concentrate on observations where the government loses or where the GDP-variable, say, is negative, as one might expect higher informational content in those cases.[6]

FIGURE 3
Norway: Net Deviation from Normal Vote

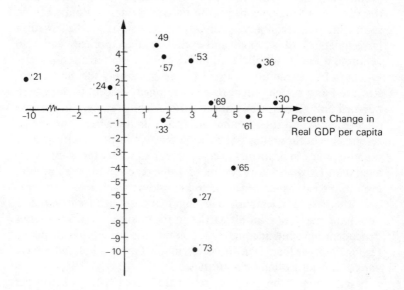

Conclusions

Earlier I ventured doubts as to the generalizability of the US evidence that '. . . election outcomes are in substantial part responsive to objective changes occurring under the incumbent party. . .'[7]

If estimates for all three countries had shown negligible effects, we supposedly would have had little difficulty in explaining the result. The countries are all extremely exposed to fluctuations in the international economy, and we might have looked at the results as corroborating a conjecture that governments had succeeded in making voters understand that; or we might have concluded that class identifications were so pervasive as to blurr the electorate's reaction.

However, the results for Sweden make any one of these interpretations problematic. It is true that Sweden perhaps more than the two other countries has taken an active interventionist role in stabilizing the economy. 'Already in the thirties the Swedish governments had adopted anti-cyclical budget policies and also ventured upon such policies', but full-fledged stabilization policies — apart from traditional fiscal policy measures, the Investment Reserve Fund system ought to be mentioned — seem to have been pursued only since the end of the fifties.[8] The argument in the case of Sweden would then be that governments have been considered responsible because they openly took on such responsibility and/or because policy instruments to counteract temporary recessions were available. However, a pronounced voter reaction appears present even in the early part of the period considered.

In the case of Denmark one might hypothesize that neither a dominant party nor an all-parties-in-the-coalition version of our dependent variable adequately represents the perception of policy responsibility which Danish voters might have had. It may have varied with parties and circumstances.[9]

In any event, the evidence seems so inconclusive and proper specification problems appear so insurmountable that further analysis may profit from less aggregate cross-section studies.

It is interesting to note that studies using micro-data and employing a model with some affinity to the implict assumption of this study have met similar problems in accounting for Norwegians' (reported) vote. Budge and Farlie's (1977) modified rational choice model of individual voting decisions, combining background characteristics with issue orientations,[10] did less well when compared to their estimates for Sweden.

The per cent correspondence between reported individual vote and the individual vote estimated by their model (using predispositions as well as cues) was 74.0 and 72.0 for the elections of 1957 and 1965, respectively, compared to 82.0 for Sweden.[11] The fact that their model, which generally yields remarkably good fits, performed comparatively less well is not, of course, tantamount to obtaining anomalous signs of parameter estimates. Their results, however, do suggest the need to look beyond the ecological fallacy argument and focus on more substantive issues.[12]

A recurring theme on Norwegian politics is the centre periphery question.[13] Our aggregate economic indices neglect distributional considerations, but we might argue that Norwegian voters in particular have been concerned about the distributional effect of economic growth, especially its differential regional impact.[14] The refusal to join the common market voted in a referendum and the ambiguous enthusiasm for the oil-boom are more recent examples of such concern. To many Norwegians, economic growth meant leaving the small coastal enclave or the small family farm and moving into larger towns or cities with a secularized culture and — since World War II — housing shortage. Provisionally, we may put forth the conjecture that economic growth in the aggregate has been accompanied by reinforcement of regional imbalances which have offset any net gain for the incumbent party/parties.[15]

THE GOVERNMENT AND THE ECONOMY

...an entertaining literature on the political business cycle...
F. Modigliani, Presidential Address, AEA 1976.

In section 1 we looked at the electoral response to macroeconomic conditions. Another set of questions provides an equally interesting aspect of this electoral economic interaction; in brief: do governments manipulate the economy in some systematic fashion? At issue here is not whether politics affects the economy — it does — but whether there is distinct short-term manipulation of the economy geared towards the pursuit of victory at the polls possibly reflecting distinct class bases of incumbent parties.[16] The answer to such questions would seem to have important bearings on the wider and more general problems of public policy determinants, in particular the role of partisan politics.[17]

Two main strains of arguments can be distinguished in the literature. On the one hand, a partisan variant theory formulated by Hibbs;[18] on the other, various partisan invariant accounts dealing with short-term changes in the economy.

Hibbs argues that incumbent political parties pursue the economic policy objectives which are in broad accordance with the objective and subjective interests of the group they represent. In general, parties of the left will be more averse to unemployment than parties of the right who are in turn more averse to inflation.[19] On the other hand, there are partisan invariant theories such as Nordhaus's in which the governmental party manipulates the short run trade-off between unemployment and inflation, the Phillips curve, in order to maximize its chances of being elected.[20]

For reasons to be explicated in a moment, Norway and Sweden only provide the empirical setting for estimating electoral cycles. It does seem clear, that some type of Phillips trade-off is discernible for at least of part of the post-war period.[21]

In regard to Hibbs' theory, the distributional consequences of various policy mixes as well as the class preferences have not been explored. The Social-democratic parties — which naturally will receive primary interest due to their dominant position — would seem to exhibit a class distinctiveness no less than that of Labour in Great Britain.[22] The conclusive test, however, clearly is provided by analysis of the economic policies. Choosing indicators of such policies meets several difficulties. First, there is a problem of neglect. For example, Maddison observes that

> ...(in post war Europe)...there has been a reluctance to apply anti-cyclical controls to (the housing sector), even though it was often a leading source of inflationary pressure and was a competing bidder for the scarce resources needed for productive investment.[23]

If an instrument has been used rarely, if at all (for the moment ignoring complex problems of deciding when which instrument should have been applied) then we can only infer that politics matter in economic policy-making, which seems an observation bordering on the obvious. Theoretical as well as statistical considerations require that any instrument for influencing electoral outcomes exhibit some variability over time.

Second, we have the problem of instrument switching. Over a span of electoral periods, different instruments may be used for attaining certain targets. A focus on one particular instrument therefore may give misleading results. This suggests giving attention to some broader economic variables reflecting the use of several instruments or to the economic targets themselves. Particularly in single equation models, properly controlling for other sources of influence then becomes important in order to avoid erroneous inferences.

I decided to give primary attention to one measure of rate of unemployment (which is available on a quarterly basis) and government final consumption expenditure (for which only yearly data exist over a longer time period). The rate of unemployment has been at the centre of interest in the political business cycle literature. It would seem to be the concern of the electorate as well, and it is in itself a not too invalid quarterly indicator of the state of the economy.

Current government spending on goods and services has a more direct instrument character and should be of interest as such. Although reduction of the public outlay can only be achieved with great difficulty in the short run — due to the quasiautomatic character of most items in the public budget[24] — varying degrees of expansion are feasible. Estimating electoral cycles for government spending has been done by Frey and Schneider.[25] Hypothesizing public expenditure cycles requires some assumption about asymmetric reaction of the electorate to taxes and expenditures — for example along the lines of a fiscal illusion argument.[26] Norway provides an especially fortuitous setting for assessing the business cycle hypotheses in one variant or another. Social Democrats and Bourgeois parties (as the Scandinavian saying goes) have alternated in office separated by constitutionally fixed elections. Hence, the endogenous timing of elections which seems to mar various estimated models in the literature is happily dispensed with. Further, Norway is a particularly strong case for testing the Nordhaus version of the political business cycle. The author noticed that among the countries included in his test sample, those economies with somewhat greater emphasis upon planning government expenditure policies showed less indication of electoral cycles; this fact made him conjecture that some planning framework would create impediments for such cycles as it would force governments

> ...to set down their policy and negotiate this policy...with labour and management and perhaps other interest groups. It would therefore be difficult for a government to persuade the other interest groups to accept a plan which deliberately projects a political business cycle or uses myopic decision rules.[27]

The Norwegian government instituted its first national plan in 1945 in order to deal more adequately with post-World War II reconstruction problems. It encompassed the public and in somewhat less detail the private sector of the economy. Since 1954 the national plan has coincided with the 4 year electoral period.[28]

Except for 1958, Swedish elections have been held at a regular interval of four years until 1970,[29] when an election was made necessary by the introduction of a new constitution; according to this, elections shall be called every three years. Denmark was excluded for consideration partly because a suspected endogeneity of some elections would impede estimation, partly because others came about by early dissolutions after defeat in Parliament.

The Models

What follows is a particularly simple way of modelling the electoral cycle. Assume a simple preference function, u_t^* indicating the level of unemployment which governments for one reason or another prefer. Following Hibbs' account

$$u_t^* = Iu_t^S + (1-I) u_t^B \tag{1}$$

Each bloc — the Social Democratic (= S) and the Bourgeois (= B) — has a preferred and distinct level. I is an appropriately defined incumbency index (with values equal to *0* or *1*). Clearly,

$$u_t^S < u_t^B \tag{2}$$

is implied by the theory. A parsimonious representation will come about if we assume that partisan unemployment targets are symmetric around some 'natural' or normal rate, say u^N, such that (1) can be rewritten as

$$u_t^* = u_t^N + PA \, u_t^P \tag{3}$$

PA being the previously defined incumbency index with values $[-1, +1]$. The partisan invariant theory may be specified as

$$u_t^* = PEu_t^E + (1 - PE)u_t^{NE} \tag{4}$$

where EL is a pre-election dummy having a value of $+1$ (and zero otherwise) for some period prior to the election. Of course

$$u_t^E < u_t^{NE} \tag{5}$$

The pre-election rate of unemployment must be lower than the rate at other periods. Like the relation in (1) it may be simplified as

$$u_t^* = u_t^N + PEu_t^E \tag{6}$$

Before elections the preferred rate of unemployment is below some normal (and possibly constant) rate

$$u_t^N: {}_t^E < 0$$

Assume further that governments — due to institutional inertia, painfulness of excessively rapid adjustments etc. — can only partially adjust to their preferred target. This adjustment process is subject to random shocks (denoted ϵ_t) arising from the international economy, the weather etc., factors which supposedly are uncorrelated through time.

$$u_t - u_{t-1} = \phi(u_t^* - u_{t-1}) + \epsilon_t \tag{7}$$
$$0 < \phi < 1$$

or alternatively

$$u = (1 - \phi)u_{-1} + \phi u^* + \epsilon \tag{8}$$

where the time index has been suppressed and lagged values appear subscripted. A relation such as (8) is almost certainly misspecified by leaving out important factors affecting the general level of employment. While we can hardly hope for a fully correct model, it would seem important to control for at least some of those factors. Small open economies are evidently dependent upon economic fluctuations in their external environment. This suggests inclusion of a factor supposedly measuring such — exogeneously given — impulses. We call this variable W and add it to the model in (8):

$$u = (1 - \phi) u_{-1} + \phi u^* + \beta_1 W + \epsilon \qquad (9)$$

Inserting (3) and (6) in (9) yields the complete model

$$u = (1 - \phi) u_{-1} + \phi u^N + \phi PAu^P + \phi PEu^E = \beta W + \epsilon \qquad (10)$$

ϕ, u^N, u^P, u^E and β are parameters to be estimated; u, PA, PE and W are variables. Some variant of (10) can be applied to Norway, whereas only (9) with (6) inserted has relevance for Sweden.

Denoting government expenditure at time t by G_t, a specification in equivalently parsimonious vein as above would simply be G_t as some function of time with an election dummy plus a random disturbance

$$G_t = g \,(\text{Time, election variable}) + \text{error term.} \qquad (11)$$

In linear form

$$G_t = \beta_0 + \beta_1 \text{TIME} + \beta_2 \text{EL} = \mu_t \qquad (12)$$

EL is a dummy, equal to _1_ in the election year, for instance, and zero otherwise. μ_t captures the effect of idiosyncratic factors in the budgetary process, manifests of the issue attention cycles, unexpected expenditure needs etc. which are assumed independent through time. The incrementalist literature has pointed out the implausibility of such assumption.[30] Accordingly we incorporate a lagged dependent variable signifying bureaucratic pressure for larger appropriations using the ones of last year as a base level and more generally representing any political pressure arising from prior expenditure commitments.

$$G = (\beta_0) + \beta_1 EL + \beta_2 G_{-1} + \nu_t \tag{13}$$

β_0 appears bracketed as it has no theoretical meaning in a strict incrementalist interpretation.[31] We a priori expect β_1 positive and β_2 larger than one. As noted previously, Swedish governments are noticed for having made use of the public budget for counter-cyclical purposes; for this reason our a priori regarding β_1 should not be too strong in this case.

The indicator of the quarterly rate of unemployment was defined as (No. of Unemployed — No. of Vacancies) as per cent of labour force deseasonalized. The inclusion of vacancies seems preferable to simply taking the number of unemployed as per cent of total labour force. The UV variant expresses the positive or negative net surplus of employment opportunities and hence reflects use of several measures to either stimulate or dampen the economy.

General Government spending employing the most recent OECD definition was expressed in fixed 1970 prices (national currencies).[32] In the case of Norway the Partisan dummy (PA) was set equal to -1 in periods with Social Democratic governments supported by a majority in Parliament, $+1$ for Bourgeois governments and zero otherwise. Various lags in this variable were entertained as we had no theoretical reason for imposing any particular one.

The quarterly election variable was set equal -1 in the quarter of election plus the preceding three quarters. The yearly election variable was defined as $+1$ in year t if election was held in the latter part of that year. The indicator of fluctuations in the world economy (W) constructed as the per cent change in total world import standardized by the US import index averaged over current and past three quarters.[33] A one quarter lag was used.

The Results

Minor variants of equations (10) and (13) were estimated for Norway, (9) cum (6) and (13) for Sweden. The results with appropriate test statistics are reported below. The Norwegian rate of unemployment has been subject to a downward trend through the period; a simple time trend was included as suggested by the residuals of preliminary estimations. Table 5 gives the final maximum likelihood results for

$$u = (1-\phi)u_{-1}+\phi u^N+\phi\beta_1 TIME+\phi PA\ u^P+\phi PEu^E+\beta_2 W+\epsilon \qquad (14)$$

The current rate of quarterly unemployment is hypothesized to be a function of its immediate past, a time specific 'normal' unemployment level, fluctuations in the world economy, the partisan character of government and a political-electoral cycle where governments succeed in lowering the rate of unemployment before the election. We expect that $u^P>0$ and $u^E<0$. The PA-variable showed anomalous signs for a lag of 1, 2 and 3 quarters (and did likewise with the EL and the W variables excluded), but the remaining coefficients were all stable across specifications, of plausible magnitude and fairly precise. There was little indication of the inadequacy of the simple error structure assumed. In comparing the partisan with the external impact we note that a 4 quarter sustained expansion of the world activity of about 0.33 per cent would offset any partisan deviation from a normal employment level. On the other hand, a contraction of a little more than 4 per cent is necessary for neutralizing the electoral cycle effect.[34] The estimates suggestively bear out the relevance of the observations Rokkan made some ten years ago.

> ...Labor leaders have not only had to cope with increasing pressures for a recognition of income differentials and hierarchies of economic status...Their concern to attract the middle class softened their ideological stands and brought them closer to the 'bourgeois' opposition....[35]

They correspond to our prior notions as well. It seems unlikely that governments in a small open economy actually can manage to keep the general level of activity at a permanently distinct level. It appears much more plausible, on the other hand, that they can succeed in accomplishing a temporary boom before the election.

TABLE 5
Norway: Estimation of Partisan, External and Electoral Effect.
Dependent Variable: Quarterly Rate of Unemployment

PA$_{-i}$	(1) i = 3	(2) i = 4
Estimate of ϕ	0.25	0.25
	(0.07)	(0.07)
u^N	1.36	1.44
	(1.26)	(0.28)
β_1	-.003	0.004
	(0.001)	(0.001)
u^P	-0.05	0.007
	(0.12)	(0.13)
u^E	-0.09	-0.09
	(0.05)	(0.05)
β_2	-0.02	-0.02
	(0.01)	(0.01)
R^2	0.83	0.83
Durbin's h	-0.68	-0.68
No of observations	77	77

Estimated Equation: (14)
Method of Estimation: Maximum Likelihood
Period: 1955.2-1974.2
Mean of Dependent Variable: 0.64
Approximate Standard Errors in Parentheses.

Equation (9) with (4) inserted only was applied to Sweden

$$u = (1 - \phi)u_{-1} + \phi u^N + \phi PEu^E + \beta_2 W + \epsilon \qquad (15)$$

The seriously correlated residuals from ordinary least squares made some other estimation procedure necessary.[36] Results are presented in Table 6. They are somewhat discouraging. The residually adjusted estimates do not generally yield parameters of expected sign, but they are in any event extremely small and uncertain. (Using the non-adjusted series by appropriate inclusion of seasonal dummies did show virtually identical results).

TABLE 6
Sweden: Estimation of External and Electoral Effect.
All Elections. Dependent Variable:
Quarterly Rate of Unemployment

	(1) OLS	(2) CO
Estimate of ϕ	0.07	0.17
	(0.04)	(0.07)
u^N	0.03	-0.04
	(0.04)	(0.05)
u^E	-0.02	0.01
	(0.04)	(0.05)
β_1	-0.02	-0.003
	(0.01)	(0.01)
ρ	—	0.52
R^2	0.07	0.20
χ^2	7.0	0.46
No of Observations	76	75

Estimated Equation: (15)
Method of Estimation: OLS, CO
Period: 1956.4 — 1975.3
Mean of Dependent Variable: -0.28

By including the 1958 election we may have misspecified the electoral variable. Accordingly, (15) was reestimated excluding this election. Table 7 gives the results. Although the estimated parameters exhibit the signs expected a priori, they are still small and imprecise. In such case, non-robustness to even minor changes of observation values is inevitable. We shall discuss this autonomy of the generally low unemployment rate more fully below. At this point we conclude that only the most tenuous evidence does support an election cycle.

The estimates of expenditure cycles are given in Tables 8 and 9. Figures 4 and 5 provide plots of per cent yearly change. Table 8 confirms the previous results for Norway. Public expenditures have accelerated during years of election adding about 1 per cent on average to a mean growth of 5 per cent.

TABLE 7
Sweden: Estimation of External and Electoral Effect.
Excluding the 1958 election. Dependent Variable:
Quarterly Rate of Unemployment

	(1) OLS	(2) CO
Estimate of ϕ	0.07 (0.04)	0.15 (0.06)
u^N	0.04 (0.04)	0.03 (0.05)
u^E	-0.05 (0.04)	-0.02 (0.05)
β_1	-0.02 (0.01)	-0.003 (0.01)
ρ	—	0.46
R^2	0.08	0.19
χ^2	9.71	2.6
No of Observations	76	75

The virtually perfect fit should of course be understood cum grano salis as one would expect a very high R^2 in this type of equation. There is little evidence of autocorrelation so we should be able to accept the OLS-estimates. A rough diagnostic type evaluation is reestimation using first order differences or per cent changes. Estimates from this correspond closely to the estimates in level form.

The precision and plausible magnitude of the parameters leave little doubt as to the existence of an electorally timed expenditure cycle the planning of which supposedly is made possible by the coincidence of the national budget horizon and the fixed electoral periods. The per cent yearly change in expenditure is shown in Figure 4.[37]

In the case of Sweden no evidence whatsoever suggests an expenditure cycle equivalent to the one found in Norway. If indeed the public budget has been used countercyclically regardless of approaching elections, we should be able to accept the result. But then there is small wonder that the relevant parameters of the unemployment equation appeared imprecise. The public budget — with total

TABLE 8

Norway: Estimation of Government Expenditure Cycles 1951-1976
Dependent Variable: General Government Expenditure in
Fixed Norwegian Kroner (1970 prices), billions

	(1) OLS	(2) CO
Estimate of β_1	79.5 (47.0)	91.0 (44.1)
β_2	1.05 (.005)	1.05 (.005)
ρ		.17
R^2	.99	.99
χ^2	.168	.381
Number of Observations	25	24

R^2 Adjusted for the fact that no constant is included.
Estimated Equation: $G = \beta_1 EL + \beta_2 G_{-1} + \mu$
Method of Estimation: OLS, CO
Mean of Dependent Variable: 8.100

tax revenue increasing from about 20 per cent to 50 per cent through the period considered — certainly should have made itself felt if employed for countercyclical purposes. In other words: the rate of unemployment has not been kept low before elections in particular, it has been kept permanently low (cf. the fact that the UV-version of the unemployment rate has an average less than zero). In small open economies, we would suspect shift in the wages' share of national income from such tight labour markets.[38] And indeed Sweden (accompanied by Denmark) does show the largest growth in the wage share of Net National Income in the period 1950-75. The Swedish wage share has grown 24.2 per cent compared to an OECD average of 17.0 per cent,[39] suggesting that the focal arena of redistributive politics is shifted from short term policies to less reversible outcomes of fights for factor shares.

TABLE 9
Sweden: Estimation of Government Expenditure Cycles 1951-1976.
Dependent Variable: General Government Expenditure in Fixed
Swedish Kronor (1970 prices), billions

	(1) OLS	(2) CO
Estimate of β_1	-.06 (.11)	-.05 (.11)
β_2	1.04 (.004)	1.04 (.004)
ρ		.09
R^2	.99	.99
χ^2	.001	.048
Number of Observations	25	24

R^2 Adjusted for the fact that no constant is included.
Estimated Equation: $G = \beta_1 \, EL + \beta_2 \, G_{-1} + \mu$
Method of Estimation: OLS, CO
Mean of Dependent Variable: 8.100

A CURVE IN SEARCH OF A THEORY

> 'Doesn't testing come to an End?'
> A. Wittgenstein, On Certainty.

Briefly recapitulating the results of section 2:

The Norwegian case shows bleak evidence of a disparate partisan impact upon employment levels and a correspondingly stronger indication of a partisan invariant effect with respect to employment as well as public expenditure: both exhibit upturns in the period preceding elections.

In the case of Sweden, on the other hand, the estimates disclose no systematic occurrence of an election cycle regarding either employment or public expenditures. In this sense, the alleged success of the counter-cyclical policies is supported. The permanently tight labour market has been associated with a rather pronounced

FIGURE 4
Norway: Per Cent Change in General Government
Expenditure: 1951-75

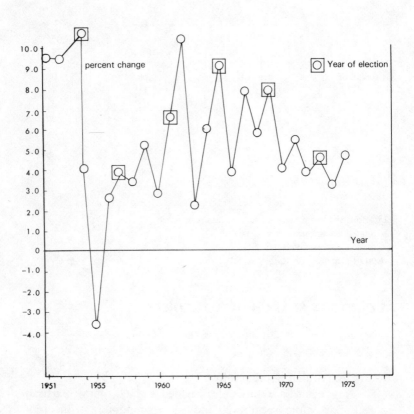

FIGURE 5
Sweden: Per Cent Change in General Government
Expenditure: 1951-75

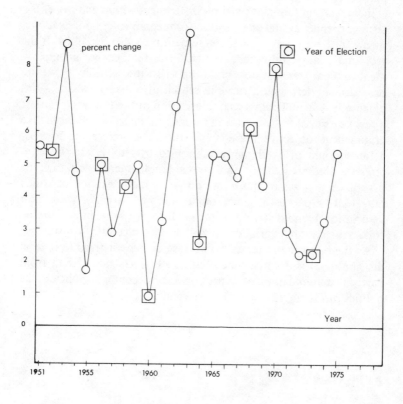

shift of factor shares supposedly to be seen as benefitting the core constituencies of the Social Democratic party.

The results for Norway seriously question the appropriateness of explaining cross national variation between unemployment and partisanship of governments, which did strike Hibbs as more than coincidental, in terms of partisan differences within countries. External dependency and competition for median voters, for example, throw further doubts upon the argument provided by Hibbs. If the cross-nationally established, empirical relation between unemployment and partisanship does stand up to further scrutiny,[40] we are provisionally left with a curve in search of a theory (which — incidentally — was Tobin's characterization of the Phillips trade-off a few years ago).[41] Conjecturally we might entertain an alternative argument: If objective interests and subjective preferences do show a fair amount of overlapping as implied by Hibbs, and those interests indeed are tied in with different employment levels, then the organized strength of those interests (one manifestation of which may well be parties in government, another, strength of interest associations) would seem of some explanatory value in accounting for across national variation as well as within country constancy.

As the opposing interests would lose or benefit from long term distributional shifts associated with such levels rather than from partisan manipulation of short run macroeconomic policies, the politics of distribution is no less relevant.

APPENDIX

Notes on Sources and Definitions of Variables

Unemployed, vacancies: OECD, 1972, 1976a.
   Consistent series could only be constructed from registered or insured unemployed.

Rate of unemployment, quarterly: OEEC, 1975; OECD, 1972, 1976a.

Labour force: Labour Force Statistics, various years.
   (Quarterly figures were constructed from yearly ones by exponential interpolation.)

Rate of unemployment: ILO, various years.

Inflation: Mitchell, 1972.

GDP: Mitchell, 1972; and OECD, 1976b.

World import, US Import Index: IFS various years.
(The figures were deseasonalized at the source and expressed in current US$. They were transformed into constant values by the US Import Price Index.)

Population: National Statistical Yearbooks, various years.

Electoral Data: Rose and Mackie, 1973; EJPR, 1974.
(The coding of the partisan variable PA was:
- 1 if S is incumbent and supported by a majority in Parliament
+ 1 if B is incumbent and supported by a majority
O otherwise.
This definition seemed necessary due to the fact that a Social Democratic government faced a Bourgeois majority in Parliament, internally split on the EEC issue from February 1971 to October 1972. After the no-vote in September 1972 an anti-EEC Bourgeois government was in office until regular elections in 1973. Both governments were coded zero).
Yearly data on economic indicators and partisan incumbency covering most Western countries for the period 1920-1975 are available in Madsen, 1978.

NOTES

Various people have kindly commented upon parts of this work. Thanks are extended to my Yale professors David R. Cameron, Ray C. Fair, and Randy Olsen, as well as to Frank H. Aarebrot who suggested various ways of testing the hypothesis set forth in section 1.5 regarding Norway, and Martin Paldam who is presently engaged in addressing questions similar to the ones of section 2.

Foremost, however, I am indebted to Professor Gerald H. Kramer of Yale for his never failing encouragement and constructive criticism.

Part of the data was collected by Anders Kretzschmer and Jorn Unnerup. Estimations were performed using the Yale version of TSP written by Jon K. Peck, and ISIS written by Henning Bunzel, Department of Economics, University of Aarhus. I would like to thank Professor Bunzel for introducing me to ISIS, and the Institute of Political Science for financial support.

Janet L. Beizer, a graduate student in Yale's French Department, presently École Normale Supérieure, made several suggestions for improvement and clarification of style. Anne Marie Christensen competently provided her usual blend of skillful typing and careful check on inconsistencies.

This list makes it even more appropriate to emphasize the sole responsibility of the author.

1. For the latest in a series of studies which examine this see R. C. Fair, 'The Effect of Economic Events on Votes for President', *Review of Economics and Statistics* 60, 1978: 159-173. A longer version of this article was published as 'On Controlling the Economy to Win Elections', Cowles Foundation Discussion Paper No. 397.
2. See G. H. Kramer, 'Short-term Fluctuations in US Voting Behaviour 1896-1964', *American Political Science Review* 65, 1971: 131-143.
3. Or he or she can abstain. See F. Arcelus and A. H. Meltzer, 'The Effect of Aggregate Economic Conditions on Congressional Elections', *American Political Science Review* 69 (4), 1975: 1232-1239.
4. Various alternative models were tried that hypothesize a 'partisan' as opposed to an 'incumbency' effect of unemployment: high or rising unemployment might benefit the Social Democratic party. However, the magnitude and precision of any estimates was small, although the parameter often had the expected sign. This may be because the reaction to unemployment is more complex than the simple models of this paper postulate. However, more complex specifications of the economic variables did not produce results closer to our own expectations.
5. See L. Lewin, B. J. Jansson and D. Sörbom, *The Swedish Electorate* (Stockholm: Almquist and Wicksell 1972), Chapters 6, 9 passim.
6. See B. S. Frey and H. Garbers, 'Der Einflus wirtschaftlicher variables auf die Popularität der Regierung — eine empirische Analyse', *Jahrbücher für Nationalökonomie und Statistic* 186, 1972.
7. G. H. Kramer, op. cit., 1971.
8. B. Hansen, *Fiscal Policy in Seven Countries 1955-65* (Paris: OECD 1969), 382, 351-357. See also A. Lindbeck, *Swedish Economic Policy* (Berkeley: UC Press 1974), Chapter 6.
9. Highly relevant in this respect in the crucial role in government formation played by one minor party in particular. See E. Damgaard, 'The Parliamentary Basis of Danish Governments: The Patterns of Coalition Formation', *Scandinavian Political Studies* 4, 1969: 30-57.
10. I. Budge and D. Fairlie, *Voting and Party Competition* (London: Wiley 1977).
11. I. Budge and D. Fairlie, ibid, 289.
12. On the so called Ecological Regression Fallacy as opposed to problems of specification see E. Hanushek, J. Jackson and J. Kain, 'Model Specification Use of Aggregate Data and The Ecological Regression Fallacy', *Political Methodology* 1, 1974: 89-107.
13. See S. Rokkan, 'Geography, Religion and Social Class: Crosscutting Cleavages in Norwegian Politics', in: S. M. Lipset and S. Rokkan, *Party Systems and Voter Alignments* (New York: Free Press 1967).
14. Indications of such concern at the elite level throughout the post-war period can be found in P. Petterson, 'Parliamentary Attitudes towards Labour Market Policies', *European Journal of Political Research* 4, 1976: 399-420. See also F. Aarebrot, 'Regional Identities, Economic Inequalities and Political Parties as Bearers of Territorial Interests: The Case of Norway', in F. Aarebrot, S. Rokkan, T. Sande and D. Unwin, *International Development, Regional Policies, and Ter-*

ritorial Identities in Western Europe (forthcoming).

15. An example of an analysis focusing on different regional impacts in explaining voting outcomes is given in T. G. Olaussen, 'The Prohibition Referenda in Norway: Stable vs Changing Peripheries as a Case of Competing or Complementary Paradigms of Center-Periphery Conflicts' (paper presented at the workshop on Economy, Territory and Identity, Loch Lomond January 1978).

16. For a review of the literature in this field see B. S. Frey, 'Politico-Economic Models and Cycles', *Journal of Public Economics* 9, 1978: 1-18.

17. See A. Heidenheimer, *Comparative Public Policy* (New York: St Martins 1975). Also I. Sharkansky (ed.), *Policy Analysis in Political Science* (Chicago: Markham 1970).

18. D. A. Hibbs, *Economic Interest and the Politics of Macroeconomic Policy* (Centre for International Studies: MIT 1975) also 'Political parties and Macroeconomic Policy', *American Political Science Review* 21, 1977:1467-1487.

19. D. A. Hibbs (1977), ibid, 1467-1470.

20. See W. Nordhaus, 'The Political Business Cycle', *The Review of Economic Studies* 42, 1975: 169-190. For a review of the literature on the Phillips curve see D. Laidler and M. Parkin, 'Inflation: a Survey', *Economic Journal* 85, 1975: 741-809.

21. See L. Calmfors and E. Lundberg, *Inflation och Arbetslöshet* (Stockholm: SNS 1974).

22. See H. Valen and W. Martinussen, 'Electoral Trends and Foreign Politics in Norway: The 1973 Storting Elections and the EEC Issue', in K. H. Cemy (ed.) *Scandinavia at the Polls* (Washington: American Enterprise Institute 1977).

23. A. Maddison, *Economic Growth in the West* (New York: Norton 1964): 111.

24. On such automaticity within the context of US Federal Expenditures see the discussion in C. Bleckman et al., *Setting National Priorities* (Washington DC Brookings 1975).

25. B. S. Frey and F. Schneider, 'A Politico-Economic Model of the United Kingdom', *Economic Journal* 88, 1978: 243-253; also 'An empirical study of Politico-Economic Interaction in the US', *Review of Economics and Statistics* 60, 1978: 174-183; and 'An Econometric Model with an Endogenous Government Sector', *Public Choice* (forthcoming).

26. That is, diversified sources of revenue, including inflationary finance, make it difficult for the average citizen to assess the tax burden. See R. Wagner, 'Revenue Structure, Fiscal Illusion and Budgetary Choice', *Public Choice* 27, 1976: 45-59; also J. M. Buchanan and R. Wagner, *Democracy in Deficit* (New York: Academic Press 1977).

27. W. Nordhaus (1975) op. cit. 189.

28. See P. J. Bjerve, 'Trends in Norwegian Planning 1945-75', *Artikler fra Statistisk Centralbyra*, No. 84 (Oslo) 1968.

29. The 1958 election was a special dissolution election which took place after a period of uncertainty about the Governments support in Parliament. See M. D. Hancock, *Sweden. The Politics of Postindustrial Change* (Hinsdale, Illinois: The Dryden Press 1972).

30. See A. Wildavsky, *The Politics of the Budgetary Process* (Boston: Little Brown 1964).

31. O. A. Davis, M. A. H. Dempster and A. Wildavsky, 'A Theory of the Budgetary Process', *American Political Science Review* 60, 1966: 529-547.

32. This includes local government expenditure. Hansen points out '...from a practical point of view the economic activities of local authorities are in many respects directly or indirectly controlled by the Central Government', B. Hansen (1969), op. cit. 340.

33. See P. D. Jonson, 'Inflation and Growth in the United Kingdom: A Longer Run Perspective', *Journal of Monetary Economics*, 1977: 1-24.

34. The relative importance of the two political variables is corroborated by Box-Jenkins-Tiao type analysis. After appropriate filtering of the unemployment series, a partisan and an electoral intervention term were estimated with various lags. Estimates of the former parameter were anomalous and/or small and uncertain. H. J. Madsen, 'The Partisan Impact upon the Rate of Unemployment: A Time Series Study of Norway', mimeo University of Aarhus. For a discussion of the technique see G. E. P. Box and G. C. Tiao, 'Intervention Analysis with Application to Economic and Environment Problems', *Journal of American Statistical Association* 70, 1975: 70-80.

35. S. Rokkan, 'Norway: Numerical Democracy and Corporate Pluralism', in R. Dahl (ed.), *Political Oppositions in Western Democracies* (New Haven: Yale University Press 1966), 103.

36. The Cochrane-Orcutt method was employed. See J. Johnston, *Econometric Methods* (Tokyo: Macgraw Hill 1972), 262.

37. In his cross national sample of 32 stable 4 year-governments from the period 1948-75 Paldam found some evidence of an electoral cycle in real government consumption peaking two years after the election. See M. Paldam, 'Is there An Election Cycle?', *Scandinavian Journal of Economics*, 1979.

38. See G. Edgren, K. Faxen and C. E. Odhner, *Wage Formation and The Economy* (Gordon: Allen and Unwin 1973).

39. See M. Paldam (1979), op. cit.

40. The relationship is rather sensitive to alternative definitions of government partisanship. See D. R. Cameron, 'Inequality and the State: A Political-Economic Comparison', paper at the annual meeting of the American Political Science Association (Chicago 1976).

41. J. Tobin, 'Inflation and Unemployment', *American Economic Review* 62, 1972: 1-18.

2 Popularity Functions: The Case of the US and West Germany

Bruno Frey and Friedrich Schneider

University of Zurich, Switzerland

I. INTRODUCTION

The purpose of this paper is to give an in-depth analysis of the influence of economic conditions on government popularity in the Federal Republic of Germany and the United States.

Popularity functions may serve three main purposes:

(1) They constitute a crucial link in politico-economic models, showing the influence of the economic sector on the political sector. The popularity index is the best and only *current* indicator for the government indicating its reelection chances. As the government is aware of the impact of economic conditions on its popularity with the voters and therewith its reelection chances, it tries to improve the state of the economy before elections in order to stay in power. The possibility for, and the existence of, such 'political business cycles' are described elsewhere.[1]

(2) Popularity functions reveal individual preferences with respect to macro-economic variables. The estimates empirically derived may be given a welfare interpretation.

(3) Popularity functions may be used by outside observers to forecast future election outcomes. Such an indirect procedure is, of course, only sensible if there is better information available about likely future economic conditions.

(4) In the US context it has been argued that a President's current popularity is an important factor of his relationship with Congress. A low Presidential popularity leads to high Congress oppositon and a high Presidential popularity has the opposite effect.[2]

Depending on which purpose is intended, popularity functions should be constructed and econometrically (politometrically) tested in a different way. If, for example, popularity functions are intended for short run forecasting, an elaborate autoregressive element may prove to be most useful. If, on the other hand, the popularity function is part of a politico-economic model, the emphasis should lie on a well developed causal structure of relationships.

The empirical results for popularity functions provided in the following have been constructed and empirically estimated with the prime purpose of inclusion into politico-economic models. Accordingly, an effort has been made to capture the influence of specific macro-economic variables on government popularity as precisely as possible.

This paper stresses *empirical* results and mostly refers to the popularity of the government. The popularity of individual parties in a government coalition is considered in a few cases only. The underlying model of individual voters' behaviour is not treated here.[3] However, an effort is made not to undertake estimation without theory. The basic framework of the 'economic theory of politics' or 'public choice' should always be visible.

Emphasis is put on the following five aspects of popularity functions:

(1) A clear identification and separation of economic and non-economic factors by appropriately specifying the estimation function and variables introduced. In particular, the popularity level of each government and its depreciation over time turns out to be of great importance.

(2) With respect to macro-economic influences on popularity, it is examined whether the population considers only current economic variables as published in government statistics and reported in the media, whether they compare it to their recent level

and trend, or whether they use expected values. It is analysed whether economic variables such as income tax receipts, government expenditures, the balance of payments, etc. exert any influence on government popularity over and above those of the 'traditional' variables; inflation, unemployment and income growth.

(3) The differential effect of changes of economic conditions on popularity according to income classes and party affiliation is studied.

(4) The effect of time lags is analysed, giving an indication about whether voters are solely or mainly concerned with current economic conditons or whether they take into account the recent past.

(5) It is investigated whether the parameters estimated are reasonably stable over different time periods. As already indicated, the results are compared among four countries.

Part II of this paper gives an extensive analysis of the German popularity function with special emphasis on the additional economic variables mentioned above and the impact of time lags. Part III makes a corresponding study of the popularity of American presidents, with a breakdown of the popularity function according to income groups and party identification. Part IV offers concluding remarks.

A POPULARITY FUNCTION FOR GERMANY

Background

The period covered extends from 1950/1 (first quarter) to 1960/3 (third quarter). In these twenty-seven years there were eight elections (including 1949) for the Bundestag (parliament of the Federal Republic). The results in terms of the share of votes and of seats are shown in Table 1.

The Table shows that the share of votes and seats of the Christian-Democrats continually grew from 1949 to 1957, while that of the Social Democrats grew from 1949 to 1972, and thereafter remained roughly constant. The shares of the small Free Democrats tend to fall. The CDU had an absolute majority in both votes and seats in the legislative period 1957-1961.

TABLE 1
Votes and Shares in the German Bundestag, 1949-1976
(Percentage shares of the three major parties)

		Parties		
Election date		Christian-Democratic Union and Christian Social Union CDU / CSU	Social-Democratic Party SPD	Free Democratic Party FDP
1949	votes	31.0	29.2	11.9
	seats	34.6	32.6	12.9
1953	votes	45.2	28.2	9.5
	seats	49.9	31.0	9.8
1957	votes	50.2	31.8	7.7
	seats	54.4	34.0	8.2
1961	votes	45.3	36.2	12.8
	seats	48.5	38.0	13.5
1965	votes	47.6	39.3	9.5
	seats	49.4	40.7	9.9
1969	votes	46.1	42.7	5.8
	seats	48.8	45.2	6.0
1972	votes	44.9	45.8	8.4
	seats	45.3	46.4	8.3
1976	votes	48.6	42.6	7.9
	seats	49.0	43.1	7.9

Source: Dieter Nohlen, Wahlsysteme der Welt, Piper (Munich and Zurich 1978),
Tables A3 and A4, pp. 386-387.

Over the period covered, there were four ideological types of government:

1949/1—1957/4 and	coalition between CDU and several small parties (FDP,
1962/1—1966/4	GB, BHE) abbreviated as CDU/o.p.;
1958/1—1961/4	coalition between CDU and the Deutsche Partei DP;
1967/1—1969/4	a 'Grand Coalition' between CDU and SPD;
1970/1—1976/4	government dominated by the SPD (coalitions with the FDP).

Figure 1 shows the development of government popularity, and Figures 2 and 3 that of economic conditions as represented by the rate of unemployment, the rate of inflation, and the growth in per capita real income.

The Influence of Economic and Non-economic Factors

Table 2 gives ordinary least squares estimation results using 107 quarterly observations. Equation (1) concentrates solely on the influence of economic variables, i.e. rates of inflation (in per cent), unemployment (in per cent), and growth rate of disposable real income (in per cent).[4] Equation (2) uses only 'political' (i.e. 'basic' popularity level) variables for the government coalitions distinguished above, and equation (3) finally shows their joint influence.

A popularity function including economic variables, only, statistically explains a low share of the variance ($\bar{R}^2 = 0.31$). The low Durbin-Watson coefficient (D.W. = 0.81) points to the existence of serial correlation of residuals, suggesting that equation (1) is misspecified. The same is true when popularity is accounted for only by level-variables, reflecting purely 'political' factors connected with each government (equation 2). A joint consideration of both economic and 'political' determinants yields clearly superior results. The statistically explained share of the variance rises to 83 per cent and the Durbin-Watson coefficient of 1.82 suggests absence of serial correlation. Both the rate of inflation and unemployment have a statistically significant impact on government

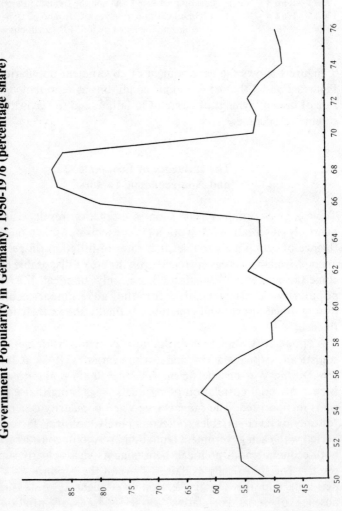

FIGURE 1
Government Popularity in Germany, 1950-1976 (percentage share)

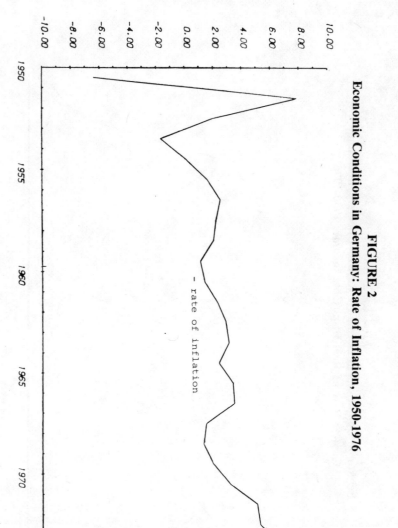

FIGURE 2

Economic Conditions in Germany: Rate of Inflation, 1950-1976

FIGURE 3

**Economic Conditions in Germany: Rate of Unemployment and
Growth Rate of Real Disposable Income, 1950-1976**

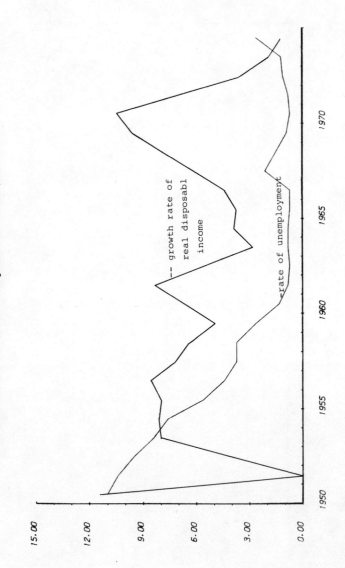

TABLE 2
The Separate and Joint Influence of Economic and Non-economic Variables on Government Popularity. Germany, 1950/1-1976/3

eq.	constant	economic variables			political variables popularity levels				test statistics		
		inflation %	unemployment	growth of real income	CDU/o.p.	CDU/DP	CDU/SPD	SPD/FDP	$\bar{R}^2$	D.W.	d.f.
1.	56.43 (13.02)	-1.17** (-3.01)	-0.80 (-1.78)	0.02 (0.28)					0.31	0.81	103
2.					58.03** (42.82)	49.61** (30.94)	91.00** (32.61)	55.70** (19.41)	0.75	1.02	103
3.		-0.71** (-3.57)	-0.82* (-2.19)	0.31 (0.96)	57.99** (48.47)	52.56** (37.21)	90.27** (55.43)	54.89** (33.92)	0.83	1.82	100

The figures in parentheses give the t-values; two asterisks (one asterisk) indicate that the respective coefficients are statistically significant at the 99% (95%) level of security (one sided). $\bar{R}^2$ is the share of the variance accounted for by the respective equation (squared correlation coefficient, corrected for degrees of freedom, d.f.); D.W. indicates the Durbin - Watson coefficient.

popularity. A rise in the rate of inflation by one percentage point (e.g. from 2 to 3 per cent p.a.) decreases ceteris paribus the popularity of the government by 0.71 percentage points (e.g. from 50.71 to 50 per cent). An increase in unemployment of one percentage point leads to a popularity decline of 0.82 percentage points. Over the period considered, a change in the real rate of growth does not have a significant effect on popularity, but it should be noted that the t-value of the respective coefficient (t = 0.96) rises strongly compared to equation (1) (where t = 0.28).

The popularity levels accounting for the differential political appeal of the parties in power are significantly different from zero. For obvious reasons, the basic popularity level of the two large parties combined in the 'Grand Coalition' is much higher (90.27 per cent) than that for other governments (where the popularity level is around 55 per cent). The popularity levels of the various governments also differ significantly *from each other*. Taking the lowest popularity level, i.e. the CDU/DP with 52.56 per cent, as the point of reference, the difference in basic popularity compared to the CDU/o.p. government is significant with a t-value of 2.84, with respect to the CDU/SPD government t = 11.49, and to the SPD/FDP government t = 2.93.

These results indicate that in Germany, over the period considered, the various government coalitions had a different 'political' appeal to the voters, irrespective of economic influences. A correctly specified popularity function has to account for this factor; it is necessary to jointly consider economic and political influences on popularity.

The estimates presented in Table 2 cover almost twenty-seven years. It may be argued that during this long period there occurred shifts in voters' reactions to changes in economic conditions. As is shown in Figure 2, economic conditions have strongly changed (unemployment has steadily decreased up to 1973, inflation has steadily increased), so that the electorate may have changed its evaluation of government in this respect accordingly. There are two ways to account for this possible shift in evaluation:

(i) The economic variables taken as determinants of government popularity are taken as *deviations* from their level in the recent past. This reflects a situation where voters have become accustomed to a prior 'base';

TABLE 3
The Influence of Adjusted Economic Variables on
Government Popularity, Germany, 1950/1–1976/3

eq.	adjusted economic variables			political variables popularity levels				test statistics		
	inflation I^A	unemployment U^A	growth of real income GYR^A	CDU/o.p.	CDU/DP	CDU/SPD	SPD/DFG	$\bar{R}^2$	D.W.	d.f.
4.	-0.76**	-0.91**	0.50	54.59**	47.91**	86.57**	52.36**	0.96	1.93	100
	(-3.39)	(-3.72)	(1.73)	(65.96)	(34.08)	(62.97)	(49.25)			

(ii) a shorter time period is selected.
These two approaches are analysed in turn.

Population's Adjustment
of Past Performance

The hypothesis is advanced that the electorate gets used to a past level of the economic variables and evaluates the government's performance relative to this benchmark. New economic variables are constructed which are defined as deviations between the current value and the average value of the respective variable over the last legislative period. The correspondingly adjusted economic variables I^A, U^A and GYR^A are used as explanatory factors in the estimate reproduced in Table 3.

The statistical properties of the estimate are quite satisfactory ($\bar{R}^2 = 0.96$, D.W. = 1.93). The adjusted rates of inflation and of unemployment are highly significant. The estimated coefficients of the adjusted inflation and unemployment variables (equation 4) are of a similar size to those of the respective non-adjusted variables (equation 3). Adjusted real income growth is again statistically insignificant at the 95 per cent level, but, as before, the t-value rises strongly compared to the previous equation. It may be concluded that transforming the variable in this fashion does not have a dramatic effect on the popularity function estimates.

The Influence of a Change in Time Periods
and Between Parties in Government

In order to account for possible shifts in the evaluation of government performance the period 1950 to 1977 is broken into two subsets:

(1) 1950 to 1966 in which the government was dominated by the Christian-Democratic party, with Adenauer and Erhard as chancellors;

(2) 1970 to 1977 in which the government was dominated by the Social-Democratic party with Brandt and Schmidt as chancellors.

TABLE 4
Popularity Functions for the Period of Christian-Democratic Rule. Germany, 1950/1-1966/4, quarterly data

eq.	dependent variable	economic variables			non-economic variables			test statistics		
		rate of inflation	rate of unemployment	rate of growth real disposable income % % %	popularity level		trend variable	$\bar{R}^2$	D.W.	d.f.
					CDU/o.p.	CDU/DP				
5.	government popularity	-0.82** (-4.81)	-0.81** (-4.02)	0.56* (2.07)	54.58** (46.07)	44.09** (23.42)	-0.04 (-1.56)	0.76	1.84	62
6.	popularity of the Christian-Democratic party	-0.63** (-4.03)	-1.31** (-4.36)	0.63** (2.84)	43.70** (48.50)	45.03** (46.90)	0.16** (6.58)	0.83	1.96	62

TABLE 5

Popularity Functions for the Period of Social-Democratic Rule. Germany, 1970/1-1977/4, quarterly data

eq. dependent variable	economic variables			popularity level SPD	test statistics		
	rate of inflation %	rate of unemployment %	growth rate of real disposable income %		$\bar{R}^2$	D.W.	d.f.
7. government popularity	-0.36 (-1.25)	-0.87** (-3.10)	0.43 (1.90)	51.10** (17.16)	0.55	1.60	28
8. popularity of Social-Democratic party	-0.63 (-1.51)	-1.20** (-3.69)	0.89** (3.44)	46.05** (13.35)	0.76	1.73	28

As the government over the periods indicated were clearly associated with the CDU and the SPD respectively, it is not only analysed how economic conditions affect government popularity, but also the popularity of the dominant party.

Tables 4 and 5 show the empirical estimates for the two subperiods. The popularity functions established perform particularly well for the period of CDU-governments. All the coefficients are statistically significant. This also applies to the time trend in equation (6) which captures the very significant continuous rise in the popularity of the Christian-Democratic party. This increase occurred at the expense of the smaller parties in the government coalition, resulting in a not significant negative trend of government popularity as a whole (see equation 5). As for the economic variables, a one percentage point increase in the rate of inflation decreases both government and CDU popularity by about -0.7 (-0.63 and -0.82 respectively) percentage points; and a one percentage point increase in the growth of real income raises government and CDU popularity by about 0.6 (0.56 and 0.63, respectively) percentage points. There is a major difference with respect to unemployment: The CDU suffers a much higher popularity loss (-1.31 per cent) than the government as a whole -0.81 per cent) when the rate of unemployment increases by one percentage point. Overall it seems that the population makes the Christian-Democratic party, the dominant coalition party, responsible for the state of the economy in the period considered.

The popularity functions for the period of SPD-governments are statistically less satisfactory with respect to the share of the variance explained, the Durbin-Watson coefficient, and the number of significant parameters. The population does not seem to make the government responsible for the rise in inflation brought about by the dramatic oil price increases of the OPEC-cartel; inflation does not have a significant effect on popularity of the government or the Social-Democratic Party. The economic variables differ markedly in their effect on the popularity of the government (a coalition between the Social-Democrats and the Free Democrats) and of the Social-Democratic party. This may be due to the fact that the Free Democrats are considered by voters to have quite a strong position in government, e.g. they occupy the positions of vice-chancellor, and certain key ministries: foreign affairs, economics and agriculture. A comparison of the estimates of equations (7) and (8) shows in particular that the SPD loses more popularity than the government as a whole when the rate of unemployment increases (-1.20 compared to -0.87 percentage points). However, the Social Democrats also benefit strongly when the growth rate of real disposal income rises: a one percentage point increase lifts their popularity in a statistically highly significant way by 0.89 percentage points. The population thus seems to hold the Social-Democratic party mainly responsible for full employment and income growth.

The Influence of Additional Economic Variables

In all the estimates presented so far the rate of unemployment has turned out to be statistically highly significant. This also applies to the rate of inflation for the overall period. German voters value full employment and price stability highly, a result which is in perfect accordance with intuitive notions, according to which the Germans are very averse to inflation and unemployment mainly due to the historical experience of the Weimar Republic which led to the rise of the Nazis.[5] The growth of real income seems to be of somewhat less importance.

Besides those three 'classical' macro-economic variables there may be other economic factors influencing voters' evaluation of government performance. In particular, they may react to both the quantity and quality of government services, as well as to the costs of providing them. It is extremely difficult to find time series data which adequately reflect the relevant aspects of the public supply of goods. The only quarterly data available are public expenditures for goods and services (in real terms) which, of course, measure the inputs in, and not the outputs of, government activity. Voters may also react to changes in government transfer payments. This is at least what many governments seem to assume when they hand out 'election presents' in the form of direct transfers to voters, an activity many German governments have been actively engaged in.

The cost of public goods supply may be measured by per capita income taxes, assuming that there is a considerable amount of fiscal illusion[6] in the sense that the burden of indirect taxes is felt less strongly than that of direct taxes.

The electorate may also be concerned about macro-economic variables such as the size of government debt — being an indicator for the fiscal responsibility of the government — and the state of the balance of payments.

The theoretical hypotheses are that an increase in government expenditures (both the supply of public goods and transfers) increases, and that a rise in income taxes decreases government popularity. A rise in government debt and in the deficit of the current balance of payments is a priori expected to decrease the popularity of the government. It is reasonable to assume that with respect to all these variables, voters have been accustomed to the prevailing level, and that they react to changes in them only. The additional variables (except the balance of payments) are therefore defined in terms of percentage growth rates (compared to the previous year).

Table 6 presents empirical estimates for the most recent periods in which there was a coalition of Social-Democrats and Free-Democrats.

Table 6 shows the estimated coefficients for two sets of estimates. Equation (9) gives the result for a popularity function without a lagged endogenous variable. It should be noted that there are few degrees of freedom[7] (only 23): the estimate statistically explains a relatively low share of the variance ($\bar{R}^2 = 0.48$). As in the previous estimates for this period, the rate of unemployment and the growth in real income are statistically significant, while the rate of inflation is not. None of the additional economic variables exerts a statistically significant effect on government popularity; the respective t-values are quite low (they lie in the range 0.4 to 1.0).

Equation (10) is based on the premise that the current value of government popularity depends on its level in the recent past. Accordingly, the popularity level in the last quarter has been included among the explanatory variables. As may be seen at once from Table 6, the size of the estimated coefficients differs but little. (Due to the lagged endogenous variable the t-value may be biased). This result applies quite generally to all popularity function estimates for Germany in the period considered.

TABLE 6
The Influence of Various Macro-economic Variables on Government Popularity. Germany, 1970/2-1977/4

explanatory variables	equations	
	(9)	(10)
political variables		
popularity level (constant)	52.08	44.43
lagged popularity level PDP$_{t-1}$	–	0.18 (1.04)
economic variables		
rate of inflation (%)	-0.19 (-0.94)	-0.19 (-0.99)
rate of unemployment (%)	-0.86** (-3.09)	-0.79** (-2.89)
growth rate of real disposable income (%)	0.41 (1.92)	0.41 (1.96)
growth of government expenditures for goods and services (%)	0.08 (0.38)	0.09 (0.43)
growth of government expenditures for transfers (%)	0.47 (0.94)	0.48 (1.03)
growth of real income taxes (%)	-0.20 (-0.70)	-0.21 (-0.77)
change in government debt	-0.37 (-0.66)	-0.40 (-0.88)
balance of payments deficit	-0.13 (-0.51)	-0.15 (-0.74)
test statistics		
$\bar{R}^2$	0.48	0.50
D.W.	1.68	1.77
d.f.	23	22

The estimation results in Table 6 suggest that the additional macro-economic variables do not affect the population's evaluation of government performance. This conclusion only applies to the *aggregate* level of popularity here considered. There can be little doubt that on a more micro-level, the supply of public goods, government transfers, and taxes strongly influences the voters. The results presented here indicate that a more disaggregated analysis is needed, and that possibility cross section data have to be used in order to be able to capture the political impact of these variables, especially in the marginal constituency.

The size of government debt and of the deficit in the balance of payments are macro-concepts with little or no meaning for the individual voters. The estimates suggest that in Germany the population is little concerned with these goals, and as a whole that they do not judge the performance of the government relative to them.[8]

Analysis of the Voters' Time Horizon

The estimates so far discussed were based on the assumption that voters have a very short memory. Essentially, they consider only the current state of the economy when they evaluate the governments' performance. Economic conditions in previous quarters or years of the election period do not seem to affect government popularity. This short memory may be attributed to various factors:

(1) Voters take the current or most recent performance of the government as evidenced by economic conditions to be the most reliable indicator of its actions in future.

(2) Individuals assume that popularity survey questions aim at their immediate, short run, evaluation of the government. They may behave differently in elections.[9]

(3) The individuals bothered by pollsters may not make the effort of seriously considering past economic conditions when they respond.

Table 7 presents estimates of the time lags involved, again for the most recent time period. In order to have sufficient degrees of freedom remaining, the influence of past values of the variable is considered for each of the three 'classical' variables in turn. Equa-

TABLE 7
Individual's Memory of Past Economic Conditions.
Germany, 1970/2-1977/4

eq. political	economic variables				test statistics		
variable	rate of inflation % I_{t-i}, i=0,..,8		rate of unemployment % U_{t-i}, i=0,..,8	growth rate of real disposable income % GYR_{t-i}, i=0,..,8	$\bar{R}^2$	D.W.	d.f.
11. 58.43	i=0	-0.96* (-2.47)	-1.99* (-2.64)	0.53* (2.51)	0.70	1.76	20
	i=1	-0.51 (-0.79)					
	i=2	-0.42 (-0.64)					
	i=3	-0.34 (-0.69)					
	i=4	-0.93 (-1.47)					
	i=5	0.47 (0.23)					
	i=6	0.45 (0.34)					
	i=7	0.23 (0.08)					
	i=8	0.39 (0.41)					
12. 69.43		-0.84* (-2.23)	i=0 -3.60** (-2.71)	0.67** (2.70)	0.78	1.89	20
			i=1 -1.46 (-0.79)				
			i=2 -0.75 (-1.43)				
			i=3 -0.79 (-0.87)				
			i=4 -0.28 (-0.15)				
			i=5 -0.30 (-0.41)				
			i=6 -0.47 (-0.52)				
			i=7 -0.51 (-0.55)				
			i=8 -0.46 (-0.49)				
13. 48.51		-0.62 (-1.94)	-0.98* (-2.21)	i=0 0.54* (2.59)	0.65	1.68	20
				i=1 0.51 (1.84)			
				i=2 0.43 (1.06)			
				i=3 0.44 (0.76)			
				i=4 0.33 (0.59)			
				i=5 0.36 (0.51)			
				i=6 0.41 (0.61)			
				i=7 0.32 (0.47)			
				i=8 0.47 (0.68)			

tion (11), for example, presents the estimated coefficients (and the corresponding t-values) for

$$POP_t = \alpha + \sum_{i=0}^{\delta} \beta_{t-i} I_{t-i} + \gamma U_t + \delta GYR_t + \epsilon_t,$$

where α, β, γ, δ are the parameters and ϵ the error term.

The estimates presented in Table 7 confirm theoretical expectations. When interpreting the table, it should be noted that there are less degrees of freedom (20). The *lagged* values of all the three variables considered have *no* significant effect on current popularity. The t-values attached to the lagged coefficients are extremely low, most of them are in the vicinity of 0.5. Germans do not seem to consider past economic conditions when they evaluate government performance in popularity surveys.

The formulation using an elaborate lag structure makes all three macro-economic variables considered in the current time period statistically significant. There is, however, multicollinearity between the lagged values of the respective variables, possibly leading to biased parameter estimates and test statistics. At least in the case of inflation and growth, the coefficients lie in a narrow range: an increase in inflation by one percentage point reduces government popularity by 0.62 to 0.96 percentage points; an increase in real income growth raises popularity by 0.53 to 0.67 percentage points.

POPULARITY FUNCTIONS FOR THE UNITED STATES

Background

In the period considered extending from 1953 (second quarter) to 1976 (third quarter) it is useful to differentiate the following Presidential administrations:

1953/1—1956/4 Eisenhower (first term)
1957/1—1960/4 Eisenhower (second term)
1961/1—1963/2 Kennedy
1963/3—1968/4 Johnson

FIGURE 4

The Popularity of American Presidents, 1953-1976

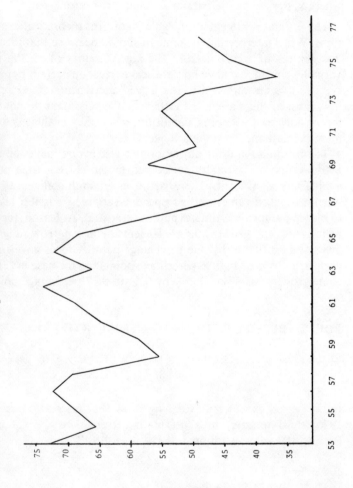

1969/1—1973/3 Nixon (first and unfinished second term)
1973/3—1976/3 Ford

These Presidents experienced the following movements of their popularity with the voters (see Figure 4).

The Separate and Joint Influence of Economic and Non-economic Variables

In the United States, it is a well known experience that Presidents suffer a continuous popularity loss over the term in office.[10] Besides the specific popularity level of each President capturing his personal appeal to the voters, it is necessary to introduce a dummy variable accounting for this 'autonomous depreciation' in popularity, which is defined to be unrelated to economic conditions. It is defined to take a steadily increasing value (e.g. in the case of President Eisenhower's first terms, the dummy variable takes the values 1, 2, 3,...for the period 1954/1 to 1956/2). An autonomous popularity loss is thus expected a priori to result in a negative estimated coefficient. The dramatic popularity loss of Nixon due to the Watergate scandal well visible in Figure 1 is captured by a special 'Watergate' dummy variable, which takes the values 1, 3, 5, 5, 5 over the period 1973/2 to 1974/2, and is otherwise zero. (Testing has shown that alternative values for the depreciation variables do not affect the results). Table 8 shows the estimates with quarterly data for the overall period 1953 to 1976.

The economic factors alone statistically explain 70% of the variance; the non-economic factors 82%; and both factors together 87%. If only economic variables are included (equation 14) the popularity function is misspecified; the Durbin-Watson coefficient indicates serial correlation of residuals, and the rate of unemployment and the growth rate of real disposable income have a statistically insignificant sign. Equation (15) shows that the popularity levels and the variable accounting for popularity depreciation are statistically significant, but that the Durbin-Watson coefficient is low.

TABLE 8
The Influence of Economic and Non-economic Variables on Presidential Popularity.
United States, 1953/2-1976/3, quarterly data.

	economic variables			con-stant term	non - economic variables											test statistics		
	infla-tion % (t-1)	unem-ploy-ment %	growth rate of real disposable income %		popularity level						popularity depreciations				R^2	D.W.	d.f.
eq.					Eisen-hower I	Eisen-hower II	Kenne-dy	John-son	Nixon	Ford	Eisen-hower	Kenne-dy/John-son	Nixon	Water-gate			
14	-2.19** (-2.87)	-0.91 (-0.68)	0.08 (0.51)	71.56 (10.19)	-	-	-	-	-	-	-	-	-	-	0.70	1.19	90
15	-	-	-	-	66.3** (32.9)	57.0** (24.9)	81.5** (44.8)	76.2** (35.4)	66.3** (24.7)	48.6** (19.4)	0.43* (2.13)	-1.81** (-9.84)	-1.29** (-3.73)	-7.64** (-9.70)	0.82	1.26	84
16	-1.58** (-2.89)	-4.07** (-6.44)	0.52* (2.19)	-	86.1** (24.6)	82.9** (19.0)	108.6** (23.7)	99.7** (23.9)	86.2** (21.3)	97.5** (11.1)	0.46** (2.91)	-2.06** (-9.91)	-0.26 (-0.86)	-5.24** (-6.31)	0.87	1.61	81

Only equation (16), which includes both the influence of economic and non-economic determinants, is satisfactory from the statistical point of view. This suggests the importance of considering economic factors jointly with 'political' factors. According to equation (15), a one percentage point rise in the rate of inflation decreases a President's popularity ceteris paribus on average by 1.58 percentage points. An increase in the rate of unemployment by one percentage point decreases Presidential popularity by 4.07 percentage points. A one percentage point increase in the growth rate of real income raises government popularity by 0.52 percentage points. Kennedy has had the highest, and Eisenhower (in his second term) the lowest popularity level. The depreciation variables of Eisenhower's first and second term, and of Kennedy and Johnson, are collapsed into one because they do not differ significantly.[11] All depreciation parameters differ from zero in a statistically significant way, except for Nixon in his first term. The positive sign of the coefficient relating to Eisenhower contradicts theoretical expectations: he is the only President who became more popular (on non-economic grounds) during his terms. Presidents Kennedy and Johnson experienced a marked autonomous popularity fall during their time in office. As expected, the dramatic popularity loss of Nixon due to Watergate is well born out by the estimate for the dummy variable.

The United States is (as far as we know) the only country for which there are available reliable monthly economic data for a sufficiently long time period. Table 9 shows the corresponding estimates.

Equation (17) in Table 9 shows the monthly estimates with all three major macro-economic variables included. It corresponds to equation (16) of Table 8 but relates to a more recent time period (1969-1976 compared to 1953-1976). The rate of inflation and the growth of real income exert a statistically significant effect on Presidential popularity. A one percentage point increase in inflation decreases the President's popularity. A one percentage point increase in inflation decreases the President's popularity by -1.36 percentage points; an increase in the growth rate of real income by one percentage point raises its popularity by 1.08 percentage points. As there is some multicollinearity between the economic variables included,[12] the statistical significance and size of a pair of

TABLE 9
Presidential Popularity Function, United States, 1969/4-1976/9, monthly data

	economic variables			non-economic variables					test statistics		
	rate of inflation %	rate of unemployment %	growth rate of real disposable income %	popularity level		popularity depreciation			$\bar{R}^2$	D.W.	d.f.
eq.				Nixon first and second term	Ford	Nixon first term	Ford	Water-gate			
17.	-1.36** (-2.90)	-1.92 (-1.75)	1.08* (2.25)	61.82** (14.02)	71.46** (9.06)	-0.28* (-2.27)	-2.46** (-2.56)	-3.12** (-8.66)	0.92	1.68	82
18.	-1.88** (-4.09)	-3.68** (-4.28)		84.20** (11.61)	99.87** (14.41)	-0.28* (-2.31)	-2.23* (-2.54)	-2.91** (-7.43)	0.91	1.69	83
19.	-1.17** (-2.89)		0.94* (2.45)	51.89** (9.48)	62.48** (9.07)	-0.36** (-3.77)	-3.49** (-3.08)	-3.49** (-9.06)	0.82	1.59	83

two among them taken alone is tested in equations (18) and (19). According to this procedure, all three economic variables have a statistically significant effect on Presidential popularity. In particular, the coefficient of the rate of unemployment turns out to be of large size and to be significantly different from zero. A one percentage point increase in the rate of unemployment depresses popularity by -3.68 percentage points.

The non-economic variables shown in Table 9 are all statistically significant. In particular, both Nixon's popularity in his first term and Ford's popularity decreased significantly while they were in office. Even more marked is Nixon's popularity fall due to the Watergate affair.

Presidential Popularity According to Administrations

The time period considered in Table 8 (1953-1976) may be broken up according to which Presidents were in power. Three subperiods are differentiated:

(a) The Republican Eisenhower administration (two terms), 1953/1—1960/4;
(b) The Democratic Kennedy/Johnson administration, 1961/1—1968/4;
(c) The Republican Nixon/Ford administration, 1969/1—1976/3.

The non-economic level variables accounting for the special voter appeal of each President refers to each President mentioned above (in the case of Eisenhower, the first level variable refers to the first term, the second to the second term). The popularity depreciation is taken to apply jointly to the three Presidential administrations mentioned above. (Due to an insufficient number of observations for Ford, the depreciation of the last administration refers to Nixon only.)

The estimation results are given in Table 10.

The popularity function estimates give statistically excellent results for the last two subperiods of Kennedy/Johnson and Nixon/Ford.

TABLE 10
Popularity Functions for Three Presidential Administrations. United States, 1953/2-1976/3, quarterly data

eq. administration	economic variables			non-economic variables					test statistics		
	rate of inflation %	rate of unemployment %	growth of real disposable income %	popularity level		joint popularity depreciation	Watergate		$\bar{R}^2$	D.W.	d.f.
				first president	second president						
20. Eisenhower (1953/2 - 1960/4)	-0.17 (-0.20)	-3.30* (-2.49)	0.47 (1.84)	80.03** (10.06)	73.40** (8.40)	0.31 (1.75)			0.69	1.73	25
21. Kennedy/Johnson (1961/2 - 1968/4)	-2.66* (-2.58)	-5.40** (-2.94)	1.84** (3.06)	89.50** (13.06)	82.10** (11.48)	-1.78** (-8.43)			0.95	1.79	25
22. Nixon/Ford (1969/2 - 1976/3)	-2.19* (-2.42)	-3.96** (-4.90)	0.61* (2.38)	74.07* (9.48)	92.48** (10.64)	-0.60** (-2.90)	-5.62** (-8.02)		0.92	1.72	23

Equation (20) for the two terms of the Eisenhower administration are less satisfactory, only 69 per cent of the variance being explained and only one of the economic variables, unemployment, exerting a statistically significant effect on Presidential popularity.

In the latter two subperiods, all three macro-economic factors affect the President's popularity in a significant way. A comparison of equations (21) and (22) shows, that during the Democratic administration of Kennedy and Johnson, voters reacted more strongly to changes in economic conditions than under the Republican Presidency of Nixon and Ford. This applies particularly to the full employment and growth goals. A percentage point increase in the rate of unemployment decreases Democratic Presidential popularity by -5.40 percentage points under Kennedy/Johnson against -3.96 percentage points under Nixon/Ford. An increase in the real growth rate of income raises popularity by 1.84 percentage points under Kennedy/Johnson, and by 0.61 percentage points under Nixon/Ford. There is some weak evidence that voters make Democratic Presidents somewhat more responsible, when employment and growth change in an unwanted direction.[13]

Population's Adjustment to Past and Expected Presidential Performance

It may (as in the German case) be analyzed whether popularity can be better explained when voters' adjustment to prevailing economic conditions is taken into account, i.e. when they evaluate the government's performance relative to what can be expected, given the general state of the economy. Data for the United States allow us to test this proposition with two different formulations:

(a) It is assumed that the electorate takes the past state of the economy (as given by average conditions over the preceding Presidential election period) as their point of reference;

(b) It is assumed that expected conditions with respect to the three macro-economic variables (which are empirically measured by public opinion surveys) are taken as the point of reference.

Table 11 presents the estimation results, with equation (23) using the difference between the actual and past values, and equation (24) using the difference between the actual and expected value, of

TABLE 11
The Influence of Adjusted Economic Variables on Presidential Popularity. United States 1954/1-1971/2, half-yearly data

eq.	type of adjustment of economic variables	adjusted economic variables			non-economic variables						test statistics		
					popularity level			popularity depreciation					
		rate of inflation %	rate of unemployment %	growth rate of real disposable income %	Eisenhower first and second term	Kennedy/ Johnson	Nixon first term	Eisenhower first and second term	Kennedy/ Johnson	Nixon first term	$\bar{R}^2$	D.W.	d.f.
23.	relative to past conditions	-1.86** (-2.09)	-1.98* (-2.07)	0.56* (2.07)	64.08** (19.15)	76.03** (15.06)	72.09** (11.02)	-0.44 (-1.21)	-4.36** (-3.72)	-3.17** (-2.94)	0.77	2.26	27
24.	relative to expected future conditions	-3.50** (3.00)	-9.47* (-2.49)	0.58 (1.79)	66.20** (22.31)	84.39** (29.08)	66.03** (11.81)	-0.45 (-1.39)	-5.13** (-9.99)	-3.02* (-2.68)	0.85	2.27	27

economic variables as explanatory variables. The estimates are in this case based on half-yearly data, because the surveys on economic expectations are undertaken twice a year only.

The period covered comprises seven years of Eisenhower's, the complete period of Kennedy and Johnson's, and two years of Nixon's Presidency. The economic variables exert (with one exception) a statistically significant effect on popularity. The size of the coefficients relating to employment and growth are similar to those reached without adjustment of the economic variables — though the influence of inflation is somewhat more marked than in the estimates shown in the preceding tables. Unemployment seems to be judged by voters relative to expected future conditions.

It may well be that the data collected on future expectations are not sufficently reliable to be used in a popularity function. In comparison, using past economic conditions as a point of reference gives sensible results, quite in line with estimates taking non-adjusted economic variables.

Popularity Functions According to Income Classes

The Gallup opinion poll data used in this study break the Presidential popularity series down according to income classes. This allows us to analyse the hypotheses that higher income groups value price stability relative to full employment differently to low income groups. It is theoretically expected that higher income recipients are more concerned about inflation because they are more seriously affected by it (e.g. their money holdings depreciate in value, there is increased uncertainty about property values). Unemployment is a less serious problem for upper groups because in general they enjoy higher job security. Low income recipients are most concerned with unemployment because they are much more in danger of being dismissed and of having to incur the cost of finding a new job (search and mobility cost, costs of uncertainty). As nominal wage rates are expected to reflect inflationary movements quite closely and automatically, and the lower income groups have little property to be concerned about they do not attach as much importance to price stability.[14]

TABLE 12
Presidential Popularity According to Income Classes. United States, 1969/4-1976/9, monthly data

eq.	income class $ p.a.	economic variables		non-economic variables					test statistics		
		rate of inflation %	rate of unem- ployment %	popularity level		popularity depreciation		Water- gate	$\bar{R}^2$	D.W.	d.f.
				Nixon first and second term	Ford	Nixon first term	Ford				
25.	0 to 2999	-1.00 (-1.64)	-4.44** (-4.13)	72.00** (13.82)	87.51** (15.61)	-0.10 (-1.09)	-1.94* (-2.15)	-2.12** (-6.63)	0.84	1.74	83
26.	3000 to 4999	-1.16* (-2.19)	-4.67** (-4.50)	74.57** (13.61)	84.19** (14.40)	-0.06 (-0.94)	-0.89 (-1.24)	-2.19** (-6.51)	0.81	1.72	83
27.	5000 to 6999	-1.43* (-2.57)	-4.29** (-4.07)	79.14** (14.34)	96.51** (16.51)	-0.21* (-2.19)	-1.43 (-1.91)	-2.09** (-6.14)	0.82	1.68	83
28.	7000 to 9999	-2.26** (-3.92)	-3.60** (-3.38)	86.04** (14.41)	95.43** (15.43)	-0.20* (-2.21)	-1.92* (-2.53)	-2.46** (-7.09)	0.86	1.66	83
29.	10000 to 14999	-2.29** (-4.04)	-2.56* (-2.24)	92.97** (16.02)	109.41** (18.45)	-0.21* (-2.31)	-2.41** (-2.94)	-2.84** (-7.23)	0.83	1.71	83
30.	15000 and above	-2.60** (-4.70)	-1.84 (-1.71)	94.02** (16.59)	116.51** (19.82)	-0.29* (-2.43)	-2.09* (-2.20)	-2.93** (-7.89)	0.86	1.68	83

The theoretical hypotheses advanced are tested with monthly data for the period 1969 to 1976 covering the Presidency of Nixon and Ford. As the growth rate of real income is highly correlated with the rate of unemployment income growth is not included among the explanatory variables in order to minimize possible biases in the estimated coefficients for inflation and unemployment. The estimation results are given in Table 12.

The empirical estimates clearly support the theoretical hypotheses advanced. Table 12 shows that the size of the inflation coefficient continuously rises from -1.00 (not significant) to -2.60 (significant at the 99% level) as we move from low to high income groups. The opposite movement holds for the unemployment coefficient. It continuously falls from -4.44 (significant at 99%) to an insignificant value of -1.84. High income recipients react more negatively to inflation and low income recipients to unemployment. This differential evaluation corresponds to their private interests.

Popularity Functions According to Party Affiliation

In line with previous empirical work[15] Republican Presidents tend to ideologically value price stability highly compared to full employment, while Democratic Presidents tend to hold the reverse ranking. It may be hypothesized that this valuation corresponds to the preferences of their respective voters. Table 13 tests this hypothesis. The voters are grouped according to whether they consider themselves to be Republican or Democratic.[16]

The estimates reported show that Republican voters react more strongly to an increase in inflation, and less strongly to an increase in unemployment compared to Democratic voters. The coefficient relating to inflation is not even statistically significant. When the rate of unemployment rises by one percentage point, Republican voters react by reducing the support of the President in opinion surveys by -2.72 per cent, while Democrats reduce it by -3.04 per cent.

TABLE 13
Presidential Popularity According to Party Affiliation.
United States, 1969/4-1976/9, monthly data

eq.	party affiliation	economic variables		non-economic variables					test statistics		
		rate of inflation %	rate of unemployment %	popularity level		popularity depreciation		Watergate	$\bar{R}^2$	D.W.	d.f.
				Nixon first and second term	Ford	Nixon first term	Ford				
31.	Republican	-1.41* (-2.60)	-2.72* (-2.09)	110.80** (15.41)	115.94** (16.01)	-0.06 (-1.07)	-1.33 (-1.22)	-2.69** (-6.04)	0.91	1.84	83
32.	Democratic	-0.56 (-0.94)	-3.04* (-2.29)	62.46** (9.41)	95.49 (12.93)	-0.44** (-3.39)	-3.88** (-4.02)	-4.79** (-6.95)	0.89	1.74	83

CONCLUDING REMARKS

The empirical analysis undertaken in this paper suggests the following conclusions:

(1) Popularity functions are correctly specified only if they simultaneously include both economic and non-economic, i.e. 'political' variables. Of these, the most important are the specific popularity level of governments (or Presidents), an autonomous decline in their popularity (United States, Australia), or a 'pure political cycle' capturing the typical U-shaped popularity movement in between election dates (United Kingdom).

(2) Macro-economic variables describing the general state of the economy exert a systematic influence upon popularity in both countries and all time periods dealt with in this paper.

(3) Of the economic variables, the rate of unemployment has by far the largest (negative) impact on government popularity, and it is consistently stastitically significant in all countries and periods. In comparison, an increase in the rate of inflation — except in Germany — decreases government popularity by a much smaller amount. The rate of growth of real income is the third macro-economic variable that has almost always a statistically significant effect on government popularity. However, the size of the effect is rather small in comparison to both unemployment and inflation in all countries and periods — the only exception again being Germany where the effect of a percentage change in the real growth rate in some estimates slightly exceeds the effect of a percentage change in the rate of growth of prices (inflation).

(4) At the level of aggregation used here, additional economic variables — such as government expenditures, taxes and the balance of payments — do not turn out to have a statistically significant effect on popularity.

(5) For Germany there is a notable difference in the effect of economic variables on government popularity as compared to the popularity of the dominant party in power. The Christian-Democratic Party CDU as well as the Social-Democratic Party SPD are subject to higher popularity loss than the government as a whole, when unemployment increases. The SPD is also made particularly responsible for economic growth.

(6) The electorate seems to have a short memory, extending over

one or two quarters only, at least in Germany.

(7) At the level of analysis undertaken, it is not possible to find any strong indication that German and American voters evaluate the government's performance relative to the recent past or expected future state of the economy.

(8) High income recipients value price stability relatively more strongly than full employment; low income recipients value full employment relatively more compared to price stability (United States). This corresponds well with their interests, suggesting rational behaviour.

(9) The parameters estimated are reasonably stable insofar as there are no sudden shifts between time periods. Within countries, the sign of the coefficients of the economic variables (and of the t-values) generally remains unchanged between different periods and for varying specifications of the popularity function.

Theoretical and empirical investigations of the popularity (and more generally, support) function undertaken here and elsewhere, suggest that future research would be most fruitfully concentrated on the following areas:

— a better understanding and specification of the non-economic influences;
— explicit studies of the influence of information, e.g. via the mass media and by propaganda (from various sources);
— a further disaggregation of the relationships between the state of the economy and the popularity of various political institutions (parties, government) with various subsections of the population;
— analyses of the output effects of government expenditures (especially in the form of the utility derived from the supply of public goods and infrastructure) on popularity;
— analyses at the micro-level of how far and concerning what economic topics the population makes the government responsible.

These and other problems can only be tackled fruitfully on the basis of a well developed theory describing the behaviour of all the actors involved; studying their interdependence, and taking explicit account of institutional conditions. This means that more extended and disaggregated studies of popularity functions should be undertaken in the framework of a complete and explicit politico-economic model.

NOTES

The authors gratefully acknowledge helpful comments by Christopher Goodrich.

1. B. S. Frey, *Modern Political Economy*, Martin Robertson (London 1978); B. S. Frey, 'Politico-Economic Models and Cycles', *Journal of Public Economics* 9, 1978: 203-220.

2. See J. A. Stimson, 'Public Support for American Presidents: A Cyclical Model', *Public Opinion Quarterly* 40 (1), 1976: 1-21.

3. See e.g. G. H. Kramer, 'Short Run Fluctuations in US Voting Behavior, 1896-1964', *American Political Science Review* 65, 1971: 131-143; G. Kirchgässner, *Rationales Wählerverhalten und optimales Regierungsverhalten*, Dissertation, University of Konstanz, June 1976; F. Schneider, *Politisch-ökonomische Gesamtmodelle: ein theoretischer und empirischer Ansatz*, Kronberg/Ts, Hain, 1978.

4. The correlations between the economic variables are: corr. $(I, U) = -0.52$, corr. $(I, GYR) = -0.39$, and corr. $(U, GYR) = -0.61$. There is thus some multicollinearity between explanatory variables. Experimentation by leaving out one of these variables in turn indicates that the coefficients stay reasonably stable, i.e. that the estimates are not seriously biased.

5. See S. M. Lipset, *Political Man*, London, H. E. B. paperback, 1978: 236ff., T. Geiger, *Die soziale Schichtung des Deutschen Volkes*, Stuttgart, 1932 and W. Kaltefleiter, *Wirtschaft und Politik in Deutschland*, Köln, Westdeutscher Verlag.

6. See W. W. Pommerehne and F. Schneider, 'Fiscal Illusion, Political Institutions and Local Public Spending', *Kyklos* 31, 1978: 381-408.

7. The additional economic variables have also been added to a standard popularity function (as presented in Tables 4 and 6) in sequence in order to retain more degrees of freedom. The size of the coefficients and t-values are practically the same as those shown in Table 6.

8. Somewhat more surprisingly, no effect on government popularity of the deficit in the balance of payments has been found for the United Kingdom.

9. See B. S. Frey and L. J. Lau, 'Towards a Mathematical Theory of Government Behavior', *Zeitschrift für Nationalökonomie* 28, 1968: 355-380; B. S. Frey, 'The Politico-Economic System: A Simulation Model', *Kyklos* 27, 1974: 227-254. Empirical estimates for the United States suggest that at least in that country individuals also have a short memory in their role as voters. See R. C. Fair, 'The Effect of Economic Events on Votes for President', *Review of Economics and Statistics* 60, 1978: 159-173.

10. See e.g. J. E. Mueller, 'Presidential Popularity from Truman to Johnson', *American Political Science Review* 64, 1970: 18-34. But see Stimson (1976, op. cit.) and Kernell, S., 'Explaining Presidential Popularity', *The American Political Science Review* 72, 1978: 506-522; for a somewhat different view.

11. Due to an insufficient number of observations, no depreciation variable is estimated for President Ford.

12. The correlations among economic variables are: corr. (I, U) = −0.79, corr. (I, GYR) = −0.32, corr. (U, GYR) = −0.68.

13. See e.g. H. S. Bloom and H. D. Price, 'Voter Response to Short Run Economic Conditions: The Asymetric Effect of Prosperity and Recession', *The American Political Science Review* 69/4, 1975: 1240-1254, also F. Arcelus and A. H. Meltzer, 'The Effect of Aggregate Economic Variables on Congressional Elections', same issue, and S. Goodman and G. H. Kramer, 'Comments on Arcelus and Meltzer', same issue.

14. See e.g. D. A. Hibbs, 'Political Parties and Macroeconomic Policy', *American Economic Review* 71, 1977: 1467-1487.

15. See B. S. Frey and F. Schneider, 'An Empirical Study of Politico-Economic Interaction in the United States', *Review of Economics and Statistics* 60, 1978: Tables 4 and 5, 181-182, and D. A. Hibbs, op. cit.

16. The estimates for the remaining group, unaffiliated voters, are not shown for reasons of space.

3 Politico-Econometric Estimation in Britain: An Alternative Interpretation

Paul Whiteley
University of Bristol, UK

There have been several articles in recent years on the relationship between aggregate economic conditions and the political popularity of the government and opposition parties in Britain.[1] In the most recent of these, Mosley makes some intereting inferences about popular rection to government economic policy-making.[2]

The purpose of this paper is to suggest an alternative explanation of the relationship between economic and political variables, which it is useful to set out in the form of the following propositions:

(1) The existing studies which have examined the relationship between economic conditions and political popularity in the UK have serious statistical deficiencies. When these deficiencies are corrected the relationships are radically changed.

(2) There are no regular political cycles in public opinion in Britain which have any substantive interpretation.

(3) If the relationship between economic variables and voting behaviour is modelled rather than the relationship between the

former and poll data, there appears to be no significant influence of economic variables on electoral support.

The first and second of these propositions are closely inter-related, so they are examined first. The third proposition is examined in a subsequent section.

POLL DATA, POLITICAL CYCLES AND ECONOMIC VARIABLES

The first article to examine the relationship between economic conditions and poll data for Britain was by Goodhart and Bhansali.[3] They concluded:

> First the level of unemployment, with a lag of somewhere around four to six months, and the rate of inflation do influence political popularity significantly, second there may be a natural path of government popularity between elections, with an immediate burst of support in addition to that actually received at elections rapidly dissipated, followed by a long run, but slow decline in popularity which in turn is sharply reversed in the run up to elections.[4]

In a later article Miller and Mackie stressed the importance of cycles in the poll data as causal factors of both government popularity and economic conditions.[5] Frey and Schneider have also found significant cyclical influences at work in political popularity.[6] However, Mosley found that the response functions of popularity to economic conditions changed between periods of high unemployment and high inflation.[7] Thus the parameters of the model shift at different time periods, and the explanatory power of the economic variables varied enormously.

In a short paper written in response to Goodhart and Bhansali, Frey and Garbers made a number of specific technical criticism of their work.[8] These criticisms have been largely ignored in subsequent work including, ironically, that by Frey and Schneider. Much of the discussion of technical problems in this present section is based on these criticisms.

The first problem concerns the technique of estimation used in these various models, ordinary least squares regression. Economic policy can be regarded as much a function of popularity as a cause of it. The use of ordinary least squares estimation in this context involves incurring simultaneous equation bias, which makes the estimates unreliable.[9] It is not easy to specify a model which makes inflation or unemployment a function of political popularity however, since there are many intervening factors. Frey and Schneider have modelled the link between economic policy making and economic variables using government policy instruments such as investment, transfer payment and loans as the dependent variables.[10] But they do not use a technique such as two stage least squares which would avoid the simultaneous equation bias, which means that their own estimates are unreliable in this respect.

A second problem with these models is that the various authors ignore the effects of autocorrelation. This refers to the correlation over time of the error terms in the various regression models.[11] This is can be illustrated in the following example of a two variable model in which the error term is a first order autogressive process.

$$Y_t = b_0 + bX_t + u_t \qquad\qquad (1)$$

where $u_t = \gamma u_{t-1} + e_t$

$$E(e_{t-j}\, e_{t-i}) = 0 \text{ when } i \neq j$$
$$= \gamma u^2 \text{ when } i = j$$

In this example the e_t term behaves like a conventional disturbance term in a model free from autocorrelation, the problem is in the u_t term of the two variable model.

The presence of autocorrelation in a model does not bias the estimates, but the value of the regression coefficients in any one sample is subject to error. As one econometrician puts it 'we may say that an "autocorrelation error" is imparted to the estimates. There is no mathematical formula for the measurement of this sort of error. However, it should be noted that the extent of this error depends on the form and the degree of autocorrelation.'[12]

Autocorrelation also influences the test statistics of the model. It leads to an underestimation of the standard errors of the regression coefficients, making it likely that a coefficient will be accepted as statistically significant, when in fact it is not.

It is however possible to correct for autocorrelation, and thus avoid these problems. This is done by applying generalized least squares estimation to the model. This involves carrying out the following transformation:

$$Y_t - \gamma Y_{t-1} = (bo - \gamma bo) + (b_1 x_t - \gamma b_1 x_{t-1}) + (u_t - \gamma u_{t-1}) \quad (2)$$

Since $e_t = u_t - \gamma u_{t-1}$ the effects of autocorrelation are removed by this transformation. However, I have shown elsewhere that poll data for the UK can be modelled by a stochastic process, specifically a first order autoregressive-moving average model.[13] In the case of governmental popularity i.e. the lead of the incumbent party over the opposition party in the polls the model is as follows:

$$G_t = 0.88 \ G_{t-1} + e_t - 0.18 \ e_{t-1}$$

$R^2 = 0.72$, residual variance $= 6.26$, $N = 348$ (January 1947—December 1975)

G_t is government popularity at time t_1 and e_t, e_{t-1} have the same properties as in (1).

Obviously if the γ coefficient in any structural equation model of government popularity approximates 0.88, that implies that a transformation of that model as in (2) would result in a purely stochastic variable. In other words the right hand side of equation (2) would equal $e_t - 0.18 \ e_{t-1}$, were the transformation to be applied to government popularity. In this event all the coefficients of the transformed model would be zero and so would the coefficient of determination (R^2).

It is possible to estimate the value of γ in a model from its relationship with the Durbin-Watson statistic, which is used to detect autocorrelation in a model.[14] Thus the value of the coefficient can be determined for Goodhart and Bhansali's estimates of the relationship between government popularity, unemployment and inflation for the years 1947-68.[15] They report a Durbin-Watson statistics of 0.40, thus γ equals 0.80. This means that a transformation of the type illustrated in (2) applied to their basic model would produce a random uncorrelated series of observations. Hence correcting for autocorrelation would make the estimate disappear.

Obviously this problem is less serious for models with a less significant degree of autocorrelation, but in the case of Miller-

Mackie and Mosley the value of the estimates and the goodness of fit would be significantly altered by an attempt to eliminate autocorrelation. There are similar problems with Frey and Schneider.[16] In most cases the results would disappear.[17] This conclusion is in fact supported by Goodhart and Bhansali's use of cross-spectral analysis to examine the relationship between govenment popularity and unemployment.[18] They failed to find any relationship between these variables which was statistically significant at the usual levels, a result which of course invalidates their own conclusions from the multiple regression models. The cross-spectral evidence is particularly important because it is not subject to the same problems of model specification, and estimation methods as multiple regression analysis.

A third problem with the existing work on poll data in Britain is a substantive rather than a statistical point. Cyclical variables appear in all of the models mentioned, and are used as explanatory variables in predicting poll movements. But the explanation of the causes of such cycles all postulate long-term learning or adaptive behaviour on the part of the public. In the United States Mueller attributes the decline in popular support for Presidents from inauguration day onwards to a 'coalition of minorities' effect.[19] This assumes that when a President makes policy decisions he alienates more voters than he pleases, and thus the longer he stays in office the more unpopular he will become if one assumes that individuals remain alienated over successive years. Alternatively, Stimson attributes cycles in Presidential support to an 'expectation — disillusionment — forgiveness' cycle in the public's attitude.[20] In Britain Miller-Mackie attribute cycles to the context in which opinion polls ask questions.[21] They argue that at times distant from elections, voters react directly to the performance of the government. However, when the elections approach they are more aware that attitudes to the government involve supporting or opposing the incumbent party at the polls. This awareness changes the context in which they reply to pollsters' questions.

For these different explanations to be plausible it is necessary to assume that voters have a long term awareness of political events either with respect to politics, or to the parliamentary life cycle of the government. There is little support for such an idea in the survey evidence on the stability of voter attitudes.[22]

A different interpretation of apparent cycles in political popularity can be stated as follows. In general individual voters have a low level of knowledge and interest in political affairs, but at the same time they react to individual events. A few people change their partisanship frequently in response to specific events relating to the behaviour of the government and opposition. Others remain loyal to one party regardless of events, and most remain loyal most of the time. Thus public opinion as a whole is characterized by a high level of inertia. A whole series of adverse events have to occur to change government popularity drastically for the worse. Public opinion is 'driven' by a series of one-off events which act like shocks to the system over time. The inertia of opinion ensures that when a government enjoys above average popularity, it will retain that position for several periods. If adverse events make it lose popularity, it will in turn remain unpopular for several periods. In this way irregular cycles are generated, but they have no substantive significance of a political nature. The public are not learning, or becoming disillusioned in a predictable way at a particular point of time in the life of a parliament. Rather they are reacting to one-off events.[23]

The empirical evidence supporting this interpretation of cycles is discussed more fully elsewhere.[24] But this explains why political popularity can be modelled by a first order autoregressive moving-average stochastic process. In the case of government popularity I have shown that once a unique event occurs to influence opinion it will take ten months before that event ceases to influence opinion, assuming it is not overtaken by other events in the meantime.[25] This is a measure of the inertia of the system.

The crucial test for this interpretation of political cycles is whether or not cycles in public opinion are regular. A first order autoregressive moving-average process will not generate cycles of regular periodicity, only irregular cycles. Thus the validity of this interpretation can be tested, at least in part, by exploring the data for regular cycles. The evidence suggests that there are none; Goodhart and Bhansali used spectral analysis to test specifically for this and concluded:

> It has also been shown that there may not be regular major cycles in these political popularity series, and that contrary to popular belief there may not be any seasonal patterns.[26]

This interpretation suggests that although several writers have used cyclical variables, in the form of crude trend terms as explanatory variables in their models these cyclical variables have no substantive interpretation. What then is the role of economic variables in this analysis? They are in fact random shocks to the system, alongside the other one-off events mentioned earlier. This implies that a given change in one economic variable, such as unemployment will have a differential impact at different periods of time. A rise in unemployment of 500,000 will have only a small political impact when it is overshadowed by exponentially rising levels of inflation, as in the period 1973-75. On the other hand if this had happened in the 1950s it would have produced a major crisis in government. The system is in a continuous state of adaptation, so that the impact of an event depends on its proximity to other events, and whether or not it represents a sharp departure from previous experience. A structural equation which tries to model this adaptive dynamic system over a long period, will merely produce estimates which are a mongrel combination of varying short term effects. Such estimates are useless for policy analysis applications.

If cycles appear to be substantively irrelevant, and the existing studies of the relationship between aggregate economic conditions and poll data unreliable, does this mean that it is impossible to estimate the influence of the economy on politics? An alternative approach is to use electoral data rather than poll data. Electoral data avoids any problems of autocorrelation since the observations are separated by several years. However, in a single equation it is still subject to simultaneous equation bias, though this is only important if it is desired to get precise estimates. In the next section we shall examine the relationship between voting behaviour and economic conditions, not so much to get precise estimates as to answer the question, is there a relationship?

VOTING BEHAVIOUR AND ECONOMIC VARIABLES 1900-1974

Several authors in the US have used voting data to examine the influence of aggregate economic conditions on the political system.

In his review of the US literature Kramer[27] concluded that:

> On the basic question of whether economic fluctuations are a major influence on election outcomes, several studies appear to indicate an affirmative answer, but others present equally strong evidence to the opposite effect.[28]

His own results tend to support the view that electoral outcomes are responsive to changes in economic conditions. In this connection he found changes in real personal income in the year prior to the election to be particularly important. 'In quantitative terms, a 10 per cent decrease in per capita real personal income would cost the incumbent administration 4 or 5 per cent of the congressional vote, other things being equal.'[29]

However, Kramer's results were strongly challenged by Stigler on both theoretical and empirical grounds.[30] On theoretical grounds Stigler questioned the rationality of vote switching on the basis of such short-term changes, especially when such changes in economic conditions might be perceived as being outside the control of the incumbent party. Stigler also re-estimated Kramer's model using changes in real income away from trend over a two-year period prior to an election. With this and other changes Kramer's findings disappeared.

Using a rather different specification of the model Arcelus and Meltzer incorporated abstention as well as vote switching, and showed that the effect of economic variables was very small.[31] Moreover, their main influence was to change participation rates, rather than to cause vote switching. Their findings generally supported Stigler's view. Another model which supported a modified version of Kramer's model was by Bloom and Price.[32] They showed that the electorate were willing to vote against an incumbent party in times of recession, but not necessarily to vote for it in times of prosperity. Thus an asymmetry existed in the relationship between economic policy outcome and voting behaviour. They argued that Stigler had mis-specified his model by examining income changes in a two year period prior to the election, rather than a one year period. In a rejoinder Arcelus and Meltzer accepted these results.[33]

Thus a consensus seems to exist in the US literature that economic conditions have an asymmetrical effect on electoral behaviour. However, these results have not been replicated in Britain using electoral data. In modelling the relationship between aggregate economic variables and electoral behaviour a variety of different variables have been used. However, in most of the literature the common measures are real income changes, money income changes, prices and unemployment.

There were twenty-one general elections in Britain between 1900 and 1974. The Conservative Party has either been in Government or has provided the main opposition throughout this period. Thus the relationship between economic conditions and support for the Conservative Party is modelled for twenty of the twenty-one general elections this century. The general election of 1918 is excluded because the party system fragmented greatly in this post-war crisis election. The Conservative vote is specified in two different ways. Firstly it is specified in terms of the Conservative percentage of the two party vote. The main opposition party to the Conservatives was the Liberals prior to 1914, and the Labour party from 1922 onwards. When this variable is used the influence of other parties or non-voting is ignored, and the focus of attention is one vote switching between the main two protagonists. Arguably, when the Conservative Party was in coalition with a rump of the Labour Party after 1935 such a specification of the variable is inadequate to take account of different voter strategies. Consequently the second specification of the dependent variable measures the Conservative vote as a percentage of the entire electorate. This is obviously influenced by all possible electoral strategies of vote switching, including abstention.

The economic variables used have already been mentioned briefly. However, before the influence of these variables on the Conservative vote can be examined it is necessary to take account of major electoral re-alignments during this period. If such shifts in the pattern of voting were ignored their influence would be felt by a distortion of the estimates; the models would be wrongly specified. During this period three major upheavals occurred in the British political system. Firstly, the 1914-18 War led to the collapse of the Liberal Party and the rise of the Labour Party as the main opposition to the Conservatives. This was a major electoral re-alignment. Secondly there was the Coalition government of 1931 which followed in the wake of the Great Depression and the General Strike. Ramsey Macdonald, the leader of the Labour Party, went into coalition with the Conservatives and Liberals and split his party, thereby condemning it to opposition until after the Second World War; this greatly favoured the Conservatives. The third major political upheaval was the Second World War, when at the general election of 1945 the Labour Party received the largest popular vote for any single political party in British history. Each of these major electoral re-alignments is modelled by a dummy variable, as described below.

The influence of economic variables on the Conservative vote clearly should depend on whether or not the Conservative Party is incumbent in office at the time of the election. If the economy is prosperous, unemployment and price inflation low this should help the incumbent party. Thus we can define an incumbency variable equal to 1 when the Conservatives were in government at the time of the election, and − 1 otherwise. This incumbency variable is used to weight each of the economic indicators on the assumption that from a popularity point of view incumbency is the inverse of opposition.

Following the US literature the influence of the economic variables is measured by changes taking place in them over the year prior to the election. The length of the time period over which economic variables influence public opinion has been disputed, although most writers have assumed it to be twelve months.[34] Accordingly we assume this to be the case.

The detailed specification of the variables is as follows:

I	is the incumbency variable and equals 1 when the Conservatives were in office at the time of the election, − 1 otherwise;
WW1	the World War I dummy variable = 0 for elections prior to 1918, 1 for elections after this year;
WW2	the World War II dummy variable = 0 for elections prior to 1945, 1 for elections from 1945 onwards;
NG	the National Government dummy = 1 for the 1931 and 1935 general elections, and 0 otherwise

$$\text{INC} = \frac{NNI_t - NNI_{t-1}}{NNI_{t-1}} \, 100$$

	where NNI_t is the net national income in the election year in money terms;
RINC	is the same as INC, except it is expressed in constant 1930 prices;
UNEM	is the rate of unemployment in the election year minus the rate in the previous year.

PRICES   Cost of living index in election year minus the cost of living index in the previous year (1930 = 100).

(*Sources*: Data up to 1968 was obtained from A. H. Halsey, *Trends in British Society Since 1900* (London: Macmillan, 1972). Net National Income from Table 3.1, p. 81, Cost of living from Table 4.11, p. 122, Unemployment from Table 4.8, p. 119, Net National Income in constant prices was calculated from Net National Income in Money Terms and divided by the Cost of living index. Data after 1968 was obtained from *The Annual Abstract of Statistics*, 112, 1975 [London, HMSO 1976]).

The estimates for four different models appear in Table 1, where the results are calculated for the two dependent variables. The first three models are estimates of the relationships for the twenty general elections. The fourth model consists of estimates for general election after 1945 on the hypothesis that the relationship between economic and voting variables may only be significant in post-war Britain. This might be argued on the grounds that the electorate only hold the government responsible for aggregate employment and price inflation during the post-war era, when through techniques of Keynesian demand management governments have sought to control these variables.

The model which uses the Conservative vote as a percentage of the two party vote fits rather better than the other specification of the Conservative vote. However, 70 per cent of the variance in the conservative vote is explained by the three re-alignment dummy variables. When the economic variables are added they explain only an additional 5 per cent of the variance. None of the estimates of the economic variables in the two party model are remotely statistically significant. Moreover the signs of the RINC and the PRICES variables are against expectations; increases in real and money income should increase the Conservative vote, similarly increases in prices should decrease the Conservative vote. Thus it appears that changes in economic variables do not significantly influence voting behaviour in Britain from 1900 to 1974. The same conclusion also applies to the post-war period, where once again none of the estimates are remotely statistically significant.

The Conservative percentage share of the electorate is much less well explained by the re-alignment dummy variables. The addition of the economic variables doubles the variance explained and this is mainly accounted for by the Conservative incumbency dummy and

PRICES, both of which are statistically significant. The sign of the PRICES variable is against expectations; however, this is not a robust result. The relationship is attributable to two outliers, the general elections of 1974 when prices were increasing at almost exponential rates. If these outliers are deleted and the models re-estimated the PRICES estimate ceases to be statistically significant. The Conservative incumbency estimate does appear to be robust to changes in the number of observations. It is significant at the 0.10 level for the specification which uses money income, and at the 0.05 level for the specification using real income. Thus incumbency alone, regardless of performance, appears to lose votes. Apart from that, the same interpretation applies as in the two party vote specification; economic variables do not appear to be significantly related to voting behaviour.

CONCLUSION

It would have been interesting to test the Bloom and Price finding of an asymmetrical relationship between economic conditions and voting in Britain. Unfortunately there were not enough observations to do this of years in which real income declined. That aside, these results support the interpretation that no significant relationships exist between changes in aggregate economic variables and electoral support. However these data are highly aggregated and the sample of necessity is small.

In the context of poll data, and following the interpretation of the nature of public opinion given earlier it may still be possible to measure the impact of individual economic events. The best way to do this would be to use the time series intervention models introduced by Box and Tiao and used by Hibbs.[35] However, such an exercise is beyond the scope of this paper. One thing remains clear though, since public opinion is a dynamic adaptive system the relationship between economic events and political popularity measured by the polls has not been adequately modelled by the existing approaches.

TABLE 1

The Influence of Economic and Political Variables on the Conservative Vote in Britain 1900-1974

Predictor Variables	Conservative Vote as % Electorate				Conservative Vote as % of 2 Party System			
I		-0.58*	-0.47			-0.17	-0.27	
		(2.38)	(1.62)			(0.93)	(1.34)	
WW1	-0.28	-0.04	-0.13		0.40*	0.40*	0.43*	
	(1.00)	(0.15)	(0.46)		(2.28)	(1.98)	(2.18)	
WW2	0.44	0.18	0.33		-0.66*	-0.62*	-0.69*	
	(1.52)	(0.58)	(1.17)		(3.65)	(2.77)	(3.44)	
NG	0.56*	0.44	0.44		0.38*	0.32	0.31*	
	(2.22)	(1.55)	(1.46)		(2.40)	(1.56)	(1.48)	
(INC)I			-0.08				0.15	
			(0.23)				(0.60)	
(RINC)I		0.28		0.06		-0.14		0.11
		(1.08)		(0.11)		(0.74)		(0.21)
(UNEM)I		0.11	0.01	0.43		-0.05	0.00	-0.30
		(0.38)	(0.04)	(0.88)		(0.23)	(0.00)	(0.59)
(PRICES)I		0.42*	0.49	0.48		0.20	0.11	0.06
		(1.80)	(1.68)	(1.18)		(1.17)	(0.55)	(0.15)
R^2	0.25	0.52	0.48	0.23	0.70	0.75	0.74	0.18
N	20	20	20	10	20	20	20	10

Coefficients are standardized, t ratios are in parenthesis
*Significant at the .05 level

NOTES

1. For a review of this field see B. S. Frey and F. Schneider 'on the modelling of politico-economic Interdependence', *European Journal of Political Research* III, 1975: 339-360.

2. P. Mosley, 'Images of the "floating voter": or the "political business cycle" revisited', *Political Studies* XXVI, 1978: 375-394.

3. C. Goodhart and R. Bhansali 'Political Economy', *Political Studies* XVIII, 1970: 43-106.

4. C. Goodhart and R. Bhansali ibid, 61.

5. W. Miller and M. Mackie, 'The Electoral Cycle and the Assymetry of Government and Opposition Popularity: An alternative Model of the Relationship between Economic Conditions and Political Popularity', *Political Studies* XXI, 1973: 263-279.

6. B. Frey and F. Schneider, 'A politico-economic Model of the United Kingdom', *Economic Journal* 88, 1978: 243-253.

7. P. Mosley (1978) 384-385.

8. B. Frey and H. Garbers, 'Politico-econometrics — an Estimation in Political Economy', *Political Studies* XIX, 1971: 316-320.

9. See J. Johnston, *Econometric Methods* (Tokyo: Mcgraw-Hill, Kogakusha 1972) 341-343.

10. B. Frey and F. Schneider (1978), 247.

11. See J. Johnston (1972), Chapter 8 passim.

12. A. Koutsoyiannis, *Theory of Econometrics* (London: Macmillan 1973), 203.

13. See P. Whiteley, 'Electoral Forecasting from Poll Data: The British Case', *British Journal of Political Science*, 9 (1979) 219-236.

14. The Durbin-Watson statistic is related to the autoregressive coefficient by the following expression.

$$d \approx 2(1 - \gamma)$$

See H. H. Kelejian and W. E. Oates, *Introduction to Econometrics* (New York: Harper and Row 1974), 200-203.

15. G. Goodhart and R.Bhansali (1970), 62.

16. In their model Frey and Schneider use government lead as their dependent variable, and include the same variable lagged one period as one of their predictors. They publish a Durbin-Watson statistic of 1.97, which appears to indicate no significant autocorrelation. However it is well known that the Durbin-Watson test is unreliable when a lagged dependent variable is used as a predictor. As Johnston points out 'Despite explicit warnings in the original paper that the Durbin-Watson test is not applicable to an equation containing lagged values among the explanatory variables it has often been applied for want of anything better to such cases.' J. Johnston, *Econometric Methods* (Tokyo: Mcgraw Hill Kogakusha 1972), 309. Frey and Schneider re-estimate the same equation without the lagged dependent variable and in this case the Durbin-Watson statistic is in the indeterminate range. This means that autocorrelation in their model can neither be demonstrated nor ruled out at the 0.05 level. See B. Frey and F. Schneider (1978), 246.

17. Another approach to the problem of autocorrelation involves incorporating sets of dummy variables to take account of cyclical and trend factors, even if (as I argue below) these have no substantive significance. Pissarides incorporates three dummy electoral variables as well as economic variables into a model of UK government popularity between 1955-75. He finds significant relationships for the economic variables and, because of the present of the dummy variables, no autocorrelation. However, he goes on to examine subperiods running moving regressions

with quarterly data for 1955 (1) — 1965 (4), 1956 (1) — 1966 (4) and so on. The coefficients of the economic variables in the submodels were not robust, but fluctuated widely. He concluded 'inflation and unemployment that were of primary importance in the 1950s and 60s ceased to be considered as indicators of the government's performance in the 1970s.' See C. Pissarides, 'Government Popularity and Economic Performance' (1978) (Mimeo, Department of Economics, L.S.E.), 7. This interpretation is consistent with the view expressed below that public opinion is a dynamic adaptive system.

18. C. Goodhart and R. Bhansali (1970), 104. A cross-spectral analysis is analogous to the analysis of covariance. It allows the researcher to determine the extent to which the two series are interrelated over time.

19. J. E. Mueller, 'Presidential Popularity from Truman to Johnson', *American Political Science Review* 64, 1970: 18-34.

20. J. Stimson, 'Public Support for American Presidents: A cyclical Model', *Public Opinion Quarterly* 40, 1976: 1-21.

21. W. Miller and M. Mackie, op. cit., 265-266.

22. For a discussion of the long term instability in voter attitudes see D. Butler and D. Stokes, *Political Change in Britain* (London: Macmillan 1974) Chapter 12 passim.

23. This is the same type of explanation of public opinion in Britain as Kernell gives for US Presidential popularity. See S. Kernell, 'Explaining Presidential Popularity', *American Political Science Review* 72, 1978: 506-522.

24. See P. Whiteley, 'Electoral Forecasting from Poll Data' (1979).

25. P. Whiteley, ibid (1979), 227.

26. C. Goodhard and R. Bhansali (1970), 97.

27. G. H. Kramer, 'Short Term Fluctuations in US Voting Behaviour 1896-1964', *American Political Science Review* 65, 1971: 131-143.

28. G. H. Kramer, ibid (1971), 133.

29. G. H. Kramer, ibid (1971), 141.

30. G. S. Stigler, 'General Economic Conditions and National Elections', *American Economic Review*, Papers and Proceedings, 63, 1973: 160-167.

31. F. Arcelus and A. H. Meltzer, 'The Effect of Aggregate Economic Variables on Congressional Elections', *American Political Science Review* 69, 1975: 1232-1239.

32. H. J. Bloom and H. Douglas Price, 'Voter Response to Short Run Economic Conditions: the Asymmetric Effect of Prosperity and Recession', *American Political Science Review* 69, 1975: 1240-1254.

33. F. Arcelus and A. H. Meltzer, 'Aggregate Economic Variables and Votes for Congress: A Rejoinder', *American Political Science Review* 69, 1975: 1266-1269.

34. See the discussion of this by H. Bloom and H. Douglas Price (1975) p. 1243 in relation to Stigler's estimates.

35. See D. A. Hibbs, 'On Analysing the Effects of Policy Interventions: Box-Jenkins and Box - Tiao versus structural Equation models', in (ed.) D. Heise, *Sociological Methodology* (San Francisco and Washington: Jossey-Bass 1977), 1467-1487.

4 Economic Conditions and Elections in France

Jean Jacques Rosa

Institut d'Etudes Politiques, Paris, France

The relationship between economic conditions and electoral behaviour has been examined for a number of countries. Much of the initial empirical work in this field was done in the United States.[1] The influence of the economy on the political system has not, however, been examined in the case of France. The purpose of this paper is to examine this relationship in France over the period 1920 to 1973, comparing the results particularly with work done on the United States.

A certain number of difficulties are encountered when comparing the case of France with that of the United States. Historically, French elections have produced results which are far more politically heterogeneous than the United States. In this situation the fundamental problem is to choose a political variable which allows the relationship between electoral behaviour and economic conditions to be rigorously examined. In the United States the number of votes recorded for the two major parties is an adequate measure for this type of model. However, this is not the case in France. The multi-party system and the government coalitions which result, many of which are extremely fragile, make it impossible to work with aggregate party votes alone. Moreover, in France there is not a clear dividing line between the Left and the Right. Only the Communist and the Right can be unequivocally identified politically. However, the Communists and the extreme Right have never represented the majority of French voters. In political terms France is most often regarded as the 'eternel marais'.

Parties other than the Communists and the Right cannot be clearly identified as a 'third force' in French politics. Furthermore it would be difficult to infer that a citizen voting for a centrist party is satisfied or otherwise with the policies of the government. The labyrinth of partisan coalitions make it very difficult for the voter to define himself clearly. He might cast a vote for a centrist party as a protest against a particular policy only to find his party in coalition repudiating its previous position in favour of an agreed coalition line. For example, voters who supported Mendes France in January 1956 may have believed that they were supporting the former President of the Council in a radical policy but, just a few months later, the same vote served to reinforce the position of Mendes-France's political adversaries. In the same way, the 'Cartel' voters who pronounced themselves in favour of the Left in 1924 very often found themselves supporting the Conservative policies of Poincaré two years later. Should they have been considered to have changed their opinions if they trusted the National Union of the President of the Council in 1928? Or were they in that event merely remaining faithful to their previous votes? These examples illustrate the difficulty of dividing the vote into two categories as in the United States, as a means of measuring the relationship between economic conditions and electoral support.

In spite of this it is clear that since 1919, except for the Liberation period when the situation was exceptionally partisan, elections for the most part took place at a time when the parties of the Left were in opposition to the ruling party's policies. For this reason a Leftist vote can be considered to be partly an expression of the electorates' discontent. Of course not all Leftist voting is a protest vote, but the link between discontent and Leftist voting is strong enough to be of use in examining the political impact of aggregate economic conditions. By the same token some of the electoral support for Right-wing groups such as the Poujadistes in 1956 or other less easily classified groups such as the RPF and UNR was undoubtedly a protest vote. But these groups had only an episodic influence, and were too ambiguous in their political positions for their support to be characterized as a protest vote, in the same way as the Left. For example, if we were to regard the RPF as a protest vote, we would have to infer that such a vote dramatically fell in 1958 after the UNR became associated with the new regime.

The Left-wing vote, on the other hand, is easily defined and can provide a useful indicator of the level of discontent amongst the French electorate. Such an interpretation, although imperfect, is rooted in the concrete reality of post-war politics in France. Thus within the framework of the present study the percentage of votes obtained by Left-wing parties as a whole in the first round of Parliamentary and Constitutent elections since 1919 is taken as a representative measure of voter discontent with the performance of the Government.[2]

There were a number of problems related to the availability of data, where economic variables were concerned, as statistical series in France are fewer, shorter and less homogeneous than the United States. Nevertheless, it was possible to compile consecutive series on prices, real income, unemployment and population for the years 1920-1973.[3] The lack of information prior to 1920 made it impossible to extend the study further back in time. Moreover, the incomplete statistics on population since 1920 made it necessary to carry out simple linear interpolations in order to obtain continuous series for the total population, the working population and the unemployed.

The complexity of the political situation in France, which was described above, makes it necessary to carry out a variety of empirical tests. The first hypothesis to be tested is that the Left-wing vote, taken as a whole, represents discontent over the economic management of the government in power. This is followed up by an examination of the relationship between economic variables and the Communist vote on the one hand, and on the non-Communist Left-wing vote on the other. It is not at all certain that economic conditions influence these various voters in the same way.

The overall results obtained do in fact seem to indicate notable differences between the Communist and the non-Communist Left.

TABLE 1
The Left as a whole — variables in level form for the election year t_0

Constant term	Prices	National Income	National Income per capita	Unemployed	Unemployed per working population	R^2	DW
55.315 (18.635)	-0.384 (1.617)	0.024 (.502)		-0.0023 (0.288)		0.684	1.746
55.317 (18.487)	-0.376 (1.632)	0.022 (0.484)			-0.0039 (0.255)	0.683	1.756
55.181 (13.474)	-0.329 (1.392)		0.017 (0.266)	-0.001 (0.124)		0.678	1.783
55.207 (13.527)	-0.326 (1.414)		0.016 (0.258)		-0.0016 (0.108)	0.678	1.788

(Note = t statistics are in parenthesis)   D.W = Durbin-Watson statistic

TABLE 2
The Left as a whole — variables in level form for year preceding election $t-1$

Constant term	Prices	National Income	National Income per capita	Unemployed	Unemployed per working population	R^2	DW
54.510 (18.408)	-0.104 (0.359)	-0.034 (0.602)		0.010 (0.969)		0.711	2.240
54.505 (17.996)	-0.143 (0.514)	-0.026 (0.486)			0.017 (0.865)	0.706	2.213
56.750 (15.906)	0.0228 (0.087)		-0.078 (1.172)	0.0137 (1.430)		0.737	2.459
56.462 (15.565)	-0.022 (0.086)		-0.066 (1.022)		0.024 (1.279)	0.727	2.408

TABLE 3
The Left as a whole — variables in level form, the mean of the current year and previous year $(t_0 + t_{-1})/2$

Constant Term	Prices	National Income	National Income per capita	Unemployed	Unemployed per working population	R^2	DW
55.385 (18.543)	-0.257 (0.905)	-0.005 (0.100)		0.0028 (0.289)		0.701	1.991
55.549 (18.373)	-0.261 (0.967)	-0.004 (0.085)			0.005 (0.292)	0.701	1.988
56.617 (14.208)	-0.182 (0.685)		-0.028 (0.397)	0.004 (0.516)		0.705	2.094
56.496 (14.257)	-0.192 (0.753)		-0.0249 (0.369)		0.0088 (0.499)	0.704	2.080

TABLE 4
The Left as a whole — variables in level form, the mean of the current year and the previous three years

$$\left(\sum_{i=0}^{-3} t_i/4 \right)$$

Constant Term	Prices	National Income	National Income per capita	Unemployed	Unemployed per working population	R^2	DW
53.737 (16.771)	-0.146 (0.732)	-0.030 (0.716)		0.0126 (1.250)		0.743	2.096
53.676 (16.458)	-0.162 (0.831)	-0.026 (0.646)			0.023 (1.222)	0.742	2.106
55.621 (15.158)	-0.042 (0.194)		-0.066 (1.133)	0.015 (1.549)		0.761	2.306
55.378 (14.805)	-0.069 (0.326)		-0.057 (1.029)		0.028 (1.480)	0.757	2.287

THE TESTS

The first series of tests applied to the Left-wing votes as a whole used the economic variables measured in level form (Tables 1, 2, 3 and 4). The percentage of variance explained by the economic variables is quite high, clearly higher than the American studies. However the regression coefficients are not statistically significant. Thus the relationship between the economic variables and the Left-wing vote is obscure. One problem with these models is the high correlation which exists between two of the independent variables, the price index and the level of National Income. This causes multicollinearity, making the estimates of the regression coefficients imprecise. This situation can be remedied by using the rate of growth of the price index, or the inflation rate, instead of the level of the price index. The former is much less highly correlated with the level of National Income than the latter. The results of this second series of tests are shown in Tables 5, 6, 7 and 8. The percentage of variance explained is rather lower in these than in the first four models, but it still remains higher than in the reference studies; also the regression coefficients become statistically significant.

The results of these models can be summarized as follows:

— The rate of inflation is significantly, and positively related to the percentage of votes going to the Left-wing.
— Per capita income is significantly and negatively related to the percentage of Left-wing votes.
— The level of unemployment, and unemployment per capita is significantly and positively related to the Left-wing vote.

These conclusions remain valid for the varying forms of the tests whether the independent variables were measured in the election year (Table 5), in the year preceding the elections (Table 6), in the mean of the election and previous years (Table 7) or in the mean of the four years up to and including the election year (Table 8).

The evidence for France seems to indicate an even closer link between economic conditions and the orientation of voters than is true of the United States. It is interesting that the best fitting model was the one with the average of the variables over the years preceding

TABLE 5
The Left as a whole — variables in level form except prices (in rate of growth form) estimates for election year t_o

Constant Term	Prices	National Income	National Income per capita	Unemployed	Unemployed per working population	R^2
44.61	0.228 (2.04)	0.003 (0.16)		0.0136 (1.29)	*	0.377
54.70	0.157 (1.99)		-0.071 (2.71)	0.012 (1.72)		0.675
55.02	0.151 (1.97)		-0.072 (2.80)		0.024 (1.81)	0.685
44.75	0.223 (2.03)	0.005 (0.23)			0.028 (1.31)	0.380

TABLE 6
The Left as a whole — variables in level form except prices (in rate of growth form). Estimates for year prior to election t_{-1}

Constant Term	Prices	National Income	National Income per capita	Unemployed	Unemployed per working population	R^2
41.81	0.299 (2.27)	0.005 (0.34)		0.024 (2.12)		0.490
53.06	0.178 (2.14)		-0.073 (3.20)	0.018 (2.62)		0.773
53.72	0.163 (2.14)		-0.076		0.038 (2.96)	0.799
41.78	0.296 (2.29)	0.010 (0.59)	(3.59)		0.050 (2.17)	0.498

TABLE 7
The Left as a whole — variables in level form, except prices (in rate of growth form). Estimates for the mean of the election and previous years

Constant Term	Prices	National Income	National Income per capita	Unemployed	Unemployed per working population	R^2
44.17	0.276 (2.05)	0.003 (0.15)		0.016 (1.42)		0.391
54.56	0.185 (2.08)		−0.075 (2.95)	0.014 (1.94)		0.708
53.24	0.158 (2.19)		−0.072 (3.24)		0.037 (2.68)	0.774
41.90	0.259 (2.33)	0.010 (0.53)			0.047 (2.03)	0.495

TABLE 8
The Left as a whole — variables in level form except prices (in rate of growth form). Estimates for the mean of the election and previous three years

Constant Term	Prices	National Income	National Income per capita	Unemployed	Unemployed per working population	R^2
38.85	0.337 (2.46)	0.012 (0.81)		0.030 (2.49)		0.551
51.53	0.199 (2.51)		−0.074 (3.35)	0.022 (2.91)		0.797
52.74	0.171 (2.35)		−0.080 (3.81)		0.044 (3.22)	0.818
39.05	0.329 (2.42)	0.017 (1.08)			0.061 (2.50)	0.553

the election (see Table 8). This supports the view that the voter judges the situation over the entire period since the previous election. The explanatory variables which maximize the variance explained are the rate of inflation, the National Income per capita and the ratio of the unemployed to the total working population. Inflation favours the Left-wing vote, as do increases in the ratio of unemployed to the total working population. An increase in per capital real income, however, is unfavourable to the Left. In the different specifications of the model these three variables are always statistically significant (see the 't' statistics) and always have the same sign. Of the three, the 'real per capita income' variable appears the most significant; although it is difficult to interpret the order of importance of the parameters because of the use of indices and index ratios as explanatory variables. When the base year is far away in time, comparisons of contemporary changes in the indices are difficult to make. Even so, these results are a striking confirmation of the original theoretical hypothesis.

A more stringent test of the relationships involves using changes in the independent variables as predictors of changes in the Left-wing vote. When this is done the results are inconclusive. However, the absence of a link between changes in economic conditions and changes in the total Left-wing vote does not refute the original hypothesis. This is because a model expressed in rate of change form assumes that the electorate has a very sensitive awareness of economic circumstances, an assumption which contradicts the evidence that voters are imperfectly informed. Such a specification also rules out the fact that the electorate may be sceptical of the abilities of different governments to finely adjust the economic situation.

The study of the Communist vote provides an additional perspective. When the Communist vote is used as the dependent variable, the tests on the variables expressed in level form show the significant and positive influence of the price level (see Tables 9, 10, 11 and 12). In every specification of the model using the Communist vote the goodness of fit (R^2) exceeds 0.55. Thus more than 55 per cent of the variance in Communist voting is explained by changes in the levels of economic variables. In addition to prices there is a significant but negative relationship between per capita income and the Communist vote. However, multicollinearity af-

TABLE 9
The Communist Party — variables in level form.
Estimates for the election year

Constant Term	Prices	National Income	National Income per capita	Unemployed	Unemployed per working population	R^2	DW
26.874	0.706	-0.123		-0.002			
(7.877)	(2.587)	(2.259)		(0.260)		0.585	1.486
26.881	0.714	-0.124			-0.004	0.585	1.489
(7.818)	(2.695)	(2.384)			(0.236)		
32.688	0.799		-0.193	-0.0007		0.664	1.859
(7.785)	(3.294)		(2.940)	(-0.09)			
32.708	0.802		-0.194		0.001	0.664	1.862
(7.817)	(3.396)		(3.064)		(0.078)		

TABLE 10
The Communist Party — variables in level form.
Estimates for the year prior to the election year

Constant Term	Prices	National Income	National Income per capita	Unemployed	Unemployed per working population	R^2	DW
27.030	1.136	-0.207		0.012		0.724	1.36
(9.306)	(3.99)	(3.755)		(1.168)			
26.970	1.101	-0.199			0.0217	0.720	1.379
(9.090)	(4.041)	(3.810)			(1.094)		
34.791	1.253		-0.3068	0.014		0.880	1.755
(14.390)	(7.084)		(6.740)	(2.274)			
34.478	1.214		-0.296		0.026	0.873	1.787
(13.876)	(6.967)		(6.641)		(2.083)		

TABLE 11
The Communist Party — variables in level form.
Estimates for mean of election and previous years

Constant Term	Prices	National Income	National Income per capita	Unemployed	Unemployed per working population	R^2	DW
27.503	0.963	-0.174		0.005		0.648	1.489
(8.437)	(3.118)	(2.847)		(0.503)			
27.449	0.950	0.172			0.00098	0.648	1.486
(8.340)	(3.225)	(2.966)			(0.489)		
34.882	1.087		-0.269	0.008		0.785	1.828
(10.225)	(4.776)		(4.434)	(1.045)			
34.668	1.066		-0.262		0.015	0.785	1.814
(10.178)	(4.856)		(4.529)		(0.992)		

TABLE 12
The Communist Party — variables in level form.
Estimates for mean of election and previous years

Constant Term	Prices	National Income	National Income per capita	Unemployed	Unemployed per working population	R^2	DW
26.550	0.718	-0.137		0.002		0.550	1.219
(6.236)	(2.698)	(2.674)		(0.172)			
26.418	0.724	-0.138			0.0056	0.551	1.226
(6.120)	(2.809)	(2.594)			(0.219)		
33.893	1.062		-0.266	0.011		0.770	1.916
(9.396)	(4.901)		(4.649)	(1.149)			
33.709	1.043		-0.261		0.021	0.769	1.891
(9.210)	(4.983)		(4.743)		(1.109)		

TABLE 13
The Communist Party — independent variables
in rate of change form

Constant Term	Prices	National Income	National Income per capita	Unemployed	Unemployed per working population	R^2	DW
16.126	23.344	7.1695		7.479		0.388	1.025
(7.532)	(1.760)	(0.465)		(0.724)			
16.269	23.455		5.455		6.404	0.376	0.964
(7.576)	(1.731)		(0.343)		(0.611)		

TABLE 14
The Communist Party — all variables in rate of change form.
Estimates for election year t_0

Constant Term	Prices	National Income	National Income per capita	Unemployed	Unemployed per working population	R^2	DW
0.033	1.170	- 0.983		-0.125		0.235	2.243
(0.272)	(1.417)	(1.042)		(0.208)			
0.031	1.184	-0.977			-0.100	0.234	2.248
(0.256)	(1.436)	(1.032)			(0.167)		
0.024	1.178		-0.976	-0.136		0.231	2.192
(0.202)	(1.417)		(1.019)	(0.225)			
0.022	1.193		-0.969		-0.109	0.230	2.196
(0.185)	(1.425)		(1.006)		(0.181)		

TABLE 15
The Communist Party. All variables in rate of change form.
Estimates for year prior to election year

Constant Term	Prices	National Income	National Income per capita	Unemployed	Unemployed per working population	R^2	DW
0.190 (1.861)	0.091 (0.147)	-3.269 (2.671)		- 0.230 (0.949)		0.448	2.896
0.189 (1.846)	0.095 (0.152)	-3.273 (2.661)			-0.224 (0.923)	0.445	2.894
0.170 (1.637)	0.145 (0.225)		-3.237 (2.475)	- 0.221 (0.984)		0.411	2.864
0.169 (1.622)	0.149 (0.232)		-3.238 (2.464)		-0.214 (0.854)	0.408	2.860

TABLE 16
The Communist Party. All variables in rate of change form.
Estimates for the mean of the election and previous years

Constant Term	Prices	National Income	National Income per capita	Unemployed	Unemployed per working population	R^2	DW
0.249 (1.798)	-0.518 (0.560)	-3.005 (2.016)		-0.285 (0.631)		0.325	2.694
0.247 (1.780)	-0.514 (0.551)	-3.002 (2.006)			-0.270 (0.598)	0.322	2.488
0.234 (1.702)	-0.490 (0.522)		-3.047 (1.924)	-0.295 (0.642)		0.306	2.505
0.233 (1.684)	-0.484 (0.513)		-3.042 (1.913)		-0.279 (0.606)	0.302	2.498

TABLE 17
The Communist Party. All variables in rate of change form.
Estimates for the mean of the election and previous three years

Constant Term	Prices	National Income	National Income per capita	Unemployed	Unemployed per working population	R^2	DW
0.228	−0.286	−6.380		1.756		0.789	2.211
(3.238)	(0.637)	(5.802)		(3.487)			
0.226	−0.274	−6.291			1.736	0.796	2.170
(3.266)	(0.623)	(5.935)			(3.598)		
0.188	−0.258		−6.470	1.666		0.794	2.251
(2.782)	(0.585)		(5.907)	3.422)			
0.187	−0.248		−6.392		1.654	0.803	2.209
(2.816)	(0.572)		(6.057)		(3.546)		

TABLE 18
The Communist Party. All variables in rate of change form.
Estimates for the change in election year relative to average
change in election and previous three years
$(M_4 - t_0)$

Constant Term	Prices	National Income	National Income per capita	Unemployed	Unemployed per working population	R^2	DW
0.086	2.288	−0.937		−0.672		0.549	2.225
(1.135)	(2.980)	(1.498)		(1.752)			
0.085	2.306	−0.960			−0.683	0.555	2.190
(1.135)	(3.018)	(1.537)			(1.799)		
0.085	2.329		−0.964	−0.687		0.552	2.186
(1.137)	(2.983)		(1.520)	(1.780)			
0.085	2.346		−0.986		−0.697	0.558	2.151
(1.135)	(3.018)		(1.556)		(1.824)		

TABLE 19
The Communist Party. All variables in rate of change form.
Estimates for the change in the year prior to elections relative
to the average election and previous three years ($M_4 - t_{-1}$)

Constant Term	Prices	National Income	National Income per capita	Unemployed	Unemployed per working population	R^2	DW
0.140 (1.329)	1.398 (0.828)	-3.136 (0.854)		-0.323 (0.752)		0.094	1.835
0.140 (1.330)	1.404 (0.831)	-3.149 (0.854)			-0.322 (0.751)	0.094	1.836
0.133 (1.211)	0.916 (0.539)		- 1.752 (0.471)	-0.220 (0.505)		0.044	1.782
0.133 (1.210)	0.917 (0.539)		- 1.748 (0.468)		-0.217 (0.500)	0.044	1.782

TABLE 20
The Non-Communist Left. Variables in level form.
Estimates for election year t_0

Constant Term	Prices	National Income	National Income per capita	Unemployed	Unemployed per working population	R^2	DW
29.596 (8.478)	-1.277 (4.571)	0.190 (3.425)		-0.015 (1.663)		0.797	2.458
29.794 (8.504)	-1.259 (4.664)	0.1858 (3.487)			-0.030 (1.691)	0.799	2.445
22.176 (6.906)	-1.304 (4.992)		0.267 (3.773)	-0.015 (1.784)		0.818	2.817
22.529 (5.027)	-1.289 (5.095)		0.261 (3.846)		-0.030 (1.821)	0.820	2.792

fects the models specified in level form. If the independent variables are expressed in growth rate from (Table 13) the goodness of fit (R^2) clearly drops, but the results still remain comparable to foreign studies, or to the tests on the Left-wing vote as a whole. The influence of the rate of inflation on the Communist vote is confirmed.

Finally, the influence of economic conditions on the Communist vote is still apparent even when all the variables are expressed in rate of change form. (Tables 14, 15, 16, 17, 18 and 19). It can be seen that in this case there exists a negative relationship between the rates of change of per capita income, and the rates of change of the Communist percentage of the total vote. It also appears that changes in the mean unemployment rate over the period between two elections significantly influences the rate of change of Communist votes (Table 17).

Table 18 is more difficult to interpret since the economic variables are expressed in the form of divergences in growth rates between the election year t_o and the average growth rates over the preceding four years. In other words the model examines the influence of off-trend changes in economic conditions on the rate of change of Communist voting. Table 19 is the same except the comparison is between trends in the last four years and the year prior to the election (t_{-1}). Even the rather elaborate specification of Table 18 demonstrates a significant relationship between the change in the Communist vote, and off-trend changes in prices and National Income per capita. However, in this specification the unemployment variable changes sign, so that off-trend increases in the unemployment rate decrease the rate of change of Communist votes.

In Tables 20-23 the relationship between economic variables and the non-Communist Left vote is examined. The results support the hypothesis that there is a differential sensitivity on the part of the Communist electorate compared with the non-Communist Left-wing electorate, as regards the economic situation. The former are clearly more sensitive to changes in economic conditions than the latter. Clearly the stable relationship between the Left-wing vote as a whole and economic conditions depends on the stability of the ratio of Communist supporters to non-Communists within the Left. This fact could undermine the earlier conclusions concerning the Left-wing vote as a whole, at a time in France when support for the various Left-wing parties is in the process of rapid change. We noted earlier that several tests that used the total of the Left votes as the dependent variable did not produce any significant results. This can easily be explained if we admit that the Communist and Socialist voters react in opposite ways to inflation, economic growth and unemployment. This would imply that economic variables are not sufficient to establish a forecast of electoral behaviour if they cannot explain the redistribution of power within the Left.[4]

One can also question the economic and political significance of the explanatory variables over time. For example, changes in the structure of the working population, and developments in the unemployment benefits system might well have changed the political impact of unemployment over time.[5] These developments throw doubt on the negative reaction of the electorate to the rate of unemployment over time. By the same reasoning a long term experience appears to influence the inflationary anticipations of the public. When inflation is correctly anticipated part of its redistributive effects, and hence its political impact, may be neutralized. In these circumstances the influence of inflation and unemployment on the election results might be less clear in recent years. The 1978 general elections were perhaps the first signs of this.

To summarize, the case of France confirms the conclusions drawn by the US studies referred to earlier. As far as we know at present, economic conditions do seem to have an effect on voting behaviour within the political context of a bipolar government-opposition system. It does, however, appear that there is a differential sensitivity of the partisan composition of the Left-wing electorate in relation to economic conditions. This means that it is difficult to use the global relationship for purposes of forecasting, during a period of substantial changes in the balance of forces within the Left.

This analysis shows that politicians are right in attaching great importance to the economic situation, but that the choice of precise election dates does not perhaps represent such a decisive advantage in electoral competition as has been suggested. This is because voters do not seem to have short memories, but rather they judge

TABLE 21
The Non-Communist Left. Variables in level form.
Estimates for year prior to election year t_{-1}

Constant Term	Prices	National Income	National Income per capita	Unemployed	Unemployed per working population	R^2	DW
26.690	-1.545	0.237		-0.023		0.809	2.331
(8.398)	(4.458)	(3.528)		(1.821)			
30.011	-1.517	0.230			-0.045	0.812	2.338
(8.454)	(4.653)	(3.689)			(1.891)		
22.606	-1.479		0.298	-0.020		0.812	2.402
(5.104)	(4.565)		(3.575)	(3.711)			
23.050	-1.464		0.292		-0.040	0.816	2.392
(5.272)	(4.775)		(3.734)		(1.803)		

TABLE 22
The Non-Communist Left. Variables in level form.
Estimates for the mean of the election and previous years

Constant Term	Prices	National Income	National Income per capita	Unemployed	Unemployed per working population	R^2	DW
29.546	-1.526	0.236		-0.023		0.818	2.367
(8.629)	(4.701)	(3.657)		(2.052)			
29.827	-1.484	0.226			-0.043	0.819	2.369
(8.637)	(4.801)	(3.714)			(2.055)		
21.365	-1.533		0.319	-0.022		0.854	2.528
(5.195)	(5.589)		(4.368)	(2.366)			
21.909	-1.499		0.308		-0.043	0.854	2.527
(5.370)	(5.698)		(4.435)		(2.377)		

TABLE 23
The Non-Communist Left. Variables in level form. Estimates for the mean of the election and previous three years

Constant Level	Prices	National Income	National Income per capita	Unemployed	Unemployed per working population	R^2	DW
31.241	-1.041	0.147		-0.012		0.714	2.471
(6.285)	(3.348)	(2.268)		(0.795)			
31.545	-1.042	0.146			-0.026	0.717	2.475
(6.290)	(3.482)	(2.364)			(0.870)		
26.419	-1.302		0.256	-0.018		0.780	2.745
(4.725)	(4.194)		(3.117)	(1.332)			
24.811	-1.285		0.250		-0.036	0.782	2.741
(4.770).	(4.319)		(3.199)		(1.369)		

performance over the entire period between elections. This is perhaps a surprising finding. On the other hand, additional variables which have not been taken into account in these tests contribute to modifying the very structure of the relationship, and might change the values of the estimates in future.

APPENDIX

By Left-Wing vote we have understood the total of votes obtained by the following parties:

1920   Socialists, Independent Socialists, Republican-Socialists Radicals and Independent Radicals

1924   Communists, Socialists, Independent Soc. Repub. Soc., Radicals and Independent Radicals

1928	Communists, Soc. Sundry Left, Independent Soc. Repub. Soc. and Radical Soc.
1932	Communists, Soc. Sundry Left, Republ. Soc. and Radical Soc.
1936	Communists, Sundry Left, Soc. and Rad. Soc.

October 1945, June 1946, November 1946:
Communists, Socialists, Radical Socialists, RGR (Rassemblement des Gauches Republicaines) and UDSR (Union Démocratique et Socialiste de la Résistance)

1951 and 1956:

	Communists, Sundry Left, Socialists, Radical Soc. RGR and UDSR
1958	Communists, UFD, Socialists, and Radical Socialists
1962	Communists, Extreme-Left, Soc. and Radical Soc.
1967	Communists, Extreme-Left, Federation of the Left
1968	Communists, PSU, Federation of the Left and Sundry Left
1973	Communists, PSU, and Extreme-Left, UGSD and Sundry Left

Sources: Before 1958 *Les Cahiers de l'Histoire*, Special Issue March 1967, *Elections in France from 1789 to the Present Day*; from 1958 to 1968, Pierre Viansson-Ponté, *History of the Gaullist Republic*, Fayard, Volumes I and II, 1971; in 1973 Le Monde.

NOTES

Part of this present article is taken from a paper published in collaboration with Daniel Amson in the *Revue Francaise de Science Politique* 26, 1976: 1101-1124. The article was translated from French by Carole Breakspear and Paul Whiteley.

1. See G. H. Kramer, 'Short Term Fluctuations in US Voting Behaviour, 1896-1964', *American Political Science Review* 65, 1971: 131-143; G. J. Stigler, 'General Economic Conditions and National Elections', *American Economic Review*, Papers and Proceedings, 63, 1973: 160-167; B. S. Frey and H. Garbers, 'Politico-econometrics on Estimation in Political Economy', *Political Studies* 19, 1971: 316-320; J. E. Mueller, 'Presidential Popularity from Truman to Johnson', *American Political Science Review* 64, 1970: 18-34.

2. See the definitions in Appendix.

3. Sources: Retail Price Index (1938 = 100) from the *Bulletin Mensuel de Statistique* 3, 1975. National Income in volume terms (1938 = 100) from *Annuaire Statistique de la France*, 1966: 561. Total population in millions, ibid, 574. Unemployed in thousands from *Annuaire Statistique de la France*, 1974.

4. Other explanatory variables can be envisaged like, for example, the population structure or the policy of political investment of the parties concerned.

5. In particular see A. Fourçans and J.-J. Rosa, 'The Mirage of Full Employment', *Review Banque*, October 1977 and March 1978.

5 Economic Conditions and Mass Support in Japan, 1960-1976

Takashi Inoguchi

University of Tokyo, Japan

INTRODUCTION

For the last few years there have been many studies of the relationship between the economy and the polity both by economists and political scientists. There are two sides to the relationship: (1) how people respond to the government's economic performance in opinion polls and elections or *the evaluation function*; and (2) how the government manipulates the economy for political purposes or *the policy function*.[1] Since there are excellent reviews of the literature in this field of study it is not necessary to repeat them here.[2] One striking thing in reviewing the literature on the evaluation function, however, is the almost exclusive empirical focus on the American, British and, to a lesser degree, West German cases. The exceptions to this are Inoguchi and Miyatake, and Madsen.[3] The fact that all these countries have the two-party system or its variation may weaken the findings of these studies, given the presumably important effects of party configurations and electoral arrangements on the evaluation function as revealed through opinion polls and elections. The mass political response to economic conditions has to go through the filter of these political rules and institutions and politically patterned practices before appearing as opinion poll results and electoral outcomes. This simple fact has often been forgotten in this field of study, presumably in part because of the almost exclusive focus on these three politico-economic systems. Thus, for instance, Fair's general model of voting behavior presupposes the two party system;[4] Frey and Schneider's politico-economic model of the United Kingdom takes as the dependent variable the government popularity lead relative to the main opposition party.[5] Despite the still unsatisfactory development of knowledge about politico-economic interdependence, the conclusion that people behave rationally and respond positively or negatively to the government, depending on economic conditions — which seems to be an emerging consensus — is a very important finding. Nonetheless, we should be able to reveal more about politico-economic interactions, however insufficient our insights and formulations may be at this stage of the field's development. More specifically, we should be able to say something more about how people express their economic attitudes and how people's economic attitudes can be — or cannot be — translated into changes in political conditions. Not only the expression of attitudes but also their translation into political facts ought to be revealed on the basis of studies of various politico-economic systems with diverse translation mechanisms.

In this paper, we will consider the Japanese politico-economic system. The Japanese case is *sui generis,* and thus interesting from a comparative perspective. There are at least three features which make it interesting. First, Japan has had a predominant party system at least since 1955.[6] The Liberal Democratic Party (LDP) has kept its power exclusively without forming a coalition with any other parties. There has been no real threat to the government emanating from the opposition parties until 1976, when the government nearly lost the House of Representatives' majority in the general election. The competition between the government and the opposition has been presumably less real than in polities with a two-party system. In this respect, the LDP government has things in common with the Congress Party government in India between

1947 and 1977,[7] the Social Democratic government in Sweden between 1932 and 1976,[8] the Labor Alignment government or its predecessors in Israel until 1977[9] and the Christian Democratic government in Italy until the 'historic compromise'.[10] All these governments are in a predominant party system or its weaker variation, the most-party (or the all-party) system, such as the one in Switzerland.[11] In a purely predominant party system like the Japanese party system, where there is no coalition partner in government, and where there is not only a strong plurality but also a safe majority, the most people can expect even when the government makes a mistake is a cabinet change or a reshuffle, unaccompanied by any major policy change.

Second, the electoral system employs a nontransferable multiple constitutency whereby multiple candidates are elected from one constituency by voters casting one vote; votes cannot be transferred even if two candidates are from the same party. This system is vastly different from the Anglo-American first-past-the-post system, or from the Continental European proportional representation system. The Irish electoral system is perhaps closest to the Japanese system, but the former does allow the transfer of votes within the same party.[12] There are at least three capital consequences of this system in relation to the evaluation function. One is the importance of the fairly fixed candidate-constituency relationship. Personal and organizational ties in residential and/or occupational environments seem to foster and cement a patron-client-like relationship.[13] The second consequence is the loose party tenets of political parties and the lack of clear party image and party identification on the part of the electorate. The third is the low salience of nationally disputed issues such as foreign policy, educational policy, or macro-economic policy in elections. In this kind of system, some may expect that the government's economic performance may not matter very much if incumbent party members can do well locally in each of their constituencies.

Third, Japan achieved a continuously high economic growth rate between the early sixties and mid-seventies. During that period, the economy grew at more than 10 per cent annually. The unemployment rate remained at about 1 per cent, until the recession started in 1974. Overall economic conditions thus continuously improved, although with many problems, such as pollution, housing and com-

muting.[4] Both high GNP (the second among non-communist countries) and high income equality (one of the top three among OECD
countries) were attained. And the overall economic management by
the government was not seriously challenged by the opposition and
did not become the major electoral issue during the sixties.[15] In
other words, economic growth was a valence issue, not a position
issue.[16] In this kind of situation, the government and the incumbent party may be expected to gain comfortable mass political
support.

From this brief enumeration of the three features of the Japanese
politico-economic system during 1960-1976, which we consider in
this paper, one might be tempted to anticipate: (1) that people are
basically positive in their economic attitudes, and (2) that fluctuations in economic conditions do not affect very much the mass
political support for the government and the incumbent party.

In what follows, we will examine whether these 'intuitive'
hypotheses are correct or not, using opinion polls and electoral
turnouts between 1960 and 1976. First, we will present in graphic
form the ups and downs of the mass political support for the
government and the incumbent party as revealed in elections as well
as in opinion polls. Second, we will point out some generally of-
fered explanations for the particular patterns of changing in mass
political support, such as the ones we find in Asahi Shimbun Yoron
Chosashitsu[17] and Soma. We hope that this section, together with
the preceding one, will help sort out some major determinants of
mass political support. Third, we will briefly describe our modeling
alternatives and basic model structure, and then list all the
variables, with their sources and anticipated signs of regression
coefficients indicated. Fourth, we will present the results of the
simple regression models comparing: (1) mass political support for
the government and the incumbent party in elections, in terms both
of votes and seats; (2) mass political support for the incumbent
party, as reflected in opinion polls, and (3) mass political support
for the government, also as reflected in opinion polls. Finally, we
will draw some tentative conclusions.

TABLE 1
Electoral Turnouts for the House of Representatives

	LDP	NLC	JSP	DSP	JCP	CGP	IND*	NPA**	TOTAL
1958	287 (61.5%)	0	166 (35.5%)	0	1 (0.2%)	0	1 (0.2%)	12 (2.6%)	467
1960	296 (63.5%)	0	145 (31.0%)	17 (3.6%)	3 (0.6%)	0	1 (0.2%)	5 (1.1%)	467
1963	283 (60.6%)	0	144 (30.8%)	23 (4.9%)	5 (1.1%)	0	0	12 (2.6%)	467
1967	277 (57.0%)	0	140 (28.8%)	30 (6.2%)	5 (1.0%)	25 (5.1%)	0	9 (1.9%)	486
1969	288 (59.3%)	0	90 (18.5%)	31 (6.5%)	14 (2.9%)	47 (9.7%)	0	16 (3.3%)	486
1972	271 (55.2%)	0	118 (24.0%)	19 (3.9%)	38 (7.5%)	29 (5.9%)	2 (0.4%)	14 (2.9%)	491
1976	249 (48.7%)	17 (33%)	123 (24.1%)	29 (5.7%)	17 (3.3$)	55 (10.8%)	0	21 (4.1%)	511

*IND: "Independents"

**NPA: No Party Affiliation

Source: Soma (1977)

MASS POLITICAL SUPPORT AT THREE LEVELS

We have to examine the mass political support for the government and the incumbent party at the following three levels: (1) elections; (2) opinion polls on the LDP; and (3) opinion polls on the government. Table 1 shows electoral turnouts by party for the House of Representatives in the Diet from 1958 to 1976. Immediately clear from Table 1 is the gradually declining trend of LDP representation in the House of Representatives. The absolute majority of the LDP was almost lost in 1976. Two concomitant trends are the gradual decline of the Japan Socialist Party (JSP) and the gradual increase in the electoral strength of minor parties, i.e., the Democratic Socialist Party (DSP), the Japan Communist Party (JCP), and the Clean Government Party (CGP) after the mid-sixties, and more recently, the New Liberal Club (NLC). Table 2 shows the electoral turnouts by party in the House of Councilors between 1956 and 1977. The three above-mentioned trends hold true also with party representation in the House of Councilors. Tables 1 and 2 are summarized in Figure 1.

TABLE 2
Electoral Turnouts for the House of Councilors

	LDP	NLC	JSP	DSP	JCP	CGP	RFC*	IND	NPA	TOTAL
1956	61 (48.0%)	0	49 (38.6%)	0	2 (1.6%)	0	5 (39%)	1 (0.8%)	9 (7.9%)	127
1959	71 (55.9%)	0	21 (16.5%)	0	1 (0.8%)	0	6 (4.7%)	1 (0.8%)	10 (7.9%)	127
1962	69 (54.3%)	0	37 (29.1%)	4 (3.1%)	3 (2.4%)	9 (7.1%)	2 (1.6%)	0	3 (2.4%)	127
1965	71 (55.9%)	0	36 (28.3%)	3 (2.4%)	3 (2.4%)	11 (8.7%)	0	0	3 (2.4%)	127
1968	69 (54.8%)	0	28 (22.2%)	7 (5.6%)	4 (3.2%)	13 (10.3%)	0	0	5 (4.0%)	126
1971	62 (49.6%)	0	39 (31.2%)	6 (4.8%)	6 (4.8%)	10 (8.0%)	0	0	2 (1.6%)	125
1974	62 (47.7%)	0	28 (21.5%)	5 (3.8%)	13 (10.0%)	14 (10.8%)	0	1 (0.8%)	7 (5.4%)	130
1977	63 (50.0%)	3 (2.4%)	27 (21.4%)	6 (4.8%)	5 (4.0%)	14 (11.1%)	0	3 (2.4%)	5 (4.0%)	126

*RFC: Ryokufu Club
Source: Soma (1977)

When we turn our eyes to opinion polls, the gradually declining trend of the LDP is also apparent. We use as our data source the Asahi survey which is conducted irregularly about once or twice a year since the immediate post-World War II years. Figure 2 shows the mass political support for the LDP and the government (MPSLDP and MPSGOV respectively) between August 1960 and Janaury 1976. Figure 2 suggests several observations. MPSLDP and MPSGOV are fairly different, although the correlation coefficient between them is 0.731 (N = 30) and indicates they are somewhat related. The basic difference between them is that MPSGOV is far more volatile than MPSLDP. The second important difference is that MPSGOV tends to go down fairly steadily as a prime minister's tenure continues, ranging between 60 per cent and 20 per cent. However, MPSGOV appears to gain a 'bonus' of 5-30 per cent after a cabinet change or reshuffle whereas MPSLDP tends to stay at the same level of 45 per cent, plus or minus 5 per cent, steadily decreasing only with the passage of time.

In order to help sort out some major variables to explain the ups and downs of MPSLDP and MPSGOV, both in terms of their long-term structural changes and short-term fluctuations, we will review some conventional explanations, such as the ones found in the Asahi opinion poll team's summary account of its opinion poll results (1976) and others found in a voluminous book on post-war Japanese elections edited by Soma (1977).

Before going into that, some remarks have to be made about our choice of the period for examination, i.e., 1960-1976. Our focus on 1960-1976 is chosen for the following reason. The whole political structure — especially political party configuration — remained more or less stable during the period; this enables us to build models without being bothered by changes in some key explanatory variables according to subperiods. The year 1960 is a clear turning point because the opposition parties lost their last opportunity to mobilize the public to throw the LDP out of power when the US-Japan security treaty was revised that year. After 1960, confrontations between the government and the opposition became less frequent and less intense. The year 1976 is a clear turning point because the LDP clearly lost its majority in the House of Representatives for the first time since 1955. One can say that the period of the LDP's safe majority ended in 1976.

Now, we will give briefly some conventional explanations of the ups and downs of political support. We start with MPSLDP, which tends to reveal more stable patterns, and follow MPSGOV, which tends to reveal more dynamic fluctuations. It is important to remind here that the following account is *not* our own interpretation but a synthetic representation of what seem to be the conventional explanations of the ups and downs of MPSLDP and MPSGOV. Thus, we are not going to try to validate or invalidate, in our own

FIGURE 1
LDP's Electoral Strength for Both Houses Combined

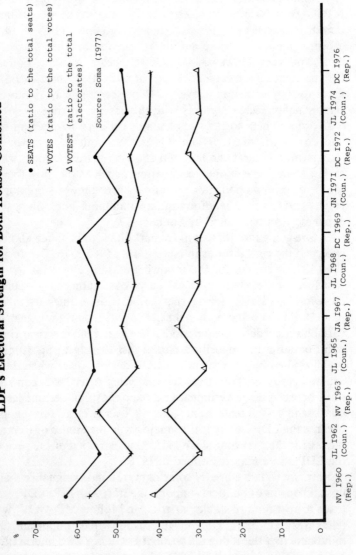

• SEATS (ratio to the total seats)

+ VOTES (ratio to the total votes)

△ VOTEST (ratio to the total electorates)

Source: Soma (1977)

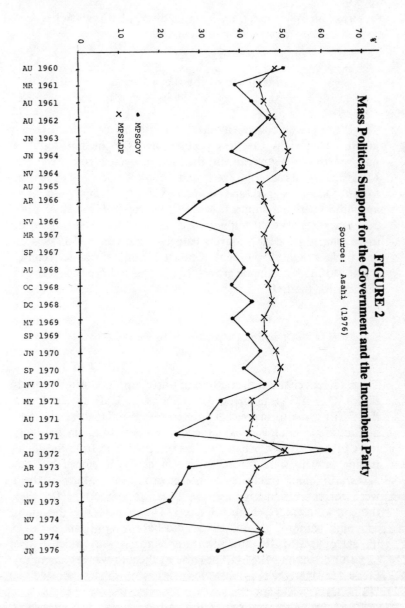

FIGURE 2
Mass Political Support for the Government and the Incumbent Party

Source: Asahi (1976)

empirical analysis in sections 3 and 4, all of what is given below in section 2 as the conventional explanations.

MPSLDP of the Ikeda Period
(1960-1964)

The Ikeda period coincided with the beginning of high economic growth. Helped by the 'low posture' and the 'income-doubling plan' of the Ikeda government, the LDP recovered from the lowest MPSLDP in its history, recorded in May 1960, when Prime Minister Kishi resigned, and went on to build up a high position of around 50 per cent support. Meanwhile, the JSP, the largest opposition party, saw its support decrease steadily from a level of more than 30 per cent — during its peak period of 1955-1959 — to one of less than 30 per cent. One of the initial political consequences of high economic growth thus seems to have been a rise in support for the LDP.

MPSLDP of the Sato Period
(1964-1972)

Three factors changed the pattern of party support during the mid-sixties. One is that minor parties, such as the DSP, the JCP, and the CGP, came to make their presence felt in Japanese electoral politics afer the mid-sixties, largely in response to the increasingly large number of new urban dwellers who migrated from the countryside or who were forced to live in newly developed but not necessarily comfortable residential environments. Many of them were not entirely happy and thus began to support parties they thought would represent their interest. The second is that the minor economic slump in the mid-sixties did have a significant negative impact on MPSLDP, and the third factor is war, which had a negative effect on MPSLDP because of the anti-war sentiment expressed fairly strongly against the government which supported the US policy in Vietnam.

Thus, during the late sixties and early seventies, two important political consequences of high economic growth manifested themselves strongly. One was the declining trend of MPSLDP, reflecting the large-scale changes in industrial and occupational structure. Although the annual rate of urban migration gradually slowed by the late sixties, its impact came to be felt most strongly after that, when the number of the accumulated migrants almost reached the saturation point. The other is that increasing dissatisfactions with negative social consequences of industrialization, namely, pollution, housing, commuting and inflation problems,[18] have negative impacts on MPSLDP. The ramifications of external problems in the late sixties and early seventies, namely, the US-Japan textile war,[19] the Okinawa reversion,[20] the dollar crisis[21] and the Japanese-Chinese diplomatic normalization issue[22] may all have eroded MPSLDP considerably.

MPSLDP of the Tanaka Period
(1972-1974)

In the first few months of the Tanaka period both MSPLDP and MPSGOV rose considerably, MPSLDP decreased steadily, if less rapidly than MPSGOV, as the period went on. Two factors explain this phenomenon. One is inflation. Inflation was universal all over the world in 1972-1973, preceded and/or accompanied by the industrial and commodity booms.[23] It was further accelerated in Japan by Tanaka's pet plan, 'Remolding the Japanese Archipelago', which encouraged speculators to raise the price of land all over the country. Then came the oil crisis of 1973-1974, which turned everything upside down and caused an extraordinary stagflation. The other is Tanaka's Lockheed scandals and the associated malaise of the LDP, which alienated many LDP supporters. Meanwhile, non-party supporters or independent voters steadily increased, amounting to nearly 40 per cent.[24]

MPSLDP of the Miki Period
(1974-1976)

MPSLDP revived from the nadir of the Tanaka period, but only slightly and steadily. It stayed around 45 per cent. Stagflation after the oil crisis continued. Urban migration slowed down. The dissatisfaction with the two major parties, the LDP and the JSP, manifested itself in the form of new splinter parties. It looked as though a new party alignment were imminent with a sort of center-right coalition forming a government. (However, as subsequent events have shown, the LDP demonstrated its resilience in the 1977 House of Councilors election and no coalition government resulted.)[25]

MPSGOV of the Ikeda Period
(1960-1964)

Most striking is a general pattern of a high plateau for quite a long period. Two factors are normally cited to explain this phenomenon. The first is that Ikeda was able to start afresh after the nightmare of the political turmoil caused by the divisive issue of revision of the US-Japan security treaty in 1960. After the period of politicization, people now wanted, and were mobilized into, something different from politics. Economic growth and improvement of life became the top priorities of the government and the principal concern of the people. The second factor, related to the first, is that economic growth was itself accelerating, producing an extended economic boom. In fact, the economic growth rate actually outran popular expectations.[26]

MPSGOV of the Sato Period
(1964-1972)

Similar observations can be made of the first and second Sato cabinets (till 1969). Two factors explain support for the Sato administration. The first is the economic growth which lasted until the oil crisis of 1973-1974. The second is Sato's skill in allocating cabinet and party posts to LDP members to strengthen and retain his position of dominance within the LDP. Sato was shrewd and skillful enough to give carrots and sticks to manipulate LDP faction leaders and followers; he was also helped by the fact that his main rivals passed away one by one during the 1960s, leaving him in quite a strong position. Cabinet reshuffle was little more than one of the means to prolong his political survival. However, during the third Sato cabinet (1969-1972), MPSGOV steadily decreased. Sato's long tenure in office made it difficult for him to satisfy everybody during that period. External changes in international economics and politics forced Sato to handle problems with two major powers, the United States and China, one after the other. These problems included the steady aggravation of the dollar's position in the world economy, the textile war with the US, the reversion of Okinawa to Japan, and the rapprochement with China. The last problem especially made it difficult for Sato to stay in power, since China kept exerting pressure to remove him in an attempt to gain favorable terms of rapprochement. At the same time Japanese public opinion was swayed by the 'immediate rapprochement' sentiment, especially after having been 'betrayed' by the US in her unilateral approach to China; taken without prior consultation with Japan.

MPSGOV of the Tanaka Period
(1972-1974)

The spectacular decline of MPSGOV during the Tanaka period is often attributed to two factors. The first is a worldwide inflation, which seemed in severity only next to the one of the immediate post-war period. The inflation reached its height in Japan when Tanaka's policy of 'Remodeling the Japanese Archipelago' prompted speculators to raise the price of land all over the country, triggering an almost logarithmic price-increase. The inflationary trend was further accelerated by the oil crisis of 1973-1974 which severely affected almost all production costs, and aggravated the already rampant inflation. Inflation set the conditions under which MPSGOV declined, because those who made their living by wage earning and who were hardest hit lost most faith in the government. Also, Tanaka's scandals and the defiance of two major aspirants for prime minister eroded government support. Though starting with an apparently solid power coalition within the LDP in 1972, Tanaka dug a hole all by himself by adopting inflationary policies which alienated the mass public, and then encouraged intra-party

power contenders to take advantage of the nation-wide dissatisfaction.

MPSGOV of the Miki Period
(1974-1976)

Like the first and second Tanaka cabinets and the third Sato
cabinet, the Miki cabinet also witnessed a steady decline in support.
The Miki cabinet had to cope with 'subversive' challenges from
within and without, because Miki did not have a normal 'mandate
of Heaven' either from the LDP or the electorate. Rather, he was
picked by an elder party figure playing the role of an adviser-cum-
arbiter to make a 'one-point rescue operation' at a critical time for
the LDP. Non-Miki party men did not cooperate well with Miki
and steadily deserted him. Miki's weak position in the LDP was
one of the two basic factors which created this pattern of
MPSGOV. The other basic factor was the stagflation associated
with the oil crisis of 1973-1974, which permeated all economic activities and did not quickly diminish.

Having presented the patterns of MPSLDP and MPSGOV and
some conventional explanations thereof, we will now turn to our
models.

MODELING ALTERNATIVES

Four things must be noted at the outset about our approach to the
model-building enterprise. First, we are concerned with short-term
fluctuations rather than long-term structural changes. Second, we
do not examine the effects of economic conditions on political outcomes at the individual level.[27] Rather the examination is made at
the aggregate level. Third, we do not develop the kind of formula
whereby the normal votes (or seats or opinion poll results) are ex-
tracted from the observed votes (or seats or opinion poll results) at
the outset so that the deviation from the normal votes (or seats or
opinion poll results) becomes the dependent variable.[28] There are
three reasons for it. (a) The Japanese case is still *terra incognita* in
this field of study and not much systematic research has been done

on Japanese electoral behavior, especially in relation to economic conditions. (b) There is no uniform definitive formula to estimate them. (c) The LDP has a fairly short history tracing back only to 1955 as far as its present party is concerned. Thus we opt for an approach which is less 'demanding' in terms of making assumptions about how they are estimated. Our formula is to put one or two major base variables in the right-hand side of the equations. We leave them to take care of what constitutes long-term structural changes and non-changes. (Needless to say, how one or two base variables are selected and used should be carefully decided. As another alternative to the normal votes extraction strategy, we can incorporate as a base variable a lagged endogenous variable of SEATS, VOTES, or VOTEST in some of the following equations.) Fourth, we do not develop the kind of formula whereby the gaps between expectation and achievement in terms of various economic performance indicators become key independent variables.[29] The reasons for this are the same as the three reasons stated above about the normal votes extraction strategy.

Basic Model Structure
and Data Sources

Our model structure is very simple. The dependent variable is either the electoral strength of the government and the LDP in terms of their votes or seats, or the public opinion poll results on the government or the LDP. The independent variables are of three kinds: base variables, economic variables and political variables. Base variables are intended to tap what constitutes structural changes and non-changes. Economic variables are related to income and price. Unemployment is not included because it was not thought to be important during most of the period dealt with. Political variables are (1) the length of tenure, which is expected to gap the depletion of power of a prime minister with the passage of time due to dissatisfactions related to intra-party resource allocation; and (2) the dummy variable to distinguish between House of Representatives and House of Councilors elections.

Two data sets are examined: (1) electoral strength of the LDP in terms of votes and seats in 1960-1976 with House of Representatives and of Councilors elections chronologically pooled (N = 11); and (2) Asahi opinion poll results on the MPSLDP and MPSGOV in 1960-1976 (N = 30). We list all the variables used in the regression models with their sources and the anticipated signs of regression coefficients indicated.

Dependent Variables

There are five variables which we want to explain separately.
(1) SEATS or the percentage of the LDP seats in the House of Representatives and the House of Councilors chronologically pooled.
(2) VOTES or the percentage of the LDP votes over the total votes in the House of Representatives *and* the House of Councilors chronologically pooled.
(3) VOTEST or the percentage of the LDP votes over the total electorates in the House of Representatives *and* the House of Councilors chronologically pooled.
(4) MPSLDP or the mass political support for the LDP as revealed in opinion polls.
(5) MPSGOV or the mass political support for the government as revealed in opinion polls.

Independent Variables

There are three kinds of variables, i.e., base variables, economic variables, and political variables, which are used as independent variables to explain each one of the five dependent variables listed above.

(1) Base Variables
A base variable is a relatively stable basis on which positive or negative increments can be accumulated.[30] By so doing we hope we can tap what constitutes long-term structural changes and non-changes. Also we can avoid problems associated with the inclusion of a lagged endogenous variable in a time series analysis.[31]

(1a) SEAT (for MPSLDP)

SEAT is a basic explanatory variable for MPSLDP. SEAT is the percentage of the LDP seats in the House of Representatives. The anticipated support is most directly expressed in voting which is in turn translated through the electoral system into parliamentary seats. This translation process is quite complicated. First, the Japanese electoral system is very unique in that it is the system of a non-transferable multiple constituency. Multiple numbers are elected in one constituency where votes for candidate A are not transferred to candidate B even if candidates A and B belong to the same party. At least three partial consequences arise from this system. Firstly, to maximize potential votes and thus seats for a particular party, the electoral strategy about how many candidates are put forward to run in a constituency matters very much. Secondly, candidates from the same party or ideologically or otherwise similar parties often compete for more or less similar voters. Thirdly, local and personality factors matter very much and national political issues tend to be played down.

According to the present electoral law, big urban constituencies are very unfavorably treated in terms of the ratio of the number of seats allocated over the population of constitutencies. This has tended to favor the LDP which is generally stronger in less urbanized constituencies. Furthermore, the translation from results in opinion polls to voting in elections is very complicated. What is fundamental is that voters may be distinguishing between questionnaire and ballot. It may be that a bulk of those who express dissatisfactions to the government are behaving like a 'good couple' occasionally expressing grievances but never thinking of terminating their marital relationship. Despite all these complexities in the translation process, SEAT is a basis which MPSLDP is built on or withdrawn from.

(1b) MPSLDP (for MPSGOV)

MPSLDP is an important variable for explaining MPSGOV. Its anticipated sign is positive. Just as SEAT is a basis which MPSLDP is built on or withdrawn from, MPSLDP is a basis which MPSGOV is built on or withdrawn from. MPSGOV is influenced more by personality and mood factors than MPSLDP is. (MPSGOV also seems to have to do with the perceived 'justness' or 'fairness' of intraparty resource allocation in which ministerial and party posts are allocated to some of LDP members.)

(1c) TREND (for SEATS, VOTES, VOTEST, MPSLDP and MPSGOV)

TREND is a base variable for SEATS, VOTES, VOTEST, MPSLDP and MPSGOV. The idea is simply to tap the long-term structural changes which cause the LDP's gradually declining representation in the Diet. Its anticipated sign is negative. The alternative for TREND as a base variable for SEATS, VOTES, and VOTEST is the lagged terms of themselves, i.e., $SEATS_{t-2}$, $VOTES_{t-2}$, and $VOTEST_{t-2}$. Since we pool both House of Representatives and House of Councilors elections, which take place alternatively during the period covered in this paper, the time subscript is always $t-2$ rather than $t-1$.

(1d) $SEATS_{t-2}$ (for SEATS)

$SEATS_{t-2}$ is the percentage of the previous LDP seats in the corresponding House. Its anticipated sign is positive.[32]

(1e) $VOTES_{t-2}$ (for VOTES)

$VOTES_{t-2}$ is the percentage of the previous LDP votes over the total votes in the election of the corresponding House. Its anticipated sign is positive.[33]

(1f) $VOTEST_{t-2}$ (for VOTEST)

$VOTEST_{t-2}$ is the percentage of the previous LDP votes over the total electorates in the election of the corresponding House. Its anticipated sign is positive.[34]

(2) Economic Variables

We have two economic variables, INCOME and PRICE.

(2a) INCOME (for SEATS, VOTES, VOTEST, MPSLDP and MPSGOV)

INCOME is the ratio of the current monthly income over that of the year before. The idea is that, if income increases over the previous twelve months, people are more likely to favor the government and the incumbent party than otherwise. Its anticipated sign is positive. The question which is justifiably asked is why a twelve month lag? It is because statistical reference in Japan is very often to a date twelve months before the month being discussed. Newspapers as well as official statistics use the similar ratio. This is in part due to the Japanese wage system whereby in June and in December a 'bonus' is paid to employees; this amounts to 1 to 4 times as much as the monthly 'regular' income each time. Thus, in June and in December, Japanese employees receive far more money than in the other months. People's reference is very often, if only implicitly, to the twelve months prior, whether it is income or price. A more sophisticated 'expectation-achievement gap' formula on the basis of various weights accorded to the past experiences will not be used in this chapter for the reasons already stated. When its application will be attempted in our next work, the formula should be modified to take into account this 'bonus' factor in the Japanese wage system.[35]

(2b) PRICE (for SEATS, VOTES, VOTEST, MPSLDP and MPSGOV)

PRICE is the ratio of the consumer price index over that of the year before. The idea is that, if the consumer price index goes up significantly over the previous year, then it is more likely to have a negative effect on the government and the incumbent party. Its anticipated sign is negative. The expectation-achievement gap formula will not be used in this chapter for the above-stated reasons.

(3) Political Variables

We have two political variables, TENURE and DUMMY.

(3a) TENURE (for MPSGOV and MPSLDP)

TENURE is the length of tenure in office of the cabinet in terms of month. The idea is that the longer the tenure, the larger the depletion of power. Its anticipated sign is negative. Under the predominant party system, the intraparty resource allocation within the LDP in terms of ministerial and party posts has a great deal to do with MPSGOV. If the same person stays in power for a long period, then dissatisfactions inevitably arise among LDP power aspirants and their followers, which are in turn amplified by the oppositon parties and more importantly by the mass media.[36] Because the LDP has been in power since 1955 without being threatened, until very recently, by the opposition, LDP parliamentary members expect that the prime minister resigns/retires after a reasonable length of tenure in office so that they can get ministerial posts or key party posts without waiting too long. This resource allocation seems to have been the most important factor of internal factional politics within the LDP by which the LDP members cluster around faction leaders to get a larger share of the pie whenever the prime minister-cum-party president resigns/retires.[37] Thus cabinet change or reshuffling means first of all the intraparty resource allocation being in tune with the perceived factional realignment during the previous period after a LDP presidential election and/or after parliamentary election, always with tactical considerations on the part of the prime minister-cum-party president. The prime minister must always be meticulous in calculating the effects of a reshuffle in terms of the longer political survival of his party of his own faction within the LDP, and most importantly of himself. If he does not give a certain number of posts to the men of 'anti-main stream' factions or within-party opposition factions, they may become more vehement and eventually side with some of opposition parties, which is likely to jeopardize the LDP's survival. Whether the prime minister can create and maintain a strong coalition within the LDP makes an enormous difference because the LDP has been a sort of coalition party itself since its foundation. Although the LDP parliamentary members are always united in the Diet, except on rare occasions,[38] LDP members tend to be far more reliant on themselves and their faction leaders than the party headquarters in election campaigning.[39] In addition, a cabinet change or reshuffle has another function — that of meeting and/or evading the oppositions' criticisms. A cabinet change or reshuffle is considered to be a fresh start for the government and thus normally boosts MPSGOV considerably.

(3b) DUMMY (for MPSGOV)
DUMMY is a dummy variable denoting whether the election con-

cerned is a House of Councilors election or House of Representatives election. In the former case, DUMMY = 1; otherwise DUM-
MY = 0. The idea is that in House of Councilors elections the LDP
tends to get less votes and seats than in House of Representatives
elections. Its anticipated sign is negative. Unlike the electoral
system for the House of Representatives, the electoral system for
the House of Councilors is a hybrid of two different formulae.
About 40 per cent of members are elected in the nationwide large
single district without a party list whereas about 60 per cent are
elected in far smaller districts in each of which 1-4 candidates are
elected very three years. House of Councilors elections take place
every three years independent of the prime minister's wishes,
whereas the timing of House of Representatives elections is up to
prime minister as long as they are within four years of the last election. Thus House of Councilors elections tend to take place
sometime in the middle of two House of Representatives elections
and often take on a character of 'mid-term' elections.[40] In House
of Councilors elections, which are characterized by lower turnouts
and less party voting, a substantial portion of nonvoters are
presumably LDP supporters in House of Representatives elections.

SOME RESULTS

Electoral Turnouts

Electoral turnouts are measured in three ways: VOTES, VOTEST,
and SEATS. The independent variables include INCOME, PRICE,
DUMMY, TREND, and the lagged endogenous variables of either
SEATS, VOTES, or VOTEST. When there are lagged endogenous
variables in the time series data, coefficients are biased and thus the
results should be taken with utmost caution. At the regression coefficients except that of PRICE in the second VOTEST equation
have the anticipated signs. Although some D.W. statistics are
slightly outside its generally acceptable range, the regression of
residuals at time t over residuals at time $t-1$ do not yield high
regression coefficients of the $t-1$ term. The regression coefficients
of PRICE and INCOME have the right signs but are not satistically
significant at the 5 per cent level. When TREND is included, the

TABLE 3
Simple Models for Seats, Votes and Votest

	1	INCOME	PRICE	$SEATS_{t-2}$	$VOTES_{t-2}$	$VOTEST_{t-2}$	DUMMY	TREND	R^2	$\bar{R}^2$	D.W.
SEATS											
equation 1	67.443	83.739 (66.268)	-97.383 (49.826)				-2.776 (2.569)		.567	.382	1.346
equation 2	59.645	36.721 (39.991)	-34.949 (32.847)				-4.291 (1.528)*	-1.010 (.260)*	.877	.795	2.391
equation 3	.103	52.323 (57.878)	-47.714 (49.750)	.838 (.385)*					.699	.570	2.109
equation 4	14.983	35.749 (49.115)	-29.601 (42.586)	.628 (.338)				-.641 (.320)	.819	.699	2.789
VOTES											
equation 1	44.138	87.537 (72.152)	-86.711 (54.250)				-3.083 (2.797)		.464	.234	1.250
equation 2	35.244	33.917 (37.830)	-15.511 (31.072)				-4.811 (1.446)*	-1.152 (.246)*	.885	.809	2.967
equation 3	-.324	51.123 (33.611)	-45.489 (25.807)		.800 (.140)*				.889	.841	2.222
equation 4	6.290	41.405 (28.112)	-32.693 (22.160)		.660 (.134)*			-.429 (.207)	.935	.892	2.431
VOTEST											
equation 1	7.265	75.155 (60.488)	-52.298 (45.480)				-6.234 (2.345)		.614	.449	.946
equation 2	-.148	30.459 (32.368)	7.053 (26.586)				-7.674 (1.237)	-.960 (.210)	.914	.857	2.685
equation 3	-34.980	70.652 (37.445)	-32.733 (28.767)			.705 (.129)*			.852	.789	1.567
equation 4	-33.492	58.775 (36.719)	-18.717 (29.337)			.664 (.127)*		-.319 (.242)	.885	.809	2.235

N = 11   Notes: 1) Asterisked coefficients mean that they are statistically significant at 5 % level.
2) Parenthesized statistics are standard errors.

regression coefficient of INCOME and PRICE become smaller, suggesting that the latter two variables contain a fairly strong 'trend' factor within themselves. The fact that the regression coefficients of DUMMY and TREND are significant at the 5 per cent level suggests that there are some other variables which we only insufficiently specified by DUMMY and TREND in the models. It seems to make sense that electoral turnouts are less affected by PRICE and INCOME than opinion polls, partly because electoral turnouts have to go through the translation mechanism of the electoral system which tends to 'stabilize' the drastic moves of opinion polls largely in favor of the incumbent party. This 'one-sided' political consequence of electoral law is an almost universal phenomenon.[41]

Opinion Polls

MPSLDP: All the coefficients have the anticipated signs. All the D.W. statistics are within its acceptable range. PRICE fairly consistently shows the statistically significant coefficients. The coefficients of INCOME are statistically significant when TREND are included in the models. It is interesting to note that the size of the regression coefficients of PRICE is generally larger than that of the regression coefficients of INCOME in the MPSLDP equations whereas the opposite is the case in the SEATS, VOTES and VOTEST equations in Table 3. This fact may suggest that the mass political support for the government and the incumbent party as revealed in opinion polls is more strongly influenced by PRICE than that as revealed in elections, which is more strongly influenced by INCOME. TENURE and TREND are fairly weak in terms of significance. R^2s are not very large. This fact suggests that there may be other variables which are only insufficiently specified by SEATS and TREND in the models. It may be necessary to consider the inclusion of some sociological varibles such as social ties in residential and occupational environment (e.g., union tie and owning or renting a house) which are recently argued to be very important in determining Japanese electoral behaviour by Flanagan and Richardson.[42]

TABLE 4
Simple Models for MPSLDP and MPSGOV

MPSLDP	1	INCOME	PRICE	SEAT	TENURE	TREND	R²	R̄²	D.W.
equation 1	71.424	16.069 (13.627)	-39.872 (14.036)*				.267	.213	1.529
equation 2	33.824	21.527 (13.318)	-33.213 (13.845)*	.414 (.217)*			.357	.283	1.551
equation 3	33.341	22.142 (13.616)	-37.704* (14.121)	.415 (.221)*	.022 (.052)		.362	.259	1.577
equation 4	53.647	22.464 (13.089)*	-27.681 (14.273)*			-.160 (.073)*	.381	.309	1.720
equation 5	42.446	23.101 (13.304)	-28.040 (14.472)*	.174 (.300)		-.119 (.103)	.390	.292	1.678
equation 6	41.928	23.324 (13.623)*	-28.442 (14.921)*	.183 (.309)	.010 (.053)	-.115 (.107)	.390	.263	1.682

MPSGOV	1	INCOME	PRICE	MPSLDP	TENURE	TREND	R²	R²	D.W.
equation 1	94.767	91.930 (42.779)	-148.690 (44.066)*				.301	.249	2.036
equation 2	-49.412	59.493 (34.236)*	-68.203 (39.195)*	2.019 (.472)*			.590	.543	1.836
equation 3	-49.527	52.972 (33.540)	-61.306 (38.355)	2.072 (.460)*	-.204 (.129)		.627	.568	1.813
equation 4	56.889	105.555 (43.087)*	-122.714 (46.986)*			-.342 (.241)	.351	.276	2.087
equation 5	-50.295	60.674 (36.847)	-67.409 (40.743)	1.998 (.523)*		-.021 (.213)	.590	.524	1.835
equation 6	-52.116	56.273 (35.901)	-58.814 (39.950)	2.013 (.508)	-.208 (.132)	-.062 (.208)	.629	.551	1.813

N = 30

Notes: 1) Asterisked coefficients mean that they are statistically significant at
          5 % level.
       2) Parenthesized statistics are standard errors.

MPSGOV: All the coefficients have the anticipated signs. D. W. statistics are within the acceptable range. R^2s are generally larger for MPSGOV than for MPSLDP. INCOME and PRICE are statistically significant when LDP or TENURE or TREND are not included in the models. Concerning the size of the regression coefficients of the economic variables, the same thing as the one stated for the MPSLDP above can be stated. The coefficients of MPSLDP are consistently statistically significant. TENURE affects MPSGOV more strongly than it does MPSLDP. These results show that MPSGOV is more susceptible to economic fluctuations than MPSLDP.

Relationships Between Electoral Turnouts and Opinion Polls

We have noted before that the mechanism of translating opinion polls into electoral turnouts matters very much. We will show their relationships and some plausible explanations of them. The correlation coefficients between SEATS, VOTES, VOTEST and MPSGOV (N = 11) are shown in Table 5. Data on MPSGOV is taken from the Jiji monthly survey.[43] Since N is very small, caution is necessary in drawing conclusions. However, these results show that the mass political support for the government as revealed in opinion polls around the election times does not have a strong relationship with electoral turnouts. It seems to suggest that although people express their economic attitude toward the government fairly in tune with economic fluctuations, they do not translate it immediately and directly into their electoral choice. The translation mechanism has also to do with the electoral system. As we have already noted, the incumbent party has been favored by the electoral system which tends to push up its parliamentary strength beyond its strength in terms of VOTES and VOTEST. Thus the electoral law tends to 'stabilize' whatever fluctuations there are in people's economic attitude toward the government. (The relationship between MPSGOV and MPSLDP has been shown before. It is 0.731 when N = 30.)

TABLE 5
Correlation Coefficients Between SEATS, VOTES,
VOTEST and MPSGOV (N = 11)

	SEATS	VOTES	VOTEST	MPSGOV
SEATS	1.000	0.917	0.809	0.271
VOTES	0.917	1.000	0.888	0.361
VOTEST	0.809	0.888	1.000	0.216
MPSGOV	0.271	0.361	0.216	1.000

TENTATIVE CONCLUSIONS

Our major, if tentative, conclusion is that, contrary to the initial
hunch, economic conditions do affect significantly the mass
political support for the government and the incumbent party. Our
initial hunch was that when there is only one party which can place
itself in power, when the electoral system tends not to highlight national issues such as macro-economic policy, and when there is an
almost continuously high economic improvement of life, economic
conditions cannot become very salient. Although the following is
very speculative and thus should be examined carefully in our
future work, it seems to be more plausible to say, however, that
one-party predominance and weak party identification, as are
found in Japan, seem to make economic conditions more salient
than otherwise. One-party predominance seem to have tended to
encourage the opposition parties to take stances on such 'lofty'
issues as foreign policy, education, and the Constitution, to make
them salient, especially in the fifties and, to a lesser degree, in the
sixties, which led some to characterize Japanese politics as a divided polity.[44] However, the truth seems to have been that these issues
were the kind of questions on which opposition parties were bound
to sharply differ from the incumbent party in order to show that
they were 'pure and upright' in their stance, even at the sacrifice of
impracticability since there was no prospect for the opposition to
take or share power in the immediate future. Although the differences were wide on these issues between the government and the
opposition parties, these issues seem to have tended to play two dif-

ferent functions: (1) the 'pure' stances on these lofty issues reassured hard core supporters of the correctness of their belief which had been shaped in the 'confrontation' period from the immediate post-World War II years to 1960; (2) the 'pure' stances did not become very salient to many other than hard core supporters and tended to be taken largely as political rhetoric: instead, more tangible, divisible and indivisible benefits ('pork barrel' of one sort and another and general economic conditions) loomed large to them. Weak party identification and weakly articulated party stances on many issues also seem to have contributed to making people more sensitive to economic conditions. Besides the divisible tangible material or political benefits Dietmen bring to their constituencies, to which people pay much attention, more indivisible economic conditions are what people can feel in daily life and thus equally care about. When the patron-client relationship has been eroded in many large urban areas, general economic conditions seem to have become all the more salient. Thus people seem to have expressed their economic attitude in accordance with the changing economic conditions even with an almost continuously high economic growth as a trend. Price especially seems to have affected people's economic attitude in the shorter term while incomes seems to have been related to people's attitude in the longer term.

Our second major conclusion is that there is a noticeable difference between the mass political support for the government and the incumbent party as revealed in opinion polls in that the former is affected more strongly by changes in economic conditions. While those who have a stronger party identification than many others express their particular party preference, are inclined to vote for that party in election, and thus express their continued support or nonsupport to the government, many others do not seem to think that way about the government which has always been the LDP government and thus they can express their evaluation of the government somewhat separately from their often weak party preference.

Our third major conclusion is that there is a noticeable difference between the mass political support as revealed in opinion polls and in elections in that, in the former, people's economic attitude is more strongly perceptible. People express in opinion polls their economic attitudes toward the incumbent party and more strongly toward the government, depending on economic conditions under which they find themselves, while in electoral choice they are much less expressive in this regard presumably because there are other factors which are as basic or important as, or more so than, short-term economic fluctuations. In other words, the translation of people's economic attitude into electoral behavior is far from direct and straightforward. It seems to suggest that this is attributed in part to the absence of viable oppositions or the lack of competition between the government and the oppositions. On the one hand, if people translate their economic attitude into electoral behavior in a continuously straightforward way on the basis of short-term fluctuations, then politics may become a near-chaos. On the other hand, if the translation is completely absent, then people may suffer in the longer term. Where the Japanese case falls on this continuum is a question that has to be answered not by a single case study like this but by cross-national studies of cases with completely different institutions.

To sum up, we have at least posed the following two questions which remain to be further researched and answered in our future work.

(1) the seeming importance of weak party competition and weak party identification as factors in highlighting economic conditions in people's attitude formation toward the government and the incumbent party;

(2) the seeming importance of the absence of viable opposition parties and the electoral law of a nontransferable multiple constituency in the process of the relatively weak translation of people's economic attitude into electoral behavior.

NOTES

1. See B. S. Frey, 'Politico-Economic Models and Cycles', *Journal of Public Economics* 9, 1978: 1-18.

2. See G. H. Kramer, 'Short-term Fluctuations in US Voting Behavior, 1896-1964', *American Political Science Review* 65, 1971: 131-143; R. C. Fair, 'The Effect of Economic Events on Votes for the President', *Review of Economics and Statistics* 60, 1978: 159-173; E. R. Tufte, *Political Control of the Economy*

(Princeton NJ: Princeton University Press 1978); D. A. Hibbs, 'Macroeconomic Performance, Mass Political Support and Macroeconomic Policy: Comparative Studies in the Political Economy of Macroeconomic Policy in Advanced Industrial Societies', mimeo (Cambridge, Mass: Harvard University 1978).

3. T. Inoguchi and N. Miyatake, 'Economic Determinants of the Popular Support for the Government: The Case of Japan 1960-76', paper presented at the European Consortium for Political Research Joint Sessions of Workshops, Grenoble April 1978. H. J. Madsen, 'Electoral Outcomes and Macroeconomic Politics: The Scandinavian Cases', in this volume.

4. See R. C. Fair, op. cit. (1978).

5. B. S. Frey and F. Schneider, 'A Politico-Economic Model of the United Kingdom', *Economic Journal* 88, 1978: 243-253.

6. See J. Watanuki, *Politics in Postwar Japanese Society* (Tokyo: University of Tokyo Press 1978); J. A. Stockwin, *Japan: Divided Politics in a Growth Economy* (New York: Norton 1974); N. Thayer, *How the Conservatives Rule Japan* (Princeton: Princeton University Press 1969); H. Fukui, *Party in Power: The Japanese Liberal Democrats and Policy Making* (Berkeley: University of California Press 1970); M. Leiserson, 'Factors and Coalitions in One-party Japan: An Interpretation Based on the Theory of Games', *American Political Science Review* 62, 1968: 770-787.

7. See R. Kothari, *Politics in India* (Boston: Little Brown 1970).

8. See B. Särlvik, 'Sweden: The Social Bases of the Parties in a Development Perspective', in R. Rose (ed.), *Electoral Behavior* (New York: Free Press 1974), 371-434.

9. A. Arian, *The Choosing People: Voting Behavior in Israel* (Cleveland: The Press of Case Western Reserve University 1973).

10. G. Di Palma, *Surviving Without Governing: The Italian Parties in Parliament* (Berkeley: University of California Press 1977).

11. H. Kerr Jr., *Switzerland: Social Cleavages and Partisan Conflict* (London: Sage 1974).

12. Soma Masao (ed.), *Kokusei Senkyo to seito seiji* (Tokyo: Seiji Koho Senta 1977). G. D. Allison, 'Japan's Independent Voters: Dilemma or Opportunity?', *The Japan Interpreter* 11, 1976: 36-55; J. H. White, 'Ireland: Politics Without Social Bases in R. Rose (ed.), *Electoral Behavior* (New York: Free Press 1974) 619-651; D. W. Rae, *The Political Consequences of Electoral Laws* (New Haven: Yale University Press 1971); G. Sartori, *Parties and Party Systems: A Framework for Analysis*, vol. 1 (Cambridge: Cambridge University Press 1978).

13. S. C. Flanagan and B. M. Richardson, *Japanese Electoral Behavior: Social Cleavages, Social Networks and Partisanship* (London: Sage 1977); N. Ike, *Japanese Politics: Patron-Client Democracy* (New York: Knopf 1972); G. Curtis, *Election Campaigns Japanese Style* (New York: Columbia University Press 1971).

14. H. Patrick and H. Rosovsky (ed.), *Asia's New Giant: How the Japanese Economy Works* (Washington DC: Brookings Institution 1976).

15. Soma Masao (ed.), op. cit. (1977).

16. D. Butler and D. Stokes, *Political Change in Britain* (New York: St Martin's Press 1969).

17. Asahi Shimbunsha Yoron Chosashitsu, *Nihonjin no seiji ishiki* (Tokyo: Asahi Shimbunsha, 1976).

18. See H. Patrick and H. Rosovsky, op. cit. (1976).

19. I. M. Destler, et al., *Managing on Alliance: The Politics of US-Japanese Relations* (Washington DC: Brookings Institution 1976).

20. A. Watanabe, *The Okinawa Problem: A Chapter in Japan-US Relations* (Carlton, Australia: Melbourne University Press 1970).

21. C. F. Bergsten, *The Dilemmas of the Dollar: The Economics and Politics of United States International Monetary Policy* (New York: New York University Press 1975).

22. C. J. Lee, *Japan Faces China: Political and Economic Relations in the Postwar Era* (Baltimore: Johns Hopkins University Press 1976).

23. See L. N. Rangarajan, *Commodity Conflict: The Political Economy of International Commodity Negotiations* (London: Croom Helm 1978) and E. R. Tufte, *Political Control of the Economy* (Princeton: Princeton University Press 1978).

24. See G. D. Allinson, op. cit. (1976).

25. M. Uchida and H. Baerwald, 'The House of Councilors Election in Japan: The LDP Hangs in There', *Asian Survey* 18 (4), 1978: 301-308.

26. See K. Ohkawa and H. Rosovsky, *Japanese Economic Growth: Trend Acceleration in the Twentieth Century* (Stanford: Stanford University Press 1973).

27. For examples of this see R. Klorman, 'Trends in Personal Finance and the Vote', *Public Opinion Quarterly* 42, 1978: 31-48; M. P. Fiorina, 'Economic Retrospective Voting in American National Elections: A Micro-Analysis', *American Journal of Political Science* 22, 1978: 426-443.

28. As do R. Fair, op. cit. (1978), Kramer op. cit. (1971), and B. Frey, op. cit. (1978).

29. As do R. Fair, op. cit. (1978) and D. A. Hibbs, op. cit. (1978). See also D. A. Hibbs, 'Political Parties and Macroeconomic Policy', *American Political Science Review* 71, 1977: 1467-1487.

30. See R. Brody and B. I. Page, 'The Impacts of Events on Presidential Popularity: The Johnson and Nixon Years' in A. Wildavsky (ed.), *Perspectives on the Presidency* (Boston: Little Brown 1975) 136-148.

31. For a discussion of this see P. Rao and R. L. Miller, *Applied Econometrics* (Belmont California: Wadsworth 1974).

32. See Soma, op.cit. (1977).

33. See Soma, op. cit. (1977).

34. See Soma, op. cit. (1977).

35. Se Sorifu Tokeikyoku, *Yearbook of Consumer Price* (Tokyo: Okursaho Insatsukyoku 1977).

36. See J. E. Mueller, 'Presidential Popularity from Truman to Johnson', *American Political Science Review* 64, 1970: 18-34.

37. See M. Leiserson, op. cit. (1968) and N. Tayer, op. cit. (1969).

38. H. J. Baerwald, *Japan's Parliament* (Cambridge: Cambridge University Press 1974).

39. G. Curtis, *Election Campaigns Japanese Style* (New York: Columbia University Press 1971).

40. S. Nisihira, 'Les elections générales au Japan depuis la guerre', *Revue francaise de Science Politique* 21, 1971: 772-789.

41. See D. W. Rae, op. cit. (1971).
42. S. C. Flanagan and B. M. Richardson, op. cit. (1977).
43. Jiji Tsushinsha, *Special Reports* (Tokyo: Jiji Tsushinsha 1960).
44. J. A. Stockwin, op. cit. (1974).

II The Political Business Cycle

6 Political Business Cycles in Britain

James Alt

University of Essex, UK

There is a growing, but relatively inconclusive where substantive findings are concerned, literature in academic journals on the subject of political business cycles. At the same time, for the last quarter of a century in Britain, the subject of pre-election booms has generated quite a bit of political and journalistic (and occasionally academic) heat, particularly in election years. The Conservative Government was commonly accused of having taken the political expedient of getting the 1955 General Election out of the way just before the economically harsh Budget of the spring. The Labour Government's holding of the 1966 General Election just before the freeze of July 1966 and the subsequent relaxing of controls on wage increases before the 1970 Election led many commentators to talk of electoral manipulation of the economy. The rapid growth of real incomes and personal consumption in 1978 similarly contributed to the widespread expectation that a general election was about to be held, even though it is now commonly forecast (as this is written) that the boom will be petering out before the election can be held. It is doubtful whether this instance, like that of 1964 before it, will prevent accusations of tampering with the economy for political gain the next time an election appears to be about to be held in times of (transitory) prosperity.

Sadly, much of the discussion of pre-election booms, is plagued by theoretical misconceptions and empirical shortcomings, and the gap is increasing between the problems and formulations discussed in academic circles and those put forward by even the most intelligent political-economic journalists. What follows is an effort to reduce the gap by suggesting which of the more abstract theoretical aspects of the political business cycle literature are most relevant, and where the worst excesses occur on both the academic and journalistic sides of the discussion. The best place to begin is with a solid, non-academic treatment of the question.

I THE CONCEPT OF A POLITICAL BUSINESS CYCLE

Writing in the Lombard column of the *Financial Times* earlier this year, Sam Brittan put forward a view of the current controversy over political business cycles (see Brittan, 1978). His argument can be reduced to about four basic points, which are listed below, and commented upon afterwards. The first point that Brittan wishes to make is that a theory of political trade cycles has been more or less fully developed, and states essentially that elections are held in a period of boom during which real income rises much faster than longer term trends. Because the inflationary effects of these real income increases are felt only somewhat later, and after the elections, the consequent corrective recession and period of stagnation occur after the election and early in the parliamentary term, while the periods of seeming prosperity or real income increases occur just before elections in the later parts of the parliamentary term. A similar view appears in Tufte (1978). Frey (1978) in presentation to the Institute of Economic Affairs, also put forward a similar view of political business cycles, save that the focus was on changes in nominal rather than real income. Nevertheless, the essence of both approaches was that a political business cycle hypothesis suggested a *temporal sequence* of boom — election — slump — boom — election — slump, and so on, with income always rising before elections, and falling after.

Brittan's second point is that — as suggested at the outset of this paper — the actual existence of these cycles is in some dispute. He adds that econometric techniques have not resolved the dispute but rather moved it to an altogether more esoteric and abstract plane. Nevertheless he also suggests that the dispute continues to generate some hostility because its implications are a 'threat to rational Chicago man', as one implication of the theory is that the electorate does not perceive these manipulations or learn from past experience, but rather is repeatedly deceived by a transitory boom into supporting the government of the day.

Brittan's third point is that in the 1950s and early 1960s the best economic guide to government popularity in Britain was the unemployment rate, which was then also a good guide to the state of the business cycle. The upward drift in unemployment since the late 1960s, with a brief exception in 1973-74, has led to the complete breakdown of the relationship between popularity and unemployment. The best predictor of political standing is now the movement of real personal disposable income, sometimes called the standard of living.

The fourth point is addressed to the evaluation of the theory. Brittan claims that the first real difficulty for the theory as applied to Britain came in 1970, when the Labour Government was defeated in spite of a rate of growth of real personal disposable income which was twice that obtaining throughout its term in office. Mr Heath's 1974 defeat, argues Brittan, is no evidence either way, not only because real incomes were rising at an average rate, but also because the confrontation with the miners dwarfed all other issues in the election. Finally, asking whether 1978 (the election was still expected when the column appeared) would be another 1970, Brittan points out that one difference is that the rise in real personal disposable income is much larger now than it was then, and that moreover, whereas Labour suffered from rising prices in 1970, the inflation rate in mid-1978, though higher than in 1970, was falling rather than rising.

To summarize what appear to be the principal points of the argument, Brittan claims that the movements in real personal disposable income are now the best economic guide to the popularity of a government. The popularity of a government is relatively high when real incomes are rising quickly, and relatively low when real incomes are growing slowly, or declining. Seizing on this relationship, governments attempt to stimulate real incomes to boost their popularity before elections, hoping that the inflation (which reduces the rate of growth of *real* incomes) attendant on this economic stimulation will come later, and not be foreseen by the electorate. Indeed, there appears to be a prima facie case for the theory, as shown in Figure 1, which is adapted from a table given in Brittan (1978) with 1966 added. Figure 1 shows that annual rate of increase in real personal disposable income obtaining in election years as against the longer-term average annual rates of increase obtaining throughout the various governments since 1951. Thus, throughout the Conservative Government of 1951-64, real personal disposable income was increasing at an annual rate of 3.5 per cent, but increased by 4.7 per cent in the election year of 1954-55, 5.1 per cent in 1958-59, and only 3.9 per cent in 1963-64 — but of course the Conservative Government lost the 1964 election. Similarly, real income was rising at an annual rate of 3.7 per cent in 1969-70, nearly double the prevailing annual rate of increase of 2 per cent from 1964 to 1970, and was rising by over 5 per cent per annum in the early summer of 1978, when the General Election was expected.

Let us first consider the equation of the theory of political business cycles with the existence of pre-election booms. It is tempting to argue that if a political trade cycle theory has been fully developed, this can't be it. It is certainly true, insofar as it goes, that any political business cycle theory would try to claim that governments try to hold elections in times of prosperity or try to engineer prosperity for times of elections. If, however, all there was to the problem was to see whether the first halves of parliamentary terms were times of stagnation and the second halves times of prosperity, there would be no empirical difficulty, as we could simply count the numbers. Indeed, others have already done so. One of the first proponents of the theory, Nordhaus (1975) did just this and came to negative conclusions. Studying parliamentary terms in nine Western countries, he discovered clear electoral-cyclical boom-slump movements of the unemployment rate in three: Germany, the United States, and New Zealand. Similarly, Paldam (1977) investigated in a relatively atheoretical way cyclical movements in a large number of economic indicators and found little evidence of electoral-cyclical variation. On the other hand, looking at real per capita personal disposable income, Tufte (1978)

FIGURE 1
Growth Rates of Real Income

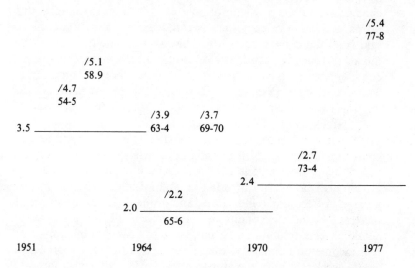

Note — This figure is modified from a Table in Brittan (1978). Broken lines indicate average annual growth rate (per cent) of real personal disposable income over long periods: for instance, an average of 3.5 per cent per annum from 1951 to 1964. Each '/' indicates the growth of real personal disposable income in the year preceding an election: for instance 3.7 per cent in the year 1969-70.

finds 'accelerations'[1] in the annual rate of growth of this indicator occurring more commonly in election years than in non-election years in a majority of parliamentary democracies. Indeed, overall, real per capita personal disposable income is about one-third more likely to accelerate in an election year than in a non-election year. This is consistent with the sort of data presented by Brittan and summarized in Figure 1: there is some tendency clear in Britain and elsewhere for the growth rate of real incomes to be higher in election years. But this finding seems so reasonable a priori that it alone could not generate the heat arising from the debate about political business cycles. There must be more to the question, and there is, but let us take up the rest of the argument first.

Holding aside for the moment the questions of the role of econometric techniques and the reasons for the hostility generated by the theory, let us consider the proposition that real income changes are a good predictor of political standing. As it stands, this proposition is hopelessly unsubstantiated. The most that can be said from the many efforts which have been made to discover the impact of economic conditions on electoral outcomes is that real income appears to have some effects in some places at some times. The United States (Kramer, 1971; Fair, 1978) appears to be a country where real income matters; Britain on the whole does not (Alt, 1979; Hibbs, 1978). This is not econometrics obscuring an obvious point, but simply a reflection of the difficulty of showing to be true something that journalists would like to believe. Looking over the recent literature, there is reason to believe in the importance to government popularity of inflation and inflation expectations, of a variety of economic indicators, and in the differential impact of different economic conditions on members of different socio-economic classes, but there is no reason to believe in the impact of real income on popularity, except perhaps in the very short term. While accelerations in the growth rate of real income may increase government popularity just around elections (Alt, 1979), so might many other factors, and it is impossible to isolate a long-term tendency for government popularity to move, ceteris paribus, with the growth rate of real income in Britain.[2]

One serious difficulty in evaluating the evidence in Figure 1 arises from confounding two totally separable aspects of the problem. It is one question whether or not governments actually *attempt* to provide booms[3] during which to hold elections: as above, there is some fairly thin evidence that they do. It is an entirely different question to ask whether the existence of these booms is sufficient to give electoral *victory* to the government of the day. In other words, 1966 is a *double* problem, because not only is the growth rate of real incomes only 2.2 per cent, about half that prevailing eighteen months earlier and no better than average for Labour's period in office (contrary to the predictions of the theory) but also, in spite of this, Labour wins a landslide (contrary to the unstated implication of the theory that governments *win* elections by electoral-cyclical economic manipulation). Now it is possible to say that Labour won in 1966 in spite of the low growth rate of real income because of their ability to blame their predecessors for the economic problems of the time (see Butler and Stokes, 1969), but this is not part of political business cycle theory, stated or otherwise. Any party would like to be able to blame its predecessors, and if they could successfully do so, there would be no need for political manipulation of the economy. Similarly, when Brittan discusses the election of 1970 as a problem for the theory, it is *not* because Labour has perversely failed to run a pre-election boom, but because they *lost* the election in boom times. But nothing in the theory (in the sense in which it entails a temporal sequence of booms, slumps, and elections) entails the further proposition that any possible manipulation will be sufficient to win the next election. That is something quite different, and very difficult to show without evidence of a systematic relationship between real income and government popularity.

The same ambiguity affects some of the other valuable points in Brittan's analysis. The point about being sensitive to whether the inflation rate, whether high or low, is accelerating or decelerating, is important, and really ought to be introduced into the rest of the analysis. Indeed, if the growth rate of real income in 1963-64 (to say nothing of 1973 to early 1974) is compared with that existing in the previous year, it looks much worse, and may be a less ambiguous guide to the downfall of the government. Similarly, in 1959 the inflation rate was low and steady, in 1964 higher and rising; in 1966 higher still but *falling*; in 1970 higher but rising again, and in 1974 higher still and still rising. This, in addition to that fact that survey evidence (Alt, 1979; Crewe, Särlvik and Alt, 1974) suggests that prices and not the miners' strike was the principal focus of public concern in 1974, echoes the point made before about considering inflation and inflation expectations in assessing the popularity or electoral success of the government. On the other hand, the methodological caveat to compare current states with recent experience only leads to further measurement problems. Real income growth in 1978 only looks rapid because the year before was a year of contraction, and growth over two years looks less dramatic. (In fact, the whole parliamentary period 1974-78 goes rather against the implications of boom-slump theories, with the slump not coming until well into the parliamentary term and the boom confined to the very last few months before the election was expected).

Finally, what are the the reasons for the hostility aroused by the theory, and the role of econometric evidence? The reason that the theory of political business cycles arouses some controversy is not that it offends 'rational Chicago man'. It is possible to show that the idea of political business cycles does not co-exist well with a 'rational expectations hypothesis': that electoral manipulation of the economy is impossible if the electorate perfectly anticipate the actions of the government. But this is a very specific result, and indeed the political business cycle hypothesis co-exists quite well with all sorts of assumptions about the forecasting of inflation and other phenomena by the electorate.[4]

What creates the hostility is really more likely to be one of two things. One is that these matters involve the activities of groups of partisans and there is always the suspicion that the *other* side is getting away with something. That is to say, some of the activities of a government, like opting for increased inflation or unemployment, benefit some groups of partisans more than others. Probably the real reason for concern with these hypotheses, however, is the argument that, correctly defined, political business cycles lead to *suboptimal* outcomes. In other words, the argument is that were the economy not interfered with for electoral gain, the actual economic outcomes that resulted would be in some sense better or more valued, be they a lower average rate of inflation, more real growth, or some such. Without the extra rider that something is actually lost by the electoral manipulation of the economy, the finding that real income growth was higher in election years would not matter. It is only if the long-term outcome is in some way inferior, or if the electorate are deceived by the pre-election boom, that the whole subject matters. But the simple holding of elections during times of atypical income growth by no means establishes either of these points.

Proofs that the incumbent politicians' gains are the electorate's losses are relatively hard to come by. If by and large, as often assumed, the electorate more or less consensually value income gains, than the timing of these gains to certain (pre-election) periods need harm no one, unless the timing means that less income is actually produced than might otherwise be the case. This cannot be shown simply by reference to the unpredictability of government activity, since the government's reactions at election time are no less predictable in principle than their reactions at any time. Similarly, as Peston (1974, Chapter 3) argues, it is not possible to show that the simple existence of cycles as opposed to steady growth paths are necessarily undesirable. Nordhaus (1975, especially pp. 175-180) does attempt such a proof, showing that the economic outcome from a democratically-controlled government will be one of higher inflation and lower unemployment than would be optimal in terms of peoples' overall preferences, but the proof is highly restrictive, and rests on a number of assumptions about popular preferences and the behaviour of elected governments.

In short, the problem is one of saying that if it were not for the activities of politicians in their own interests the economy would have continued to work in such a way, and produced a different (better) outcome overall. In other words, *political* cycles consist in the activities of governments doing other than what 'neutral' economists would recommend; that is, the outcomes must be viewed relative to the workings of an assumed economic model. This is an enormous complication, to insist that political business cycles can only be detected relative to an economic model, and not simply by investigating the activities of governments at certain times, but it does show why it is *not* the case that econometric evidence has simply made the debate more esoteric. Even if econometric models do not always perform well. Econometric evidence is simply essential to any informed discussion of political business cycles.

Thus, there are a number of important but separate questions to deal with. First, there is the question of whether or not the government actually does manipulate the economy, an interesting empirical politico-economic question. There is limited evidence that real income does rise unusually fast in pre-election periods. On the other hand, almost all economic advisers were united in suggesting economic stimulation in early 1978, so nothing about electoral ambitions or manipulation can be really deduced from the fact that stimulation ensued. Was the stimulation greater than a 'neutral' economic observer would have recommended? This sort of question cannot be answered by looking merely at time paths or growth rates of income, but requires answering in the conext of an economic model. Even if real income gains turn out to be concentrated in pre-election periods, does the electorate actually lose anything? If they do lose something, does the government of the

day actually gain anything? In principle, the theory of political
business cycles should have something to say about all of these.

II A MODEL OF POLITICAL BUSINESS CYCLES
   IN BRITAIN

Let us sketch how one fills in the salient points of a political
business cycle model.[5] On the one hand, assume that the government is not simply crisis-averse,[6] but actually confronts the problem of maximizing welfare, or minimizing its unpopularity, with
respect to popular preference distributed continuously across all
ranges of values of economic variables. On the other hand, assume
that the working of the economy is not really exogenous to the problem, but that the government faces known tradeoffs among
economic variables which it is manipulating in the interest of its
popularity. We now have the model in the form of a utility-
maximizing government confronted by an economic constraint. A
number of such models have been proposed: they differ to some extent only in detail. As an example we shall consider a model proposed by Macrae (1977), and extend the analysis to Britain in the
period 1951-74.

In Macrae's model, there are two fundamental relationships, and
a number of extra assumptions and tests. The model proposes a
simple economic system in which there are only two relevant
economic variables, inflation and unemployment. These are related
to each other through an expectations-augmented Phillips-curve
relationship:

$$I_t = aI_{t-1} - bU_t + c \qquad\qquad (1)$$

so that inflation is produced by the current level of unemployment
(negatively) and positively by last period's inflation rate (expected
by wage setters to continue) and, if anything, increased further
because exogenous shocks are hostile to the government (the constant term). This represents the economic constraint under which the
government operates: essentially, any reduction in unemployment
produces inflation.

This matters because the government of the day faces a vote loss function in respect of the levels of unemployment and inflation:

$$V_t = \tfrac{1}{2}qI^2_t + \tfrac{1}{2}rU^2_t \tag{2}$$

so that any levels of inflation and unemployment cause unpopularity, but that the relative penalties attaching to each (q and r) determine the penalty suffered in respect of any combination of inflation and unemployment. The penalty weights q and r are assumed to be fixed, at least for some period; obtainable values of inflation and unemployment are constrained by (1) above. In this model the penalty weights reflect assumptions made by the government about the beliefs of the electorate.

The question of a cycle arises because elections arise at regular intervals. Thus, in order to keep the ultimate combination of I and U as low as possible, the government has an incentive to push unemployment up early in its term, in order to keep inflation down, and then to reduce unemployment as the election approaches, in order to optimize the combination of I and U at election time. The existence of the cycle rests on periodic elections:[7] the assumption that the electorate are more concerned (or at least not less concerned) with the recent past than with the more distant past, and on what assumptions the government makes about some characteristics of the electorate, or about its own purposes.

It is clear that if people forgot the past after a year or two — or the government believed that they did — unemployment could be pushed up very high in the early years of a government, as only the (low) values of inflation and unemployment of election time would count. More significant is what the government believes about the future. There are three possibilities. First, the government could assume the electorate to be *myopic*, that is, incapable of looking forward, and therefore attaching no inflation expectations to low levels of unemployment at election time. This is equivalent to believing that the future is entirely discounted by the electorate: a government believing this could be assumed to be minimizing its vote loss with a one-term horizon, or, equivalently, maximizing its probability of winning the next election.

As an alternative, the government could believe in a *strategic* electorate, capable of seeing tomorrow's inflation in today's low unemployment. Belief in a strategic electorate would moderate the 'political' aspects of the cycle, for there would be less benefit in driving unemployment down just at one particular (election) time. In other words, the strategic electorate hypothesis is equivalent to the case of a government which wants to maximize the probability of winning an election at any time; in short, a government with an indefinite time horizon. Of course, analytically the government also has the alternative of doing nothing at all, a *naive* hypothesis in which unemployment will continue to take its own past values autogressively, disturbed only by exogenous shocks. Under this naive hypothesis, the relative penalties q and r are undefined.

There are therefore a number of parameters to estimate. The three parameters of the economic model, a, b and c of (1), must all be estimated over a reasonably long term. Given the parameters a, b and c there are values of q and r from (2) which optimize the fit of observed data on unemployment and inflation to each of the myopic and strategic hypotheses. The best fit of all can be used as a test of adequacy of each of these hypotheses for a particular government. Having determined the optimal hypotheses, one can look at shifts in the values of q and r over time. Third, one can seek confirming evidence from government popularity data and economic conditions to support (by triangulation) any conclusions about shifts in the perceived relative costs of unemployment and inflation which emerge from the first exercises. Macrae concludes that in the United States the government appeared to assume myopia from 1969-68, but a strategic electorate before and after; moreover, the apparent perceived penalty for inflation peaked in 1969-64 and was lower both before and after, falling in 1968-72 to a point where the penalties for inflation and unemployment were nearly equal. For Britain, let us provide (i) estimates of the parameters of the economic constraint, (ii) the optimum q and r weights, (iii) the vote loss function, and provide (iv) a short discussion of the results.

Economic Constraint

The estimation is actually done in the following manner. We first require estimates of the Phillips-curve parameters a, b and c. These

TABLE 1
Political Business Cycles 1951-74

Government	Coefficient of:			Best-fitting q/r ratio under:		Poll-estimated q/r vote loss weights
	I_{t-1} a	U_t b	Constant c	Myopic Hypothesis	Strategic Hypothesis	
1951-55	0.88 (9.5)	-1.48 (1.5)	3.02 (1.9)	0.06 (1.05)	0.02 (0.11)**	-0.01*
1955-59	0.86 (13.4)	-0.86 (2.1)	1.65 (2.4)	0.20 (5.22)	0.15 (1.94)	0.11
1959-64	0.78 (8.6)	-0.69 (2.3)	1.87 (2.8)	0.50 (0.48)**	0.25 (0.08)**	0.20
1966-70	0.86 (11.9)	-0.41 (1.5)	1.70*** (2.1)	0.42 (7.59)	0.16 (1.14)	0.09
1970-74	1.00****(12.7)	-0.31 (1.0)	0.59 (0.8)	0.54 (0.64)	0.05 (0.62)	0.73

* Wrong sign
** Good fit
*** Include a post-1966 variable
**** Actual coefficient 1.08, insignificantly different from theoretical maximum of 1.0

Note—Bracketed figures in columns 1-3 are t-statistics, equations estimated by OLS over the period of the current and previous government. Bracketed figures in columns 4-5 are goodness-of-fit statistics representing the ratio of the error sums of squares of the hypothesis in the column to the naive hypothesis. Column 6 shows the ratios of the coefficients of the squared values of I and U when quarterly estimates of vote loss were regressed on them, with the constant constrained to zero.

can be obtained by regressing the annual price inflation rate on itself lagged one period plus the current unemployment rate. Other research indicates that the unemployment rate should be allowed to float upwards after the fourth quarter of 1966, to reflect the effects of increased unemployment benefits, so the constant term is altered by a binary variable D_{66} taking the value 1 after this quarter and zero otherwise. When this is done, we obtain the equation, over quarterly data from 1947.3 to 1974.1,

$$I_t = .91\, I_{t-1} - .56 U_t + 1.1 D_{66} + 1.3 \tag{3}$$

While this approach to estimating the coefficients of an expectations-augmented Phillips-curve may seem overly simple, the coefficients have the virtue of plausibility, are not very different from other published estimates, and replicate Macrae's approach exactly.[8] Certainly the signs are exactly as expected, the coefficients are all highly significant, and the R^2 exceeds 0.9.

We could employ the estimates a = .91, b = .56, and c = 1.3 (2.4 from 1966 onwards) in evaluating Macrae's model. However, the Phillips curve was thought to be shifting in this period, and it might therefore be preferable to estimate the tradeoff faced by each government separately. We therefore give in Table 1 (columns 1-3) the estimates of a, b and c derived from quarterly data, where the tradeoff faced by each government[9] is taken to be that holding over the period of its incumbency plus the previous government. This is an arbitrary choice, but has the virtue of keeping moderately long periods for estimation while allowing ample scope for the relationship to change. As the estimates show, the coefficient a attaching to I_{t-1} does not move all that much until the final period, but the magnitude of the coefficient of U_t drops sharply and continuously, implying that the benefit of a per cent of unemployment in reduced inflation was at the end of a fifth (0.31/1.48) of what it had been at the beginning. This slippage approximates the sort of information governments could have had at their disposal (there is no certainty to be had in these matters) and so the evaluation of the model will be carried out with these separate estimates. Importantly, it has been shown elsewhere that the estimates obtained for the optimal values of q and r are relatively stable for moderate changes in the values of a, b and c (Alt, 1978).

Optimal Weights

Given a, b and c, Macrae describes an iterative process for determining the optimal q/r weights under the myopic and strategic hypotheses, and determining the predictive success of each hypothesis by comparing the best fit (error sum of squares) obtainable under it with the fit of the naive model.[10] Columns 4 and 5 of Table 1 give the q/r ratios which provide best fit under each hypothesis for each government since 1961, with the degree of fit (low values equal best fit) below each. The results can be summarized as follows.

The myopic hypothesis never significantly outperforms the strategic hypothesis, and indeed, only twice outperforms the naive null hypothesis of no change. The strategic hypothesis outperforms the naive hypothesis on three occasions, twice very significantly so, and only once (1955-59) provides a substantially poorer fit. On this occasion, as in 1966-70, Nordhaus (1975, p. 189) has suggested that preoccupation with the balance of payments may have led governments to ignore the unemployment-inflation tradeoff. Some of the poor fit of the myopic hypothesis also derives from the exaggerated speed of response to government policy which is demanded of the unemployment rate. Nevertheless, the results suggest clearly that, at least before 1970, while on some occasions the government may indeed have manipulated unemployment with a vote loss or social welfare function in mind, there is no evidence that the desire merely to win the next election — as distinct from remaining in office as long as possible — was the motivation.

The pattern of q/r (relative penalties for inflation and unemployment) weights are also interesting. Taking the better fitting strategic hypothesis in each case, we see that the vote loss penalty of inflation in 1951-55 was one fiftieth that of unemployment. This accords well with Milne and Mackenzie's (1954) description of the electorate at the time: great concern with unemployment and no attention at all to other economic matters. The relative weight of inflation rises to 0.15 during the next government, and to 0.25 in the years 1959-64, but falls back to 0.16 in 1966-70. The same trends can be observed from the best-fitting values under the myopic hypothesis, with inferior fits. After 1970, however, the implications diverge, and we can only say (with equal probability) that the

Heath Government appeared to follow either a myopic hypothesis with an unprecedently large penalty seen to attach to inflation, or a strategic hypopthesis with an extremely small penalty seen to attach to inflation. We discuss these results further in a moment.

Vote Loss Estimates

Recall that the government's assumed vote-loss function is given by

$$V_t = \tfrac{1}{2}\, qI^2_t + \tfrac{1}{2}\, r\, U^2_t,$$

where I_t is the twelve-month price inflation rate, U_t the unemployment rate in per cent, and V_t is the vote loss at the time, which the government seeks to minimize. V_t can be estimated by taking the difference in any period between government popularity in the opinion polls at that time, and in their share of the poll at the time of the previous election. This V_t can then be regressed in the usual way on I^2_t and U^2_t: the results of this estimation are given in Table 1, column 6. The regressions were performed without allowing a constant term, and on quarterly data, but the results shown in the Table are consistent with those obtained from monthly data, and by unrestricted regression. Column 6 gives the *ratios* of the estimates of q and r in the above equation: these can be thought of as independent empirical estimates of the q/r ratio actually *obtaining* in each of the periods discussed above, and can be compared with the government's perceived q/r ratios derived from the business cycle model.

The results suggest that there is a very close fit before 1970 in the q/r ratios actually obtaining in government popularity and those upon which the governments of the day appeared to base their vote-maximizing behaviour (insofar as their behaviour was vote-maximizing). In 1951, the estimate of q (from poll popularity regressed on inflation and unemployment squared) was negative and not significantly different from zero: in all other cases the signs are correct and almost all estimates are highly statistically significant. The 1951 estimate suggests that a vote-maximizing government should have assumed inflation was more or less free of penalty, and unemployment was all that counted in popularity: as column 5 showed, this is exactly what the government of the day appeared to believe. By 1955, inflation should have appeared much more expensive, though still cheap compared to unemployment, and again this is what appeared to happen, though the fit of the business cycle model was poor. In 1959, a shrewd government would have taken account of a further rise in the price of inflation in the vote loss function (estimated at about 0.2 relative to r in the popularity estimates), and again, this is exactly what column 5 suggests the government of the day did. Now the vote loss attaching to inflation appears to have become relatively less in 1966-70, when Labour was in office, and again this is exactly (though the fit is indifferent) what their behaviour in office appeared to reflect. The trends in the estimated vote (or popularity) loss attaching to each of inflation and unemployment up to 1970 are very closely reflected in the trends in the perceived vote loss ratios deduced from fitting the political business cycle model, under the strategic hypothesis.

Discussion

The models discussed above also lead to an interesting, though speculative, account of the defeat of the Heath Government in 1974. Poll evidence (column 67) suggests that the penalty attaching to inflation was very high in the years 1970-74. Survey evidence suggests that the assumption of myopia with regard to inflation in 1974 would have been inappropriate, and that the electorate had clear and pessimistic expectations of continuing inflation. The belief in a high penalty for inflation, however, emerges only from the further assumption of myopia on the part of the government. If the government had in fact not had a short time horizon then the data suggest that they must have underestimated the penalty attaching to inflation (see the optima ratio of 0.05 under the strategic hypothesis). A 'strategic', but vote-maximizing government, believing in a q/r ratio of even 0.5 would have aimed at an unemployment rate nearer four per cent in 1973-74 than the level of 2.5 per cent which prevailed. It is therefore a plausible interpretation of these years that either the government recognized the increasing penalty attaching to inflation, but not the ability of the electorate to forecast inflation in assessing government performance, or that they recognized the ability to forecast, but not the increasing penalties attaching to inflation. Both these interpretations are consistent with Table 1, and either would have facilitated the Conservative defeat in February 1974.

The model employed above is highly restrictive, allowing only a single tradeoff and only two economic variables, inflation and unemployment, and assuming that the government knows the tradeoff relationship and also the rates at which votes are lost for units of each economic variable. The model also assumed very quick and controlled response on the part of the economy to government decisions, and furthermore, the model is sensitive to misspecification — and indeed, to the choice of annual versus quarterly data, and so on. All this, along with the impossibility of proving, no matter how good the fit, that the government intentionally did the things the model implies, render any conclusions extremely tentative. The model contains a specification for expectation formation which is demonstrably naive, and the assumption that myopia is an all-or-nothing business is also difficult to accept. Moreover, most governments arguably have long-term and short-term interests, and blends of these are not deducible under the existing model. It is difficult to accept a model which sometimes works and sometimes does not, though the independent confirmation of perceived weights is a help in this context.

Perhaps most interesting is that the replication of Macrae's model in Britain leads to conclusions further from electoral manipulation of the economy and closer to support for the role of electoral constraint on economic policy. In this sense, by providing some link in micro-structures between electorate and government, the model deserves extension and replication. Some other results echo the findings reported in this paper: Tufte (1978) claims that the real income increases so evident in the American cycles he reports are financed by increases in government transfer payments (particularly social security benefits). Results reported elsewhere (Alt and Chrystal, 1978) cast doubt on the existence of regular electoral-cyclical variations in transfer payments in Britain, and in that respect reiterate the lack of any clearly recurring evidence of political manipulation of the economy. There are many other questions which deserve investigation before these models can be said to be well-investigated, not the least of which is the matter of whether there is a 'demand' for inflation as well as the supply of inflation implied by the models discussed above. While some interesting work is in progress the subject of politico-economic interaction will be in debate for some time to come.

NOTES

1. Searching of Table 1-1 in Tufte (1978) and surrounding text does not clarify whether the income growth 'accelerations' are relative to the previous or to long-term trends rates of growth.

2. The best-fitting long-term popularity model from Alt and Chrystal (1978):

$$G = 41.1 \quad -.36T \quad -.45C \quad -.31EI \quad -.97U \quad +.04R$$
$$(t = 19.5) \quad (4.0) \quad (1.8) \quad (1.6) \quad (1.6) \quad (0.2)$$

where G is government lead in the polls, T a time trend and C a cycle within government incumbencies as defined by Frey and Schneider (1978), EI the expected rate of inflation minus an average past rate (see Alt, 1979, ch. 6 for details), U the rate of unemployment and R the annual rate of growth of real disposable income, and the observations are quarterly, 1959.1 to 1977.3. Estimation is by GLS (rho = 0.56) and the unadjusted $R^2 = 0.70$.

3. Or, as Tufte (1978) points out, attempt to hold elections in periods of boom. The fact that British elections do not occur at regular intervals, but rather are held at times chosen by the government, may have directed attention toward the short-term boom end of political business cycle theory. On the other hand, most governments since the war have lasted four or five years, and it does not seem unreasonable to assume that newly-incumbent governments expect a four-year term, with the fifth year seen as a sort of contingent reserve. Whatever assumptions one makes, the idea that a new government in Britain (except one without a majority) has an expected time in office of four to five years is reasonable, and therefore no special problem for the theory.

4. On the rational expectations hypothesis, see Gordon (1976). The relationship between a political business cycle hypothesis and the rational expectations hypothesis is examined by McCallum (1978), and commented on by Kirchgässner and Frey (1977).

5. The evidence presented in this part is drawn from Alt (1979), Chapter 7) which should be consulted for further details.

6. On crisis-aversion, See Mosley (1978).

7. On the assumption of a period of 4-5 years, as in note 3, above.

8. It could be arued that the parameters a, b and c should be estimated non-linearly or in the context of a multi-equation economic model. Indeed, Macrae has re-estimated some of his earlier findings in just such a way, and found that the results do not change appreciably. This need not occasion too much surprise, as all that is important is the relative size of a and b, and there is no reason why their ratio

must be affected by the omission of simultaneous equations, though the possibility remains.

9. The answer to a Parliamentary question in March 1971 suggested that the government was already aware of increased errors attaching to the 'Phillips curve' for Britain, so the idea of each incumbent government having a view of the tradeoff terms it faced may not be so far-fetched.

10. The ratio of error sums of squares is called Theil's inequality coefficient. The computer program written by the author to perform the iterative search for optimal q/r ratios is available on request.

REFERENCES

ALT, J. (1978) 'Political Business Cycles in Britain Since 1951', Paper presented to the Joint Sessions of the European Consortium for Political Research, Grenoble.

ALT, J. (1979) *The Politics of Economic Decline*, Cambridge: Cambridge University Press.

ALT, J. & CHRYSTAL, A. (1978) 'Modelling the Growth of Government Expenditure in Advanced Industrial Societies', Paper presented at the Annual Conference of the American Political Science Association, New York.

BRITTAN, S. (1978) 'The Election and the Economy', *Financial Times*, 26 June 1978, p. 8.

BUTLER, D. and STOKES D. (1969) *Political Change in Britain*, London: Macmillan.

CREWE, I., SÄRLVIK, B. and ALT, J. (1974) 'The How and Why of the February Voting', *New Society*, 12 September 1974.

FAIR, R. (1978) 'The Effect of Economic Events on Votes for President', *Review of Economics and Statistics* 60: 159-173.

FREY, B. (1978) 'The Political Business Cycle', Paper presented to the Conference on the Economics of Politics sponsored by the Institute of Economic Affairs, London.

FREY, B. and SCHNEIDER, F. (1978) 'A Politico-Economic Model of the United Kingdom', *Economic Journal*, 243-253.

GORDON, R. (1976) 'Recent Developments in the Theory of Inflation and Unemployment', *Journal of Monetary Economics* 2: 000-000.

HIBBS, D. (1978) 'Why are US Policy Makers so Tolerant of Unemployment and Intolerable of Inflation?', Mimeo.

KIRCHGÄSSNER, G. and FREY B. (1977) 'A Political Model of the Business Cycle: A Comment', Mimeo.

KRAMER, G. (1971) 'Short-term Fluctuations in US Voting Behavior 1896-1964', *American Political Science Review* 65: 131-143.

MACRAE, D. (1977) 'A Political Model of the Business Cycle', *Journal of Political Economy* 85: 239-263.

McCALLUM, B. T. (1978) 'The Political Business Cycle: An Empirical Test', *Southern Economic Journal* 44: 504-515.

MILNE, R. and MACKENZIE, H. (1954) *Straight Fight*, London: Hansard Society.

MOSLEY, P. (1978) 'Images of the "Floating Voter": or, The "Political Business Cycle" Revistied', *Political Studies* 26: 375-394.

NORDHAUS, W. (1975) 'The Political Business Cycle', *Review of Economic Studies* 42: 167-190.

PALDAM, M. (1977) *Is There an Electoral Cycle? A Study of National Accounts*, Aarhus, Inst. of Economics, no. 8.

PESTON, M. (1974) *Theory of Macroeconomic Policy*, London: Phillip Allan.

TUFTE, E. (1978) *Political Control of the Economy*, Princeton: Princeton University Press.

7 The Political Business Cycle: Alternative Interpretations

Polytechnic of Central London, UK

Somewhere along the line the marriage of Political Economy divorced into Political Science and Economics. Though Adam Smith would have been pleased by the resulting increase in output from this division of labour, product quality may well have diminished. Now we are seeing a renewal of the old acquaintance. In some fields of activity a tentative holding of hands has galloped along into a passionate affair. The study of Political Business Cycles (PBC) is one such instance. The problem is that as the two partners hotly embrace each other they have no time to reflect, to ask are we doing the right thing? Extravagant plans are formulated with no heed to their capital.

The purpose of this paper therefore is to take a deep breath by raising issues, questioning foundations and proposing alterntives in the hope of improving the relationship, the sort of thing Ma or Pa might do. The guidance to all this prodding is something Grandpa once said (actually Stigler): 'The fact that economic conditions influence voters is a leading commonplace of conversation in election years. The question is: Is this fact in fact a fact?"[1]

Undoubtedly an understanding of PBCs or just business cycles is important to different sections of the community — forecasters, advisors, politicians and the media.[2] But they can be interpreted in many ways depending on one's perception of the underlying assumptions. Here the contrasting views of Kalecki and the 'Modern' interpreters of PBCs are examined, followed by a general discussion of the newer works before looking more closely at popularity functions. After making some suggestions the true political nature of the debate over PBCs is raised. Hopefully this should complete the circle which will not be a fruitless exercise if on the way we have decided we were right or wrong to have had the banns posted.

KALECKI

Michael Kalecki, a comparatively unknown though significant figure in the social sciences, first introduced the term Political Business Cycle in 1943. Working independantly he had anticipated many of the conclusions found in Keynes's 'General Theory' but he came to the gloomy opinion that:

> The assumption that a government will retain full employment in a capitalist economy if it only knows how to do it is fallacious. In this connection the misgivings of big business about the maintenance of full employment by government spending is of paramount importance.[3]

Both Kalecki and Keynes had identified the importance of aggregate demand in the operation of the business cycle and the possibility of smoothing the passage of the cycle by government spending. This idea broke with the traditions of the 'Classical School' and their firm belief in balanced budgets for such spending was to be financed by running up a deficit. Keynes was confident about his analysis and after a lag the implementation of his proposals. But Kalecki saw great difficulties in eradicating the business cycle, rather seeing its replacement by the PBC, largely because of the above mentioned influence of business interests. Working from a Marxist perspective he was conscious that capital was not only a quantity but also a coercive social power. Further, he was aware of the institutional datum that workers do not own capital or the means of production. Thus he proffered three reasons for business opposition to the maintenance of full employment.

The first concerns 'business confidence', a notion central to Keynes's marginal efficiency of capital, it being the psychological attitude of those making investment decisions. Keynes wrote, 'The state of confidence... is a matter to which practical men always pay the closest and most anxious attention'.[4] Any actions, especially by government, that unsettle an entrepreneur's degree of belief will effect a downward revision of investment plans. Consequently, business interests have considerable indirect control over governments wary of destabilizing confidence. If governments make good any shortfall in investment expenditure the ties of this indirect control are loosened. When public spending maintains the level of investment required for full employment business control-through-confidence becomes a mere bagatelle. Quite understandably business interests oppose full employment when it is achieved by the diminution of their authority and influence.

Kalecki's second reason concerns the direction of public expenditure, i.e. on public investment and subsidizing mass consumption. Outlets for public expenditure on 'public goods' are extremely limited. The natural fear arises that investments will eventually be made in areas whose output will compete with privately produced goods and services, concomitantly cutting into private profitability. On subsidizing mass consumption, the argument rests on the social relations prevailing under capitalism and its imperative that workers must sell their labour. Subsidies to the masses weaken this compulsion and threaten the social relations.

This point is developed in Kalecki's third reason for business opposition. He noted that even if opposition to creating full employment is overcome, policies directed at sustaining this condition would effect social and political changes unacceptable to business interests. There would be a fundamental shift of power in the factories and stability would be threatened. Clearly a 'reserve army' of workers is essential to the system.

Developing Kalecki's argument George Feiwel commented:

Implied here is a fourth reason which first and foremost underlies business opposition to full employment policies: the intrinsic apprehension of resulting redistribution of income. The fact that such a redistribution might be long in coming... does not matter. Its ultimate threat is sufficient.[5]

Taken together these factors constitute a powerful source of business opposition to the maintenance of full employment. But they do not produce total opposition to government interference. Some stimulation of the economy in a slump and some forms of expenditure, like investment grants, are quite acceptable. But opposition hardens if intervention proceeds to perpetuate full employment. Consequently Kalecki predicted a PBC where governments would undertake ameliorating policies in a slump but pressure from big business would induce cuts in government expenditure in near full employment conditions. The cuts would reproduce the slump conditions necessitating the reintroduction of public expenditure and so generating a business cycle whose cause is primarily political.

Feiwel crystalises this process when he observes:

> In this situation (full employment) a powerful block is likely to be formed between big business and the rentier interests, and they would probably find more than one economist to declare that the situation was manifestly unsound. The pressure of all these forces, and in particular of big business — as a rule influential in Government departments — would most probably induce the Government to return to the orthodox policy of cutting down the budget deficit. A slump would follow in which Government spending would come again into its own.[6]

Looking behind this interpretation of the PBC we can find three central features. Firstly, the construct is class based. The capitalist class are opposed to full employment because it harms their class interest; for the condition enhances the position of their class enemy, the working class. Under slump conditions workers' agitation for reflationary policies will gain business support but this will be withdrawn as full employment is approached. Instead business will demand deflationary policies and their dominance over government ensures that this follows. Clearly, Kalecki views the government as an instrument of the dominant class. This leads to the second feature.

Unless 'political' is interpreted as 'electoral', Kalecki disregards party politics and changes of governments. Whichever party is elected the relationship between government and business interests remains unchanged. Though there is some uncertainty as to the outcome of an election and initially some problems may arise, in order to survive its term of office the old relationship must be reconstituted. Business interests have been known to take somewhat violent extraparliamentary action in order to preserve this special relationship.

Finally, throughout Kalecki's interpretation runs the notion of ideology and in particular the primacy of 'soundness' in economic affairs. In modern parlance this amounts to the 'hegemony' of business interests over economic thinking, where 'soundness' entails a balanced budget (or small deficit), a belief in the existence and efficacy of free markets and a limited role for government activities.

Given the above perspective PBCs can be interpreted as the conscious actions of governments obeying business interests. By alternating its expenditure it causes oscillations in employment levels generating cycles. To be more correct we also need the assumption that governments are unable to maintain a level of unemployment that just satisfies both classes, perhaps due to lags, leads or informational difficulties. However, even this degree of stability may raise worker consciousness and therefore become unacceptable to employers.

The above is a somewhat harsh exposition of Kalecki which can be toned down. For Kalecki class was an objective reality, perhaps producing unequal access to government. Thus, PBCs can be seen not as the outcome of conscious actions by government but rather as a groping process in response to sectional pressures, some more intense than others. Whether we choose conscious (linked to business pressure) or unconscious (linked to various pressures) conduct on the part of governments producing fluctuations in the level of economic activity the explanation under 'modern' theories of the PBC are markedly contrasting, as we shall now see.

'MODERN' THEORIES

The 'modern' body of literature on PBCs can trace its lineage from Hotelling, Downs, Black, Buchanan and Tullock,[7] all of whom point to, in varying degree, the interrelationship between the polity and the economy. From these the concepts of party competition, popularity and reaction functions have evolved and been incorporated into the most sophisticated of the modern studies.[8] Superficially the current studies, representatives of which are included in this volume, differ from Kalecki in that they have fruitfully injected econometric techniques into the debate. But the difference goes deeper than that. Firstly, they involve a far more complex set of relationships than Kalecki's class based analysis. Further, they include time. But most importantly they accuse governments of deliberately generating business cycles, pushing the economy from a social optimum, in order to achieve the goal of re-election. Consider this small sample of comments:

> Should it be possible...for politicians to advance their own interests by acting contrary to the promotion of stability, it is likely that they will merely curtsy to macroeconomic stability and then proceed to ignore it.[9]

> There is growing evidence...that the business cycle has become to a large degree a 'policy cycle' in which macroeconomic policy causes fluctuations rather than eliminating them.[10]

> The basic hypothesis advanced is that the governing party aims to stay in power and therefore seeks to increase its popularity with the electorate when its (perceived) re-election chances are low. For this purpose it undertakes an expansionary policy expected to lead to a popularity increase and an improvement in its election prospects.[11]

Not only do the above contrast starkly with Kalecki's concept of the PBC but also with the perceived wisdom of many in the economics profession.

The essence of the modern PBC is:

(a) a popularity function measuring the incumbent party's degree of support and indicative of its re-election prospects. Usually popularity is considered to be determined by key economic variables; and

(b) a reaction function being the government's response to the popularity function. The incumbent has available to it certain economic policy instruments, the use of which is triggered when popularity falls below some critical level.

This very simple definition of the PBC will be developed later in the paper.

The mechanism of the PBC is represented diagramatically in Figure 1 following a formulation suggested by Wagner.[12]

FIGURE 1

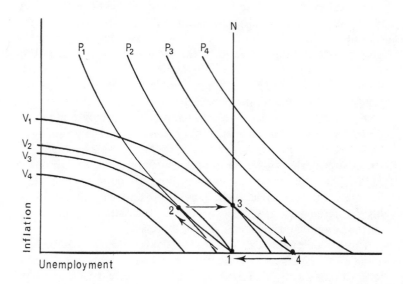

The horizontal axis measures the unemployment rate and the vertical, the rate of inflation. The concave indifference surfaces V_1, V_2 etc. represent the popularity function, being degrees of voter support. Their value declines as we move from the origin for it is assumed that neither unemployment nor inflation are desired by the electorate. The economy is described by the two curves P_1 (plus the associated set through to P_4) and N. The P curves represent Phillips type short run combinations of inflation and unemployment. In this respect they are the set of available policy instruments available to the government. If the economy is on, say, P_2 budget manipulation can move the economy to any position on P_2 in the short run. N represents the 'natural rate of unemployment' consistent with the real forces in the economy and accurate perceptions.[13] Unemployment can only be kept below this long run rate by accelerating inflation. Assume an election is imminent: starting from point 1 on Figure 1, the government can improve the value of its popularity function by engineering a movement along P_1. Unemployment falls, inflation increases until 2, a point of tangency is reached on V_2, which is more favourable for re-election. However, as the new rate of inflation becomes anticipated by the electorate, labour is withdrawn, unemployment rises and the economy creeps to point 3, with an accompanying decline in the popularity function. However, if the use of the policy instruments succeeded in gaining re-election this loss of support is not crucial. It does, however, stimulate the government to react so that by the time of the next election the economy is back at 2. To achieve this goal, policy instruments are used to move the economy along P_2 to point 4 giving rise to an even greater loss in popularity. But once again when the new (zero) rate of inflation becomes anticipated, the labour market swells, unemployment falls and the natural rate holds. Thus, the economy completes the cycle returning to point 1 in time for another cycle. As long as the government can get its timing right re-election is fairly probable. The outcome is the synchronization of business and electoral cycles.

Though simplistic, this description does by implication include some of the issues involved in the PBC. Firstly, time is an important variable with respect to voters' memory and to the use of policy instruments. The above assumes that voters make their decisions only on the basis of current economic performance. We could lag this one period holding the election at point 3 with voters reflecting on point 2. Alternatively, some weighted assessment of performance could be introduced. Also it is clear that the range of policy instrument options open in any period is limited by the options used in previous periods. Thus, government is really involved in a dynamic programming problem. Finally, note that party competition is non-existent. Oppositions do not win elections; only incumbents lose them when they get their timing wrong. These and other issues are briefly discussed in the next section.

IDEOLOGICAL FACTORS

Ideology is almost completely absent from the Downsian-type analysis of politico-economic interdependence. It is necessary to note that parties are more than just political entrepreneurs, willing to produce any policy output to get elected but also have ideological beliefs. It has been suggested that governments try to maximize utility,[14] defined as a function of implementing ideological conceptions and of being popular, rather than merely maximizing popular support. Nevertheless, governments must remain in office to carry out their ideological goals so that the popularity function becomes a constraint on ideological action. A niggling temptation must persist to delay ideological objectives in favour of more popular practices. Various rules have been proposed to deal with the possibility of putting beliefs into practice which are discussed later.

Time enters the popularity (or lead) functions by way of voters' memories. Kramer[15] and Frey and Schneider[16] use one year as the length of memory. Stigler[17] proposes two years and a long-memory model with weights for variables exhibiting a steady trend. Fair[18] generalizes all these perspectives. There seems no a priori time period to base economic performance on and this has considerable implications. It is not just a measurement problem that is at issue but how voters form their expectations. Decisions based on a one period performance of the economy can be vastly different from those mellowed over time. If we use a model to predict election outcomes then a freak value for a key variable may lead us to predict either a landslide or annihilation with a short memory but not necessarily with a long one.

There is ample evidence that the exercise of policy instruments now delimits choice in the future and of course that the present is itself affected by past decisions. The Phillips Curve-Natural Rate analysis shows that after reducing unemployment below its sustainable position persistent inflation arises and we are stuck with it. This rate is then fed into policy calculus at the next round. Public Sector borrowing means Public Sector debt servicing and public expenditure can be on consumption or investment. At the heart of policy instruments then is an intertemporal trade-off between current and future welfare, a matter discussed by Nordhaus[19] and MacRae[20] in the PBC context.

Finally, time can enter the PBC when the length of the election period is itself a policy instrument, for a 'snap-election' is certainly one way of avoiding deteriorating economic conditions.

An implicit assumption when including economic variables in

PBCs is that governments control them, that voters know this and 'blame' politicians. I doubt if any economist, however arrogant, would support this notion. Governments in implementing policy are basing their judgements on a set of aggregate behavioural assumptions, theory advising them how voters 'should' behave. Even the simple ones fall apart occasionally. Further, the economy will be sensitive to external shocks, heightened by increasing international interdependence. On top of this we have a plethora of cycles of varying duration from the Kondratieff[21] to the Seasonal of adjusted fame. Only an autarkic command economy really fits the bill and such States have little need for elections.

Non-economic sociological factors have also been included in PBC analysis. US studies usually contain an 'incumbency' dummy variable or some 'coattailing' effect of victory in Presidential elections on Congressional elections.[22] In the UK Miller and Mackie[23] have added a purely non-economic electoral cycle to the normal economic variables which Frey and Schneider[24] have formulated into political capital stock, which depreciates, and the number of periods to the nearest election. These are better descriptions than explanations and more thought is required on this matter.[25] Okum[26] raises the pertinent question of 'party image', it being the association in the voters' mind between parties and types of bias in policy. Ideology thus returns as does party competition since it would be a rational strategy to attempt to stigmatize the opposition. In fact an opposition must necessarily raise other issues whenever the economic performance of the government is satisfactory. Concerted effort on the role of trade unions, immigration, nuclear energy, foreign policy, law and order, even environmental pollution by dogs, backed by media exposure may elevate any of these above the state of the economy.

The data applied to the studies are either votes actually cast or surveys of voting intentions. There are few doubts concerning the former, except institutional factors, the peculiarity of war and the accuracy of early economic statistics but questions can be posed to the latter. Surveys are sensitive to recent media coverage and the manipulation of issues by politicians. Governments with developed propaganda machinery and excellent access to the media may be able to shift the 'blame' to external factors, ethnic groups, supranational bodies or the garden paraphenalia who inhabit Zurich.

Further, it is easy to be fickle when casting a hypothetical vote and sophisticated sections of the electorate could even use the surveys in a strategic fashion. When 'leads' are a dependent variable the number of 'don't knows' in surveys may render any results meaningless.

Finally, the 'rules of the game' must be examined in this section of general issues. Propositions have been made about voters' and parties' behaviour. These rules criticially affect the validity of models of politico-economic interdependence. It may be a cheap question, but why do people vote? Rational theorists assume a voter calculus akin to consumer behaviour. Tullock states:

> Voters and customers are essentially the same people. Mr Smith buys and votes; he is the same man in the supermarket and in the voting booth. There is no strong reason to believe his behaviour is radically different in the two environments. We assume that, in both, he will choose the produce or candidate he thinks is the best bargain for him.[27]

Difficulties arise if the cost of voting exceeds the expected benefits especially when the probability of a vote 'counting' is included. Riker and Ordeshook[28] enlist the support of 'psychic income' to get round this chicane. Non-rationalist explanations cover political mobilization by elites and the use of threshold costs not exceeded by voting. The paradox of participation was discussed by Whiteley[29] but the fact remains, people do vote. Given this we can regard voters as undertaking information gathering and processing before reaching a decision based on self-interest. Like shareholders, they then vote for the party closest to their own position in terms of policy outputs. Recognizing the practical difficulties of such a process Kramer[30] introduces a 'satisficing' model, supported by Nordhaus.[31] Linking past experience and expectations voters make judgements on whether a government's performance has been 'satisfactory'. If it is thought to be unsatisfactory, the government gets the thumbs down and the opposition gets a 'chance'. To disregard the opposition's ability in this way especially if it has no track record, is not a totally sound judgement. Further, through aggregation, expectations and the definition of 'satisfactory' the predictive powers of the model are weakened. Nevertheless, if by assuming voters behave 'as if' we can examine the behaviour of the incumbent.

Ideological factors and their sensitivity to popularity leads were mentioned earlier. It has been hypothesized, quite reasonably, that if the incumbent's lead is considerable ideological goals will be implemented. Similarly, if the government has no hope of gaining reelection the goals will be pursued with vigour.[32] At other times policy instruments react to the popularity function, including the pure electoral cycle. When the lead falls below some critical level expansionary policies are triggered. It is over the nature of the response that questions can be raised. Would a rational government attempt to improve its popularity in either a safe or hopeless constituency? Would it be better to stimulate all spheres of economic activity or just the labour intensive ones? Though a government will stimulate demand generally, this may be achieved with a high degree of selectivity, aiming at a particular target population of popularity. This amounts to an alteration in the structure of relative prices which could, by its dysfunctional impact, effect a business cycle. This view has been discussed by Wagner[33] and contrasts with the models that concentrate solely on the inflation-unemployment trade off.

All the above questions illustrate the complexities involved in modern PBC analysis, many of which should be included in any total model of interdependence. It would be far easier to formulate a model where the government was a manager of the national football team. The World Cup would provide a readily comprehensible and discreet measure of satisfactory performance but unfortunately the social sciences are not that simple.

POPULARITY FUNCTIONS

Skeletal popularity functions are composed of three elements: unemployment, inflation and growth. The first two are linked through a trade-off and the latter is influenced by the others. Frey and Schneider have found that in the UK between 1959 Q4 and 1974 Q4,

> A rise in the rate of inflation by 1% reduces the government's lead by about 0.6% and an increase in unemployment by 1% reduces the government's lead by about 6%, and an increase in the growth rate of disposable real income by 1% increased the lead by about 0.8%.[34]

These elements are now dissected to ascertain the theory of how they affect voting. So often models include statements like

> Votes for or against the party in power are influenced by many things, but to some degree they are influenced by ecomomic variables, inflation and unemployment in particular.[35]

and —

> The two most obvious economic variables to consider as possible measures of performance are some measure of the rate of inflation and some measure of real output or employment.[36]

Why?, a cynic might say, because data are readily available for these variables. But for the model to be robust it is essential to explain the reasoning behind such hypotheses.

It must be noted that governments allegedly control these variables or are perceived to do so. This provides the first building block and may be regarded as a shaky foundation. Sitgler comments:

> In general, there is no direct or easily traceable link between national economic policy and a specific person's employment status. A failing company may simply fail a little sooner than in a period of stable aggregate demand, or the appearance of a new firm may simply be delayed.[37]

Certainly, governments through their investment decisions, have considerable control over government employment levels, the prices of nationalized industries and, in some respect, growth. There are linkages from such government management to the rest of the economy. But there are many others in the economy also making similar decisions who could be held responsible for performance, particularly high profile multi-national corporations. The three key variables are now examined in more detail.

Generally, for economic variables to affect voting they must be 'felt' by households. We can assume that voters do not allocate resources to an investigation of others' welfare so changes must be experienced by the voter's family. Overlooking questions of thresholds of perceptions and learning effects we are still concerned with voter psychology as performance is measured by some deviation from an 'expected' standard. Expectations are usually only applied to growth but there seems no reason to exclude the other variables. As unemployment and inflation are held to be inversely related in the short run, higher than expected unemployment with lower than expected inflation involve voters in a complex calculus. The outcome will depend on the importance of each to the voter plus, of course, the deviation of growth from that expected. But, if the voter does not experience unemployment, the good of lower inflation may be decisive. This brings us to an obvious but often overlooked point. Each voter has only one vote, though intensities (i.e. for or against) may differ considerably. Someone ranking employment highest who becomes unemployed may favour the opposition. If that same person is then hard hit by inflation his support for the opposition may increase but this will have zero impact on the government's lead. Perhaps the popularity function is one of those cases where the whole is less than the sum of the parts.

Stigler[38] expresses some doubts about the inclusion of unemployment as a bad. Certainly it is very unevenly experienced with the highest incidence in the 'disadvantaged sector'[39] of a dual labour market. Using aggregate unemployment rates obliterates the fine categorizations involved. Concentration of unemployment among the young, unskilled and single begs the question of their participation in the electoral process. Should the rate be adjusted for the 'unemployables'? Is the bad of unemployment reduced by the good of social security payments? And do these payments induce people to register or quit to take advantage of the good, making unemployment statistics unreliable. One way round this is to treat unemployment in probabilistic terms. Thus, someone in employment will reduce his support for the government when unemployment rises because it increases the probability of his becoming unemployed i.e. it influences his personal expectations.

In the above sense we are assigning unemployment a micro-importance; Nordhaus and Okun consider its macro-importance. Here it is used, without micro-foundations, as an indicator of cyclical conditions. Okun sees it as:

> . . . reflecting cuts in real labour income through shorter working weeks, reduced participation in the labour force, slower movements up promotion ladders, and reduced mobility to better jobs, and even the curtailment in property income that accompanies slack and recession.[40]

And Nordhaus:

> In short, a movement in the aggregate unemployment rate will be felt, directly or indirectly, by a very large fraction of households.[41]

Even when employed voters experience any of these and blame the incumbent, unemployment rates involve huge short term flows. These may be indicative of a healthy economy with a great deal of mobility and self-improvement.

There appears no clear cut a priori theory of the influence of unemployment on voters as a pure bad. It may be the price to be paid for a good, i.e. lower inflation rates. Employment, however, is a good which, in conjunction with an appropriate denominator and, adequately defined, may provide a better theoretical basis for PBC models.

Inflation also suffers from measurement problems. Yearly inflation rates can be falling whilst the six-month rate is rising. The Retail Prices Index gives most weight to food but households of different incomes and size spend considerably different proportions of income on food. Again, we have a variable with a differential impact. Palpably, inflation is a bad if incomes are fixed or consistently lag behind. It is not so bad for those at the head of the income race, especially if they are in debt at fixed rates. Nordhaus[42] accepts it as a bad because of possible balance of payments problems; disruptive implications for resource allocation and the arbitrary redistribution of income that may follow. The first two reasons have no obvious micro-foundations except with an exceptionally well educated electorate but the third has considerable validity. Again, though, it might be the price to be paid for a good, employment.

A major factor that needs to be incorporated into PBC analysis is the existance of a 'demand for inflation' where it is considered a good. Inflation is not demanded per se but rather for its consequences. It is now typically accepted by economists that in the long run 'inflation is always and everywhere a monetary phenomenon', the outcome of persistent budget deficits (i.e. of policy instruments). Spending in excess of revenue, thereby inflation, is 'supplied' by governments, but it is central to PBC that this is a reaction to demand by voters rather that something forced upon

them. It is an indirect demand, by by-product of demands for other
goods. Thus Gordon states:

> While no group in society explicitly 'demands' more inflation, pressures for the
> government to pursue a more inflationary policy, or not to pursue and anti-
> inflationary policy, emanate from taxpayers who resist tax increases made
> necessary by increases in expenditures...beneficiaries of government programs
> who resist expenditure reductions, groups attempting to obtain an increase in
> their share of national income, and, in open economies, from price increases and
> inflows of money from abroad. These pressures constitute an implicit, if not ex-
> plicit, demand for inflation.[43]

Gordon argues that the considerable literature on 'cost-push' inflation, particularly of European origin, supports this notion of a demand for inflation. Of significance here is the role of trade unions,
their 'pushfulness' and 'militancy' which manifests itself in a desire
for the redistribution of income and wage increases as governmen-
tally supplied goods paid for by a tax on money holdings.

The above does not imply a reverse Say's Law, demand creating
its own supply. The sensitivity of the reaction function (i.e. supply)
is related to the expected vote loss if demand is resisted, plus many
other factors, including the short-term unemployment-inflation
trade-off and the cost of raising revenue through taxes. Though
Brunner[44] criticizes Gordon's approach, particularly for its lack of
theoretical foundations, Burton[45] has teased out those factors
which may lead a voter to place a positive or negative valuation on
inflation. They are whether on balance he is a creditor or debtor;
whether on balance he benefits from government spending and the
cost borne by all from the dysfunctional consequences of inflation.
Given this type of calculus many votes will be in favour of inflation
over a certain range.

There are alternative sources of a demand for inflation. Voters
may suffer from an illusion, being unable to recognize that current
benefits from budget deficits must be set against lower future levels
of welfare than would obtain in the absence of a deficit. Of course,
voters may apply a very high discount to future benefits in which
case they are expressing their distaste for deferred gratification.
The initial analysis predicts an explosive demand for inflation
unless there is some learning effect (rentiers and foreign creditors
will surely undertake a missionary role) when the disruptive effect

of inflation outweighs the other two factors.

Alternatively voters may have informational problems, ignorance, believing that the short run trade-off is sustainable when in fact the Natural-Rate hypothesis holds. Seeing unemployment rise for a given inflation rate they will demand larger deficits and generate even higher unemployment for given rates of inflation.

The conclusion must be that whether through illusion, ignorance or a desire to confiscate, a demand for inflation is a natural phenomenon and rightly must be included within models of the PBC. With this interpretation inflation is partly a good produced through the interaction of the popularity and reaction functions.

Growth is the least contentious of the three key variables. However, the distribution of an increase in national product will influence voters. Rapid growth where all the new output is appropriated by the 'haves' will win very few votes from the 'nots'. Similarly negative growth achieved by a redistribution from rich to poor could lead to re-election as would zero growth under the same circumstances.

Summing up, unemployment at the micro level is difficult to rationalize as being of great importance to voters' decisons, but at the macro level is an adequate indicator of the general level of economic activity. Inflation can be a good or a bad but it is central to the PBC that it is demanded. Growth, or deviations from the expected path, is quite satisfactory if accompanied by the 'right' distributions. Researchers have variously and frequently found significant statistical relationships between these variables and popularity. Further they have deduced that governments respond to such functions. Here, in the spirit of honest cynicism, we ask should such statistical results be elevated to the status of 'fact' in the absence of clear cut theoretical foundations?

By shaving the three variables with Occram's Razor, the economic content of popularity functions can be whittled down to one. Share prices respond to unemployment, implying spare capacity and reduced profits; they also adjust to inflation and are sensitive to growth. Further, they are affected by expectations, confidence and even the balance of payments. It can therefore be argued that share prices encapsulate the full complex gamut of economic factors that influence popularity. The author is in the process of testing a popularity function that includes share prices but it is difficult to suggest any rationale of why they should affect a government's standing. This points to the necessity of a more robust explanation of the linkages between the variables included in any PBC model.

Having raised so much flak it is, of course, de rigueur to propose alternatives. The starting point is to confine selection to those variables over which the government has a fair degree of control, which influence as many voters as possible and are 'felt'. The number of people employed in government services is an obvious candidate as is welfare spending. Both are more under the governments' aegis than are the conventional variables, they involve large sections of the community and at little informational cost. A less obvious though equally satisfactory variable is the mortgage rate. The growing number of owner occupiers in the UK, the responsiveness of mortgage rates to monetary policy and its political sensitivity make research in this area potentially fruitful. This basically micro-approach, using government employment, welfare payments and mortgage rates, is based on quite a firm set of justifiable assumptions. At least the results of this on-going research will throw light on the usefulness of this type of methological interpretation. As yet, though, the central and dark issues at the heart of the PBC have not been broached. This is discussed in the final section, where the true 'political' character of the PBC is brought out.

THE POLITICAL ASPECT

We have seen that Kalecki believed in the dominance of business interests in economic affairs. Politico-economic action in this perspective was the transmission of their doctrine through policy instruments. Keynes had a different view. He could hardly be described as a man of the people, he couldn't fathom Marx and his perspective was certainly elitist. He implicitly conceived of policy as being directed by a well-meaning few, guided by the star of 'public interest'. His radical proposals were quite simple — the symmetrical employment of budget deficits and surpluses — the quantity and direction of which are related to the underlying business cycle. The expected outcome would be stability of employment and prices plus, over a longer period, nearly balanced budgets. But the evidence does not support this prediction.[46] There has been a persistent bias towards budget deficits and it is these that are central to the ferocious political debates that encompass the Western economies. Why the bias? Quoting Hayek, marginally out of context:

> The reason is that it is now generally taken for granted that in a democracy the powers of the majority must be unlimited, and that a government with unlimited powers will be forced, to secure the continued support of a majority, to use its unlimited powers in the service of special interests...[47]

That is, the tool kit provided by Keynes coupled with our type of democratic organization produce a predilection for government spending in excess of receipts. Buchanan and Wagner add:

> Old-fashioned beliefs about the virtue of the balanced-budget rule and of redeeming public debt during periods of prosperity became undermined by Keynesian ideas, and lost their hold on the public. In consequence, debt reduction lost its claim as a guiding rule. Budget surpluses lost their raison d'être. Deficits allow politicians to increase spending without having directly to raise taxes. There is little obstacle to such a policy. Surpluses, on the other hand, required government to raise taxes without increasing spending — a programme far more capable of stimulating political opposition than budget deficits, especially once the constraining norm of debt retirement had receded from public consciousness.[48]

Thus, the truly political aspect of PBCs is not concerned with the internal logic of Keynes's model but his implicit assumptions concerning the men who executed his prescriptions. The PBC arises because 'Keynesian economics has turned the politicians loose; it has destroyed the effective constraint on politicians' ordinary appetites to spend and spend without the apparent necessity to tax'.[49] The primary goal of budget deficits is stability of employment — a good. But the price is future bads, inflation and worsening unemployment.[50] However, Frey and Schneider have found that popularity is generally far more sensitive to unemployment than inflation for both the UK and the US,[51] indicating Keynesian prescriptions are supportable. Thus, we have two fundamental connected political questions:

(a) What is the best economic model, Keynesian or Monetarist, to adopt for maintianing full employment?
(b) Is the model appropriate to our form of democratic organization?

No attempt is made to answer either here, only to point out that after an extended period of full employment in most Western economies and faced with the current levels of unemployment, the debate revolves around the balanced-budget rule and whether it should be embodied constitutionally. Are those who favour such a rule the 'business interests'? Was Kalecki right?

NOTES

1. G. J. Stigler, 'General Economic Conditions and National Elections', *American Economic Review* 63, 1973: 160-167, especially 160.

2. For a rather crude analysis of the interest of PBCs for Trade Unions see G. Locksley, 'Trade Unions and the Political Business Cycle', *Political Quarterly* 49, 1978.

3. M. Kalecki, 'Political Aspects of Full Employment', in *The Last Phase in the Transformation of Capitalism* (New York 1972), 75.

4. J. M. Keynes, *General Theory of Employment Interest and Money* (London 1936).

5. G. R. Feiwel, 'Reflections on Kalecki's Theory of the Political Business Cycle', *Kyklos* 27, 1974: 21-48, especially p. 33.

6. G. R. Feiwel, ibid, 35.

7. For example, see H. Hotelling 'Stability in Competition', *Economic Journal* 39, 1929: 41-57; A. Downs *An Economic Theory of Democracy* (New York 1957); D. Black, *The Theory of Committees and Elections* (Cambridge 1958); J. M. Buchanan and G. Tullock, *The Calculus of Consent* (Ann Arbor 1962) and D. Robertson, *The Theory of Party Competition* (London 1976).

8. For a review of the different types of PBC studies see B. S. Frey and F. Schneider, 'On the Modelling of Politico-Economic Interdependence', *European Journal of Political Research* 3, 1975: 339-360; and for a review of results see G. H. Kramer, 'Short-Term Fluctuations in US Voting Behaviour, 1896-1964', *American Political Science Review* 65, 1971: 131-143.

9. R. E. Wagner, 'Economic Manipulation for Political Profit: Macroeconomic Consequences and Constitutional Implication', *Kyklos* 30, 1977: 394-410, quote p. 396.

10. D. MacRae, 'A Political Model of the Business Cycle', *Journal of Political Economy* 85, 1977: 293-363, quote, p. 239.

11. B. S. Frey and F. Schneider, 'A politico-Economic Model of the United Kingdom', *Economic Journal* 88, 1978 (a): 243-253, quote p. 244.

12. R. E. Wagner, op. cit.

13. For a more thorough exposition of these notions see J. Burton, 'The Demand for Inflation in Liberal-Democratic Societies', this volume.

14. B. S. Frey and F. Schneider, op. cit., 1978.

15. G. H. Kramer, op. cit.

16. B. S. Frey and F. Schneider, op. cit. 1978 (a).

17. G. J. Stigler, op. cit.

18. R. C. Fair, 'The Effect of Economic Events on Votes for President', *Review of Economics and Statistics* 60, 1978: 159-173.

19. W. D. Nordhaus 'The Political Business Cycle', *Review of Economic Studies* 42, 1975: 160-190.

20. D. MacRae, op. cit.

21. N. D. Kondratieff, 'The Long Waves in Economic Life', *Lloyds Bank Review* 129, 1978: 41-60.

22. See G. H. Kramer, op. cit., 136-137.

23. W. L. Miller and M. Mackie, 'The Electoral Cycle and the Asymmetry of Government and Opposition Popularity: An Alternative Model of the Relationship between Economic Conditions and Political Popularity', *Political Studies* 21, 1973: 263-279.

24. B. S. Frey and F. Schneider, 1978 (a) op. cit., 245-246 and 'An Empirical Study of Politico-Economic Interaction in the United States', *Review of Economics and Statistics* 60, 1978 (b): 174-183.

25. See David Butler's comments in the *Sunday Times*, 6 August 1978.

26. A. M. Okum, 'Comments on Stigler's Paper', *American Economic Review* 63, 1973: 172-177.

27. G. Tullock, *The Vote Motive* (London 1976).

28. W. Riker and P. Ordeshook, 'A Theory of the Calculus of Voting', *American Political Science Review* 62, 1968: 25-42.

29. P. Whiteley, 'The Political Economy of Electoral Support', paper given at the ECPR workshop on Formal Political Analysis, University of Grenoble 1978.

30. G. H. Kramer, op. cit.

31. W. D. Nordhaus, op. cit.

32. B. S. Frey and F. Schneider, 1978 (a) 244.

33. R. E. Wagner, op. cit.

34. B. S. Frey and F. Schneider, 1978 (a), 250-251.

35. D. MacRae, op. cit. 240.

36. R. C. Fair, op. cit., 164.

37. G. J. Stigler, op cit., note 162.

38. G. J. Stigler, ibid.

39. See P. B. Doeringer and N. Bosanquet, 'Is there a Dual Labour Market in Great Britain?', *Economic Journal* 83, 1973: 421-435 for a discussion of the concepts involved here.

40. A. M. Okun, op. cit., 174.

41. W. D. Nordhaus, op. cit.

42. W. D. Nordhaus, ibid.

43. R. J. Gordon, 'The Demand and Supply of Inflation', *Journal of Law and Economics* 18, 1975: 807-836, quote p. 808.

44. K. Brunner, 'Comment', *Journal of Law and Economics* 18, 1975: 837-857.

45. J. Burton, op. cit.

46. See J. Burton, 'Keynes's Legacy to Great Britain: Folly in a Great Kingdom', in J. M. Buchanan, J. Burton and R. E. Wagner, *The Consequences of Mr Keynes* (London 1978) for the statistics on the bias towards deficits.

47. F. A. Hayek, *Economic Freedom and Representative Government* (London 1973) 9-10.

48. J. M. Buchanan and R. E. Wagner, 'Democracy and Keynesian Constitutions: Political Biases and Economic Consequences', in J. M. Buchanan, J. Burton and R. E. Wagner op. cit., 18.

49. J. M. Buchanan and R. E. Wagner, ibid.

50. M. Friedman has suggested that the natural rate of unemployment may become endogenous and shift outwards in response to persistent high inflation; see his Nobel lecture, *Inflation and Unemployment: The New Dimensions of Politics* (London 1977).

51. B. S. Frey and F. Schneider, op. cit., 1978 (a) and (b).

III Politics, Inflation and Economic Policy

8 Public Choice, Monetary Control and Economic Disruption

Richard E. Wagner

Auburn University, USA

With the Keynesian-inspired denial of Say's Equality, the coordination of the economic activities of the various participants in the economic process was no longer regarded as something that would naturally take place smoothly and continuously. Smooth and continuous coordination became an exceptional state of affairs, the creation of which became a task for macroeconomic engineering. For at least a generation, therefore, an important element of macroeconomic analysis has been the development of a basis for government to use its monetary and budgetary controls to promote economic stability.

This literature on macroeconomic policy has developed largely in innocence of the possible inconsistency between the conduct of policy in such a manner — assuming for now that it is even possible to conduct such policy — and the requisites for rational political action. In large measure it has been tacitly assumed either that politicians will act selflessly to promote economic stability or that their interests in their own political survival will require them to act in this manner. Herschel Grossman, in reviewing the contributions of James Tobin to macroeconomics, described clearly this failure of economics to treat seriously the relation between politics and macroeconomic policy. While particular references were to Tobin, Grossman was speaking of economists in general when he noted:

> Tobin presumes that the historical record of monetary and fiscal policy involves a series of avoidable mistakes, rather than the predictable consequences of personal preferences and capabilities working through the existing constitutional process by which policy is formulated. Specifically, Tobin shows no interest in analysis of either the economically motivated behavior of private individuals in the political process or the behavior of the government agents who make and administer policy.[1]

Should it be possible for politicians to advance their interests by undertaking policies that create economic instability, they are likely merely to pay lip service to macroeconomic stability, while proceeding to pursue their own contrary interests. In recent years several people have become interested in the possibility that politicians might enhance their survival prospects by using their monetary and fiscal powers to promote economic instability.[2] In stark contrast to the common, normative view of government as a balance wheel, government might actually act to destabilize the economy. The rational pursuit of political self-interest commonly takes place within an institutional context in which government possesses a monopoly over money. This monetary monopoly serves to create a natural link between economics and politics, and the intent of this paper is to explore some aspects of this linkage.[3] There are strong grounds for suggesting that macroeconomic ills are a by-product of the mixture of democratic politics and a central government with a monetary monopoly, and that is large enough to produce macroeconomic consequences in its pursuit of political ends.[4]

STATE MONOPOLY OVER MONEY

As a point of departure, financial policies should be regarded as a product of the rational actions of people undertaken in light of the knowledge generated by and the incentives created by particular institutions. One such institution is the monopoly over money, for this institution creates a link between politics and monetary control. It is well recognized that economic instruments are employed by government to advance the purposes of those in control of the apparatus of the state. Government monopoly over money is simply one such instrument, and this monopoly will certainly be used when suitable in the pursuit of political gain. The literature on the political business cycle is one sign of recognition of this property of state action.[5] This literature raises the possibility that the deliberate creation of economic instability can sometimes be sound political strategy. What makes political business cycles possible is the government's control over the supply of money, though this control is less immediate in some nations than in others.[6] When government monopoly over money is combined with the pursuit of political self-interest, macroeconomic discoordination can result because of the non-neutral character of monetary disturbance.[7]

Government monopoly over money is, of course, advocated not because of its harmful consequences, but because of hypothetical gains in economic efficiency. As compared with a commodity standard, a purely fiduciary or fiat system of money holds out the promise of a potential social saving. With a commodity standard, specific commodities must be produced and then reserved for monetary purposes. Resources must be devoted to the production of gold, if this is a monetary commodity, and this gold will subsequently serve as a medium of exchange. A fiduciary or fiat system obviates the need for this type of production. Pieces of paper can serve as substitutes for the gold or other commodities that would serve as money under a commodity standard. The adoption of a fiduciary standard instituted by government fiat offers, in other words, the potential of an outward shift in the production capabilities within the economy. The services formerly supplied by the money commodity, and which require the dedication of stocks of that commodity to that use, can now be supplied costlessly through government fiat, at least in principle.

A substantial chasm, however, separates the proposition about the potential benefits from an ideal monopoly over money from the proposition that state monopoly is preferable to other, non-monopoly monetary institutions. A rationalization for state monopoly over money should never be confused with an explanation of the essential properties of state monopoly. While a rationalization can be developed for government monopoly to institute a fiduciary standard, this act of rationalization does not guarantee that government monopoly will actually yield the potential social saving. A statement about the desirable conduct of a monetary monopoly generally has little bearing upon actual conduct.

It is contrary to reason and to experience to expect that a monopoly position will fail to be exploited for the benefit of those in a position to practice such an exploitation. It is the costlessness with which fiduciary money can be created, the very source of its rationalization, that creates difficulties of monetary control when government possesses a monopoly over money. One must sweat to produce gold or silver, but little effort is required to print currency. A fiduciary standard, in other words, makes it possible to produce claims to real resources at nearly zero cost. Counterfeiting becomes a profitable activity, one that the state customarily tries to reserve for its own use. One could mine an ounce of gold and exchange this gold for a television set. Alternatively, one could simply print up $400 worth of currency, fiat money, to trade for the television. A fiduciary system is obviously subject to strong forces of corruption. The temptation to counterfeit is easily understandable, whether it is done by private citizens or by the state. A private citizen might print because he did not want to work to gain the desired purchasing power. A government might print because it did not want to tax to gain the desired purchasing power, perhaps because it believed that the higher taxes would reduce its likelihood of success in future elections.

PUBLIC POLICY, VOTE BUYING, AND MONEY MONOPOLY

In a democracy, citizens will be able periodically to choose among candidates. To continue in office, an incumbent must secure more votes than a challenger. In this context of political competition, politicians may be viewed as creating policies so as to increase their electoral support, though the taxes that must be assessed to finance those policies will lose support.[8] Within this context of using policies to buy votes, there are strong analytical grounds for understanding both the temptation by government to resort to money creation and the resulting harm of such money creation. With a commodity standard, an increase in the benefits promised to one set of citizens necessarily requires a decrease in the benefits promised to another set, for this is how the increased benefits must be paid for. Government monopoly over a fiduciary standard, however, severs this link between positive and negative benefits. It now becomes possible to enact or expand a program designed to benefit one set of citizens without having either to curtail a program designed to benefit another set or to increase taxes. Positive promises can be made without negative offsets, for the excess of desires to spend over the means to pay for such spending can be bridged through money creation.

Several efforts have been made both to assess empirically and to understand conceptually the use by governments of their money monopoly to strengthen their survival prospects. In several different studies, Bruno Frey and Friedrich Schneider examined the determinants of the popularity of incumbent politicians in West Germany and in the United States. Their evidence suggested quite strongly that the popularity of incumbents declined as rates of inflation and unemployment increased, which would seem to indicate that macroeconomic variables can influence the survival prospects of politicians. Moreover, the popularity of incumbents was found to vary directly with the rate of growth in real per capita consumption. In turn, the incumbent party can use such instruments as government spending, transfer payments, government employment, and wages paid to public employees to influence its popularity.[9] Other studies have found only one or two of these three variables to have explanatory power. Gerald Kramer, for instance, found that the share of the popular vote going to the incumbent party in congressional elections varied positively with the rate of change in real income and negatively with the rate of inflation. He found the rate of unemployment to be insignificant.[10] Allan Meltzer and Marc Vellrath also found two of the three variables used by Frey and Schneider to be significant in explaining the division of the vote, only these were the rate of unemployment and the rate of inflation.[11] Ray Fair found that only the rate of growth of real income had a significant impact on election outcomes.[12] George Stigler similarly found only one variable to be significant in determining election outcomes, the rate of inflation.[13]

These various arguments have attempted to relate votes to policy outcomes, and these studies have been backward-looking or historical in orientation. Actually, it is the beliefs of politicians that matter, for it is these beliefs that get translated into action. That is, what matters is not whether macroeconomic manipulation has created political gain in the past, but whether politicians believe such gain can be created and promoted in the future through the appropriate timing of macroeconomic policy. To the extent politicians possess such beliefs, efforts at macroeconomic manipulation will be timed, assuming politicians are able to exert some control over monetary-fiscal instruments, with an eye to the occurence of elections. In this respect, for instance, Yoram Ben-Porath found in Israel during the 1952-73 period that per capita consumption was allowed to rise far more rapidly in the years close to an election than in the years immediately following an election.[14] This finding might suggest that politicians believe that the timing of peaks and troughs in employment will influence their survival prospects. Despite differences in particular details among the various empirical studies, the central proposition that the incumbent government will attempt to use economic policy to serve its political purposes seems unassailable. What is at issue is *not* the general proposition that politicians will use to their advantage their ability to enact policy, but only the specific form that such policy takes.

One of the earliest formulations of the use of the state's money monopoly for political gain was by William Nordhaus.[15] He assumed that the economy can be described as possessing a Phillips curve trade-off, though differing as between the short-run and the long-run. Moreover, politicians were regarded as being able to select that combination of unemployment and inflation that they prefer. The general character of this policy choice is illustrated by Figure 1, though the presumption of a vertical Phillips curve in the long run is mine, not Nordhaus'. It is assumed, in line with some of the empirical studies cited above, that individuals regard both unemployment and inflation as undesirable, so the indifference surface rises toward the southwest; the curve i_1u_1 represents a higher rate of voter approval than the curve i_2u_2, and so on. For instance, i_1u_1 might represent, say, 56-44 odds in favor of the incumbent party, while i_2u_2 represents, say, 52-48 odds, and so on. In the long run, the optimal choice of inflation and unemployment is described by the corner solution at a.

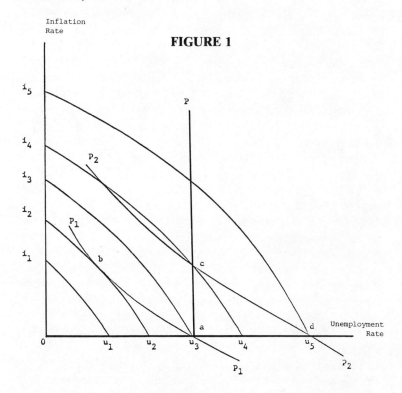

A series of short-run Phillips curves, pp, are also described in Figure 1. Starting from point a, the politician can move from the lower indifference curve i_3u_3 to the higher indifference curve, i_2u_2 by moving the economy up the short-run Phillips curve, p_1p_1 to the tangency position described by b. As people come correctly to anticipate the inflation, the short-run curve will shift upward to p_2p_2. As indicated by c, a temporary reduction in unemployment will have been purchased at the price of a permanent increase in the rate of inflation. The level of voter satisfaction, however, is lower at c, i_4u_4, than it was at a, i_3u_3. Assuming the incumbent party has survived the election, it could follow a deflationary policy to allow the economy to contract along the short-run Phillips curve, p_2p_2 to d.

Initially, the party's popularity will decline still further, as indicated by the movement to i_5u_5. But as people come once again to anticipate correctly the change in inflation, the short-run Phillips curve will shift downward to p_1p_1 until a is attained once again. An electoral cycle has occurred. Movement from a to b is instituted before the election to gain votes. The long-run harm done by the permanent inflation described by c is eliminated by incurring still greater disfavor by the deflationary policy that moves the economy to d after the election, but long before the next election. And when the next election draws near, the politicians stand ready to repeat the cycle again.

The dichotomy between short-run and the long-run, at least in this framework, reflects voter myopia. The memory of voters is assumed to decay over time. In evaluating politicians, voters weight recent experiences more heavily than more distant experiences. In this setting, a macroeconomic policy that provides for a constant rate of unemployment or inflation over the entire electoral period will be dominated by a stop-and-go policy that contracts the economy after an election and expands it before the next election. Unemployment is raised immediately after an election to combat the inflation that follows the stimulatory policies applied before the election. And as the next election approaches, unemployment is lowered in an effort to buy votes, although this policy will generate inflation after the election.

A similar framework was developed by Duncan MacRae.[16] Once again, a dynamic trade-off between inflation and unemployment is posited, and a business cycle emerges as a consequence of the rational behavior of politicians in the face of this trade-off. Myopia is also present in MacRae's analysis, for the evaluation by the electorate of the incumbent's performance is based wholly on experience during the past period. While a regular cycle emerges from the mathematics of the analysis, the political value of such macroeconomic manipulation would seem likely to decline as it becomes more regular because regularity would enhance the ability of voters to discern such manipulation.[17] MacRae went on to compare the explanatory power of this presumption of myopic voting with a presumption that such myopia is absent. During the Kennedy and Johnson administrations, the hypothesis that the administration acts as if voters are myopic had the better explanatory power, while during the second Eisenhower and the Nixon administrations, the hypotheses that the administration acts as if voters exhibit no myopia had the better explanatory power. Is there a lesson to be learned from comparing the relative success of the two parties?[18]

RATIONAL POLITICAL ACTION
AND THE STRUCTURE OF MARKET PRICES

The literature on the political business cycle which has developed in recent years is valuable because of its recognition that the conduct of macroeconomic policy must be understood as the product of rational political action. Such political action, moreover, typically takes place in the context of state monopoly over money. This literature, however, seems to be excessively aggregative in its orientation. Consequently, the common interpretation of rational political action seems in need of modification, as does the framework for understanding the economic consequences of such political action.

Rational political action will focus on the *structure of relative prices*, not on something called the level of absolute prices.[19] Simple coalition theory suggests that a policy of attempting to act on truly aggregative variables will be dominated by a policy of attempting to act on individual variables. Discrimination among citizens is the very essence of majoritarian politics, and such discrimination is facilitated by such institutions as government monopoly over money. A simple illustration should suffice to make the general point. Suppose an electorate consists of three persons, and further suppose there exists two alternative programs for potential political action. One program would provide equal benefits to all, say $1 per person. The other program would concentrate benefits by giving $1.50 to each of two persons. Within a majoritarian political setting, the latter, discriminatory program would dominate the former, nondiscriminatory program.

A policy that affected all prices proportionately would be dominated by a policy that affected some prices more strongly than others. If the policy were financed by money creation, it would be inflationary in either event. In the former case, however, it is the intent of political action to influence only the state of the aggregate variables. In the latter case, by contrast, it is the intent of political action to influence the state of variables affecting particular individuals, with the aggregate consequences emerging merely as a by-product. In the former case, political action is intended to influence the stream of total spending; in the latter case political action is intended to influence the structure of relative prices, with the changes in total spending that result being but a secondary consequence.

It is difficult even to conceive of what are commonly referred to as macroeconomic policies that do not affect the structure of relative prices, let alone actually to find historical instances of such nondiscriminatory policies. Particular patterns of tax reductions are advocated, and other particular patterns of tax reduction of the same aggregate magnitude are rejected. Particular programs of public expenditure are advocated, while other programs of equal magnitude are rejected. In all such instances, the structure of relative prices is being influenced. While the level of absolute prices may increase, this increase is simply incidental to the change in the structure of relative prices. In the operation of the process of money expansion, the money balances of particular persons are increased. If all that were of interest to politicians were the aggregate impact of the monetary-fiscal change, they would be indifferent among all policies that yield the same aggregate impact. Their demonstrated lack of indifference suggests strongly that politicians want to design policies that create particular patterns of benefit. To fail to use the state's monopoly over money in a discriminatory fashion is to refrain from the efficient use of available instruments. Such reluctance tends to turn politicians into statesmen. As Harry Truman put it so well: 'A statesman is a defeated politician.' And politicians generally wish to be known as statesmen only in the memoir-writing stage of life.

Many people seem prone to ask: 'What causes inflation?' It might seem as though a reasonably correct answer is 'money creation'. Obviously, a sustained rise in prices must be accompanied by sustained money expansion, practically everyone will agree. But to attribute the rising prices to money creation is not to provide an explanation as to *why* the money creation takes place. Must not the printing presses turn because it is profitable under existing institutional arrangements for those in control to turn them? When seen from this perspective, different monetary institutions can be looked upon as creating different patterns of ownership over the printing presses. Space is too scarce here to raise these issues of property rights in relation to banking and the supply of money, but it is clear that the pattern of monetary expansion that results will depend upon the particular structure of ownership, along with the anticipated pattern of costs and gains to the owners from their printing activities. Moreover, different monetary institutions can influence both the pattern of ownership and the pattern of costs and gains.

An understanding of how political action may influence economic coordination requires a reasonable interpretation of political motivation. Policies that are truly aggregative in nature must be nondiscriminatory; they cannot influence the relation among the prices of specific products or factors. In any struggle for political dominance, such aggregate policies would be dominated by policies designed to influence the structure of relative prices. Actions that alter all prices by the same percentage will be dominated by policy actions that alter the structure of relative prices. Alternatively, actions that increase some people's money balances relatively more than others will tend to dominate actions that increase all money balances at the same rate. It may well be that such policies end up being financed at least partly through money creation, which inflates the average level of prices. To look upon the average level of prices as the desired object of political manipulation is, however, inappropriate because it presumes irrationality in political conduct. Even the debates over such alternative macroeconomic policies as spending changes versus tax changes, as well as the choice among competing tax or expenditure programs are fundamentally debates over what modification in the structure of relative prices to achieve, not over what level of aggregate prices to attain.

POLITICS, INFLATION, AND ECONOMIC COORDINATION

This focus on rational political conduct as concerned mainly with the structure of relative prices fits in nicely with an emphasis on the non-neutral character on monetary change, a thesis developed in the history of economics by such persons as Richard Cantillon, Henry Thornton, Knut Wicksell, Ludwig von Mises, and Friedrich Hayek. The emphasis in this line of analysis is on how monetary change brings about systematic changes in the structure of relative prices. Rational political action similarly will aim at bringing about systematic alterations in the structure of relative prices.

Whether politicians aim indiscriminately to influence aggregate prices or whether they aim discriminately to influence particular prices represents a matter of perspective closely related to the distinction Gottfried Haberler described between the monetary and the monetary over-investment theories of the business cycle.[20] With both theories, business cycles have their origin in monetary disturbances. With the monetary theory of the cycle the primary phenomena to be explained are variations in the absolute level of prices. In this instance, monetary disturbance is assumed to be neutral; it may affect the distribution of wealth, but it will have no impact upon the allocation of resources. Some people will be wealthier and others poorer as a result, but no macroeconomic discoordination will result. Wealth will be transferred to the early recipients of the newly created money from the remainder of the populace. With the monetary over-investment theory, by contrast, the primary phenomena to be explained are the inflation-induced shifts in relative prices and their consequences.[21] In this instance, monetary disturbance is non-neutral, for it influences the allocation of resources, as well as modifying the distribution of wealth. Within the context of a political business cycle, variation in the level of absolute prices would be regarded as merely a by-product of political efforts designed to modify the structure of relative prices.

While political action to enhance survival prospects will aim at the structure of relative prices, not at the level of absolute prices, the resulting modifications in the structure of relative prices may contribute to cyclical fluctuations in the coordination of economic activities. While economic coordination is continually being disrupted through changes in wants, resources, and knowledge, there seems to be no reason for assuming that such discoordination will be concentrated in time. Cycles, however, are characterized by a concentration of such discoordination, so such phenomena as the political business cycle must be explained in terms of the concentration of politically generated sources of discoordination or instability at particular points during the election cycle.

As originally formulated by Hayek, cycles result from a process set in motion by credit expansion. The monetary expansion brings about systematic variation in the structure of relative prices.[22] As formulated by Hayek, the structure of relative price shifts systematically in favor of a lower price of time. As a result of the market rate of interest falling below the natural rate, the economic process leads to a lengthening of the structure of production. With the fall in the rate of interest, the discounted marginal value product of factors engaged in more roundabout processes of production will rise relative to those engaged in less roundabout processes of production. In his initial efforts in the 1930s, Hayek described the inflation-induced shift in relative prices as one in which the structure of relative prices shifted in favor of capital goods of relatively high order.[23] The resultant lengthening of the structure of production, however, is inconsistent with the underlying data of wants, resources, and knowledge because this lengthening does not result from a reduction in the rate of time preference. In the absence of an increase in voluntary saving, this lengthened structure of production cannot be maintained without an acceleration of the inflation. But a continually accelerating inflation is not sustainable as a long-run feature of an economic order. In the absence of such acceleration, the economic expansion will eventually be reversed, and the structure of production will revert to its former state. This process of readjustment will typically bring about some unemployment. A recession becomes the price of the political activities that produced the inflation. Reallocations of labor must take place before the economy's structure of production will once again reflect the underlying data to which the economy adapts. The mistakes that resulted because people responded to the nonsustainable price signals that were generated by inflation must be worked out before the economy can return to normalcy. Recession is an inherent part of the recovery process.[24]

In terms of the specific historical experience when Hayek wrote, this particular process of expansion and cyclical reaction seems reasonable. When Hayek wrote, government was small and the source of instability seemed to reside primarily in money expansion as a result of an elastic currency facilitated by existing bank institutions. In our present institutional setting, however, this process may operate somewhat differently. For this reason, it is possible to accept the essential point of Hayek's emphasis without accepting his specific description of that process. Today, government is large and its actions are a prime source of money expansion. The specific relation between the Treasury and the banking system differs among nations, of course, but in most cases it is generally recognized that a failure by government to meet all of its expenditure promises by tax extractions will be validated to some extent by money creation. Moreover, transfer programs, along with other programs that encourage consumption, seem increasingly to represent the margins of government spending. In consequence, the expansion may lead initially not to an artificial lengthening of the structure of production, but to a shortening. While the particular description of the discoordination will thus be different, macroeconomic discoordination will arise all the same.

Legislative enactments seem also capable of bringing about economic discoordination, even though monetary creation may not be taking place. By altering the pattern of net returns to various employments of resources, such legislation encourages some employments and discourages others. Should such vote buying through legislation be spaced evenly over the election cycle, the economy would be subjected continually to disturbances in the pattern of economic coordination, but there would be no concentration of such discoordination. But should such political action come to be concentrated in time, cycles will be created in the sources of discoordination at work in the economy. In other words, while monetary expansion can produce systematic shifts in the structure of relative prices, legislation can potentially have the same impact. In either event, the temporal concentration of such disturbances in relative prices can generate cycles in economic activity.

ECONOMIC WASTE THROUGH MONETARY INSTABILITY

Why, however, should concern about the discoordinative properties of government monopoly over money be limited to cyclical fluctuations in such aggregate variables as unemployment rates and price levels? Does not this very limited focus itself illustrate the erroneous conceptual foundations of much of contemporary macroeconomics?[25] To illustrate, consider a typical Hayekian-type cycle in which the structure of production lengthens at first and then subsequently shrinks again. To provide concreteness, this process might initially entail a shift of resources from raising chickens to growing hickory trees, with a subsequent shift back to raising chickens again. It certainly should cause an economist no difficulty to postulate a set of circumstances under which the necessary shifts in labor will take place without affecting the unemployment rate. To the extent such shifts in employment take place without intervening intervals of unemployment, the rate of unemployment will not be affected by the monetary disturbance. But this constancy of the rate of unemployment should not be taken as a sign of a smoothly-working economy. The chickens that initially were raised with the intention of producing eggs, then subsequently destroyed, or perhaps eaten prematurely, to make room for trees, along with the myriad other plans that necessarily were altered in the switch from raising chickens to raising timber are all wasted. The ability to satisfy wants that would have resulted from the completion of those production plans is lost forever. A similar waste results when the structure of production reverts to its initial state, changing this time from growing timber to raising chickens. Mistakes cannot be corrected costlessly, even though labor may be fully employed in the process of correcting those mistakes. All those plans that are revised in response to the changing structure of relative prices entail waste, for what could have been produced had the disruption of plans not taken place is lost forever. All of this wastage of what could have been produced to satisfy human needs had the monetary expansion not taken place to discoordinate individual plans is also a cost of that expansion, even though the rate of unemployment may have remained unchanged.

A different illustration may solidify the point, at least for such literary types as professors and students. Suppose someone had in a fit of extraordinary excitement or under the harassment of a deadline worked around the clock to write an article. Upon completing the last sentence of the manuscript 24 hours after starting, a pot of coffee sitting on the desk gets knocked over. Because a felt-tipped pen had been used in writing the manuscript, the manuscript smears so much that it cannot be submitted to a typist without first being rewritten. Looked at in terms of labor supplied, by the time the manuscript was finally submitted for typing, the writer was fully employed for 48 hours. Only 24 of those hours were engaged in truly worthwhile production. The other 24 hours were devoted to correcting a mistake. What could have been produced in those 24 hours had the coffee not been split, has, however, been lost forever.

Monetary manipulation for political gain inherently involves alternations in the structure of relation prices. The resulting adaptations in the structure of production involve economic waste, even if unemployment is unaffected. And even if unemployment does occur, an assessment of the extent of economic discoordination by looking at the rate of unemployment will understate the amount of loss from such discoordination. Moreover, it does not seem to be an unreasonable conjecture that the loss due to such shifts in the structure of employment exceeds considerably any losses due to unemployment. Measures of the economic success of political programs in terms of measures of the rate of unemployment are, in other words, fraudulent, for they misrepresent what is at stake in choosing among different courses of political action.

It seems tempting to suggest that such waste could be detected through the national income accounts, either as a lower level of national income or as a slower rate of growth. Neither type of detection, however, seems likely. As these accounts are kept, resources devoted to the correction of error are valued in the same manner as are resources devoted to other production. Resources devoted to destroying chicken farms are valued in the same manner as are the resources devoted to raising chickens; the resources devoted to the second writing of the manuscript are valued in the same manner as are those devoted to the first writing.

Differences in measured rates of economic growth would not seem likely to appear either. In principle, we are speaking of two different economies under two different institutions, with the economy with unstable monetary institutions producing an output mix in which more effort is devoted to rectifying mistakes or malinvestments. Rates of growth refer conceptually to rates of expansion along different rays of production. There is no reason to presume that technological progress will be any slower with regard to the correction of malinvestment than it would be for other economic activities. The particular structure of economic production will vary as institutions create more or less instability, but there is no inherent reason why the rate of expansion will be greater or smaller for one structure of production than for another. Measures of national income and of rates of growth might not differ, although the economy with institutions that increase malinvestment would have a lesser ability to fulfill human wants.[26]

MONETARY STABILITY AND ECONOMIC COORDINATION: SOME CONCLUDING THOUGHTS

Common representations of macroeconomic policy have looked upon govenment as a balance wheel that acts to keep stable an otherwise unstable economy. Recognition that public policy emerges from a political process has rarely been incorporated into macroeconomic analysis, and such an effort at incorporation makes it readily apparent that political activity may create or intensify business cycles. To focus exclusively upon aggregate variables, however, is to set aside a substantial part of the phenomenon to be examined. There is far more to the political business cycle, or to macroeconomic disruption through political action generally, than the use by government of changes in aggregate spending at different points in the electoral cycle to buy votes. Political manipulation revolves around individual rather than aggregate variables. Cycles result as a by-product of the efforts of politicians to buy votes through what are customarily called macroeconomic policies which, to be compatible with political rationality, necessarily generate readjustments in the structure of relative prices. Even when unemployment is addressed politically, it is never in the form of an indifferent selection among different programs for achieving the same increase in aggregate demand. It matters to politicians which program is selected because different programs affect differently the real income of different people, and such differentiation among citizens is an essential feature of majoritarian or non-Wicksellian democracy.[27] Macroeconomic consequences may result *ex post*, but the *ex ante* impetus for policy is microeconomic or micropolitical in orientation. Moreover, the waste resulting from changes in plans is an important part of these consequences, even though these consequences are not normally considered macroeconomic in nature.

State monopoly over money was not supposed to contribute to macroeconomic discoordination, but a growing body of literature suggests that it does and explains why it does. While rationalizations can be advanced for anything imaginable, a chasm separates rationalization from explanation. While one may concoct rationalizations for government monopoly over money, macroeconomic discoordination can be explained quite sensibly as a product of such monopoly. The pursuit of political gain in conjunction with an institutional setting of state monopoly over money leads to politically-induced disturbances in the organization of economic activity. The kinds of monetary and fiscal institutions in existence can affect both the information possessed by transactors and the frequency and magnitude of economic disturbances. Recognition of the non-neutral character of monetary disturbance combined with an awareness of the patterns of rational political action allows one to understand more clearly how existing institutional arrangements contribute to macroeconomic discoordination. This examination of the relation between monetary stability (instability) and economic coordination (discoordination), by itself and in isolation from a more general consideration of economic instability, lends support to Hayek's call to separate public finance from monetary control. As he put it in *Denationalisation of Money*:

> If we are to preserve a functioning market economy (and with it individual freedom), *nothing can be more urgent than that we dissolve the unholy marriage between monetary and fiscal policy*, long clandestine but formally consecrated with the victory of Keynesian economics.[28]

NOTES

I should like to acknowledge my gratitude to Gordon Tullock for helpful suggestions and to the National Science Foundation for its support of the project on 'The

Institutional Framework for Controlling Politicians', of which this paper is one product.

1. Herschel I. Grossman, 'Tobin on Macroeconomics: A Review Article', *Journal of Political Economy* 83, August 1975: 845-846.

2. For a survey of this literature, both conceptual foundations and empirical evidence, see Bruno S. Frey, 'Theorie und Empirie Politischer Konjunkturzyklen', *Zeitschrift für Nationalökonomie* 36 (1), 1976: 95-120.

3. The dispute over monetary policy and fiscal policy is inconsequential here. Matters can be kept in clearest focus by assuming that budgetary expansions or contractions are accommodated by increases or decreases in the stock of money.

4. On some of these topics, see Richard E. Wagner, 'Economic Manipulation for Political Profit: Macroeconomic Consequences and Constitutional Implications', *Kyklos* 30 (3), 1977: 395-410.

5. Besides the references described below, see Gebhard Kirchgässner, 'Zur Struktur politish-ökonomischer Konjunkturzyklen', manuscript, Zurich, 1978; Hans Jürgen Ramser, 'Anmerkungen zur Theorie politischer Konjunkturzyklen', manuscript, Konstanz, 1977; and Edward R. Tufte, *Political Control of the Economy* (Princeton: Princeton University Press, 1978).

6. With respect to the Federal Reserve System in the United States, see James M. Buchanan and Richard E. Wagner, *Democracy in Deficit: The Political Legacy of Lord Keynes* (New York: Academic Press, 1977) 107-124; and William P. Yohe, 'Federal Reserve Behavior', in *Crisis in Economic Theory*, ed. by William J. Frazer (Gainesville: University of Florida Press, 1974), 189-200. See also, Keith Acheson and John F. Chant, 'The Choice of Monetary Instruments and the Theory of Bureaucracy', *Public Choice* 12, Spring 1972: 13-34; and idem, 'Bureaucratic Theory and the Choice of Central Bank Goals', *Journal of Money, Credit, and Banking* 5, May 1973: 637-55.

7. The reasons for the non-neutral character of monetary disturbance are summarized in Friedrich A. Lutz, 'On Neutral Money', in *Roads to Freedom* ed. by Erich Streissler et al. (London: Routledge & Kegan Paul, 1969) 101-116.

8. Anthony Downs, *An Economic Theory of Democracy* (New York: Harper and Row, 1957) inspired a voluminous subsequent literature.

9. Their general framework is detailed in Bruno S. Frey and Friedrich Schneider, 'On the Modeling of Politico-Economic Interdependence', *European Journal of Political Research* 3, December 1975: 339-360. See also, idem, 'An Empirical Study of Politico-Economic Interaction in the US', *Review of Economics and Statistics*, forthcoming.

10. Gerald H. Kramer, 'Short-Term Fluctuations in US Voting Behavior, 1896-1964', *American Political Science Review*, March 1971: 131-143.

11. Allan H. Meltzer and Marc Vellrath, 'The Effects of Economic Policies on Votes for the Presidency: Some Evidence from Recent Elections', *Journal of Law and Economics* 18, December 1975: 781-798.

12. Ray C. Fair, 'On Controlling the Economy to Win Elections', manuscript, New Haven, 1975.

13. George J. Stigler, 'General Economic Conditions and National Elections', *American Economic Review*, Proceedings 63, May 1973: 160-167.

14. Yoram Ben-Porath, 'The Years of Plenty and the Years of Famine — A Poltical Business Cycle?' *Kyklos* 28 (2), 1975: 400-403.

15. William D. Nordhaus, 'The Political Business Cycle', *Review of Economic Studies* 42, April 1975: 169-190.

16. C. Duncan MacRae, 'A Political Model of the Business Cycle', *Journal of Political Economy* 85, April 1977: 239-263.

17. Robert J. Gordon, 'The Demand for and Supply of Inflation', *Journal of Law and Economics* 18, December 1975: 807-836.

18. Empirical suport for what is called myopia is presented in Fair, 'On Controlling the Economy', op. cit. note 12.

19. On this point, along with some brief consideration of who it relates to the literature on the political business cycle, see Richard E. Wagner, 'Economic Manipulation for Political Profit', op. cit. note 4.

20. Gottfried Haberler, *Prosperity and Depression*, 3rd edition (London: George Allen & Unwin, 1958).

21. While, as noted above, the non-neutral character of monetary disturbance has been discussed by such authors as Richard Cantillan, Henry Thornton, Knut Wicksell, and Ludwig von Mises, the seminal statement for our purposes is contained in Friedrich A. Hayek, *Monteary Theory and the Trade Cycle* (New York: Harcourt Brace, 1932); and idem, *Prices and Production*, 2nd ed. (London: Routledge & Kegan Paul, 1935). For an excellent description of Hayek's work on economic coordination, see Gerald P. O'Driscoll, Jr., *Economics as a Coordination Problem: the Contributions of Friedrich A. Hayek* (Kansas City: Sheed Andrews and McMeel, 1977).

22. For an empirical examination a price changes under inflation, showing not only that some prices will increase more rapidly than others, but also that these price changes will be highly shewed rather than being symmetrically distributed, see Daniel R. Vining and Thomas C. Elwertowski, 'The Relationship between Relative Prices and the General Price Level', *American Economic Review* 66, September 1976: 699-708.

23. Hayek, *Prices and Production*, op. cit. note 21.

24. One particular point of comparison between monetary and monetary over-investment theories of the business cycle is sketched in Robert E. Lucas, Jr., 'An Equilibrium Model of the Business Cycle', *Journal of Political Economy* 83, December 1975: 1113-1144.

25. For a brief survey of these conceptual difficulties, see Ludwig M. Lachmann, *Macroeconomic Thinking and the Market Economy* (London: Institute of Economic Affairs, 1973).

26. On many of these problems of comparing economic growth among economies, along with an explanation of why such comparisons necessarily reflect value judgments, see G. Warren Nutter, 'On Economic Size and Growth', *Journal of Law and Economics* 9, October 1966: 163-188.

27. Knut Wicksell, 'A New Principle of Just Taxation', in *Classics in the Theory of Public Finance*, ed. by Richard A. Musgrave and Alan T. Peocock (London: Macmillan, 1958), 72-118. See also, James M. Buchanan and Gordon Tullock, *The Calculus of Consent* (Ann Arbor: University of Michigan Press, 1962).

28. Friedrich A. Hayek, *Denationalisation of Money* (London: Institute of Economic Affairs, 1976), 89 (Hayek's emphasis).

9 The Demand for Inflation in Liberal-Democratic Societies

John Burton

University of Birmingham, UK

I THE POLITICAL ECONOMY OF INFLATION

Naturally enough for an 'Age of Inflation' (as the contemporary era has been so described), the causes of wage and price inflation have become the subject of both much controversy and a massive and still-growing literature. The focus of this literature, at least within the discipline of economics, has been upon the question of the relative contribution of different economic variables — such as the rate of growth of the money supply, productivity growth, unemployment and union militancy — to the explanation of variations in the rate of inflation both over time and across countries. That is, the limelight has for most of the post-war period been upon the question of the identity of the 'proximate' determinant(s) of inflation.

Questions as to the role of political factors in the generation of inflation have inevitably, given this focus of research, been relatively ignored, less adequately treated, or discussed only in a tangential

fashion. However, the unfolding of the controversy over the proximate determinants of inflation has increasingly led back to these
relatively ignored questions, on all sides of the debate.

The controversy centred around the claims of two rival poles of
thought — the monetarist and the union-push school.[1] The former
hypothesized that the main determinant of the rate of inflation was
the rate of growth of the money supply (relative to the rate of
growth of real aggregate output), while the latter hypothesized that
it was instead the degree of union wage 'pushfulness'. The large
body of empirical research that has been conducted to test these
competing hypotheses has been successful in clarifying these issues
in considerable degree. The main results of this research are, in
summary, that:

(a) There is a very close statistical relationship between the rate
of growth of the money supply (relative to the growth rate of real
output) and the rate of change of the price level. This relationship
has now been corroborated for a large number of individual countries, and for historical data extending as far back as millenia B.C.[2]

(b) All variants of the union-cause-inflation thesis perform empirically far less well by comparison. For instance, the most well-
known version, the Hines (1964) hypothesis (which proxies union
militancy by the rate of growth of union density) does not replicate
well outside the UK, and does not work well at the industry level
within it. Furthermore, both the rate of growth of unionization and
alternative (strike activity) proxies for union militancy are correlated with economic variables such as price inflation and productivity growth, suggesting that union wage-bargaining behaviour is
not an independent force in inflation, but rather an endogenously-
determined variable.[3]

The balance of evidence, as currently available to us, thus seems
to lie strongly in favour of the monetarist hypothesis. However,
this has led both monetarists and union-militancy theorists straight
back to the question of the role of the polity in inflation, because
the question now becomes: why do governments expand the money
supply in an inflationary manner? Union-push theorists, faced with
the evidence, now commonly admit that an expansion of the money
supply is a *necessary* condition for *continuing* inflation (e.g., Kahn,
1976), but then go on to argue that it is union pressure that indirectly causes governments to undertake expansive monetary actions.

That is, modern governments, with policy or statutory commitments to 'full' (or 'high' or 'tolerable') employment, yet faced with a union wage push, find it necessary to 'validate' the higher rate of wage (and thus price) inflation, in order to sustain their employment goal. Many monetarist writers (e.g., Hutt, 1975; Rees-Mogg, 1974) agree with this in general, if not in specifics. Between such monetarists and such union-push theorists, then, the issue is one of semantics, or self-labelling, only.[4] However, many other monetarists would disagree with this diagnosis of the political factors behind the choice of inflationary finance. Friedman (1970) has recorded the view that the factors leading to deficit finance and money creation by governments vary widely from particular historical circumstance to circumstance, so that no simple analysis apparently holds true for all situations. Others still, such as Brunner (1975), would reject this implicitly electic view, and seek to provide a uniform analysis of the political causes of inflationary finance. However, whichever variety of monetarist is examined, there is no denial that the discovery that 'money matters' (indeed, 'most of all') in inflation only gives rise to further questions as to the political sources of inflationary finance, and that this is a separate and important question in its own right.

In summary then, the development of research into the proximate determinants of inflation has increasingly led back to the formerly relatively-ignored question of what has been called variously the 'fundamental' determinants of inflation, or the 'political economy' of inflation. Friedman (1977) has himself recorded his hunch, in his 1976 Nobel lecture, that the next major development of research into inflation 'will have to include in the analysis the interdependence of economic experience and political developments. It will have to treat at least some political phenomena not as independent variables — as exogenous variables in econometric jargon — but as themselves determined by economic events — as endogenous variables.'[5] He further adds his belief that this next major development will be greatly influenced by the application of economic analysis to political behaviour (variously termed as public choice theory, the new political economy, positive political theory and formal political analysis).

Of course, theoretical and empirical research into the political economy of inflation exists already in the form of the existent

literature upon the political business cycle, to which further contributions are being made rapidly.[6] This research explores the question of whether governments peopled by individuals who have job-
security interests — as is normally assumed in economics for all
other employees — can, and do, manipulate variables subject to
their (possibly only short-run) influence — such as the rate of inflation, unemployment and average real disposable income — in order
to enhance their prospects of survival under the electoral system. A
further literature of relevance that has grown up is that relating to
the 'political economy of bureaucracy' (e.g., Niskanen, 1971;
Tullock, 1965; Downs, 1967). This analyses bureaucratic (government periodic grant-financed) supplier behaviour, and
bureaucratic-government exchange interaction, in a rational choice
framework, breaching tradition with both 'public
interest'-maximization and (moralistically-inspired) 'evil official'
views of administrators that litter the preceding academic and
literary discussion of bureaucratic behaviour. Although the implications of the political economy of bureaucracy research for
budget (im)balance and inflationary finance have yet to be
developed in detail, it adds a further presumption in this direction
to the government-centred political business cycle literature. That
is, the new political economy of bureaucracy analysis predicts a
bias towards the expansion of bureau size, due to the interaction of
bureaucratic motivations (as all arguments in the bureaucratic utility function are positively related to bureau size) and bureau-
government negotiation over bureau-budget size, in which the
more-permanent and well-informed bureaucrats have an informational advantage over government decision-makers. The implication of this analysis is that bureaucratic endeavour adds a further
impetus towards budget expansion — and thus, given voter
resistance to tax increases, budget deficits and inflationary finance.

Both the political business cycle and economics of bureaucracy
literatures examine the political economy of inflation from what
may be termed the 'supply-side' of the question. That is, they are
predominantly concerned with the behaviour of 'suppliers' —
governments and bureaucrats — in the political market-place. The
behaviour of the 'demand-side' (i.e., voters) in the political market-
place is either implicitly ignored, or, more commonly, it is assumed
that here the suppliers have the ability to manipulate the

demanders, in quasi-Galbraithian fashion, or that one set of suppliers (bureaucrats) can manipulate, through informational advantages and free rider factors, other 'higher-level' groups of suppliers in the political market-place (legislators, ministers, cabinets, etc.).

The purposes, 'positive' and 'negative', of this paper may now be enunciated. It is concerned with the question of the 'political economy' of inflation. But it ignores the 'supply-side' factors that may lead to an inflationary bias under democracy that have been outlined above. However, it is *not denied* that these supply-side factors may yield some, if not the predominant, explanation of the contemporary tendencies of representative democracies towards budget deficits and inflation. The purpose of this paper is simply to explore — in a purely theoretical manner, but with a view to both testable predictions and the explanation of the 'stylized facts' of inflation — the 'demand-side' of the political economy of inflation under democracy. That is, ignoring supply-side factors in the political market-place, are there any pure demand-side factors that would lead us to predict an inflationary bias under democracy? What are they? What, specifically, is predicted about the nature of the resultant inflation — is it stable, accelerative, volatile? Indeed, under what set of assumptions is it valid to talk of a 'demand' for inflation (usually treated as a 'bad' rather than a 'good')? These, then, are the sorts of questions explored in this paper.

The rationale for exploring these questions may be described as a political generalization of the Marshallian 'scissors principle'. That is, the predicted outcomes of interaction between demanders and suppliers in pecuniary markets (in enforceable private property rights bundles) is in general determined by both 'demand' and 'supply' factors. Let us presume, then, on analogical grounds, that the outcomes in political markets will likewise be influenced in general by both demand and supply-side factors. Certainly, political and pecuniary markets work according to different specific rules, but it is assumed that this 'general' rule — that both demand and supply may have influence — is common. As most analysis to date has been on the 'supply-side' of inflation, there is at least a presumption for evening-up the balance: for examining the demand-side. As with any market outcome, the result will be determined (in greater or lesser degree, respectively) by both 'demand' and 'supply'. It is the task of empirical analysis, of course, to *identify* the relative importance of both sides in the 'real world'. This paper does not tackle that issue.

The structure of the rest of the paper may be itemised as follows. In Section II the basic assumptions of the analysis, necessary to give us a 'pure' and not vastly-complicated analysis of the demand for inflation, are elaborated. The subsequent Sections — III, IV, V and VI — explore variations, given different assumptions about demanders in the political market-place. Section VII offers some final conclusions.

II BASIC ASSUMPTIONS OF THE ANALYSIS

It is here assumed that inflation is determined in the political system, in the 'fundamental' sense that budget deficits and inflationary finance are, in contemporary democracies, governmental decision variables. That is, under the now widespread Keynesian monetary-fiscal constitution, elected governments exercise direct and (commonly) unconstrained control of the central bank and the domestic money supply. But what determines the governmental choice of budget imbalance and the rate of growth of the money supply?

Under political democracy, the roles of three groups suggest themselves for inspection in answer to this question: voters, the government, the bureaucracy. The potential role of the latter two groups is here ignored for the reasons given in Section I. We concentrate upon the role of the former group in the 'demand for inflation'.

The further assumptions of the analysis may be detailed as follows:

A1: The monetary-fiscal constitution is Keynesian in nature. That is, there are no rules embedded in the constitution constraining the choice of budget imbalance, or the rate of growth of the money supply (with the exception of A.9).

A2: The budget deficit for each period is chosen in a referendum of all voters on this single issue. The budget deficit (B) is here defined as:

$$B_t \equiv G_t - T_t \tag{1}$$

where

> G is total government expenditure
> T is total tax revenue
> t is a time subscript

A3: The criterion for the selection of each period's budget deficit is that of majority vote.

A4: Each voter seeks to maximize his own utility.

A5: Voter utility-functions are well-behaved and single-peaked.

A6: Government and bureaucracy exercise no influence on deficit size either directly, or indirectly via influence upon, or manipulation of, voters. This is a model of 'pure democracy': government and bureaucrats merely carry out the 'will of the people (majority)'.

A7: Voting in the referendum is compulsory.

A8: The economy is closed — there is no international trade or capital movements.

A9: The proportion of the budget deficit that is financed respectively by additional government borrowing from the public and by money creation is fixed. That is, the budget deficit decomposes as:

$$B_t = \Delta D_t + \Delta M_t \tag{2}$$

where ΔD is the addition to the national debt held by the public,

ΔM is the addition to the stock of base of high-powered money,

and we are assuming that:

$$\frac{\Delta M_t}{\Delta D_t} = \frac{k}{1-k} \qquad 0 < k < 1 \tag{3}$$

These simplifying assumptions are rationalized as follows. A1 avoids the extra complications that would be introduced if variety of monetary and fiscal constitutional constraints were to be introduced to the analysis.[7] A6 concentrates the analysis upon the demand-side of the political economy of inflation. A2 keeps us in one-dimensional policy space, and A3, A4 and A5 together make the outcome of the vote process determinate; all three serve to divorce the analysis of the Pandora's box of manifold complications that open up once such assumptions are relaxed.[8] A7 likewise steers us away from the issues pertaining to the rationality of voting.[9] A8 serves to delete the further complications opened up by the consideration of inflation in the open economy under either fixed or dirty floating exchange rates, in the contemporary world of highly integrated international markets for both commodities and finance.[10] Finally, A9 sidesteps complications relating to the effect of the composition of the budget deficit on inflation. There are two major views on this. Briefly, the Friedmanite position (e.g., Friedman, 1970) is that it is *only* the ΔM component of the budget deficit that has implications for the rate of inflation, whilst the fiscal monetarist position (e.g., Brunner and Meltzer, 1972; Brunner, 1976; Fratianni, 1977) is that ΔM and ΔD will have an inflationary effect, but the time-profile of the effect of the two variables on the rate of inflation differs. Thus, on either view, a change in the composition of deficit finance will, for a given size of budget deficit, affect the trajectory of the inflation rate. The fixture of the parameter k in equation (3) avoids these complications.

III THE DEMAND FOR INFLATION UNDER PERFECT INFORMATION

We start with a model in which voters have perfect, costlessly-acquired information; or, more specifically, we introduce the assumption that:

A10: All voters are perfectly-informed concerning the consequences of alternative values of B_t for their utility position. There is no voter 'ignorance', 'error' or 'illusion'. We introduce the further assumption that:

A11: Voter utility (V) is negatively related to both the rate of inflation ($\dot{P}$) and the aggregate unemployment rate (U); that is:

$$V^i = V(\dot{P}, U) \quad \frac{\partial V^i}{\partial \dot{P}}, \frac{\partial V^i}{\partial U} < 0 \tag{4}$$

for all i.

The rationale for such a utility function in this sort of analysis has been discussed by Nordhaus (1975). A rise in U is taken to negatively affect family income through the increased probability of job loss and temporary lay-off, reductions in part-time and over-time work, and reduced profits. Nordhaus has, however, some difficulty in rationalizing the other assumed element of the utility function, $\dot{P}$, and admits that he finds the reason for an aversion by households to inflation to be 'less apparent' than is the case with U. This is certainly true if we adopt the standpoint of the orthodox economic analysis of inflation, which visualizes a (fully-anticipated) inflation as merely a tax on holdings of money. However, recent developments in the economic analysis of infla-tion have now thrown some new light on this issue. That is, if Friedman (1977) is right that the volatility of inflation is related to the (secular) trend of the inflation rate, then inflation is easily ra-tionalizable as being negatively-valued, due to its effects on uncer-tainty, in the manner that Leijonhufvud (1977) has explored.

Different voters are, of course, likely to have different subjective trade-offs between inflation and unemployment; the indifference curves mapping their $V(\dot{P},U)$ functions will have different slopes. However, given our assumptions A3, A4 and A5, we know from Black's (1958) median voter theorem that the outcome of the vote process will be the optimum for the median voter. We therefore do not here need the devices of aggregate constant voter curves which some others have employed in government vote-maximizing models of inflation and unemployment policy-selection (Lepper, 1974; Nordhaus, 1975). To determine the outcome of the vote process in the present model, all we need to know is the utility function of the median voter. This is represented by the series of concave-to-origin indifference curves I_1, I_2, etc., in quad A of Figure 1.

Voter choice of B will, of course, also depend on the trade-offs and constraints facing the voter in the real world. Two polar possibilities as regards the latter suggest themselves for investiga-tion: a 'Keynesian-Phillips Curve World' and a 'Quantity-Theory — Natural Rate' World.

The Keynesian-Phillips Curve World

Here it is assumed that the government can manipulate the level of unemployment via the budget:

$$U_t = f(B_t) \qquad f' < 0 \tag{5}$$

and then the inflation rate is determined in a simple or naive Phillips curve manner:

$$\dot{P}_t = g(U_t) \qquad g' < 0 \tag{6}$$

Equations (5) and (6) are graphed respectively as the curves bb and cc in Figure 1. The inflation rate resulting from the assumed democratic choice process is shown in the diagram by $\dot{P}*$ — the optimal rate of inflation for the median voter — and the selected budget deficit by $B*$.

Given that neither the median voter's utility function nor the Phillips curve shifts over time, this variant of the model thus generates a prediction of persistent but stable inflation and deficit finance.

A Quantity Theory — Natural Rate World

We now jettison equations (5) and (6) and replace them with a simpliste version of a 'quantity theory — natural rate' world. That is, following Vanderkamp (1975) we might simplify Friedman's model of inflation and unemployment in the following way:[11]

$$\dot{P}_t = a(U_t - U^n) + w\dot{P}_t^e \qquad a < 0; \ w = 1 \tag{7}$$

$$\dot{M}_t = \dot{P}_t + \dot{y}_t \tag{8}$$

$$U_t = U^n + h(\dot{y}_t - \dot{y}^n) \qquad h < 0 \tag{9}$$

$$\dot{P}_t^e = \dot{P}_{t-1} \tag{10}$$

where U^n is the natural (equilibrium) rate of unemployment in the economy

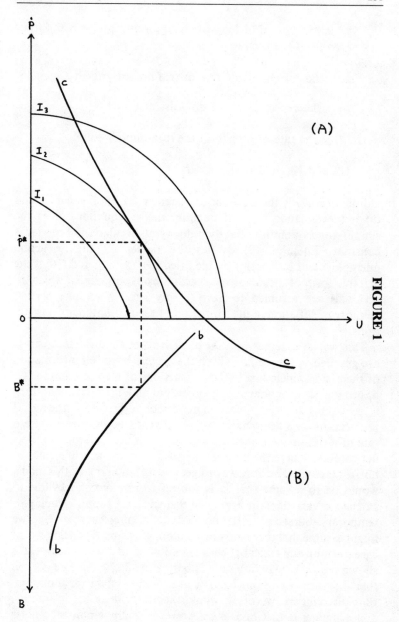

FIGURE 1

$\dot{y}^n$ is the natural or long-run equilibrium rate of real output growth of the economy

$\dot{y}_t$ is the current actual rate of real output growth

$\dot{P}_t^e$ is the expected rate of inflation at time t

$\dot{M}_t$ is the rate of growth of the total money supply

U^n and $\dot{y}^n$ are assumed fixed.

Equation (7) is the expectations-augmented Phillips curve, and (8) is the dynamic form of quantity theory equation, given the simplifying assumption that the velocity of circulation of money is constant. Equation (9) defines the movement of the actual unemployment rate in this simple Friedman system, and (10) is the extreme form of the adaptive expectations hypothesis, in which individuals are assumed to have a very short (i.e., one period) memory of inflation in the formation of their inflationary expectations.[12]

This world, together with the median voter's indifference curves are graphed in Figure 2.[13] Given that voters have full information of the system, including long-run reactions of a change in the rate of growth of the money supply on output and unemployment, then if we assume also that voters do not discount the future, the model predicts that the democratic choice process would generate a *zero* rate of inflation — as median voter utility is maximized at the corner solution where the natural rate of unemployment line cuts the horizontal axis. The only way to get any inflation out of this model would be to assume that $\dot{y}_t$ is subject to random shocks due to stochastic variations in aggregate demand and supply, leading to temporary bursts of inflation and deflation. Alternatively, we might assume that there is dynamic money illusion (w < 1), in which case the long-run trade-off between inflation and unemployment is shown not by $U^n U^n$ in Figure 2, but by the dashed line $C_L C_L$ on that diagram. Long-run equilibrium of the system (assuming no time-discounting by voters) would then be with inflation rate $\dot{P}'$, and a budget deficit of B'. As, however, many empirical studies suggest that w is not significantly different from unity — or is ex-

tremely close to it — this does not seem like a really profitable line
of investigation.[14]

FIGURE 2

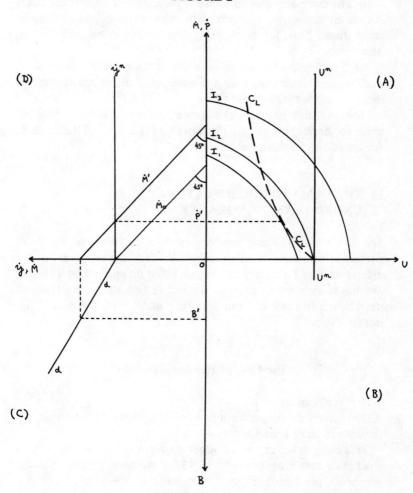

Neither version of this model of the demand for inflation is in
fact satisfactory in providing a potential explanation of the stylized
facts of inflation in democratic polities with a Keynesian monetary-
fiscal constitution. This is the most clearly so with the QT-NR ver-

sion. But neither, in fact, is the Keynesian-Phillips curve version satisfactory. Although it predicts a persistent inflation, it fails to account for such stylized facts as:

(i) The extremely high and erratic inflations of democratic Latin American countries, twinned with high unemployment: 'superstagflation'. This, for example, typified the experience of Chilean democracy.[15]

(ii) The accelerating inflation of the advanced-economy Western democracies, combined with the emergence of higher unemployment, in the Sixties and Seventies.

However, this first model has provided us with a jumping-off point for developing potentially more useful models of the demand for inflation. To these we now turn.

IV THE DEMAND FOR INFLATION UNDER VOTER IGNORANCE

We now relax A10 and assume instead that voters do not have perfect information of either the workings of the economy, or the effects of their budgetary choices on inflation and unemployment. We might view voters as being subject to two alternative types of defective information: 'random ignorance' and 'systematic ignorance'.

The Case of Random Ignorance

A10 is replaced by:

A12: 'Ignorance' (imperfections of information) is distributed in a random manner across voters.

This case, however, does not generate any results of interest. As Buchanan and Wagner (1977, p. 129) have noted, 'so long as the errors of perception made by individuals are distributed symmetrically, or roughly so, around some idealized "true" assessment of alternatives, the model that generally ignores errors in perception will not yield false results.' In other words, we get the same predictions (at least in the long run) as in the earlier perfect information models.

The Case of Systematic Ignorance

A12 is replaced by:

A13: All voters have systematic misconceptions about the nature and workings of the economy. That is, voters are 'ignorant', not in the sense of *imperfect* information, but in the sense of having *systematically incorrect* 'information'.

The precise predictions that are generated by combining A13 with A1 through A9 and A11 will, of course, depend on the precise assumptions made concerning the systematic ignorance of voters. One particular possibility that suggests itself is that voters believe the world to be of K-PC type, when, *in fact*, it is of a QT-NR type.

This possibility is analysed in Figure 3. The pre-referendum scenario is one where the economy is at the natural rate of unemployment, with both $\dot{P}_t$ and $\dot{P}_t^e$ zero. Voters in the budget referendum believe that the (permanent) trade-off between inflation and unemployment is shown by c_1, the short-run Phillips curve for $\dot{P}^e = O$. As before, the outcome of the referendum is determined by the median voter choice: a budget deficit of B_1 and an inflation rate of P_1. This will eventually affect, through equations (7) and (10), the position of the short-run Phillips curve, which will shift out. If voters simultaneously, witnessing the rise in unemployment for a given inflation rate, revise their notion of equation (5) in a like manner[16] — that is, they recognize that it is somehow 'incorrect' and that a larger budget deficit is now necessary to generate any given fall in unemployment — then the system will behave in an explosive manner, with budget deficits and inflation rates showing a secular tendency to rise in perpetuity. This model, with systematic voter ignorance, thus has the ability to offer something towards the explanation of the experience of democratic politics in both advanced-economy and Latin American democracies.

The assumption of persistent systematic voter ignorance has, however, been criticized by Johnson (1973, 1975) on the grounds of implausibility. Writing specifically with regard to Latin America, he argues that 'the answer cannot be that, after generations of experience, the public and its politicians have simply not learned that deficit budgeting and financing by money creation cause inflation; they know it very well...' (Johnson, 1975, p. 864).

FIGURE 3

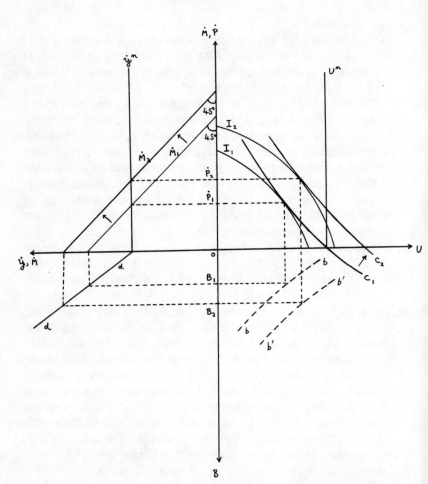

However, this criticism is not necessarily a valid one. First, survey evidence indicates that voters do, in fact, have considerable ignorance of the causes of inflation (e.g., Behrend, 1971). Second, give the cost of acquiring information on the causes of inflation and the workings of the economy, the persistence of voter ignorance may be quite rational, as Downs (1957) has noted in a more general context.

Such a model based on systematic ignorance may thus at least explain in part the experience of advanced countries such as the UK, which has experienced a generally accelerating inflation, growing unemployment rate, and mounting budget deficits over the past two decades.[17] This seems especially plausible given the fact that economic policy has been operated, for much of this time period, on the assumption of an inflation-unemployment trade-off, and the electorate had been 'informed' of this analysis by establishment economists, politicians and the media alike. The notion that the Keynesian-Phillips view of the world may be seriously wrong has only relatively recently started to gain support in the UK, and alternative ideas have yet to fully percolate throughout the adult population.

Systematic voter ignorance of the inflationary consequences of deficit finance thus can by no means be ruled out as one plausible political factor behind stagflation, at least in the advanced-economy democracies, where inflation is, although showing accelerative tendencies, as yet of a generally milder and younger nature than in many Latin American countries. However, it must also be admitted that the *degree* of systematic voter ignorance of the role of deficit finance and money creation in the generation of inflation is plausibly a declining function of both the duration and severity of the inflationary experience. That is, the longer the duration of inflation, and the higher the secular rate of inflation, the more readily apparent (the lower the costs of acquiring a correct information 'image') does the process of inflation, and the role of deficit finance, become to the voter. Not many people, for example, who have experienced daily life under a hyper-inflation will need to read esoteric discourses in economic journals in order to inform themselves that the situation has something to do with massive increases in the stock of money.

The hypothesis of an *unchanging* degree of systematic voter ignorance thus seems to become less plausible when we consider countries such as Chile where the secular rate of inflation has been extremely high and of a very long duration. This suggests that we must turn to further hypotheses if we are to provide an adequate explanation of the failure of inflation to diminish in such countries.

V THE INFLUENCE OF VOTER 'ILLUSION' ON THE DEMAND FOR INFLATION

Voters may suffer not only from 'ignorance' but 'illusion'. The distinction here drawn is that voter 'ignorance' results from information difficulties (the costs of acquiring information), whereas 'illusion' results from perception problems within the voter's own mind. As with voter ignorance, voter illusion may be analyzed for both the random and systematic cases. And, as before, it is the case of systematic voter illusion that is of interest. We now, therefore, introduce the following assumption in place of A10, A12 or A13:

A14: All voters have systematic 'illusion' regarding the costs and benefits of budget imbalance.

As with the case of systematic ignorance, the precise predictions of the analysis will depend upon the nature and degree of the assumed illusions. One particular hypothesis of voter illusion has been put forward by Buchanan and Wagner (1977, 1978) which rests upon the perceptual difficulties in comprehending the *indirect* consequences of budget imbalance. Their argument is most readily approached by comparing the creation of a budget surplus and a budget deficit.

The Budget Surplus Case

Starting from an initial situation of budget balance, the generation of a budget surplus implies either a reduction in G or an increase in T (or some combination of the two). Either (or a mix) of the two will generate *direct* losers in the voting population. That is, in the case of a reduction in G, a fall in the consumption of governmentally-provided goods and services will be created; an increase in T will likewise cause a fall in privately-provided goods and services. But the costs thus fall in either case on *currently-enjoyed* goods and services. The benefits of a surplus, on the other hand, are of an *indirect* character: 'it takes the form of the hypothesized or imagined gains from *avoiding* what would have otherwise been a [more] inflationary experience' (Buchanan and Wagner, 1978, p. 21).

The Budget Deficit Case

Starting from an initial situation of budget balance, the generation of a budget deficit implies either an increase in G or decrease in T (or some mix of the two) leading respectively to an increase in the consumption of governmentally-provided or privately-provided goods and services. That is, there are *direct* gains from the budget deficit. The *indirect* costs of the deficit relate to future conjecture — a reduction in future well-being at some future date, which must be creatively imagined.

Formalization of the
Buchanan-Wagner Illusion Hypothesis

Formal incorporation of this particular illusion hypothesis within the framework of the present analysis of the demand for inflation requires a revision of our earlier assumption regarding the form of the voter utility function. That is, the Buchanan-Wagner analysis visualizes voter utility not as a function of macro economic variables as in (4) above, but instead of the costs and benefits (both direct and indirect) yielded to the individual by the budget. We therefore replace A11 by:

A13: All voters have a utility function of the form:

$$V^i = V^i(F_g^i, \Theta C_g^i) \tag{11}$$

where F_g^i is total benefits to voter i of government spending
C_g^i is the total cost to voter i of financing government
Θ is an illusion index, with a range of $0 \leq \Theta < 1$ and we
also assume that:

$$\Theta = \Theta(b) \qquad \Theta' > 0 \tag{12}$$

where $b = B/G$, the proportion of total government spending
financed by deficit creation.

However, as here set up, this illusion hypothesis implies that the
democratic choice process, if unconstrained by constitutional rules
or international factors etc., will always result in the selection of a
budget deficit equal to 100 per cent of total government spending.
For if the *perceived* cost of a unit of government spending is lower
to the voter when financed by deficit than by taxation, then the
former will always be selected over the latter in an unconstrained
democratic choice process.

The hypothesis might, however, be revised to yield $b < 1$ in the
following fashion. We might plausibly assume that voter illusion is
related not only to b but also (negatively) to the rate of inflation,
once this exceeds some threshold level. That is, the experience of inflation beyond this threshold will erode the voter's fiscal illusion;
the 'creative jump' involved in the recognition of the indirect consequences of deficit finance will be reduced. That is, we might
reformulate (12) as:

$$\Theta = \Theta(b, \dot{P}) \qquad \frac{\partial \Theta}{\partial b} > 0, \quad \frac{\partial \Theta}{\partial \dot{P}} < 0 \tag{13}$$

But of course in a QT-NR world $\dot{P}$ is determined by B through (7)
through (10). Combining (13) with (11) we might then visualize median voter utility to vary with B, for a given level of G, as graphed
by the curve xx in quadrant B of Figure 4. That is, median voter
utility is maximized with a budget deficit of B*, leading to an inflation rate of $\dot{P}$*. This version of the voter illusion hypothesis thus

provides us with a potential explanation of the source of the demand for inflation in democracy.

FIGURE 4

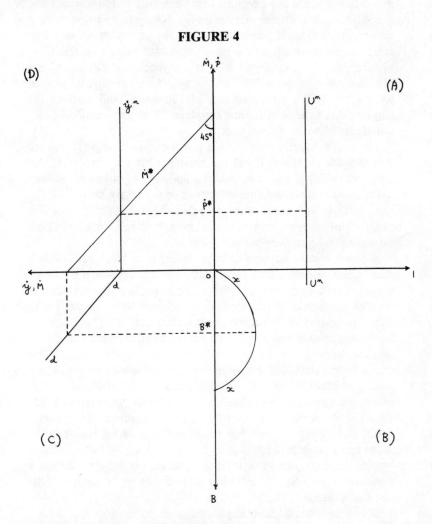

VI INFLATION AS CONFISCATION

The orthodox assumption in the analysis of the political business cyle (e.g., Nordhaus, 1975) is that, as specified in equation (4), inflation is a negatively-valued good — a 'bad' — to all voters. As shown in Section III, this leads to difficulties in rationalizing a demand for inflation if we assume that voters are fully-informed and non-illusioned, that the world is of QT-NR type, and that there is no dynamic money illusion. To explain the generation of inflation from the demand-side of the political market-place then leads, inevitably, to the consideration of the hypothesis that voters are systematically 'ignorant' or 'illusioned'. Alternatively, of course, we might drop a pure demand-side approach and turn to the supply-side of the political market-place for an explanation of persistent inflation in democracies.

There is, however, a yet further possibility to be explored on the demand-side of the political market-place. It may be, as H. G. Johnson (1975) has argued, that the majority of voters are neither ignorant nor illusioned, but in fact have a positive stake in inflation, at least over some range of inflation rates. That is, over this range of inflation rates, inflation is not a 'bad' to the majority, but rather a (net) positively-valued good.

A now standard analysis of inflation initiated by Bailey (1956) is that (stable) inflation may be visualized as a tax on the holdings of money balances, analogous to an excise tax on a normal commodity. The prediction of this analysis is that the inflation tax, under fully-anticipated inflation, causes a redistribution of wealth from holders of money balances to the *government*. In other words, the implicit assumption of the inflation tax literature, as it has developed to date, is that the motive for the use of inflation as a means of taxation lies on the supply-side of the political market place, with government. The latter, it is commonly assumed, has difficulty in meeting its expenditure needs by means of ordinary taxation, and is therefore 'forced' to resort to deficit finance. Or, in the more generalized Bailey analysis (Gordon, 1975) it is led, in a benign attempt to maximize the 'public interest', to adopt a measure of taxation by inflation in order to minimize the social costs of taxation.

But there is the additional possibility to be considered of an explanation of the inflation tax arising from the demand-side of the political market-place. Inflation may be conceivably used by the majority of voters to redistribute wealth to themselves through the polling booth. That is, inflation may be visualized as a form of confiscation that is more easily conducted than by open taxation. In that case, the majority may have a fully-rational (derived) demand for inflation, and even though they are not subject to 'ignorance' or 'illusion'.

R. J. Gordon (1975) has initiated the exploration of the demand for inflation via redistribution. However, his seminal analysis is vitiated somewhat by two factors. First, he assumes ad hoc that it is only members of trade unions that have a redistribution motive for inflation. Second, his analysis may be criticized on the grounds that the specific model that he adopts does not provide a clear theoretical rationale for the demand for inflation by even the unions (Brunner, 1975). It therefore seems useful to turn to a more general analysis of the redistributory demand for inflation than that specifically adopted by Gordon.

What determines the valuation that a voter will put on inflation? Three major factors suggest themselves from economic theory:

(i) The 'net monetary status' of the voter (N_m^i): that is, given his holdings of monetary assets and liabilities (the value of which are specified in *nominal* terms), whether he is a net monetary creditor or a net monetary debtor (Kessel and Alchian, 1962);[18]

(ii) The 'net government benefit status' of the voter (N_g^i): that is, whether he is a net beneficiary of government spending and taxing, or a net negative beneficary; and

(iii) the volatility of inflation (v): that is, the greater the volatility of inflation over time, the greater will be the economic dislocations caused by inflation, which will affect all voters. The volatility of inflation is also plausibly related to the level of inflation (Friedman, 1977; Burton, 1979).

Given these assumptions, we may reformulate the voter's utility function, equation (4), as:

$$V^i = V^i \{ \overset{\bullet}{P}(N_m^i, N_g^i, v), U \} \qquad (14)$$

It is thus possible that the median voter's indifference curve map is not that as portrayed in quad A of Figure 1, but as in quad A of Figure 5. Under these conditions, assuming a QT-NR world, the outcome of the democratic choice process will be as shown in the latter diagram: persistent budget deficits of size B*, and inflation

FIGURE 5

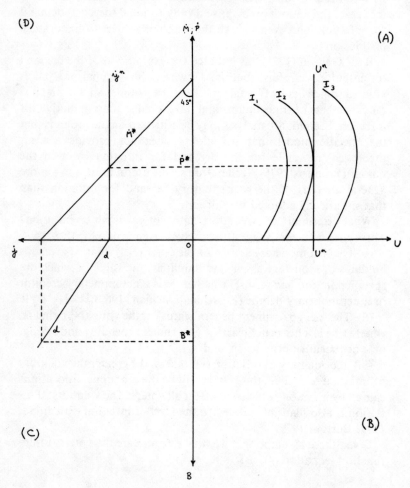

rate (displaying some degree of volatility) of amount $\overset{\bullet}{P}*$, even though voters have neither 'ignorance' nor 'illusion'.

Such a model, I believe, may help us to understand the history of inflation in countries such as Chile, given the alignment of voter interests prior to the collapse of democracy in that country (Davis, 1963, 1965).

VII CONCLUSION

This paper has sought to explore the possibility of rationalizing inflation in democracies from the perspective of the demand-side of the political market-place. It has been shown that, even if governmental and bureaucratic biases towards deficit finance are absent, factors on the demand-side of the political market-place, such as fiscal illusion, voter ignorance, or the attempt by one group of voters to redistribute wealth to themselves via inflation, may independently generate an inflationary bias in democratic countries. This is not to suggest, however, that supply-side influences can be ignored. A full analysis of the generation of inflation in democracies requires that both sides of the political market-place be brought into the picture.

NOTES

1. Neither school of thought is in fact as internally homogenous as the brief treatment here given would seem to imply; see Addison and Burton (1980).

2. For a more adequate discussion, see Laidler and Parkin (1975) and Meiselman (1975).

3. See Burton and Addison (1977) and Burton (1980) for extensive discussions of the evidence.

4. At the level of causal explanation, at least. The policy implications that are derived often remain at variance.

5. Note, however, that Friedman's primary concern in his Nobel lecture is with a different aspect of the political economy of inflation to that here treated: the feedback effects of inflation on the politico-institutional framework, and further consequences of this interaction for the natural rate of unemployment (in the intermediate

run) and for politico-economic evolution (in the long-long run).

6. Witness the other contributions to this Volume.

7. In the limit, if a classical monetary-fiscal constitution is assumed, i.e., a balanced budget (G = T) and the money supply is determined by some automatic mechanism or rule, then the political system could play no causal role in inflation.

8. See Whiteley (1978) for a conspectus of issues.

9. Note, however, that the alleged irrationality of voting entangles itself in methodological difficulties. First, the purpose of rational choice theory is to generate *predictions* about behaviour, and it is to these that we should be primarily concerned. Second, the predictive power of any hypothesis cannot be judged by examining its assumptions. Finally, it is in any case impossible to empirically judge the validity of the assumption that voting is a rational activity, for this would require that we can directly observe the mind of the voter. That is, it cannot be shown either a priori or empirically that the net return to voting is negative.

10. Much of the literature on the international transmission of inflation has ignored the political economy aspects. For one paper that integrates these two aspects of the inflation problem, see Lindbeck (1976).

11. A more adequate formalization of Friedman's analysis is developed in Addison and Burton (1980), ch. 3.

12. The more general form of the adaptive expectations hypothesis is:

$$\dot{P}^e_t = r\dot{P}_{t-1} + (1-r)\dot{P}^e_{t-1}, \text{ where } < r \leqslant 1.$$ Our simplifying assumption is thus that r = 1.

13. As we are here in a Friedman world we assume that only the M component of B has implications for inflation. Graph dd in quad C of Figure 2 is arrived at by collapsing equations (3) and (4) into one, and adding the further assumption that the rate of growth of the total money supply (M) is realted to M — the rate of growth of high-powered money — by some fixed money supply multiplier.

14. See Laidler and Parkin (1975) for a discussion of the evidence regarding the value of w, Addison and Burton (1980), ch. 3.

15. The Chilean inflation is now about one century old. It has over this period exhibited large fluctuations — sometimes reaching rates of 70 per cent p.a. — but has at no time degenerated into hyper-inflation. See Davis (1963) for further discussion.

16. Note that this equation does not exist 'really' if the 'world' is described by (7) through (10).

17. See Burton (1978) for a detailed discussion of the post-war British experience of the growth of budget deficits and the inflationary consequences.

18. Monetary assets and liabilities are those whose yield are fixed in money terms (e.g. money itself, unindexed fixed-interest bonds). Note that in the case of unindexed bonds, the redistribution of wealth from the lender to the borrower caused by inflation occurs if the inflation is unanticipated; if the inflation were fully anticipated borrowers would have to offer a higher money rate of interest to compensate fully for inflation, and no redistribution of wealth would occur. Even under fully-anticipated inflation, however, redistribution would still occur via the inflation tax on money-holdings. See Bailey (1956), Kessel and Alchian (1962), for fuller discussion.

REFERENCES

ADDISON, J. T. & BURTON, J. (1980), *The Explanation of Inflation*. London: Macmillan, forthcoming.

BAILEY, M. J. (1956), 'The Welfare Cost of Inflationary Finance', *Journal of Political Economy* 64 (2): 93-110.

BEHREND, H. (1971), ' "What Does the Word Inflation Mean to You?" and "What is the Connexion between Wage Claims and Prices?": Findings from two National Sample Surveys in 1966 and 1971', *Industrial Relations Journal* 2 (3), Autumn.

BLACK, D. (1958), *The Theory of Committees and Elections*, Cambridge: Cambridge University Press.

BRUNNER, K. (1975), 'Comment', *Journal of Law and Economics* 18 (3), December: 837-857.

BRUNNER, K. (1976), 'Inflation, Money, and the Role of Fiscal Arrangements: An Analytical Framework for the Inflation Problem', in MONTI, M. (ed.), *The 'New Inflation' and Monetary Policy*, London: Macmillan.

BRUNNER, K. and MELTZER, A. H. (1972), 'Money, Debt, and Economic Activity', *Journal of Political Economy* 80, September/October: 951-977.

BUCHANAN, J. M., BURTON, J. and WAGNER, R. E. (1978), *The Consequence of Mr Keynes*, London: Institute of Economic Affairs.

BUCHANAN, J. M. and WAGNER, R. E. (1977), *Democracy in Deficit*, New York: Academic Press.

BUCHANAN, J. M. and WAGNER, R. E. (1978), 'Democracy and Keynesian Constitutions: Political Biases and Economic Consequences', in BUCHANAN, BURTON and WAGNER (1978) op. cit., 11-27.

BURTON, J. (1978), 'Keynes' Legacy to Great Britain: "Folly in a Great Kingdom"', in BUCHANAN, BURTON and WAGNER (1978), op. cit., 29-75.

BURTON, J. (1979), 'Inflation: A Revised Friedman Theory with a Reverse Phillips Twist' , Birmingham: University of Birmingham, Faculty of Commerce and Social Science, Discussion Paper Series A.

BURTON, J. (1980), *Trade Unions and Inflation*, London: Macmillan, forthcoming.

BURTON, J. and ADDISON, J. T. (1977), 'The Institutionalist Analysis of Wage Inflation: A Critical Appraisal', *Research in Labor Economics* 1, June: 333-376.

DAVIS, T. E. (1963), 'Eight Decades of Inflation in Chile, 1897-1959: A Political Interpretation', *Journal of Political Economy* 71, August: 389-397.

DAVIS, T. E. (1964), 'Inflation and Stabilization Programs: The Chilean Experience', in BAER, W., and KERSTENETZKY, I. (eds.), *Inflation and Growth in Latin America*. New Haven: Yale University Press, 360-364.

DOWNS, A. (1957), *An Economic Theory of Democracy*, New York: Harper and Row.

DOWNS, A. (1967), *Inside Bureaucracy*, Boston: Little, Brown and Co.

FRATIANNI, M. (1977), 'Price and Output Adjustments in a Closed Economy', *Journal of Money, Credit and Banking* 4 (1), Part 2, February: 151-164.

FRIEDMAN, M. (1970), The Counter-Revolution in Monetary Theory, London: Institute of Economic Affairs.

FRIEDMAN, M. (1977), 'Nobel Lecture: Inflation and Unemployment', *Journal of Political Economy* 85 (3), June: 451-472.

GORDON, R. J. (1975), 'The Demand and Supply of Inflation', *Journal of Law and Economics* 18 (3), December: 807-836.

HINES, A. G. (1964), 'Trade Unions and Wage Inflation in the United Kingdom, 1893-1961', *Review of Economic Studies* 31 (88), October: 221-252.

HUTT, W. H. (1975), *The Theory of Collective Bargaining, 1930-1975*, London: Institute of Economic Affairs.

JOHNSON, H. G. (1973), *Inflation and the Monetarist Controversy*, Amsterdam: North Holland.

JOHNSON, H. G. (1975), 'Living with Inflation', *The Banker*, August: 863-864.

KAHN, R. (1976), 'Inflation — A Keynesian View', *Scottish Journal of Political Economy* (1), February: 11-15.

KESSEL, R. A. and ALCHIAN, A. A. (1962), 'Effects of Inflation', *Journal of Political Economy* 70 (6): 521-537.

LAIDLER, D. and PARKIN, J. M. (1975), 'Inflation: A Survey', *Economic Journal* 85, December: 741-809.

LEIJONHUFVUD, A. (1977), 'Costs and Consequences of Inflation', in HARCOURT, G. (ed.), *The Microfoundations of Macroeconomics*, London: Macmillan.

LEPPER, S. (1974), 'Voting Behaviour and Aggregate Policy Targets', *Public Choice* 18, 67-81.

LINDBECK, A. (1976), 'Stabilisation Policy in Open Economies with Endogenous Politicians', *American Economic Review* 66, Papers and Proceedings, May: 1-19.

MEISELMAN, D. (1975), 'Worldwide Inflation: A Monetarist View', in MEISELMAN, D., and LAFFER, A. B. (eds.), *The Phenomenon of Worldwide Inflation*, Washington, DC: American Enterprise Institute for Public Policy Research.

NISKANEN, W. A. (1971), *Bureaucracy and Representative Goverment*, New York: Aldine-Atherton.

NORDHAUS, W. D. (1975), 'The Political Business Cycle', *Review of Economic Studies* 42, April: 169-189.

REES-MOGG (1974), *The Reigning Error: The Crisis of World Inflation*, London: Hamish Hamilton.

TULLOCK, G. (1965), *The Politics of Bureaucracy*, Washington, D.C.: Public Affairs Press.

VANDERKAMP, J. (1975), 'A Simple Friedman Theory with a Phillips Twist', *Journal oF Monetary Economics* 1, 117-122.

WHITELEY, P. (1978), 'The Political Economy of Electoral Support', paper given at the ECPR workshop on formal political analysis, University of Grenoble 1978.

IV Formal Approaches to the Analysis of Political Systems

10 Equilibrium in a Political Economy

Norman Schofield
University of Texas, USA, and University of Essex, UK

Here I will consider two competing 'research programs'[1] which are relevant to the analysis of a political economy.

Equilibrium Theory is a generalization of microeconomic theory, and is concerned with the existence of various kinds of stationary states, whether price equilibria or the core, under appropriate assumptions. The more restricted results of the theory suppose the existence of a price mechanism and 'convexity' in both preference and power ('decreasing returns'), and show the existence of an equilibrium price vector where supply and demand of all commodities are equalized. Hahn[2] has argued most forcibly for the general core model which does not rely on a price mechanism.

In the general theorems the power of a coalition is represented in terms of its 'characteristic set': the core consists of those outcomes with the property that no coalition has the power and inclination to move to another point. In an exchange economy, for example, if it is assumed that each individual is 'private want regarding', i.e. concerned only with personal commodity consumption, then the core will exist.

To comment on these theorems, we may distinguish between technical and fundamental assumptions. As I understand the results, convexity of preference or power is a technical assumption, in the sense that when this assumption is dropped, the core is still essentially retained. For example, as Hahn observes, increasing returns which are small relative to the scale of the economy 'perturb' the Arrow-Debreu price equilibrium. Furthermore, if the number of agents is enlarged then the core collapses down to the price equilibrium for certain limiting processes.

However, the whole characteristic function formulation and the assumption of 'private' preferences is much more fundamental. With private preferences the representation of power in terms of a characteristic function is quite reasonable. However, if publicness occurs in the political economy, then the characteristic function formulation may not be capable of fully representing the 'power of actors'. The more subtle point is whether or not a slight modification of the assumption 'private want regarding' is compatible with the existence of a set of core equilibria.

Whether or not a 'real' political economy actually exhibits core equilibria is a question which cannot easily be determined by empirical observation. As Lakatos[3] has indicated, data which might refute a central result of a research program can generally be accounted for by ad hoc hypotheses. In the case under discussion, the observation of extreme fluctuations in currency exchange rates could be accounted for in terms of exogenous changes (i.e. rapid technological or social transformations). Indeed one difference between natural sciences and social sciences is the extent to which events may be conveniently associated with closed subsystems. Consequently ad hoc hypotheses may be more readily constructed in the social sciences.

Feyerabend[4] has argued that observations relevant to the 'refutation' of a particular theory A may be in principle unconceivable until a competing theory B is available. Indeed the competing theory B may well be inferior to theory A, in the sense of having no explanatory power for observations 'covered' by A.

Arrowian social choice theory produces qualitatively quite different results from equilibrium theory. In general some technical assumptions are made (pareto optimality and unrestricted domain), and a fundamental assumption (independence of irrelevant alternatives or binary independence).[5]

With these assumptions strong *consistency* properties require concentration in power: if weak preference (including indifference) is transitive, then the process must be dictatorial, and if strict preference is transitive then the process must be oligarchic.[6] Since these assumptions are appropriate to voting games, the results can be regarded as generalizing the classical voters paradox with three individuals, where A prefers a to b to c, B prefers b to c to a, and C prefers c to a to b. The theorem only implies, however, that for a non-oligarchic process there is *some* pattern of preferences such that intransitivity occurs. Consequently there was analysis of general exclusion principles,[7] so that if the preference pattern was suitably restricted then transitivity occurred. Unfortunately for these consistency results, Kramer[8] showed, under simple majority rule in a policy space of at least two dimensions, that the exclusion principles almost always failed. While this result did not prove conclusively that inconsistency occurred, it did indicate that inconsistency was likely.

It could of course be the case that a voting process was intransitive, but that a core existed nonetheless. Plott[9] however had obtained a characterization, in the case when utilities are smooth, which indicated that the core would be empty when the policy space was two dimensional. The equilibrium results of Downs[10] in the one dimensional case did not seem to carry through in higher dimensions. Consequently the classical pluralist model[11] of the political system faced a possible fundamental critique.

Notwithstanding the negative results on voting games, Tullock[12] argued that although 'cycles' would exist in voting games, they would become less important as the number of choosing individuals increased. Various results were obtained on conditions for the existence of a core in a voting game with a suitably distributed continuum of players.[13]

Recent results show that with a finite number of players, and with the assumption of smooth utilities (or preferences), simple majority rule is in fact very badly behaved.[14] Recently I have shown[15] with a population of size n, under simple majority rule on a policy space W of dimension w, that, for *almost all* preferences:

(i)   if n odd and w $\geqslant 2$, the core is *empty* and cycles exist, and if w $\geqslant 3$ then these cycles fill the whole of W.

(ii)   if n even and w $\geqslant 3$, the core is empty and cycles exist, and if w $\geqslant 4$ then again the cycles fill the space.

Indeed, for any symmetric voting game similar results obtain, although higher dimensionality is required. Furthermore, I conjecture that any decision process which is essentially non-oligarchic and for which the independence axiom is appropriate will display endemic cycles.[16]

It should be clear from this discussion that, within the 'Social Choice' research program, a major point of disagreement over the relevance of the inconsistency results has only just been resolved. The study of voting processes on policy spaces required the development of more 'geometric' mathematical tools than was required in Arrowian social choice, and since economic equilibrium theory also makes use of geometric tools, it is now conceptually possible to compare the assumptions and results of the two research programs. My own attitude is that the difference between the 'equilibrium' orientation of the one and the 'inconsistency' of the other is in fact a deep epistemological conflict between those who hold that behavioral systems are 'equilibriating' or well behaved, and those who consider them to be 'chaotic'. With reference to my remarks above on empirical analysis, if behavioral processes are chaotic but deterministic (non-probabilistic) then no statistical procedure can distinguish them from random ones. Consequently 'chaos' will be obscured in the 'random error' of an analysis.

It is surprising that similar results in abstract mathematical analysis of multivariate processes indicate that 'chaos' is typical. For example Li and Yorke[17] and Oster and Guckenheimer[18] obtain chaos in discretely changing processes. These results precisely parallel the 'discrete' cyclicity of voting processes.[19] In a differential ecological model of three competing species, May and Leonard[20] have shown the existence of an odd limit cycle, where each species in turn almost totally dominates the others. This parallels Kramer's result[21] for n = 3 in two dimensions. Finally, in an extraordinary paper Smale[22] has shown that if there are at least five species (so the state space is five dimensional) then 'chaotic' systems can be typical.

Any process which can be regarded, at least qualitatively, as differential is in a certain sense local or myopic, and would satisfy some kind of independence axiom. Any such process which is non trivial (i.e. non oligarchic, involving many actors or 'species', in a complex environment) would seem, from these results in social choice and mathematical ecology, to be *chaotic*.

If these results are indeed relevant, then the expectation that ecological, genetic, social, political and even economic processes display 'law governed' behavior is confounded.

My purpose in this paper is to discuss a number of aspects of the political economic system to see whether chaos (or at least some kind of internal inconsistency) is indeed endemic. I shall consider first the nature of a bargaining game between a 'government' and a 'client' (which could be a state bureaucracy or an economic actor such as a large corporation). It seems that a certain indeterminancy is possible. I then contrast equilibrium and social choice approaches in general. Finally, I consider the decision process associated with a house of representatives, in the light of the Arrowian conclusion that consistency is only possible if power is concentrated.

THE POLITICAL 'FIRM'

Niskanen[23] has adopted a simple model of bilateral monopoly to study the problem of the provision of a public good Q, let us say, by a governmental agency or bureau which operates under a budget constraint. In this case the budget is determined by an administrative decision: thus for a level of output q of Q by the agency the government administration is willing to provide a budget or *total revenue* TR(q).

The administration may be regarded as the *consumer* for the good. In microeconomics, decreasing marginal utility by consumers for a good gives a demand curve for the good with certain features. If the good is supplied by a monopoly producer then, for each level q of the good, this firm can determine the price p(q) at which it can dispose of the good. At this level the firm's total revenue is:

$$TR(q) = q \cdot p(q) \tag{1}$$

In the political situation the government administration plays the role of the consumer and the agency is in the role of the firm: thus we may refer to the agency as a *political firm*.

Obviously from (1) the effective price of the good is

$$p(q) = \frac{TR(q)}{q} = \frac{\text{budget}}{\text{production}} \tag{2}$$

The typical demand assumptions referred to above imply that the TR curve has decreasing gradient, in other words marginal revenue (MR = dTR/dq) decreases in q. Niskanen supposes that the choice of the political firm over output is determined by a bureau head who values the perquisites of office, reputation, patronage etc., all of which are related to the size of the budget.

Assuming that

$$TR = aq - bq^2 \tag{3}$$

for example, TR is maximized when MR = O, or q = a/2b.

Of course the costs TC may constrain the agency, forcing TC $\leq$ TR. Since TR increases for q < a/2b, the optimal level is obtained by equating TC = TR. For example if TC = cq + dq^2 (with increasing marginal cost) then the optimal level of output for the agency is

$$q = \frac{a-c}{b+d} \tag{4}$$

Note that under this model the administration is a channel for the demands of the consumers (electorate) for the good. If the budget (total revenue) curve is derived in some way from a demand curve, then the trade offs involved at different prices between Q and other costly goods are incorporated.

Since it may be the case that $\frac{a-c}{b+d} > \frac{a}{2b}$, the agency may 'oversupply' the good, i.e. produce more of q than maximizes the electorate's 'utility'. Migue and Belanger[24] suggest that the firm may well maximize the difference between the budget constraint and total costs. This they call the managerial discretionary profit:

$$\pi(q) = TR(q) - TC(q) \tag{5}$$

With TC, TR as above, $\pi(q)$ is maximized at

$$q = \frac{a-c}{2\ (b+d)} \tag{6}$$

Under this optimization rule of course the production of the good is *inefficient*, since some of the budget assigned to the agency is squandered. Whereas in the economic situation one expects that profit maximization would provide incentives to invest some of these profits to decrease total costs, a political firm might not have such an incentive. In any case the political firm is in a monopolistic situation and other competitors may not enter into production, thus having the effect of transferring the benefits of productivity increases on to the consumer.

Breton and Wintrobe[25] have developed the model further by supposing that the administration imposes control devices to offset the agency's inefficiencies. This immediately suggests that one regard the eventual level of good produced as a result of a bargaining process between the two institutional actors.

Whereas the two earlier models gave 'equilibrium' results, it is clear that the administration was not 'active'. In a bargaining situation the budget offer (TR) could reasonably be expected to be dependent on the expected behavior of the agency. Miller[26] has developed this possibility. Suppose that an administration provides a budget C_j to $j = 1, \ldots, n$ agencies, leading to the (vector) production of goods q. To this production vector q is associated a utility $U(q)$. The decision problem for the agency is to maximize

$$G(q) = U(q) - R \tag{7}$$

where R is the constraint

$$R = \Sigma C_j$$

Consider for the moment the choice by the administration of C_i, for a good q_i (which we shall write as C,q). Given C, the agency devotes a proportion h of its budget C to the production of the good, and thus chooses q such that

$$TC(q) = hC. \tag{8}$$

The *payoff* H(q) to the agency may be regarded as partly the value of the output (through prestige etc.) and partly profit

$$\pi(q) = (1-h)C.$$

Thus the administration can only compute the optimal level $C = gR$ of its budget offer if it knows the response (h) of the agency.

To illustrate consider Miller's example:

$$\begin{aligned}
G(g,h) &= G(q) = aq - bq^2 - gR \\
H(g,h) &= H(q) = cq - dq^2 + (1-h)gR \\
TC(q) &= \ell q
\end{aligned} \tag{9}$$

Here $U(q) = aq - bq^2$ is the value to the administration of the level q of production of the good, $V(q) = cq - dq^2$ is the value assigned by the agency to the production level, and $(1-h)gR$ is the profit of the agency. Both G,H may also be regarded as functions of g, h, since g, h both determine q from equation (8).

The 'response curve' of the *agency* is the curve $h = h(g)$ found by setting

$$\frac{\partial H}{\partial h}(h,g) = 0,$$

and similarly for the administration G.

The equilibrium outcome is that (g^*,h^*) such that $g^* = g(h^*)$, $h^* = h(g^*)$. In this case it is a *Nash equilibrium* with the property that

FIGURE 1
The Agency Sponsor Bargaining Game

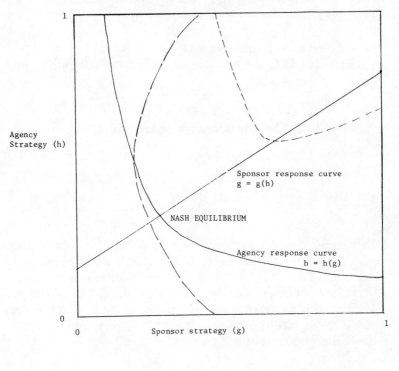

Agency
Strategy (h)

Sponsor response curve
g = g(h)

NASH EQUILIBRIUM

Agency response curve
h = h(g)

Sponsor strategy (g)

Indifference contour of agency   — — — — —
Indifference contour of sponsor   —— —— ——

$$G(g^*,h^*) > G(g,h^*) \text{ all } g \neq g^*$$
$$H(g^*,h^*) > H(g^*,h) \text{ all } h \neq h^* \qquad (10)$$

See Figure 1.

In Miller's example with $(a,b,c,d) = (200,.5,50,.125)$, $(\ell,R) = (48,4800)$ we obtain the array of payoffs $(G(g,h),H(g,h))$:

TABLE 1
The Administration-Agency Game

	h' = 1.00	h* = 0.25
g' = 1.00	(10200,3750)	(−112.5,4771.75)
g* = .32	(4352,1472)	(32,1544)

Here both players may 'cooperate' by fixing $h = 1$, $g = 1$ to mutual advantage. While the Nash equilibrium would be expected were each player to act competitively, there in general exist mutually preferred outcomes (in this case $(h,g) = (1,1)$). The question is whether such mutually preferred (pareto optimal) outcomes are stable. Note that this game is structurally very similar to the classical prisoners' dilemma:

TABLE 2
Prisoners' Dilemma

	C	N
C	(100,100)	(10,150)
N	(150,10)	(20,20)

Suppose G and H do agree to cooperate: H might well be tempted to set $h = 0.25$ instead of the agreed $h = 1$. If G has available no retaliation then there would be every reason for H to do just that. In general, however, one would expect G to have some redress, and to change g to 0.32, say, as soon as possible. From the point

$$(g^*, h^*) = (.32, .25)$$

there is a pareto preferred move to $(g,h) = (1,1)$. As I shall argue in the next section, the sequence of moves

$$(1,1) \rightarrow (1,.25) \rightarrow (.32,.25) \rightarrow (1,1) \qquad (11)$$
$$ H \qquad G \qquad (G,H)$$

constitutes an Arrowian *cycle* (see Figure 2).

FIGURE 2
The Bargaining Domain and Cycle in the Agency Sponsor Game

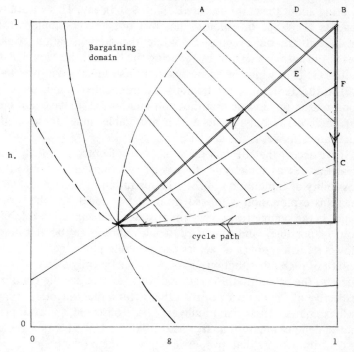

However if the agency plans ahead, then it can fairly readily calculate that the eventual result of its non-cooperative move (from h = 1.0 to 0.25) is the inferior outcome (g,h) = (.32,.25). Consequently it is rational for H to resist its selfish inclinations and stay at the cooperative position (g,h) = (1,1).

This is the theoretical argument behind the *core*. In this framework one outcome is dominated by another via some actor if the latter outcome can be guaranteed by the actor whatever other actors choose to do. In the agency-administration game, each actor can only 'guarantee' the Nash Equilibrium (g*,h*), payoffs. Consequently the *core* consists of the boundary arcs AB and BC since these are the pareto optima which give each player more than the (g*,h*) payoffs.

However, there is a serious conceptual ambiguity associated with the notion of 'guarantee'. Consider an initial core point D = (0.9,1.0) in figure 2, and suppose that the agency reduces h, to bring about the new outcome E = (0.9,0.8), say. This naturally benefits H. While the sponsor has lost out, the possibilities for retaliation are quite complex. While the administration could 'teach the agency a lesson' by reducing the budget, this would also reduce G. Thus while the agency cannot 'guarantee' the move (0.9, 1.0) to (0.9,0.8), since the administration could respond, there is good reason to suppose that the 'non-guaranteed' move could occur. Indeed the only points which are stable under these 'non-guaranteed' moves is the arc BF.

If we accept that BF is a reasonable set of outcomes, then it is clear that the asymmetry in the payoff functions gives rise to the possibility of exploitation of the administration by the agency, and that this exploitation is missed by the core model. On the other hand, in the symmetric two person prisoners' dilemma no exploitation is possible, and the core would appear to be relevant. However, if a number of actors can generate public goods to the benefit of each other, but one actor A is a sufficiently effective producer to the extent that it is rational for it to produce the good irrespective of the behavior of the other actors, then the others may well exploit A. Russett and Sullivan[27] have observed, for example, that in defence alliances a large actor, like the United States, tends to contribute more than proportionately to the public good.

Indeed it is only in the symmetric, bipolar situation that the stability associated with the core is reasonable. If many actors are involved in what is essentially a bargaining game, then the existence of cycles, or indeterminacy in the outcome, is a very real possibility.[28] At the same time the existence of asymmetries between the players can lead to exploitation.

While the agency in this asymmetric model was regarded as a state bureaucracy, this is no reason why a similar relationship may not hold between a single economic enterprise (or group of enterprises) and an administration. In this context it is worthwhile mentioning Lieberson's[29] analysis of the US economy, using Leontief input-output analysis. He estimated that a 20% cut in US armaments expenditure would lead to considerable losses for a small number of industrial sectors, namely aircraft (10%), ordinance (15%), research and development (13%), electronics (5%). Other sectors gained, with agriculture benefitting the most (2.1%). On the basis of this analysis, a few possibilities suggest themselves. Because of geographical location factors one would expect a certain communality of interest between economic enterprises deeply involved in these sectors and certain political interests. Lieberson indicates for example the close connection in 1969 between Senate Committee membership and State involvement with the sector of concern to the Committee. Given the concern of certain states with particular sectors, one would expect, through the log rolling process, for this concern to find representation in the 'social preference' of the sponsoring administration. Consequently one might expect to find a certain exploitation of the concerned political interests *by* the economic enterprises involved.

On the other hand, if we consider the relationship between economic enterprises involved in this bargaining game with the administration, then the input output model indicates there is a degree of conflict between them, since after all the nature of the game is the division of a budget. To some extent of course the fact that the budget may be constantly increased modifies somewhat the degree of conflict. The existence of negative externalities in this game indicates perhaps that exploitation of the unconcerned by the large occurs. This is the converse of the exploitation of the great by the small which we observed above in pure public goods games with *positive* externalities.

Until now we have assumed that the administration is a unitary actor. In the final section we shall study the *political* decision process in an attempt to see whether the supposition of 'consistent' preferences on the part of an administration is reasonable. Before doing this, however, we shall discuss in more detail the differences between Arrowian social choice and game theoretic equilibrium theory.

SOCIAL CHOICE AND EQUILIBRIUM THEORY

In this section I wish to deal with the notion of *power* as developed in the theory of games and social choice.

First of all suppose that every member i of a society, N, has a preference ordering, p_i, representing that individual's preference on a set W of possible alternatives. The pattern of all individual preferences will be written p and called a preference profile. A social preference function, $\mathcal{6}$, is a function which assigns to each preference profile p, a preference relation $\mathcal{6}(p)$ on W, called the *social preference*.

A *coalition* M is a subset of N. Say that a coalition M is decisive for x over y, and write x $\mathcal{6}_m$y whenever it has the *power* to change y to x. Consequently if x $\mathcal{6}_m$y and xp_my we may write x $\mathcal{6}_m(p)$y, to indicate that the coalition M has the power and inclination to implement x over y. If, for some M, x $\mathcal{6}_m(p)$y then x $\mathcal{6}(p)$y.

In a *characteristic function game* power is represented in a simple form. Using the terminology of Bloomfield and Wilson,[30] an alternative x is called *conclusive* for a coalition M if the coalition is decisive for x over any y. The characteristic *set*, V(M), of M is the set of conclusive alternatives of M. A coalition M is called *winning* if all alternatives in W are conclusive for M (viz. V(M) = W). A *simple* game is one determined completely by a fixed class of winning coalitions.

Say that an alternative y is dominated by x via the coalition M, and write $xd_m(p)$y, if xp_my and x ϵ V(M). A *characteristic function game* is a social decision process d(p) such that xd(p)y iff $xd_m(p)$y for some M.

For example consider a pure exchange economy with a set J of commodities $(w_1,\ldots,w_n)$ and n individuals. An *initial endowment* is an allocation scheme $(w_{ij})_{i \epsilon N, j \epsilon J}$ where w_{ij} is i's endowment of the jth commodity. For a coalition M let V(M) be the set of feasible distributions (x_{ij}) subject to the constraint:

$$\sum_{i \in M} (x_{ij} - w_{ij}) \leqslant 0 \text{ for each } j \in J \tag{12}$$

Then for two exchanges x,y which both satisfy the feasibility condition (12) for M, we see $xd_m(p)y$ whenever $(x_{ij})jp_i(y_{ij})j$ for each $i \in M$.

In general the *core* of a game is the set

$$C(d,p,W) = (x:yd(p)x \text{ for no } y \in W) \tag{13}$$

In such a characteristic function game the core is the set of *undominated* outcomes.

As we mentioned in the first section, the core of a pure exchange economy exists, contains the competitive price equilibrium and under certain limiting conditions collapses to the competitive price equilibrium.[31]

To indicate the orientation of Arrowian social choice, consider the following axioms:

T_i : *Individual transitivity*: each individual i has transitive preference: i.e. xp_iy and $yp_iz \Rightarrow xp_iz$

A_i : *Individual acyclicity*: for each individual i, if $x_1p_ix_2 \ldots p_ix_r$ then not $(x_rp_ix_1)$

T_s : *Social transitivity*: $\delta(p)$ is defined and transitive for each profile p whose components are transitive

A_s : *Social acyclicity*: $\delta(p)$ is defined and acyclic for each profile p whose components are acyclic.

P : *Pareto optimality*: If everyone prefers x to y then so does society: xp_iy, all i in N implies $x \, \delta(p)y$. Alternatively $x \, \delta_N y$, for all x,y.

More important of all, Arrow orginally formulated an axiom known as the independence of irrelevant alternatives, which guaranteed that the choice of a process from some feasible set V was to be *independent* of preferences on alternatives outside V. To make this clear we should perhaps have written $\mathcal{6}^V(p)$ for the social preference given by the rule $\mathcal{6}$ together with the profile p, on the *feasible set* V.

Suppose we write $\mathcal{6}^V(p)/U$ for the restriction of $\mathcal{6}^V(p)$ to U in V. Then in general there may be no relationship between $\mathcal{6}^{V_1}(p)/U$ and $\mathcal{6}^{V_2}(p)/U$ for $U \subset V_1 \cap V_2$. However, this possibility was forbidden by requiring that $\mathcal{6}^V(p)$ be derived from *binary choice*.

I: Binary Independence

For any feasible V_1, V_2, if $(x,y) \subset V_1 \cap V_2$
then
$$\mathcal{6}^{V_1}(p)/(x,y) = \mathcal{6}^{V_2}(p)/(x,y) \tag{14}$$

While this axiom forbids the utilization of interpersonal companions of utility, it also involves a certain formalization of power, as I shall indicate below.

One form of the impossibility result is that if a social preference function satisfies T_S, P and I then there is an oligarchy (some winning coalition which belongs to all winning coalitions). If T_S is weakened to A_S, then there is a collegium (some coalition, not necessarily winning) which belongs to all winning coalitions.[32]

How do these impossibility results relate to economic equilibrium theory? In the oligarchy result, if $x \, \mathcal{6}_m y$, for some x, some y, then the coalition M is *winning*. But this obviously does not hold for an economy, since in general only the whole society is winning. In the economic model, in any case, preferences are not unrestricted, but are generally assumed to have certain features. When the economic model is generalized to incorporate externalities then there are results that for certain cases the core is nonempty.[33] Again a core may exist even though cycles are present.

To try to reconcile these two approaches consider again the administration-agency game of the previous section, and the path

$$(1,1) \longrightarrow (1,.25) \longrightarrow (.32,.25) \longrightarrow (1,1) \tag{11}$$
$$\quad H \qquad\quad G \qquad\quad (G,H)$$

Certainly H has the 'intrinsic power' to make the first move. Suppose that $(1,1)$ and $(1,.25)$ were the *only* two outcomes possible. Obviously G would have no retaliation. Consequently the move would be rational in this restricted situation, and by the independence axiom rational, in the Arrowian sense, no matter what the feasible set. Similarly for the next two moves, so that (11) represents an *Arrowian* cycle. However, it is *not* the case that $(1,.25)d_H(p)(1,1)$ since, as we have shown, a rational retaliation by G is possible. Now consider the second case:

$$(0.9,1.0) \rightarrow (0.9,0.8) \rightarrow (.32,0.8) \qquad (15)$$
$$\delta_H(p) \quad \delta_G$$

While the first move is (Arrowian) rational for H, the second is not. That is to say, while the second move by G is *possible*, it is not rational. Nonetheless, under the characteristic function formulation, the second move 'blocks' the first. Again it is *not* the case that $(0.9,0.8)d_H(p)(0.9,1.0)$.

This discussion suggests that we can relate the dominance and Arrowian social preferences by:

$$xd_H(p)y \langle = \rangle x\delta_H(p)y \text{ and there is} \qquad (16)$$
$$\text{no } z \text{ such that } z\delta_G w \text{ and}$$
$$yp_H z, \text{ where G is disjoint}$$
$$\text{from H.}$$

Thus if $x\delta_H(p)y$ but some coalition G has the power to move to z and z is worse for H than y, then the move from y to x is blocked, so not $(xd_H(p)y)$.

Note that (11) indicates that Arrowian preference is too *rich*, since it implies change when none is rational; whereas by (15) dominance is too *scarce* since it implies no change when change is in fact possible. A more reasonable social preference relation $\gamma(p)$ may be defined by slightly modifying (16) to require blocking retaliation to be rational:

$$x\gamma_H(p)y \langle = \rangle x\delta_H(p)y \text{ and there is} \qquad (17)$$
$$\text{no } z \text{ such that } z\delta_G(p)x$$
$$\text{and } yp_H z$$

$x\gamma(p)y \langle = \rangle \ x\delta_H(p)y$ for some H.

Here G may be some coalition disjoint from H, or more generally 'δ_G' may in fact be change resulting from a sequence of 'rational' blocking moves.[34]

In general

$$d(p) \subset \gamma \ (p) \subset \delta \ (p) \tag{18}$$

The dominance notion, d, embodies a kind of omniscience on the part of actors, or alternatively a presumption that the actors are extremely risk averse. On the other hand the richness of Arrowian social preference is the result of myopia, or risk preference, by the actors. Neither is really completely satisfactory. However in an exchange economy, with private regarding wants, $\gamma = d$ since no coalition may 'hurt' another. In typical voting games, no coalition, disjoint from a winning coalition, has any power so $\gamma = \delta$. The results mentioned in the first section are then certainly relevant for political institutions that use some kind of voting process. Only if the voting process is constrained by some kind of veto structure, either through an oligarchy, collegium or more generalized veto hierarchy[35] can 'consistency' be expected.

In political economies one would expect bargaining to be the general characteristic of the decision process. It would seem that the decision process would be neither as stable (equilibrating) as characteristic function theory suggests, nor quite as unstable as Arrowian social choice theory implies. However, it is plausible that there would exist a 'fuzzy' set of possible outcomes within the bargaining domain. Consequently a system involving some degree of asymmetry between actors, who can form impermanent coalitions, *can* display instabilities. While these may be restricted by the imposition of a veto or authority system, this very imposition may also generate instabilities. It is this possibility that we will discuss in the final section.

POLITICAL ECONOMIC STABILITY

A political system is, essentially, a means whereby information about the demand for public goods may be transmitted to various political firms who provide these goods. The government presumably acts as a kind of 'actioneer' testing out the demand characteristics of the electorate and attempting to coordinate the supply.

Coalitions do form in the political system, and one would not expect them to be permanent. If political systems are essentially voting systems and if more than a few domains of policy are involved then the decision process must exhibit the kind of instability mentioned above. This would have the consequence that there was *no* single governmental 'utility function' as assumed in the second section. To see whether this is a likely consequence consider the relationship between a constituency electorate and its representative. In the US political system, local political competitors have to put together fairly complex coalitions of individuals with different interests. Unlike the British system there would not seem to be a single dimension of conflict (left-right continuum). Consequently there need be no unambiguous equilibrium position for a candidate to adopt. I infer then that the electoral choice is more a matter of imponderables, like personality, luck or strategic insight than anything else.

The decision process in a house of representatives can, it seems to me, take one of four, possible forms.

(i) It can be a formal voting process. Since each incumbent depends for re-election on his ability to supply certain political goods to his electorate, he has to engage in log rolling so as to provide these goods. It is well known that this type of process generates instabilities.[36]

(ii) On the other hand since it is in the interests of all incumbents to supply public goods, then this political game might well be more of a bargaining process than a voting process. One mechanism would be a 'pricing mechanism' for votes. It is not at all clear how this would operate however. In the absence of a pricing mechanism one could use a characteristic function form and deduce the existence of a core. However the difficulty of enforcing 'contacts', which I have alluded to in the previous section of the paper, might in fact mean that the process was fairly indeterminate.

(iii) The representatives might coalesce into a small number of groups or proto-coalitions.[37] These would be the analogue of

Nozick's protective associations.[38] An analysis of 1969 voting
behavior in the US Senate[39] indicated that senators could be
clustered into about fourteen cliques, characterized by similarity of
voting: typically each clique was organized round a senior senator
or committee chairman.

(iv) Finally, strong authority relationships may be present: see,
for example, the analysis by Lindblom[40] of political processes in
terms of authority or influence structures. An authority structure
can be interpreted as a veto hierarchy or 'pyramid' of collegia. If
the authority system is highly structured then this would be sufficient to ensure consistency[41] and thus equilibrium.

Lindblom has made a good point about authority structures.
They may of course be based on exchange relationships, so that
authority is preserved by the ability to generate 'political goods'.
On the other hand authority may be *given*. To delve into this
possibility, consider a pure voting system as in (i). Since the decision problems are complex, one would expect the process to be
chaotic.[42] Nobody may predict outcomes, and the situation closely
resembles the 'State of Nature' of Hobbes.[43] One line of argument
is that it is rational for individuals in such a prisoners' dilemma to
give up autonomy to a sovereign who has the authority to enforce
contracts etc. Obviously enough an authority structure is a kind of
generalized *sovereign* able to ensure rationality or consistency in
the decision process.

As I understand it, however, an authority structure is potentially
unstable. Presumably members of a political institution may be
willing to forego autonomy, if the authority structure ensures a
reasonable distribution of political goods. If the members feel that
they are being insufficiently recompensed then they may withdraw
support (the exit strategy in Hirschman).[44] Indeed it is rational for
members to buck the system where possible, by putting together
coalitions if they can, to serve their special interests. Thus the
potential instabilities of the prisoners' dilemma or the bargaining
game may make themselves manifest.

A possible half-way stage between the authority system (iv) and
the chaos of (i) is an oligopoly system, combining some of the
features of (ii) and (iii). Suppose a number of powerful political actors play the role of brokers. They put together packages of bills using the voting support of their clients. In this case one may well im-

agine that each 'vote' has its value, and that individual senators 'buy' public goods in the political market place.[45] However it would seem to me that the 'price equilibrium' in this market is dependent on the nature of the budget constraint. As long as voters acquiese to the taxation system, then the public goods are of 'low cost' to the senators. When the growth rate of the economy slows down, the budget constraint facing the political system for dams, aircraft factories etc. may become more severe. The power of the economic actors able to produce these goods may make it difficult to reduce the cost of the goods. Consequently the value of the senators' votes is reduced. This of course is *inflation* in the political market place. The natural result of inflation is a 'strike'. Since there may well be groups in the senate who were not involved in the vote buying process, there would be a temptation for others to join them to put together special interest packages. Eventually the full chaos of an unrestricted voting process may occur.

While this discussion has been purely abstract and conjectural, it is relevant to Dodd's[46] argument that the US Congress has displayed a *structural cycle*: with the authority system dominant in the 1960s breaking down, and eventually giving rise to choas. Realizing that they are in a non-cooperative stage of a prisoners' dilemma, the participants gradually give up autonomy and an authority system develops. Eventually the process may be repeated.

It is interesting to speculate how the relationship between the political decision making body and its economic and agency clients changes as the system proceeds through the structural cycle conjectured by Dodd. With a formal authority structure one might expect the highly concerned political interests to concentrate their energies on accumulating power: this is compatible with the clique pattern noted in stage (iii) above. Presumably these interests would be successful in guaranteeing a proportion of the budget for the respective sectors. As the authority system breaks down and develops into the decentralized form that we called the 'state of nature', these interests might be less successful in controlling that aspect of the budget that concerns them. Consequently one might find surprising reversals of policy. One would also expect lobbying organizations to become more important. The complexity of uncontrolled log rolling would also imply that no obvious 'rationality' could be discerned in the decision-making process. It is of interest to note the frequent exclamations in the US that the 'public interest' has not been served by the recent emphasis on private interest.

One can regard the structural cycle in another light however. If the decision process is restricted by the adoption of an authority or influence structure, in the form of a hierarchical veto system, then rationality or consistency can be imposed. However, this rationality may well be attained at the cost of adaptability. In this regard Lindblom has characterized authority systems by the phrase 'strong thumbs, no fingers'. This failure of adaptability in a political authority system may be, in a sense, the cause of its own collapse. Any decision making system may also exhibit similar oscillations between a tightly organized consistent form, and a loosely organized more chaotic structure.

In the US Senate instance what may have 'triggered' the collapse of the formal pattern may well have been 'exogenous' shocks from the economic environment. More generally it is conceivable that such 'exogenous shocks' may dramatically change the structure of a decision making process. For example one may note the instabilities in a number of contemporary western democracies, or consider the rapid escalation of wage demands a few years ago in Great Britain.

CONCLUSION

I have argued that political economies need neither be as 'stable' as the general equilibrium theorems indicate, nor quite as 'chaotic' as social choice theory suggests. However the γ representation of change which I suggested in the third section has built into it a conception of rational retaliation. For an actor (or group of actors) to choose to implement some change which is feasible, some reasonable model of the nature of retaliation (and thus a model of the empirical and subjective world) is necessary. All this was subsumed, in a somewhat facile way, by the use of the operator '$\delta_G(p)$' in equation (17). Since exogenous shocks may presumably considerably change a subjective model of the world, the preference relation γ may also change even though the underlying 'power relationships' (as represented by Arrowian preference δ) remain more or less unchanged. Consequently even though there is a certain amount of 'chaos' associated with the δ-relationship, as there certainly is in a voting system but also in any kind of bargaining situation, this may not become immediately apparent in the actual behavior of the system.

NOTES

This material is based upon work supported by the National Science Foundations Grant No. Soc 77-21651.

I greatly benefited from conservations with Larry Dodd, John Gray, Kenneth Shepsle and Hannu Nurmi in developing the ideas presented in this essay.

1. I. Lakatos, 'Falsification and the Methodology of Scientific Research Programmes', in I. Lakatos and A. Musgrave (eds.), *Criticism and the Growth of Knowledge* (Cambridge: Cambridge University Press, 1970).

2. F. H. Hahn, *On the Notion of Equilibrium in Economics* (Cambridge: Cambridge University Press, 1973).

3. Lakatos, op. cit.

4. P. Feyerabend, *Against Method* (London: New Left Books, 1975).

5. K. J. Arrow, *Social Choice and Individual Values* (New Haven: Yale University Press, 1951).

6. A. P. Kirman and D. Sondermann, 'Arrow's Impossibility Theorem, Many Agents and Invisible Dictators', *Journal of Economic Theory* 5, 1972, 267-277; B. Hansson, 'Existence of Group Preferences', *Public Choice* 28, 1976, 89-98.

7. A. K. Sen, 'A Possibility Theorem on Majority Decisions', *Econometrica* 34, 1966, 491-499; A. K. Sen and P. K. Pattanaik, 'Necessary and Sufficient Conditions for Rational Choice under Majority Decision', *Journal of Economic Theory* 1, 1969, 178-202.

8. G. H. Kramer, 'On A Class of Equilibrium Conditions for Majority Rule', *Econometrica* 37, 1973, 285-297.

9. C. R. Plott, 'A Notion of Equilibrium and its Possibility under Majority Rule', *American Economic Review* 57, 1967, 788-806.

10. A. Downs, *Economic Theory of Democracy* (New York: Harper and Row, 1957).

11. A. F. Bentley, *The Process of Government: A Study of Social Pressures* (Evanston: Principia Press of Illinois, 1949); D. B. Truman, *The Governmental Process, Political Interests and Public Opinion* (New York: Alfred Knopf, 1951); R. Dahl, *Preface to Democratic Theory* (Chicago: Phoenix Books, University of Chicago Press, 1956).

12. G. Tullock, 'The General Irrelevance of the General Impossibility Theorem', in G. Tullock, *Towards a Mathematics of Politics* (Ann Arbor: University of Michigan Press, 1967).

13. O. A. Davis, M. J. Hinich and P. C. Ordeshook, 'An Expository Development of a Mathematical Model of the Electoral Process', *American Political Science Review* 64, 1970, 426-448.

14. R. D. McKelvey, 'Intransitivities in Multidimensional Voting Models and Some Implications for Agenda Control', *Journal of Economic Theory* 12, 1976, 472-482; L. Cohen and S. Matthews, 'Constrained Plott Equilibria, Directional Equilibria and Global Cycling Sets' (mimeo, Cal. Tech., 1977); N. Schofield, 'Instability of Simple Dynamic Games', *Review of Economic Studies* 45, 1978, 575-594.

15. N. Schofield, 'Generic Instability of Voting Games', presented at the Public Choice Meeting, New Orleans, March 1977; N. Schofield, 'Generic Properties of Simple Bergson-Samuelson Welfare Functions', forthcoming in *The Journal of Mathematical Economics*.

16. N. Schofield, 'The Theory of Dynamic Games', in P. Ordeshook (ed.), *Game Theory and Political Science* (New York: New York University Press, 1978).

17. T.-Y. Li and J. A. Yorke, 'Period Three Implies Chaos', *American Mathematical Monthly* 82, 1975, 985-992.

18. G. Oster and J. Guckenheimer, 'Bifurcation Phenomena in Population Models', in J. E. Marsden and M. McCracken (eds.), *The Hopf Bifurcation and its Applications* (New York: Springer Verlag, 1976).

19. See G. H. Kramer and A. K. Klevorick, 'Existence of a "local" Co-operative Equilibrium in a Voting Game', *Review of Economic Studies* 41, 1974, 539-547, for 'discrete' cycles even in the one-dimensional case, and R. D. McKelvey (op. cit., note 14) for discrete cycles in two dimensions.

20. R. M. May and W. J. Leonard, 'Non Linear Aspects of Competition between Three Species', *SIAM Journal of Applied Mathematics* 29, 1975, 243-253.

21. G. H. Kramer, op. cit., note 8.

22. S. Smale, 'On the Differential Equations of Species in Competition', *Journal of Mathematical Biology* 3, 1976, 5-7.

23. W. A. Niskanen Jr., *Bureaucracy and Representative Government* (Chicago: Aldine Atherton, 1971).

24. J. L. Migue and G. Belanger, 'Towards a General Theory of Managerial Discretion', *Public Choice* 17, 1974, 27-43.

25. A. Breton and R. Wintrobe, 'The Equilibrium Size of a Budget-Maximizing Bureau: A Note on Niskanen's Theory of Bureaucracy', *Journal of Political Economy* 83, 1975, 195-207.

26. G. H. Miller, 'Bureaucratic Compliance as a Game on the Unit Square', *Public Choice* 29, 1977, 37-51.

27. B. M. Russett and J. D. Sullivan, 'Collective Goods and International Organization', *International Organization* 25, 1971, 845-865.

28. N. Schofield, 'Dynamic Games of Collective Action', *Public Choice* 30, 1977, 77-105.

29. S. Lieberson, 'An Empirical Study of Military Industrial Linkages', *American Journal of Sociology* 76, 1971, 562-585.

30. S. Bloomfield and R. Wilson, 'The Postulates of Game Theory', *Journal of Mathematical Sociology* 2, 1972, 221-234.

31. K. J. Arrow and F. H. Hahn, *General Competitive Analysis* (San Francisco: Oliver and Boyd, 1971); G. Debreu and H. Scarf, 'A Limit Theorem on the Core of an Economy', *International Economic Review* 4, 1963, 235-246; Aumann, R. J., 'Existence of Competitive Equilibria in Markets with a Continuum of Traders', *Econometrica* 34, 1966, 1-17.

32. D. J. Brown, 'Acyclic Choice' (mimeo, Yale University, 1973).

33. L. S. Shapley and M. Shubik, 'On Market Games', *Journal of Economic Theory* 1, 1969, 9-25; H. E. Scarf, 'The Core of an N-person Game', *Econometrica* 35, 1967, 50-69; Hildenbrand, W. and A. P. Kirman, *Introduction to Equilibrium Analysis* (Amsterdam: North Holland, 1976).

34. N. Schofield, 'The General Relevance of the Impossibility Theorem in Dynamical Social Choice', presented at the Annual Meeting of the American Political Science Association, New York, August 1978.

35. J. H. Blau and R. Deb, 'Social Decision Functions and the Veto', *Econometrica* 45, 1977, 871-879; J. H. Blau and D. J. Brown, 'The Structure of Social Decision Functions', presented at the Public Choice Meeting, New Orleans, March 1977.

36. T. Schwartz, 'Collective Choice, Separation of Issues and Vote Trading', *American Political Science Review* 71, 1977, 999-1010; see also T. Schwartz, 'The Universal Instability Theorem' (mimeo, University of Texas at Austin, 1979).

37. B. S. Rundquist and G. S. Storm, 'Explaining Legislative Organization' (mimeo, University of Illinois, 1978).

38. R. Nozick, *Anarchy, State and Utopia* (Oxford: Basil Blackwell 1974).

39. J. Alt and N. Schofield, 'Representation of Complexity in Voting Bodies: The Example of the U.S. Senate' (mimeo, University of Essex, 1973).

40. C. Lindblom, *Politics and Markets* (New York: Basic Books 1978).

41. See Blau and Brown, op. cit., note 35.

42. See the results referred to in notes 14 and 15.

43. W. C. Bush, 'Individual Welfare in Anarchy', in G. Tullock (ed.), *Explorations in the Theory of Anarchy* (Blacksburg, Va.: University Publications 1972).

44. A. O. Hirschman, *Exit, Voice and Loyalty* (Cambridge, Mass.: Harvard University Press 1970).

45. K. J. Koford, 'An Economic Theory of Legislature: Centralized Exhcnage under Competition and Monopoly' (mimeo, Vassar College, 1978).

46. L. C. Dodd, 'Congress and the Quest for Power', in L. C. Dodd and B. I. Oppenheimer (eds.), *Congress Reconsidered* (New York: Praeger, 1977).

11 A Note on the Political Economy of Pure Space

Hans Schadee

University of Liverpool, UK

INTRODUCTION

Weber defines politics as:

> striving to share power or striving to influence the distribution of power, either among states, or among groups within a state.[1]

and the state is defined as:

> a human community that (successfully) claims the monopoly of the legitimate use of physical force within a given territory. Note that 'territory' is one of the characteristics of the state.[2]

These two fairly standard definitions relate, through the use of the word territory, and stressing territory as a characteristic of the state, space to politics. Four aspects of this relation are potentially relevant:

— first, what are the effects of purely spatial factors, such as
  distance and area on politics;
— second, territory is potentially 'land', an economic term indicating a production factor in the classical trinity of land,
  labour and capital, which leads to discussions of spatial political
  economy;
— third, what is the impact of actual geographical features on
  politics, a question which should be answered by political
  geography;
— fourth and last, how do groups of people and human com-
  munities identify a territory as being *theirs*, a problem in the
  study of myth, philosophy and law.

This note is mainly concerned with the first aspect of the relation
between space and politics, and, to some extent also with the second aspect. It can be argued that these two aspects, space in
politics and the political economy of 'land', are part of a
theoretical prologue to political geography, the third aspect
distinguished here. The paper does not deal with the fourth aspect
at all; it merits a separate discussion since it is, in any case, rather
different from the three other aspects.

A MODEL FOR GOVERNMENT OVER SPACE

This section contains an attempt to construct an elementary model
for government over space. The model falls into the loose category
of rational choice models in as far as its style is somewhat deductive
and it is assumed that some actors inside the model have a utility
maximizing attitude.

The model assumes that politicians exist, a category of entrepreneurs who seek profit through the activity of government and
administration. How government arises or how politicians come into being is of no concern to this model. Politicians are profit maximizers, subject to the constraints inherent in the nature of government. The major constraint used in the model is that the activity of
governing is considered to be indivisible: politicians can not perform one activity, for example collect taxes, without also having to
perform other activities, for example defense or road-building.

The model does not deal with the rest of the population. It assumes that they produce certain goods on which tax or tribute can be levied and that they supply, where needed, politicians at a certain location. The population is assumed to be homogeneous. These assumptions are specifically intended to bar two arguments. Within the model population differences can not be used to increase or decrease the costs of governing and, secondly, the population does not engage in tax bargaining with politicians. Perhaps this last feature of the model is unsatisfactory. Plausible and interesting models can be set up where tax bargaining between populations and politicians in governments provides a good part of the dynamics of the model. However, such models would be mainly concerned with the amount of tax to be paid and the level of goods and services provided by the government, and less with spatial aspects which are the main concern in this note.

The second component of the model is space. Space has various meanings in the model. One meaning is that of land; space is supposed to produce a good. As land space is homogeneous; one bit of space producing as much as another bit of space. In this sense space is not only land, but also the population living in and on the land. Another meaning of space in the model is area; area measures quantities of space. A third meaning of space is distance between two points in space; a distance can be determined.

Politicians form governments which control or govern over space. But a government is located at one point in space, the capital, hence areas in the space controlled by the government can be characterized by their distance from the capital. A government together with a capital and the area over which it governs will be called a state.

A government takes goods from an area and uses these for its own benefit. But the further away the area is from the capital the less good it contributes. This assumption is a simple argument concerning transport costs. The model in the next section represents these costs by a linear function of distance, but this is not necessary, other functions which increase monotonically with distance are also suitable. What is necessary is the assumption that transport costs can increase to such an extent that, after subtracting the costs of governing, politicians make no profit from areas beyond a certain distance from the capital.

In governing a government incurs costs. Three elements of such costs can be distinguished. The first is a fixed cost incurred by any government, independent of the area it controls. It could be called the cost of being a government, having a capital, the fixed costs of a defense necessary to resist attacks from other states and so forth. A second element is the cost of administrating any area. The third element are administration costs which increase the further an area is from the capital; these costs are assumed to increase monotonically with the distance from the capital. In the model of the next section a linear function is used to represent these costs, but other functions would also be suitable.

It is interesting to try to specify some of the variable costs of governing. Tung, in discussing the advantages and disadvantages of centralization, distinguishes four components connected with the handling of information:

— the costs of collecting information. Information about an area far away is likely to be more expensive to collect;
— the cost of transmitting information;
— the cost of processing information;
— the cost of making decisions and the time spent in decision making.[3]

The first two of these costs are obviously related to distance and probably increase with increasing distance of the governed area from the capital. The last two are not related to distance, though they may be related to the total area in the sense of increasing more than linearly with area. The last argument has been used by those who favour decentralization and regional self-government. They point out that a government can become inefficient through the sheer size of the task it must deal with. But the argument is double-edged, one could just as well point to economies of scale favouring centralization.

For the modern period the assumption of transport and communication costs may seem slightly overdone, though even nowadays these costs are not negligible, but historically these costs have been very high. Using data for eighteen democracies on the relative size of the central government to all governments in a country Dahl and Tufte present the following correlations with population size and area:[4]

TABLE 1
Government Centralization with Size

Aspect of government	Correlations with population	area
Employment	− .49	− .83
Expenditure	− .10	− .66
Revenue	.00	− .56

Source: Dahl and Tufte 1973, p. 38, Table 3.1. Data from Dahl 1971, p. 248.

Dahl and Tufte comment that the high negative correlations of government centralization with area rather than population size might reflect the historical importance of distance as an obstacle to communication. They continue:

> To be sure, the barriers imposed by space on direct communication have been radically reduced...Communication costs, though not independent of distance, are a fraction of what they once were. How much the decentralization in countries with a large territory reflects historic costs of communication rather than present costs it is difficult to say. Yet the need for decentralization shows no signs of disappearing.[5]

A general form of the model has now been stated. A government is linked to space by functions of distance specifying costs and benefits with governments trying to maximize their benefits. The general form specifies a class of models. Some assumptions will have to be added about the behaviour of politicians when they are faced with a possibility to increase profits, so as to allow an analysis of developments over time. The criterion used here is not the profit of each government, but the sum of all profits of all governments in the space under consideration. The assumption is the following: if, given a set of capitals with their associated areas and a total profit an alternative set of capitals with associated areas exists with a greater total profit, then that alternative set will replace the first set, provided that the new profit is sufficiently larger to pay for the cost of transformation within the lifetime of the politicians who have to effect the transformation. The tail end of the condition insures that not every little fluctuation results in changes of the location of capitals or changes in the boundaries of states. If the cost of an overall change is sufficiently high, then a historically given configuration will be fairly stable. Additional restraints might make the behaviour of the system conform more closely to the historical behaviour of states. Examples would be the requirement that a rearrangement of capitals and boundaries involving a large number of states needed a greater total surplus than a rearrangement which involved only a few states, or the requirement that the break up of an existing state needed less surplus than the formation of a new state taking area from two or more existing states and straddling a previous boundary.

The last assumption of the model may be interpreted in terms of politicians in a capital being threatened continuously by groups of would-be politicians located outside the capital. But the threat only becomes real when the potential challengers can raise more resources than the existing group of politicians. But the resources which can be raised are, presumably, related to the total profits which can be realized, so in the end that distribution of capitals and boundaries which maximizes total profits of all states, will prevail.

SOME CONSEQUENCES OF THE MODEL

Having stated the model its consequences can be investigated. First the conditions under which the model gives rise to an equilibrium will be looked at, together with the nature of that equilibrium. After that some other issues are discussed.

The results on equilibrium given here depend on work by Rader.[6] Let a set of states, i, with their areas, A_i, and the locations of their capitals, L_i, be given. Each state has a profit which is a function of its area and the location of its capital $P(A_i, L_i)$. Consider an alternative set of states j, with their areas A_j, their locations of capitals L_j and the associated profits $P(A_j, L_j)$. Any area that has no government over it is considered a state in its own right, but one with no profits from political entrepreneurship. The states then are disjoint and together they constitute the whole available space.

Given the condition determining the dynamics of the system a condition both necessary and sufficient for the internal stability of each state is that for a set of disjoint regions j^* which together make up the area of state i

$$\sum_{j^*} P(Ai,Li) > \sum P(Aj^*,Lj^*) \text{ for all possible sets } j^*$$

The reason for this is straightforward. A state is internally stable if there is no way of splitting it up such that the total profits of the combined parts exceed the profits of the state as a whole.

A necessary condition for a global equilibrium is, given a set of states i, that there is no alternative set j with a higher total profit:

$$\sum_i P(Ai,Li) > \sum_j P(Aj,Lj) \text{ for all possible sets } j$$

This states that the profit from the existing set of states must be greater than the profit from any alternative set of states. This condition has the condition for internal stability as a corollary. For if state i is split up into j^* regions, then by the general condition:

$$\sum_{k \neq i} P(Ak,Lk) + P(Ai,Li) > \sum_{k \neq i} P(Ak,Lk) + \sum_{j^*} P(Aj^*,Lj^*) = \sum_j P(Aj,Lj)$$

This relates internal stability to global equilibrium. But global equilibrium does not mean that an equilibrium exists between pairs of states. For consider a situation with two states i and j where the state j consists of two regions R and R^l such that:

$$P(Ai + R^l,Li) > P(Ai,Li) \text{ and}$$
$$P(Ai,Li) + P(Rj + R^l,Lj) > P(Ai + R^l,Li) + P(Rj,Lj)$$

So state i makes more profit with region R^l than without it, hence there exists a great temptation for the politicians of state i to expand into R^l. But in the long run such an expansion would be unstable since government j makes even more profits out of area R^l than government i and hence would be willing to commit more resources to reconquest of R^l than i could commit to defend it.

In stating the conditions determining the dynamics of the system in terms of overall profits for all governments such forms of external instability have been ruled out. If that is considered satisfactory then the necessary condition for the global equilibrium also becomes a sufficient condition. But the motivations given to politicians by the model, the search for profit, do not extend to considerations of global peacefulness. So, provided the conditions given above are met, external local instability could occur. More interestingly, in a further specification of the model to be discussed later, it can be shown that the necessary condition for global equilibrium implies external instability of the local kind just mentioned. The fate of the French possessions of the English Angevin kings may well be an example of the situation just discussed. The switching of the Elzas between France and Germany may be another example.

It remains to be shown that the conditions for a global equilibrium can be realized. This requires that the boundaries between the areas over which the governments rule are arranged in such a way as to maximize profit. Provided that the profit function is continuous, and with the assumptions already made that areas without a government make no profit, and that there is at least one government which makes a profit, it can be shown that the necessary condition for a global equilibrium can be met. The idea of the proof is simple, one approaches the condition as a limit of distributions of governments with areas making increasing profits. *Proof*: The statement above is a restatement of a theorem by Rader. The proof is identical.[7] Two trivial corollaries of this may be noted. For given boundaries profit maximizing locations of capitals can be found. And also, with the locations of the capitals given, it is possible to determine boundaries which maximize total profit.[8]

The investigation of the equilibrium properties of the model shows that when none of the parameters on which the model depends change a stable configuration of states will arise. But while the overall configuration is stable local instability can occur. Since these properties are independent of the homogeneity assumptions in the model they should hold for non-homogenous spaces, such as real, physical territories, as well.

The following presents a realization of the model on the plane. For purposes of simplification the distance measure used is the city block metric. The reason for doing this is that the 'normal' euclidean distance metric leads to messy formulas. Ideally, under the assumption of a homogeneous space and using euclidean distance, the shape of the areas of states would be a circle. But circles do not cover a surface when they are disjoint. Simple considerations of symmetry and reasonable assumptions about competition would then lead to hexagons as the 'natural' shape for states: in the literature on economic location hexagons do indeed abound.[9] But the difficulty with hexagons is that not all the points on the boundary are equally far from the centre. Use of the city block metric avoids this problem for then the locus of points at an equal distance from the centre forms a square, and squares can cover a surface completely without overlap. The simplification has no effect on the conclusions, as the interested reader can verify.

The following symbols are defined:

* c is the cost of having a capital and a government in it;
* d is the distance as measured from the capital;
* q is the quantity of good produced in an area of space;
* b is the fixed cost of governing an area;
* t is the transport cost per unit distance of q;
* a is a coefficient relating to the cost of governing at distance.

From the meaning of the symbols it is clear that they are all positive.

The cost of governing an area at distance d from the capital will be: $b + ad$. At distance d from the capital there is a quantity $4d$ of area, so the total cost of government is:

$$\text{Total Costs} = c + \int_0^d 4d(b + ad) = c + 2bd^2 + \tfrac{4}{3}ad^3$$

The revenue of an area at distance d from the capital will be: $q\text{-}td$. The transport process embodied in this linear assumption may be envisaged as the transport of a fixed quantity of good from an area to the capital, with the payments for the transport not being taken out of the amount of good during the transport. With this assumption the revenue of the government becomes:

Total revenue = $\int_0^d 4d(q-td) = 2qd^2 + \frac{3}{4} td^3$

The profit made by politicians is revenue minus costs, so:

Profit = $-sd^3 + rd^2 - c$, where
    *s = $\frac{3}{4}$ (a + t) and
    * r = 2(q - b).

The profit function expresses the profit of the politicians as a function of the distance of the boundary from the capital. For each state the profit will be maximized when the distance $d = \frac{2r}{3s}$; the profit will then be $\frac{4r^3}{27s^2} - c$. Unless $r^3 > \frac{27}{4} s^2 c$ there will be no profit at all for politicians and no states will be formed. This also implies that $q > b$; there will only be a government when the cost of governing an area is less than its product.

    The profits of all states will be maximized when the average profit on the area of each state is maximized. The average profit on the area of each state is:

Average profit = $-sd + r - \frac{c}{d^2}$

which is maximized for $d^3 = \frac{2c}{s}$. When the profit for each state is at a maximum $d^3 = \frac{8r^3}{27s^3}$, combining these two conditions and simplifying results in: $r^3 = \frac{27}{4} s^2 c$. But this is precisely the condition under which no state makes any profit at all. It follows from this that when the total system of all states makes a maximal profit, then the individual states, while still making a profit, are not making as much profit as they could make; grabbing some of the area of their neighbours would increase their individual profit. So, in this realization of the model, a global equilibrium implies, inevitably, a local, external instability.

    Though the details of the result above depend on the realization of the model used the general conclusion does not. The general features which are relevant are the following. Firstly, the second derivative of the average profit function is negative for $d > 0$. This means that there is a diminishing marginal return for a real expansion; a condition which is likely to hold for a large number of plausible average profit functions. The second relevant feature is that the maximum of the profit function is reached for a value of d greater than the value of d for which the average profit function reaches its maximum. But, under the assumption that both functions have a single maximum, which is very plausible, and that the second derivative of the average profit function is negative, this will always hold.

Proof: write P(d) for the profit function, which will reach its maximum for d* when the first derivative $P'(d^*) = 0$. The average profit function can then be written as $\frac{P(d)}{d^2}$ and its derivative is

$-\frac{2P(d)}{d^3} + \frac{P'(d)}{d^2}$ which will be negative at d*. Hence the average profit function must reach its maximum for a value of d, $d^{**} < d^*$.

From the way the problem has been set up it is clear that each state has the same area and its capital located in the centre of that area, as long as no special conditions on the total amount of space available in relation to the size of states or on boundaries obtain. The mathematics just analyzed imply that each state is smaller than its politicians would like, and presumably kept so by the pressures on its borders. But a state which had a safe border, or a boundary on which there is no pressure would give its politicians a possibility for additional profit. For in the case of the safe border they could position the capital further away from the border than would be possible otherwise, the only restriction being that it should not be possible for another group of politicians to set up a state between the capital and its border. In the case of a boundary without pressure on it the politicians could expand the area under control till no additional profit was to be made, or till the internal stability of the state was threatened. These considerations suggest that peripheral states can sometimes have an advantage over a heartland. Rokkan, for example, has pointed out that early Western state formation began at the periphery, and that the big states in Europe were peripheral to the belt of rich trading cities in the centre.[10]

Some further features of the model deserve mention. The size of states depends only on the s and c parameters in the model, since the distance from the border at which average profit is maximized is $d = \frac{2c}{s}$. Since the c parameter, the cost of having a capital, is related to the costs of defense, this implies that when the costs of defense increase states become bigger. Similarly, when transport costs increase or when the cost of governing at a distance increases states become smaller, or, more precisely, average profits will be maximized by smaller states. In recent periods transport costs have certainly gone down precipitately, but the same is not necessarily true for the cost of governing at distance. On the contrary, one could well argue that, with the expansion of the tasks of governments, the cost of governing at distance has increased, leading to growing pressures for regional autonomy up to and including regional independence.

The last observation points to a problem of the model used so far. It is assumed that there is a single size which is optimal for a state. But this seems improbable, different tasks require different size units. In discussing democracy, though the point applies generally, Dahl and Tufte write:

> Rather than conceiving of democracy as located in a particular kind of inclusive, sovereign unit, we must learn to conceive of democracy spreading through a set of interrelated political systems, sometimes though not always arranged like Chinese boxes, the smaller nesting in the larger. ...they need to adapt...to the fact that different problems are best met by units of different sizes.[11]

Different tasks would have, in terms of the model, different values of a, the coefficient relating to the cost of governing at distance, and thus have different sizes for which profits are maximized. In effect this would create different capitals for different governmental functions. Of course the assumption of a single capital may break down in another way as well. If the cost of governing at distance is not great, but the transport of the good produced in space is very expensive, politicians might move the capital around. In modern times this has not happened, but travelling courts, summer and winter palaces and similar forms of moving capitals are relatively frequent in history and deserve to be looked at from this perspective.

An unsatisfactory feature of the model as it stands is that the formation of states and their size do not depend on the total level of productivity. This is a consequence of using a linear function for revenue. A non-linear function, such as qt^d, representing a transport process where a certain proportion of the good, $1 - t$, is used for transporting it over a unit distance, solves this. But the solution carries a price tag with it, the functions for profit and average profit become much more complex. Exploration of such complexities and other, further problems must wait for another paper.

NOTES

This paper is a severely cut and drastically changed version of a paper presented at the ECPR workshop on formal political theory in Grenoble, April 1978.

1. H. H. Gerth and C. Wright Mills (eds.), *From Max Weber* (New York: OUP, 1946) 77-78.

2. Gerth and Mills, ibid, 78.

3. T. H. Tung, 'The Spatial Pattern of Decision Making Authority and Organization' in Isard et al., *General Theory, Social, Political, Economic and Regional* (Cambridge, Mass.: MIT Press, 1969) 79-84. See also T. Marschak, 'Centralization and Decentralization in Economic Organizations' *Econometrica* 27, 1959, 399-430 and J. Marschak 'Towards an Economic Theory of Organization and Information' in R. M. Thrall, C. H. Coombs and R. L. Davies (eds.), *Decision Processes* (New York: Wiley, 1954) 187-220.

4. R. Dahl and R. E. Tufte, *Size and Democracy* (Stanford: Stanford University Press, 1973) and R. Dahl, *Polyarchy* (New Haven: Yale University Press, 1971).

5. Dahl and Tufte, ibid, 38.

6. Trout Rader, *The Economics of Feudalism* (New York: Gordon & Breach, 1971).

7. Rader, ibid, 51-63.

8. Rader, op. cit, 46-54.

9. See W. Christaller, *Central Places in Southern Germany* (Englewood Cliffs NJ: Prentice Hall, 1966) and A. Losch, *The Economics of Location* (New Haven: Yale University Press, 1954).

10. S. Rokkan, 'Dimension of State Formation and Nation Building: a Possible Paradigm for Research in Variations within Europe' in Charles Tilley (ed.), *The Formation of National States in Western Europe* (Princeton: Princeton University Press, 1975), Chapter 8.

11. Dahl and Tufte, op. cit., 135.

12 Modelling Uncertainty in Political Decision-Making

Hannu Nurmi

University of Turku, Finland

INTRODUCTION

This essay deals with political decison-making and the ways in which uncertainty relates to it. More specifically, the paper discusses the modelling devices that are being used in describing in a relevant and yet analytically convenient manner the impreciseness that surrounds human decision-making. We outline a decision-model in which the source of uncertainty differs from the one from which the customary modelling apparata derive their motivation. Specifically, I shall argue that while uncertainty in the sense of randomness can be formally accounted for by employing probabilistic conceptualizations, there are other sources of uncertainty pertaining to political decision-making that may be more naturally interpreted as vagueness or a combination of vagueness and ambiguity than as randomness or stochasticity. The theory of fuzzy notions seems particularly suitable for modelling vague notions. Therefore, we outline a decision-model that utilizes notions from fuzzy set theory which by now is well-known in the field of modelling imprecise notions. Hence, it seems only natural to extend the domain of application of the theory into political decision-making.

In the well-known model of Downs which deals with the optimal location of candidates in one-dimensional issue space the optimal strategy of a candidate in an electoral contest is to take a stand in the issue dimension that corresponds the median position.[1] The justification of this proposed strategy is dependent on the assumption that each voter votes for the candidate who occupies the position that is closest to the voter's optimum. In other words, one assumes that the voters reveal their preferences sincerely. Throughout this paper we stick to this undoubtedly somewhat unrealistic assumption. Another questionable assumption of the Downsian model is the unidimensionality of the issue space. We shall make this assumption as well in the following but as will be argued later, dropping it causes no particular difficulties in the model that will be outlined in this paper.

It has been pointed out by Downs that the one-dimensional deterministic model overlooks a feature that is well-known to every voter (let alone campaign expert), viz. it may be beneficial for a candidate to be somewhat ambiguous on what exactly is his stand on the issue that is being discussed.[2] In other words, it is not always so that the crucial matter for a candidate in planning the campaign strategy is to decide where to stand in the issue dimension. That decision must be logically preceded by a decision concerning whether or not to reveal one's stand exactly to the voters. In the model that will be discussed next, there is assumed to be no communication barrier so that if a candidate so wishes he can bring to every voter's awareness where exactly he stands on the issue. Furthermore, if he resorts to a randomized strategy, the probability 'mixes' can also be communicated with perfect accuracy to each and every voter. In the following model we stick to the one-dimensional case and investigate a special case: a two candidate contest in which one of the contestants is called the incumbent and the other the challenger. These are the basic underlying assumptions of the model that has been formulated by Shepsle.[3] We now turn to the model.

THE LOTTERY MODEL

Being an incumbent in an electoral contest undoubtedly affects the amount of manoeuvre space one has along the issue dimension. The incumbent can obviously represent continuity in the policy issue at hand. At any rate — indeed a fortiori — the incumbent is naturally the one of the two contestants who has a definite or exact stand on the issue, one could assume. In Shepsle's model we assume that the position of the incumbent is fixed while the challenger can occupy any position in the issue dimension. It is known that if the preference function of the voters is either unimodal and quasi-concave or symmetric, the optimal position for the incumbent to locate himself is the median most-preferred point.[4] By so doing the incumbent can be sure to beat any challenger who chooses an exact location along the dimension. Now it obviously pays for the challenger to make some other campaign strategy choice than the one that implied taking a definite stand on the issue. He may make deliberately ambiguous statements about the issue in public so that his location in the issue dimension becomes ambiguous. In Shepsle's model ambiguity is — quite correctly I think — interpreted as randomness. Making ambiguous statements is, consequently, interpreted as randomization of the challenger's position in the issue dimension. Let us consider the case in which the issue dimension consists of a finite set of points $X = \{x_1, \ldots, x_r\}$. Now the incumbent's strategy consists of choosing one of the x_i's, i.e. taking an unambiguous stand on the issue. The challenger's strategy, on the other hand, is a probability mixture of the x_i's $(p_1 x_1, \ldots p_r x_r)$ with $0 = \leqslant p_i = \leqslant 1$ and $\sum_{i = 1}^{r} p_i = 1$. In other words, the challenger's strategy is to locate himself at x_1 with probability p_1 etc. and at x_r with probability p_r. As will be argued shortly, the only reasonable sense I can give to the randomized campaign strategy is the one according to which the above strategy means that the challenger gives to $p_1.100\%$ of the electorate the impression that he stands at x_1 on the issue, etc. to $p_r^{\cdot}100\%$ of the electorate the impression that he is at x_r.

We can assume that each point in the unidimensional issue space has a certain utility value for each of the voters. In symbols $U_j(x_i)$ $(j = 1, \ldots m; i = 1, \ldots r)$ denotes the utility for voter j of the policy x_i. On the assumption that the incumbent has to take a definite stand on the issue, we can predict that he locates himself at the median most-preferred position (on the assumption that it is known) x_k. This guarantees a victory to the incumbent no matter which unambiguous position is chosen by the challenger. Hence, there is a presumption that the challenger refrains from taking a definite or unambiguous stand on the issue. Instead, it is rational for him to choose a probability mixture of the locations along the dimension. To be specific let us assume that the challenger chooses a probability mixture of the end-points x_1 and x_r with probabilities p and $1 - p$, respectively. Now, $(px_1, (1 - p)x_r)$, may be considered as a lottery with a well-defined expected utility value for each individual voter j: $pU_j(x_1) + (1 - p)U_j(x_r)$. Depending on the shape of his utility function, j may prefer the lottery $(px_1, (1 - p)x_r)$ to the median most-preferred point x_k or vice versa or be indifferent between the two. The crucial observation here is that when lotteries are allowed the median most-preferred point may not, simply be the Condorcet winner, if the voters are expected utility maximizers. The winner is determined by the number of voters possessing a utility function of a given type: convex, concave or linear.

We now briefly summarize the results obtained by Shepsle:[5]
(1) If all voters have concave utility functions over X, then x_k defeats all the other alternatives, lotteries or otherwise.
(2) If the majority of voters possesses a concave utility function, then for any lottery of alternatives there is always a position in X that beats the lottery by a simple majority.
(3) If a majority of voters possesses a convex range of the utility function in the interval containing x_k (the utility function of these voters in toto may still be quasi-concave), then any lottery $(px_q, (1 - p)x$ where $x_q < x_k < x_s$ defeats x_k.

WHAT KIND OF UNCERTAINTY

From the view-point of the present paper it is important to pay attention to the role and nature of impreciseness or the uncertainty notion in the above analysis. In particular, one should focus on the meaning of the idea of a lottery. The authors referred to above consider quite explicitly this impreciseness as ambiguity. In my opinion this is a plausible interpretation as ambiguity does seem to pertain to concepts lacking unequivocal meaning.[6] In other words, ambiguity is a property of concepts that refer to different things. There is not necessarily anything imprecise in the things themselves. In particular, there need not be any border-line cases of the application of an ambiguous concept. If there are some borderline cases, then there is some additional and different sort of impreciseness involved. Ambiguity construed in this sense is, I think, what is involved in Shepsle's analysis: a lottery is imprecise by comparison with specific positions in the sense that in a lottery any one of a set of positions can 'occur' (be the true one) with a given probability. So, the impreciseness quite obviously takes the form of randomness.

Dwelling a little further on the concept of lottery of positions, one might ask in which sense the concept of probability is being used here. Surely, it would be impossible to resort to the limiting relative frequency interpretation and, I think, to any objective interpretations of probability. The concept of probability distribution over positions in the issue domain clearly refers to subjective considerations and, therefore, subjective probability is apparently the one that is being used. Indeed, the introduction of lotteries, explicitly based on the idea that the voters are expected utility maximizers, amounts to assuming that the probabilities are the same in lotteries and in individual utility calculations.[7] What guarantees, however, that the same probability values are being used by candidates and by all voters? By assuming a uniform perception of probabilities one is making a very strong assumption indeed. It should be noticed that this assumption is to be dealt with separately from the justification of assumptions concerning the shape of voter utility functions. In other words, in assuming that the probability values in lotteries are perceived in the same way by all voters we are making a genuinely new assumption in addition to those related to the shapes of the utility functions.

Another problem that has to do with the lottery model concerns the view of the voter rationality. It is assumed that the voters are expected utility maximizers. Of course, there is nothing inherently objectionable in this assumption: it may very well be the case that the electoral process is usually concerned with issues for which this type of criterion is most plausible. But still one cannot help feeling slightly strained in speaking of lotteries of policies. In particular, one is led to ask: is this type of uncertainty in some respects a typical sort of impreciseness in the electoral process? In my opinion the answer is negative at least as far as the examples of issue dimension given in spatial modelling literature are concerned. Often the positions in the dimension represent amounts of public spending for a given purpose or similar types of things. In real life it may be difficult to find parties or candidates deliberately randomizing their policies so that one gets the impression that the candidate would spend the amount of x_l with probability p and x_r with probability $1 - p$ for a given purpose if the amounts are so far apart that the opposing candidate (the incumbent, say) may locate himself between these two positions. It seems to me that the randomized policy would appear as blatantly inconsistent to the voters, no matter how gambling-minded or risk-acceptant they are. The only realistic sense I can think of applying to a randomized policy is where for one part of the electorate the party or candidate gives the impression that its or his policy is x_l and the rest of the electorate is given the impression that the position is x_r.[8]   Then, depending on whether or not the preference density of the electorate in toto is convex or concave in $(x_l \ldots x_r)$, the randomized policy defeats intermediate positions or is defeated by them. In this interpretation the probabilities do not refer to voters' subjective degrees of belief but to the candidate's partitionings of the electorate into groups $n_l \ldots n_w$. To each group the candidate gives a different impression of his position. We notice immediately that the probabilities now enter the candidates' calculations only. Hereby we are exempt of the discomforting assumption that the lottery probabilities are perceived as the same by all voters.

In my opinion a more common or 'natural' type of uncertainty surrounding electoral decision-making is vagueness instead of ambiguity. In the following I shall discuss this type more closely.

VAGUENESS AND FUZZINESS

A more realistic picture of the electoral competition in spatial terms is obtained when we assume that both voters' optima and candidates' locations are ranges instead of single points in the issue dimension. The common complaint about the 'vagueness' of the candidates in taking stands on electoral issues is often translatable into a statement that instead of a single point in the issue dimension, the candidate represents a range of points. For example, in the issue of public spending on a given social program the 'big spenders' can be viewed as a range of the dimension representing the amount of public spending. Indeed, the more 'precise' or 'exact' the measurement scale of the dimension, the more difficult it is to locate candidates as single points in it. Rather we can characterize the candidates by indicating for each value of the dimension, to what extent the value characterizes the candidate. In other words, we can 'define' the candidate in terms of the degree to which various points in the issue dimension characterize that candidate or are favored by him or applicable to him. We, graduate, so to speak, the truth of claims that the candidate represents a given stand on the issue. This is, therefore, a truth-functional view of vagueness.

In this interpretation each candidate is expressed by means of a characteristic funtion of a fuzzy subset in the set of points of the issue dimension. Let S be a finite set and A a fuzzy subset of S. A is defined in terms of the characteristic function f_A which expresses for each argument $s_i \epsilon S$ the degree to which s_i belongs to A. The original motivation of the fuzzy set theory was to generalize the characteristic function of the classic set theory.[9] For a nonfuzzy set $B \subset S$:

$$g_B(s_i) = 1 \text{ if } s_i \epsilon B$$
$$g_B(s_i) = 0 \text{ otherwise.}$$

In the case of fuzzy sets the range of f_A may be any lattice. In the following we shall, however, be dealing with only those characteristic functions which have as their range the closed real number interval [0,1]. A fuzzy set A in S may be defined as follows:

$$A = \sum_{s_i \epsilon S} f_A(s_i)/s_i$$

where Σ denotes union rather than an algebraic sum. The definition amounts to listing all elements of S with their characteristic function values. The latter are also called membership degrees or values of the membership function.

If we have two fuzzy sets A and C in S, their union and intersection are defined as follows:

$$f_{A \cup C}(s_i) = \max \, (f_A(s_i), f_C(s_i)) \text{ for all } s_i \in S,$$

$$f_{A \cap C}(s_i) = \min \, (f_A(s_i), f_C(s_i)), \text{ for all } s_i \in S.$$

The complement of a fuzzy set A, $\bar{A}$, is defined as follows:

$$f_{\bar{A}}(s_i) = 1 - f_A(s_i) \text{ for all } s_i \in S.$$

PROBABILITY vs. FUZZINESS

One of the most hotly debated issues in fuzzy set theory is whether the very notion of fuzzy set is needed at all in the methodology of human sciences. In particular, many authors have felt that the formal properties of fuzzy sets are so similar to those of probability that there is no need — let alone necessity — to employ fuzzy concepts. Let us investigate this claim a little further.

At first it is convenient to make a distinction between interpretations of probability and the formal properties of probability. In the early discussion on fuzzy set theory the main motivation of developing the theory was given in intuitive terms thereby focusing upon issues that pertain to interpretation rather than formalism. In the discussion on this level it is important to bear in mind that there are several interpretations of probability and, consequently, also several ways in which probability and fuzziness can be distinguished. Let us, however, first cite an authoritative statement related to the intuitive distinction between fuzziness and probabilty: 'Essentially randomness has to do with uncertainty concerning membership and non-membership of an object in a nonfuzzy set. Fuzziness, on the other hand, has to do with classes in which there may be grades of membership intermediate between full membership and nonmembership.'[10] The quotation suggests an important point: in the case of randomness it is always possible — in principle if not physically — to determine whether the event has occurred or not in the past. In the case of randomness the uncertainty concerning the occurrence of the event in the given trial vanishes when the 'experiment' is conducted and its result is observed. This is not the case when uncertainty takes the form of fuzziness: the observation of the object in a given trial does not necessarily make its membership degree in a given set either 0 or 1. Fuzziness refers to the difficulty of classification of an object.

When confronting fuzziness with one particular interpretation of probability, viz. the limiting relative frequency interpretation, it seems that the distinction can easily be made. One can argue that fuzziness has nothing to do with frequencies whereas the latter are conceptually linked with probability in this interpretation. In other words, one could maintain that no evidence to a statement containing fuzzy concepts can be given by invoking statements containing information on relatively frequencies. On the other hand, when the limiting relative frequency interpretation is adopted, probabilistic statements become decidable — in principle — in the light of data on relative frequencies of events.[11] Upon closer inspection, however, this argument needs further elaboration. It has been pointed out by De Luca and Termini that there is a way in which fuzziness appears to become conceptually related to frequencies.[12] I briefly restate their argument. We denote by L(S) the set of all fuzzy sets defined over S, i.e. the set of all mappings from S to the real number interval [0,1]. A decision D over L(S) can be defined as follows: D: $Sx[0,1] \rightarrow (0,1)$. Here the range of D consists of two values which represent classes into which the objects of S can be assigned. In other words, the decision consists of grouping the objects of S having a given membership degree to either one of the classes denoted by 0 and 1. De Luca and Termini set a following requirement for D

$$D(s,0) = 0 \text{ and } D(s,1) = 1 \text{ for all } s \epsilon S.$$

The coherent decisions are defined as follows:
D is coherent if and only if

$$D(s,x) = 1 \text{ implies } D(s,y) = 1 \text{ for all } y \rangle x \text{ and for all } s \epsilon S.$$

Now the result relating membership degress and frequencies can be stated: for any fuzzy set f the membership degree f(s) of an element s∈S equals the average of D(s,f(s)) with respect to all coherent decisions. In other words, if we take the average of all coherent ways of assigning the value 0 or 1 to an element of S, we get its degree of membership in the fuzzy set f. It should be noticed that what is coherent is, of course, relative to f.

Now this result apparently contradicts what was said above in indicating that frequencies are related to membership degrees and, consequently, to fuzziness. Upon closer inspection, however, the contradiction disappears due to the fact that the reference class with respect to which the frequencies are calculated for any s and f to obtain f(s), is the class of all coherent decisions with respect to f(s). As De Luca and Termini point out, the membership value f(s) can be interpreted as the frequency with which a coherent decision will give an answer 1. On the other hand, when calculating a probability of an event as a limit of its relative frequency, the reference class is wholly unrelated to decisions. It consists of the past occurrences of the event. Hence, the reference classes of the membership degree and probability assignment are different. Therefore, the distinction pointed out above can be made.

The most straight-forward way of attacking the demarcation problem of probability and fuzziness is to look at the respective measures in order to find out whether there exist measurement-theoretical differences between the two concepts. This is what I have attempted to do at greater length elsewhere.[13] I briefly summarize the main point. According to Terano and Sugeno, fuzzy measure in a set X and in a sigma-algebra H defined on it, can be defined as follows: if there is a function f with the following properties, we call f a fuzzy measure:

1. $f(\emptyset) = 0$ and $f(X) = 1$
2. If $A, B \in H$ and $A \subset B$, then $f(A) \leqslant f(B)$.[14]

Let now G be an algebra of sets on non-empty set X and let $>$ be a 2-place relation in G ($>$ may be read 'is at least as probable as'). If there exists a mapping $P: G \longrightarrow Re$ with the following properties:

  i. $P(A) \geqslant 0$,
  ii. $P(X) = 1$ and
  iii. if $A \cap B = \emptyset$, then $P(A \cup B) = P(A) + P(B)$

then (X,P,G) is called a finitely additive probability space.

We immediately notice that measures f and P have the same properties except that conditions 2 and iii differ. In the case of fuzzy measure we require monotonicity (condition 2) whereas in the case of probability we require additivity (condition iii). Hence, from a measurement-theoretical point of view fuzziness is a more general property than probability as the measure of the latter can be derived as a special case of the former.

Obviously this conclusion depends on the concept of probability as an additive measure. Were we to employ a nonadditive probability measure, we would end up with a different conclusion. To this objection there is a straight-forward reply: dropping the assumption of additivity would be tantamount to giving up the axiom system of Kolmogoroff. There is no a priori reason why we should not do that. The crux of the issue is, however, that it is a matter of interpretation which formal properties we want our probability measure to possess. Of course, we can construct many types of measures and call them probability measures. Similarly, we can interpret our probability measures in such a way that they have nothing to do with our intuitive notion of probability. The same applies, of course, to fuzzy measures.

FUZZINESS IN DECISION-MAKING

Similarly as the candidates' positions may be interpreted as fuzzy sets in the issue dimension, the voters' optima may be so regarded. Each voter's action may, then, be analyzed as decision-making in a fuzzy environment, a setting that was first discussed by Bellman and Zadeh.[15] The voter's optimum is in this view a fuzzy goal-set in the issue dimension. According to Bellman and Zadeh a decision in a fuzzy setting like the present one may be seen as a confluence of goals and constraints. By confluence one may mean the intersection of the two fuzzy sets. This is by no means necessary, but depends on the interpretation of the situation. The flexibility in this respect may be regarded as one of the virtues of the fuzzy set model of the decision-making.

For the sake of simplicity let us consider the example adapted from Weisberg and Fiorina.[16] The issue dimension consists of points representing public expenditure on a given social security program, say. In the electoral contest there are two candidates, A and B, who — on the basis of their public statements, writings etc. — can be represented as fuzzy sets in the issue dimension. The vertical axis thus indicates the membership degrees of each point of the horizontal axis in the fuzzy set representing the candidate. Let us assume that candidate A has given the impression to the electorate that he stands for a 'moderate' spending on the program in question, whereas candidate B has been ambiguous giving one part of the electorate the impression that he stands for small spending and the other part the impression that he favors large spending. Hence we get the result seen in Figure 1.

FIGURE 1
Candidates A and B as fuzzy sets in a policy-dimension.
The membership degrees are measured by the vertical axis

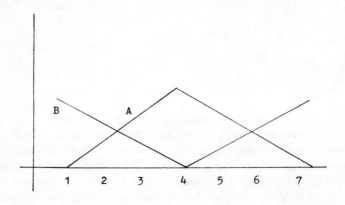

The fuzzy policy sets of A and B may — in accordance with Figure 1 — be defined as follows:

A = 0.0/1 + 0.4/2 + 0.8/3 + 1.0/4 + 0.8/5 + 0.4/6 + 0.0/7
B = 1.0/1 + 0.7/2 + 0.3/3 + 0.0/4 + 0.3/5 + 0.7/6 + 1.0/7

Now, the voter faced with the choice between these two candidates may have somewhat conflicting or 'mixed' motives about the social security program in question. These may be reflected in the following two goal-sets of the voter:

U = 0.0/1 + 0.3/2 + 0.4/3 + 0.5/4 + 0.6/5 + 0.3/6 + 0.0/7 and
V = 1.0/1 + 0.8/2 + 0.6/3 + 0.4/4 + 0.2/5 + 0.0/6 + 0.0/7.

The set U may be interpreted as reflecting somewhat favorable attitude on the part of the voter towards the program. He seems, however, to oppose the largest possible spendings. One could think this to be due to his opportunity cost calculations despite his in principle favorable attitude towards the program. The fuzzy set V, in turn, may quite straight-forwardly be interpreted in economic terms: the more spending on the program, the more costly it will become to the tax-payers. We can assume that the voter prefers less taxes. The voter's decision-making results now in a decision set which may be constructed so as to consider U as the goal, V as the constraint and confluence as the intersection of U and V.

	1	2	3	4	5	6	7
f_U	0.0	0.3	0.4	0.5	0.6	0.3	0.0
f_V	1.0	0.8	0.6	0.4	0.2	0.0	0.0
$F_{U \cap V}$	0.0	0.3	0.4	0.4	0.2	0.0	0.0

The fuzzy decision set $f_{U \cap V}$ can be given the interpretation 'vote for the candidate located at about 3 or 4'. This would be an optimizing decision in the case where the candidates have a single position in the issue dimension. Of course, this is not the only possible way of constructing the decision set. Some voters may tend to emphasize the closeness of alternatives to either one of the goal sets. In the constructions of the corresponding decision set one could, then, perhaps use the union instead of the intersection of the component goal sets. If the voter tends to emphasize both goals equally, then perhaps the arithmetic mean of the membership values would do best. In some other cases the algebraic product would be the most suitable construction etc.

But the act of voting still consists of picking out one alternative despite previous considerations. How could this crucial feature be accommodated in the framework of decision-making in the fuzzy environment? Obviously one has to consider now both the decision set and the candidates' policy sets. If the latter are non-fuzzy, the optimum voting strategy would be to vote for that candidate whose location has the largest value in the voter's decision set. If in the present example A's location is at 4 and B's at both 1 and 7, a rational voter would vote for A as 4 has the membership value 0.4 in the decision set, whereas the value of both 1 and 7 is 0.0.

In the case of genuinely fuzzy policy sets, the optimal decision is more difficult to determine. The problems are essentially similar as in the context of decision set construction. But it would — at least in some cases — be plausible to assume that the voters take into account the intersection of their decision set and the policy set of the candidates. Intuitively there would be some grounds for arguing that the voter who votes for the candidate having the maximum intersection set value is rational. This, at any rate, would be in accordance with the nonfuzzy policy set case discussed in the preceding paragraph. One readily notices that this strategy also suggests that the voter should vote for A.

The above example may be sufficient to point out the flexibility of the fuzzy set considerations in spatial analysis. Not only is it possible to consider several goals simultaneously, but it is also possible to translate constraints of decision-making into the same 'language' as goals. Moreover, there is no difficulty in incorporating the salience of certain goals into this framework. One simply considers convex combinations of goals and constraints so that the relative importance of each becomes visible. Further, the introduction of several issue dimensions does not cause any particular difficulties for the analysis of fuzzy goals and policy sets.

A REINTERPRETATION OF THE RESULTS OF THE FIORINA-PLOTT EXPERIMENT

As a more relevant illustration of a situation where the above calculus can be applied we shall briefly discuss the experiment conducted by Fiorina and Plott.[17] By saying that the calculus can be applied to that experiment I mean that the experimental results can plausibly be interpreted as ensuing from the application of a fuzzy decision-making by the subjects of the experiment.

In the experiment each of the five subjects was given an optimal point in a two-dimensional space as well as a set of indifference curves indicating the payoffs accruing to the player from any point of the space being chosen as the outcome of the collective decision making process. Simple majority rule was being applied. Each experimental run consisted of a search sequence whereby the subjects made amendments to proposed outcomes and then voted upon them. When no further amendments were proposed, the winner of the last ballot was considered as the final outcome. In one of the three series of experiments the configuration of voters' optima was that as shown in Figure 2.

FIGURE 2
Optimum point configuration in the Fiorina-Plott
game without a core (series 3)

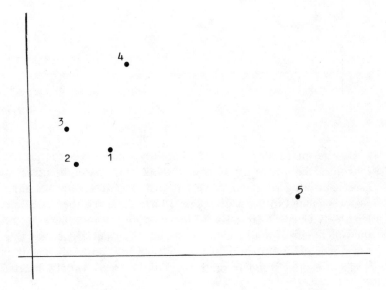

In this series the indifference curves are, by construction of the experimenters, circular, i.e. the loss functions are monotonically increasing with the euclidean distance of the collectively chosen outcome and the individual optimum point. Also by construction there is no voting equilibrium or — what amounts to the same thing in the present context — core. Fiorina and Plott report the distribution of final outcomes in 15 runs of the experiment (Figure 3).

FIGURE 3
The distribution of outcomes (x)

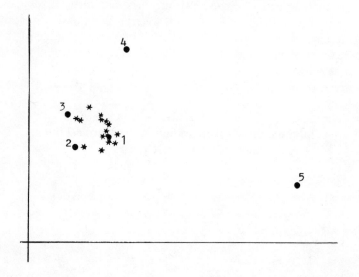

Despite the result proven by McKelvey which suggests that the outcomes should scatter all over the outcome space, we notice a clear clustering of them.[18] This is just one of several puzzling features related to the experiment. I have discussed them at some length elsewhere.[19] Here I shall focus on the curious clustering of the outcomes 'around' points 1, 2 and 3. I shall argue that this phenomenon is in principle explicable by postulating fuzzy decision-making behavior on the part of the experimental subjects.

Indeed, a very crude type of fuzzy calculus of 'satisficing' is sufficient to explain the clustering.

Suppose that each voter has a fuzzy goal set called 'satisfactory outcome'. We denote this set by $f_i (i = 1, \ldots 5)$. In three-dimensional representation the f_i's become surfaces over the two-dimensional issue space. We assume that for each voter i there is a critical value $\bar{f}_i$ of f_i such that for all $f_i(x,y) < \bar{f}_i$, the voter i deems the outcome (x,y) unsatisfactory. It is quite natural to assume, furthermore, that $f_i(x,y)$ is monotone non-increasing function of the distance of (x,y) and i's optimum. We now define for each voter i a function $h_i(x,y)$:

$$h_i(x,y) = \begin{cases} f_i(x,y) \text{ if } f_i(x,y) \geqslant \bar{f}_i \\ 0, \text{ otherwise} \end{cases}$$

Let us now form for any fixed point (x,y) the intersection of the fuzzy goal sets of those three voters having the largest $h_i(x,y)$ value. By definition, the membership value of (x,y) in the intersection set is the minimum of those three membership degree values $h_i(x,y)$. Let us denote the resulting intersection surface over the Re^2-space by $D(x,y)$ if the membership value of the point (x,y) in the intersection set is different from zero. Elsewhere $D(x,y)$ is undefined. The projection of $D(x,y)$ on the Re^2 – plane indicates those sets of points in the outcome set which are considered satisfactory by at least a simple majority of voters. Furthermore, the $D(x,y)$ values give the degree in which the worst-off person in the minimal winning coalition regards each point to belong to his or her goal set.

For some values of $\bar{f}_1$, $\bar{f}_2$ and $\bar{f}_3$ in Fig. 3 the set of predicted outcomes (the set of satisfactory ones from the view-point of a simple majority of voters) contains the set of observed outcomes in the Fiorina-Plott experiment. This can be verified by drawing circles with points 1, 2 and 3 as centers and radii of various lengths (Figure 4).

FIGURE 4
Satisficing outcomes for players 1, 2, 3 and 4 with
simple majority equilibria

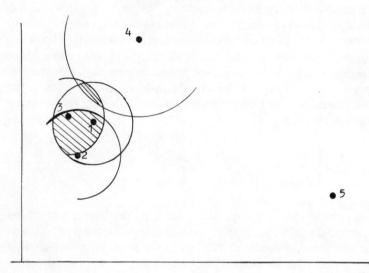

The shaded area in Figure 4 represents the outcome set if the voters 1, 2, 3 and 4 resort to the above outlined crude fuzzy decision-making. Incidentally, one of the experimental subjects reportedly told the experimenters that he was actually using the above kind of intellectual short-cut. Of course, as long as we have no idea of the f_i — values and f_i — functions of voters, Figure 4 is just one of many possible ones. What is interesting to see is that by changing the relative lengths of the radii of the circles we get a configuration that very closely coincides with the circumscribed area of observed outcomes in the Fiorina-Plott experiment.

COMBINED RANDOMNESS AND FUZZINESS

As was pointed out above it is intuitively clear that there is a difference between fuzziness and randomness: the latter deals with the uncertainty pertaining to the occurrence or non-occurrence of an event which in itself is entirely unambiguous and non-vague, whereas the former relates to difficulties in the classification of events. Events are fuzzy in virtue of the difficulties in classifying them. This intuitive distinction will do in the present context.

It was argued above that the notion of probabilistic or randomized policy appears somewhat unrealistic and counter-intuitive. If one is uncertain of whether the candidate is located at x_i or x_j in the issue dimension, it would be strange indeed in most cases if one knew or believed that the candidate was precisely at x_i with probability p and precisely at x_j with probability $1 - p$. The strangeness is the more conspicuous the more points there are in the issue dimension. The uncertainty most often seems to pertain to the exact location of the candidate in the neighborhood of some point in the dimension so that candidates can be interpreted as fuzzy sets in the issue dimension. It may be the case that there are several such points for a candidate in the dimension. In that case we would have both random and fuzzy policy as experienced by the voter. I would claim that in electoral competition the uncertainty facing the voter is either of a purely fuzzy nature or is both random and fuzzy. For example a voter may perceive a candidate's policy as follows 'the candidate would spend a large amount of public funds on a social welfare program T with probability 0.7'. 'Large amount' would in this case be a fuzzy set with some subjectively determined membership function defined over the dimension of, say, integers from 0 to 1 billion representing the sums of money in some currency.

Suppose that the candidate has managed to randomize his policy over a given issue dimension so that the voter perceives that the candidate may be representable as one of several fuzzy sets with given (subjective) probabilities. In general, the voter may not be interested in very fine distinctions, that is, he may not care whether the candidate is at x_i or x_j if these points are very close to each other. Hence, the voter is only interested in knowing which of the fuzzy sets characterizes the candidate. In the example discussed above the voter would try to determine which of the two fuzzy sets 'small spending' or 'large spending' really characterizes B. What would the voter, then, do? I think one can plausibly assume that he would attempt to eliminate the uncertainty concerning B's ambiguous position by reading and listening to the statements B had made on social security as well as collecting other evidence to the same purpose. Assuming that the voter perceives the candidate's position as both random and fuzzy along the policy dimension consisting of points representing e.g. expenditure on social security, we can now briefly outline a model of this type of decision-setting, that is, a situation in which both randomness and fuzziness are present as sources of uncertainty. The model has recently been devised for a slightly different situation by Asai, Tanaka and Okuda.[20]

We start with denoting by $X = \{x_i, \ldots, x_r\}$ the (finite) set of points in the policy dimension as done earlier in this paper. Let the voter be faced with an uncertainty concerning which one of two fuzzy sets A and B in X characterizes the candidate (whether he is big spender or small spender, say). The fuzzy sets A and B are defined by means of their characteristic functions f_A and f_B. We assume that the voter has an a priori probability distribution $p(x_i)$ $(i = 1, \ldots, r)$ over X. This may be interpreted as reflecting his hunches or previous experiences concerning the candidate's location. We make the assumption that each of the statements or rather the speeches or writings of the candidate can be characterized unambiguously by means of a variable $Y = [y_1, \ldots, y_v]$ i.e. a set of values (indicating the amounts of spending, say). Moreover, we assume that the conditional probability distribution $g(y_i|x_j)$ $(i = 1, \ldots, v; j = 1, \ldots, r)$ is known. This assumption is not entirely without justification: it is usually the case that when a candidate occupies a given position in the issue dimension, this fact restricts the possible range of variation of his statements. Depending on the kind of relationship in which X and Y are to each other — in the voter's opinion — the conditional probability distribution may be of a different shape. It reflects the voter's conception of how accurate an observation device Y he has at his disposal with respect to the underlying property X in which he is interested when contemplating his voting decision. In order to make his decision the voter needs to aggregate this probability density so that $g(y_i|A)$ and $g(y_i|B)$ can be constructed. The voting decision rule can, thereafter, be derived in accordance with Bayes' principle.

A more detailed account of the procedure can now be given. We define the probability of the fuzzy sets A and B

$$p(A) = \sum_{i=1}^{r} f_A(x_i) p(x_i)$$

$$p(B) = \sum_{i=1}^{r} f_B(x_i) p(x_i)$$

Furthermore, the joint probability of y_j, on the one hand, and A or B, on the other, for each $j = 1, \ldots, v$ is given by:

$$p(y_j \& A) = \sum_{i=1}^{r} f_A(x_i) \, g(y_j|x_i) \, p(x_i)$$

$$p(y_j \& B) = \sum_{i=1}^{r} f_B(x_i) \, g(y_j|x_i) \, p(x_i)$$

Now the conditional probability distribution of y_j given A or B is obtained as follows:

$$g(y_j|A) = p(y_j \& A)/p(A)$$
$$g(y_j|B) = p(y_j \& B)/p(B), \text{ for all } j = 1, \ldots, v.$$

Next the probability distribution of y_j is calculated by means of the following formula:

$$g(y_j) = g(y_j|A) \, p(A) + g(y_j|B) \, p(B).$$

The a posteriori conditional probabilities for A and B are derived as follows:

$$p(A|y_j) = p(y_j \& A)/g(y_j)$$
$$p(B|y_j) = p(y_j \& B)/g(y_j), \text{ for all } j = 1, \ldots, v.$$

Suppose now that the voter has a sequence of information

$\overline{y} = (y_{h(1)}, \ldots, y_{h(m)})$ of length $h(m)$ $(y_{h(i)} \in \{y_1, \ldots, y_v\}$ for all $i = 1, \ldots, m)$

at his disposal. This may simply be understood to mean that he has

listened to h(m) speeches or gained h(m) pieces of some other information about the candidate. The conditional probability of the sequence $\bar{y}$ given A or B can be calculated as follows:

$$g(\bar{y}|A) = \frac{1}{p(A)} \sum_{i=1}^{r} f_A(x_i) g(\bar{y}|x_i) p(x_i)$$

$$g(\bar{y}|B) = \frac{1}{p(B)} \sum_{i=1}^{r} f_B(x_i) g(\bar{y}|x_i) p(x_i)$$

Obviously we now need the conditional probabilities of observation
sequences given exact locations in the issue dimension. Using
Bayes' formula we obtain:

$$p(A|\bar{y}) = \frac{p(A) \, g(\bar{y}|A)}{p(A)g(\bar{y}|A) + p(B)g(\bar{y}|B)}$$

$$p(B|\bar{y}) = \frac{p(B) \, g(\bar{y}|B)}{p(A)g(\bar{y}|A) + p(B)g(\bar{y}|B)}$$

We notice that each of these conditional probabilities has the same
denumerator value. Hence, the comparison of probabilities is a
matter of comparing the numerators. It can be shown that the decision rule minimizing the average error probability in making decision about the candidates' locations leads to the decision A, if
$g(\bar{y}|A)p(A) \geqq g(\bar{y}|B)p(B)$ and to decision B otherwise.[21] This
would, then, mean that a voter attempting to find out a general
method for making decisions about the candidates' fuzzy locations
in the policy dimension would use the above expression if he wants
to minimize his average error probability. This is, thus, a picture of
a Bayesian voter in the spatial model of the electoral process.

CONCLUSIONS

In the preceding sections we have discussed probabilistic and fuzzy
models of uncertainty facing the voter and policy-maker in the
decision-making situation. While randomness is a fairly extensively

studied source of uncertainty, I have argued above that it would be somewhat counter-intuitive to consider randomness as the only source of uncertainty. Rather, vagueness seems to be involved in almost all electoral and other decision-making situations. The theory of fuzzy sets is particularly suitable for dealing with vague notions. In the preceding we have touched upon some possible ways of utilizing this theory. The previous sections show that while there is a conceptual distinction between probability and fuzziness, one can also distinguish methodologically between the two in some cases.

In the preceding sections we have deviated somewhat from the ordinary problem-setting of the spatial modelling approach. Instead of discussing the electoral equilibria resulting from given types of preference configurations of voters, we touched upon the problem of how rational voters form an opinion about the candidates' positions in a given issue dimension. In that context the problem of voter rationality was discussed in Bayesian terms. Thereby we introduced one more explication of rationality in addition to those commonly encountered in the literature: expected utility maximizer, minimax-regretter etc. It seems promising to dwell more deeply on the dynamic and sequential view of the decision-making process. The puzzling 'irrational' features sometimes encountered in empirical research could perhaps thereby become intelligible, resulting from the fact that in reality the decision-maker rarely is confronted with a choice of a single well-defined position in a policy domain, given a probability distribution of the alternatives over the domain. The 'givens' may be essentially more vague than the spatial modelling literature suggests.

I have not dealt with the problems of the empirical measurement of probabilities and membership degrees. Yet in this field there seems to be many open problems. Initial steps have, however, been taken in special areas of research.[22]

NOTES

The author wishes to thank Norman Schofield for comments on an earlier version of this paper. The suggestions made by Paul Whiteley have also been most helpful. The revisions were made during the author's stay as a British Academy Wolfson Fellow at the University of Essex.

1. A. Downs, *An Economic Theory of Democracy* (New York, 1957).
2. Ibid., 136.
3. K. Shepsle, 'The Strategy of Ambiguity', *The American Political Science Review* LXVI, 1972, 555-568; and 'Parties, Voters and Risk Environment', in R. Niemi and H. Weisberg (eds.), *Probability Models of Collective Decision-Making* (Columbus, 1972).
4. C. Plott, 'A Notion of Equilibrium and Its Possibility Under Majority Rule', *American Economic Review* 57, 1967, 787-806; C. Black, *The Theory of Committees and Elections* (Cambridge, 1958).
5. Shepsle, 'The Strategy...', op. cit.
6. See K. Fine, 'Vagueness, Truth and Logic', *Synthese* 30, 1975, 265-300; H. Nurmi, 'Probability and Fuzziness', *Sixth Research Conference on Subjective Probability, Utility, and Decision-Making* (Warszawa, September 1977); H. Nurmi, 'Modelling Impreciseness in Human Systems', *Fourth European Meeting on Cybernetics and Systems Research* (Linz, March 1978).
7. Shepsle, 'Parties...', op. cit., 280.
8. H. Weisberg and M. Fiorina, 'Candidate Preference Under Uncertainty', *IPSA* (Edinburgh, August 1976).
9. L. Zadeh, 'Fuzzy Sets', *Information and Control* 8, 1965, 338-353.
10. R. Bellman and L. Zadeh, 'Decision-Making in a Fuzzy Environment', *Management Science* 17, 1970, B142,
11. Nurmi, 'Probability...', op. cit.
12. A. De Luca and S. Termini, 'Measures of Ambiguity in the Analysis of Complex Systems', in: J. Gruska (ed.), *Mathematical Foundations of Computer Science 1977* (Berlin 1977).
13. Nurmi, 'Modelling...', op. cit.
14. T. Terano and M. Sugeno, 'Conditional Fuzzy Measures and Their Applications', in: L. Zadeh et al. (eds.) *Fuzzy Sets and Their Applications to Cognitive and Decision Processes* (New York, 1975).
15. Bellman and Zadeh, op. cit.
16. Weisberg and Fiorina, op. cit.
17. M. Fiorina and C. Plott, 'Committee Decisions under Majority Rule', *The American Political Science Review* LXXII, 1978, 575-595.
18. R. McKelvey, 'Intransitivities in Multidimensional Voting Models and Implications for Agenda Control, *Journal of Economic Theory* 12, 1976, 472-482.
19. H. Nurmi, 'A Fuzzy Solution to a Majority Voting Game', manuscript (October 1978).
20. K. Asai, H. Tanaka and T. Okuda, 'On Discrimination of Fuzzy States in Probability Space', *Kybernetes* 6, 1977, 185-192. For a general discussion on probability and fuzziness in decision making, see R. Capocelli and A. De Luca, 'Fuzzy Sets and Decision Theory', *Information and Control* 20, 1973, 446-473.
21. See Asai et al., op. cit., 187.

22. See P. Macvicar-Whelan, 'Classification of Human Heights', mimeo (Toulouse, May 1976); M. Nowakowska, 'Methodological Problems of Measurement of Fuzzy Concepts in the Social Sciences', *Behavioral Science* 22, 1977, 107-115; H. Nurmi, *Rationality and Public Goods* (Helsinki, 1977) 53-67.

V Strategic Behaviour at the National and International Levels

13 Strategic Voting: An Empirical Analysis with Dutch Roll Call Data

Menno Wolters

State University of Utrecht, The Netherlands

Since Arrow published his *Social Choice and Individual Values* in 1951,[1] American roll-call analysts (and scholars with a formal orientation towards decision-making processes), have been interested in the phenomenon of strategic voting. Empirical writers have noted and sometimes shown its occurrence in American national and state legislatures. Others have analysed strategic voting as a wilful and calculated endeavour of legislators to create an instance of the 'Voters' Paradox' (which is alternatively known as the 'Paradox of Condorcet' or 'Arrow's Paradox').

The main analytical technique for studying roll-calls has, up to now, been Guttman scaling. It is not surprising, then, that the first and, so far, only techniques for highlighting patterns of strategic voting in a set of roll-calls are to be used against a background of Guttman scaling. These techniques are found in a contribution by McCrone to *Legislative Studies Quarterly*.[2] We leave it to him to unfold four Models of Strategic Voting:

To some extent, all voting is strategic; only the situation and possible alternatives differ. As Ferejohn and Fiorina[3] note: 'Legislators are goal-seeking agents who choose from available strategic alternatives to further their ends'. The simplest, and probably most frequent, strategy is the straightforward one of *sincere voting*. Sincere voting occurs when voters vote directly in accordance with their personal preference scale (Farquharson).[4] If a voter prefers A to B, and B to C, he will vote for A. Failing to achieve his desire for the victory of A, if A is eliminated from a subsequent ballot, he will vote for B over C.

More complex voting strategies yield patterns of voting which do not reflect, directly, the voter's personal preference scale (Niemi and Riker).[5] The voter may vote for B, in the first instance, because he believes that A has no chance of winning or that it is possible to eliminate C (his least preferred outcome) and then vote for A against B.

We will consider, verbally and graphically, four major voting strategies. First, in Figure 1a, we have an instance of *simple sincere voting*. As a voter's support for a particular policy dimension increases, his propensity to support (or oppose) a bill or amendment designed to strengthen (or weaken) that policy increases. For example, on an amendment to extend the coverage of a minimum wage bill from large to small businesses, the greater a congressman's support for minimum wages in general, the more likely he is to support the amendment.

Second, in Figure 1b, we display a case of *simple reverse voting*. As a voter's support on a policy dimension increases, his propensity to support (or oppose) a bill or amendment designed to strengthen (or weaken) that policy decreases. For example, as a Congressman's support for minimum wages in general increases, the more likely he is to reject an amendment to increase the bill's coverage from large to small businesses. Why? The amendment, whatever its source, is seen by both proponents and opponents of minimum wages to be a threat to the prospects of the bill's passage into law. Opponents of minimum wage legislation vote for the amendment in the belief that the adoption of this amendment will kill the bill. Proponents of minimum wage legislation vote against the amendment to avoid killing the bill.

Third, in Figure 1c, we have the first of two complementary non-linear forms of strategic voting. In *concave strategic voting*, strong proponents and strong opponents of a policy dimension combine in an attempt to strengthen legislation reflecting that dimension or to prevent attempts to weaken the legislation. For example, opponents and proponents of minimum wages both vote to expand coverage from large to small business. Conversely, they both may vote against an amendment to reduce coverage from large and small businesses to large businesses only. The proponents of minimum wages are voting sincerely, i.e. in accordance with their preference scale. The opponents are engaged in reverse voting. Why? The opponents of minimum wages believe that the comprehensive bill will be defeated, while the weaker bill will pass. In order to prevent the increase of minimum wages, they are willing to gamble on the failure of the entire bill. The proponents of minimum wages are willing to risk the defeat of the strong bill in order to gain maximum coverage.

Fourth, in Figure 1d, we have our second type of nonlinear strategic voting. In *convex strategic voting*, strong opponents and strong proponents of a policy dimension combine in an attempt to weaken or to defeat a bill reflecting that dimension. For example, proponents and opponents of minimum wages may vote to reduce coverage or to defeat a weakened minimum wage bill. The opponents of minimum wages are voting sincerely, but the proponents are engaged in reverse voting. Why? The proponents of mimimum wages believe, in the first case, that only through weakening the bill will it have a chance of passage. If they vote to defeat a weakened minimum wage bill, they may have concluded that it is better to produce maximum continuing pressure for strong minimum wage legislation, rather than settling for partial results. They are willing to gamble that strong minimum wage legislation will result, eventually, from defeat of a weak bill. Opponents of minimum wages are willing to settle for a weakened bill.

In this discussion of these types of strategic voting, we have tried to provide illustrative, rather than exhaustive, rationales for these voting patterns. Whatever the rationale, we need some method for identifying simple sincere voting, simple reverse voting, concave strategic voting and convex strategic voting.

In the remainder of his article, McCrone proposes first- and second-degree polynomial regression techniques. Simple sincere and reverse voting should correspond to first-degree regression with positive and negative coefficients, respectively. Both forms of curvilinear strategic voting should correspond to second-degree polynomials, with, again, appropriate signs for the coefficients. Concave strategic voting yields a negative regression coefficient for X and a positive one for X^2. Convex strategic voting produces a positive coefficient for X and a negative one for X^2.

In summary, McCrone proposes a battery of techniques, consisting of, in sequence, Guttman scaling a set of roll-calls to uncover the underlying policy dimension and the scale scores of the legislators, first-degree polynomial and one-term regression analysis of voting behavior against Guttman scale scores to highlight instances of simple reverse voting (i.e. roll-calls with negative regression coefficients), and second-degree polynomial and one-term regression analysis of voting behavior against Guttman scale scores to single out both forms of curvilinear strategic voting (discriminating between them according to the signs of the regression coefficients).

STRATEGIC VOTING AND THE PROXIMITY SCALE

Guttman scaling is just one of a range of related scaling techniques to describe a set of roll-calls according to various models of roll-call

FIGURE 1
McCrone's models of strategic voting. Borrowed from
D. J. McCrone (1977)[2] with minor adaptations

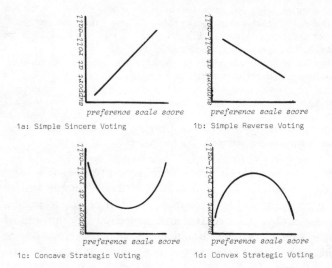

1a: Simple Sincere Voting   1b: Simple Reverse Voting

1c: Concave Strategic Voting   1d: Convex Strategic Voting

Note: As a voter's preference scale score increases, his/her support for the
policy dimension increases.

behavior.[6] If the dimension underlying the voting behavior of the legislature cannot be detected by means of Guttman scaling, Mc-Crone's observations do not apply. His approach is very fruitful, however, as third- and fourth-degree polynomial regression analysis appear useful tools for the detection of strategic voting.

In an ongoing study of the Dutch Parliament that takes into account all roll-calls held in both Chambers between 1963 and 1971, the present author has found that over 80 per cent of the roll-calls on bills (excluding amendments, resolutions and motions of order), taken under each of the subsequent cabinets, can be fully explained as unidimensional proximity voting.[7] The exact rank order of the parliamentary parties on the dimension varies slightly over the years, but is clearly of the form *extreme left — moderate left — 'government' — christian-democrats — liberals — extreme right*. Though the government as such is not represented in either

Chamber (ministers and secretaries of state are not allowed to be members of parliament), it advises the parliamentarians how to vote; these recommendations can be conceived as the government's roll-call behavior in order to locate the cabinet on the dimension.

The central position of the government on the dimension deserves more comment. Practically all bills are introduced by the government into parliament, and the government has the right to withdraw its bill whenever it threatens to be amended in a way unacceptable to the government. It does not happen, therefore, that the government advises against a bill, since it would rather withdraw it than object to it. Technically, therefore, the government's position on the dimension is the combined positive anchor point of two Guttman scales, a scale of the parties of the right (global rank order *'government'* — *christian-democrats* — *liberals* — *extreme right*), and one of the parties of the left (global rank order *'government'* — *moderate left* — *extreme left*). The extreme parties are the ones casting nays most of the time; the more moderate a party is, the more it tends to cast ayes — especially if the party is represented in the cabinet. The rank order of the bills on both Guttman scales differs; this indicates that the salience of the issues varies, and that some bills are regarded as more left-wing and others as more right-wing.

The pervasiveness of the unidimensional left-right structure in all 100 per cent of the roll-calls on bills (again, excluding amendments, resolutions and motions of order) is strikingly high. The present author removed all roll-calls that fit both Guttman scales perfectly, and thus retained only roll-calls with error on one or both scales. The same Guttman scales were found with reasonable (significant) scalibility and reproducibility coefficients. This is something of a crash test to show that the impact of the left-right dimension is general and not confined to any one policy domain, such as economic policy, social security, nationalization or free enterprise. Conversely, roll-call voting in any one policy domain can be expected to conform to the general left-right dimension.

According to McCrone, simple sincere voting occurs when legislators vote directly in accordance with their personal preferences. The meaning of this observation differs slightly when the context is that of proximity scaling rather than Guttman scaling. In proximity voting, legislators compare the bill at the vote to

FIGURE 2
Models of sincere proximity voting. Support at roll-call
against preference scale score on a LEFT-RIGHT continuum

2a: Right-sided Linear Sincere Voting

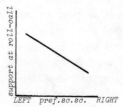

2b: Left-sided Linear Sincere Voting

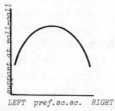

2c: Convex Sincere Voting

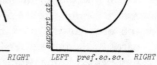

2d: Concave Sincere Voting

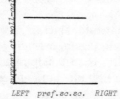

2e: Unanimous Sincere Voting (aye)

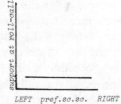

2f: Unanimous Sincere Voting (nay)

Note: Both forms of Unanimous Sincere Voting (2e and 2f) are bastard forms
      of Linear Sincere Voting (2a and 2b), which in turn are bastard forms
      of Convex and Concave Sincere Voting (2c and 2d).

some internal reference point (e.g. their political ideals or platforms or the party line) rather than to one or more alternative proposals. Basically, the extremes of left and right combine to vote against the bill which is backed by some coherent set of parties in the center: this might be called 'convex sincere voting'. Instances of unanimous and 'linear sincere voting' must be regarded as simplifications of the curvilinear pattern. Figure 2 portrays the basic and bastard models of sincere voting in a way similar to McCrone's Figure 1.

Figure 2 also depicts concave sincere voting: the extremes of left and right vote for a proposal which is rejected by the government and the center. In this case, one might think of a move to dismiss the cabinet, or an amendment to lower taxes so that the government's budget will fall short. Of course, the opposition parties rather than the government would introduce such proposals.

It seems to be the case, then, that both first- and second-degree polynomial regression may correspond to sincere voting, if the underlying model of roll-call behavior is that of proximity voting. More specifically, the linear models should be regarded bastard forms of the quadratic models.

Each of these models of sincere voting has its corollary in the range of reverse voting. There is a model of convex reverse voting and one of concave reverse voting, and there are bastard forms of linear reverse voting and unanimous voting. From McCrone's discussion of reverse voting, quoted above, it will be clear how these models relate to sincere voting. Since content analysis of proposal and debate is the only way to make out whether a specific roll-call is an instance of reverse voting rather than of sincere voting, and since content analysis must remain beyond the scope of this paper, reverse voting will be left out of focus in the sequel.

It is a characteristic feature of McCrone's curvilinear models of strategic voting that strong proponents and strong opponents line up against moderates. How should this idea be elaborated in the area of proximity voting? In order to keep the discussion simple and straightforward, the example is that of an amendment to a bill introduced by the government; the government is among the strong opponents of the amendment.

Imagine first that, if the parties would vote sincerely, the roll-call would be a case of concave sincere voting. That is, the extreme parties of left and right are among the strong proponents of the amendment, the government and the constituting coalition partners are among the opponents, whereas the moderate opposition parties of left and right (and perhaps a disloyal government party) are rather indifferent. Cut the underlying dimension at its anchor point ('government') and analyse the constituting Guttman scales separately. If the government is among the sincere voters, whereas the extreme party on either scale is voting strategically, the result on each scale is convex strategic voting. Considering the whole dimension rather than its parts, we may term this 'double convex strategic voting'. If, on the other hand, the government is among the strategic voters and the extreme parties vote sincerely, the result will be an instance of 'double concave strategic voting'. Moreover, the case may be that the extreme left is involved in strategic voting whereas the extreme right is not (left-sided convex strategic voting or left-sided concave strategic voting) or vice-versa (right-sided convex strategic voting or right-sided concave strategic voting). Figure 3 shows all double and one-sided forms of strategic voting.

It will be clear from Figure 3 that fourth- and third-degree polynomial regression analysis does the job of detecting examples of double and one-sided strategic voting. Double convex strategic voting produces a fourth-degree polynomial with a negative coefficient for X^4; double concave strategic voting yields a fourth-degree polynomial with a positive coefficient for X^4. The one-sided cases correspond to third-degree polynomials.[8] Left-sided convex strategic voting and left-sided concave strategic voting yield positive coefficients for X^3; both forms of right-sided strategic voting produce negative coefficients for X^3. One-sided convex strategic voting stands out from its concave counterpart in that the government's vote is against rather than for the motion.

In the Dutch case (i.e. a multi-party system with strong party cohesion) the cumbersome repeated use of polynomial regression analysis is not necessary. A simple sign test is sufficient. Just write down the parties in the rank order found along the underlying dimension, and note how many runs (sets of adjacent parties casting identical votes) are found for the roll-call. An nth-degree polynomial yields n + 1 runs.[9]

Two caveats are in order at this point. First, the discussion was deliberately limited to the case of an amendment against the

TABLE 3
Models of strategic proximity voting. Support at roll-call against preference scale score on a LEFT-RIGHT continuum

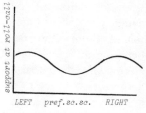

3a: Double Convex Strategic Voting

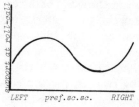

3b: Left-sided Convex Strategic Voting

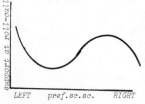

3c: Right-sided Convex Strategic Voting

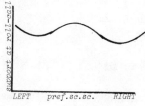

3d: Double Concave Strategic Voting

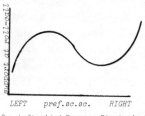

3e: Left-sided Concave Strategic Voting

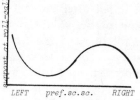

3f: Right-sided Concave Strategic Voting

Note: All of these models are based on the assumption that sincere voting would yield a concave curve. A comparable series of models can be drawn for the case of convex sincere voting.

government's plans. The reader should go through it again for the case that the government is among the proponents of the motion, or is neutral — and arrive at the same conclusion: in general, strategic voting is equivalent to fourth- or third-degree polynomial regression. Second, both regression analysis and analysis of runs (but especially the latter) are subject to a tendency to underestimate the number of runs (the number of maxima and minima in the case of regression). Underestimation occurs when one run is missing so that those at either side coalesce, reducing the manifest number of runs by two. In the subsequent analysis, there may be cases of strategic voting among the roll-calls registered as first- or second-degree polynomials; and there may even be roll-calls registered as third- or fourth-degree polynomials which do not fit the unidimensional model.[10]

THE CABINET-MARIJNEN (1963-1965)

The cabinet headed by Minister-President V. G. M. Marijnen ruled from 25 July 1963 until 27 February 1965, and was a coalition of ARP, CHU, KVP and VVD. It came into power after regular elections; it fell after internal disagreement between VVD and the religious parties. The Cabinet-Marijnen ruled with demissionary status till 14 April 1965; no roll-calls were taken after its fall in February. Table 1 shows the composition of Second and First Chambers in those days; it should be stressed that there was no right-wing opposition in the First Chamber.

All roll-calls on bills (excluding amendments, resolutions and motions of order) are exposed in Table 2. The table shows the results of the search for Guttman scales: as stated above, there is a scale of the left (*Government* — *moderate left* (PvdA) — *extreme left* (CPN, PSP)) and one of the right (*Government* — *christian-democrats* (ARP, CHU, KVP) — *liberals* (VVD) — *extreme right* (BP, SGP)); various statistics are given in the bottom of the table. There are slight differences between Second and First Chambers such as the order of CPN and PSP; the former seems to be less oppositional. KVP is located to the right of the Government to ensure optimal similarity to scales under later cabinets; the same is, in fact, true for ARP and CHU.

TABLE 1
Political Parties in the Dutch Parliament

party	full name	description	N FC 1963	N SC 1963	N SC 1967
KVP	Katholieke Volks Partij	Roman Catholic People's Party	26	50	42†
PvdA	Partij van de Arbeid	Labor; Social-Democratic Party	25	43	37
VVD	Vereniging voor Vrijheid en Demokratie	Association for Freedom and Democracy; Conservative Liberals	7	16	17
ARP	Anti-Revolutionaire Partij	Anti-Revolutionary Party; Protestant party opposed to French revolution	7	13	15
CHU	Christelijk-Historische Unie	Christian Historical Association; conservative Protestant party	7	13	12
CPN	Communistische Partij Nederland	Communist Party of The Netherlands	1	4	5
PSP	Pacifistisch Socialistische Partij	Pacifistic Socialistic Party; left-wing Socialists	2	4	4
BP	Boerenpartij	Peasants' Party; right-wing protest party	0	3	7√
SGP	Staatkundig Gereformeerde Partij	Political Reformed Party; theocrats	0	3	3
GPV	Gereformeerd Politiek Verbond	Reformed Political Union; Protestant party more opposed to French revolution	0	1	1
D'66	Demokraten '66	Democratic party founded in 1966; left-wing Liberals	0	0	7
PPR	Politieke Partij Radikalen	Political Party of the Radicals; left-wing Protestants and Catholics	0	0	3†

N FC 1963 = number of seats in First Chamber from May 16, 1963 on

N SC 1963 = number of seats in Second Chamber from May 15, 1963 on

N SC 1967 = number of seats in Second Chamber from February 2, 1967 on

† in 1968 3 members (out of 42) of KVP split off to constitute PPR

√ between 1967 and 1971 BP suffered from various splits, re-splits and reunions

TABLE 2a
Roll-calls on Bills, Cabinet-Marijnen (1963-1965)

Second Chamber. Coalition of KVP, CHU, ARP, and VVD.

bill	date	PSP	CPN	PvdA	Gov	KVP	CHU	ARP	VVD	GPV	SGP	BP	N of runs
6831	631022	+	+	+	+	+	+	+	+	+	-	-	2
7019	631022	+	+	+	+	+	+	+	+	+	-	-	2
7232	631128	+	+	+	+	+	+	+	+	+	-	-	2
7400	631210	-	-	+	+.	+	+	+	+	+	+	+	2
6811	640129	-	-	-	+	+	+	+	+	-	-	-	3
7535	640212	-	-	+	+	+	+	+	+	+	+	+	2
6188	640225	-	?	-	+	+	+	+	+	+	-	-	3
7559	640304	?	+	+	+	+	+	+	-	-	-	-	2
4800	640318	-	-	-	+	+	+	+	+	+	-	-	3
4108	640428	-	-	+	+	+	+	+	+	+	+	+	2
7591	640526	+	+	Δ	+	+	+	+	+	?	+	?	3†
5380	640527	-	-	-	+	+	?	?	?	?	?	?	2
5380	640527	?	-	-	+	+	?	?	?	?	?	?	.2
7074	640623	-	-	+	+	+	+	+	+	+	+	+	2
7202	640624	+	+	+	+	+	+	+	+	+	-	-	2
7582	640701	+	+	+	+	+	+	+	+	-	-	Δ	3†
7613	640701	-	-	+	+	+	+	+	+	+	+	-	3
7643	640916	+	+	+	+	+	+	+	Δ	+	+		4†
7736	641117	+	+	Δ	+	+	+	+	+	+	+	-	4†
7800	641125	-	-	+	+	+	+	+	+	+	+	+	2
7733	641201	Δ or Δ	+	+	+	+	+	+	+	+	-	-	4†
7813	641202	-	-	-	+	+	+	+	+	+	-	-	3
7800	650202	-	-	+	+	+	+	+	+	+	+	+	2
7540	650210	-	-	+	+	+	+	+	+	?	+	+	2
7187	650223	-	-	+	+	+	+	+	+	+	+	+	2
7203	650223	Δ	-	-	+	+	+	+	+	+	+	-	4†

There are 6 errors in 6 roll-calls in 4 or 5 parties. N = 26.

The following statistics are calculated as if the full scale were a Guttman scale:

Coefficient of Reproducibility = .98   *Minimum Marginal Reproducibility = .77*

Percent Improvement = .21   *Coefficient of Scalability = .91*

Δ erroneous vote   † erroneous roll-call

TABLE 2b

First Chamber. Coalition of KVP, CHU, ARP and VVD.

bill	date	PSP	CPN	PvdA	Gov	KVP	CHU	ARP	VVD	N of runs
6512	631008	+	?	+	+	+	-	-	$\overset{+}{\Delta}$	3†
6611	631105	-	?	-	+	+	+	+	+	2
7400	640204	-	-	+	+	+	+	+	+	2
7400	640218	-	-	+	+	+	+	+	+	2
7400	640218	-	-	+	+	+	+	+	+	2
7400	640317	-	-	+	+	+	+	+	+	2
7400	640317	-	-	+	+	+	+	+	+	2
7533	640324	-	-	-	+	+	+	+	+	2
7533	640324	-	?	-	+	+	+	+	+	2
7400	640526	-	-	+	+	+	+	+	+	2
7400	640602	-	-	+	+	+	+	+	+	2
4800	640616	-	-	+	+	+	+	+	-	3
7591	640623	-	-	-	+	+	+	+	+	2
4108	640714	-	-	+	+	+	+	+	+	2
4108	640714	-	-	+	+	+	+	+	+	2
7613	640908	-	-	+	+	+	+	+	+	2
7636	640908	-	-	+	+	+	+	+	+	2
6811	640929	-	-	-	+	+	+	+	+	2
7074	641117	-	-	+	+	+	+	+	+	2
7643	641201	-	+	+	+	+	+	+	-	3
5380	641208	-	$\overset{+}{\Delta}$ or $\overset{-}{\Delta}$	+	+	+	+	+	+	4†
5380	641208	-	$\overset{+}{\Delta}$ or $\overset{-}{\Delta}$	+	+	+	+	+	+	4†
7603	641208	+	+	+	+	+	+	$\overset{-}{\Delta}$ or $\overset{+}{\Delta}$	+	3†
7896	641222	-	$\overset{+}{\Delta}$ or $\overset{-}{\Delta}$	+	+	+	+	+	+	4†
7813	650119	-	-	-	+	+	+	+	+	2
7733	650202	-	-	+	+	+	+	+	+	2
7733	650202	-	$\overset{+}{\Delta}$ or $\overset{-}{\Delta}$	+	+	+	+	+	+	4†
7800	650223	-	-	+	+	+	+	+	+	2
7800	650223	-	-	+	+	++	+	+	+	2

There are 6 errors in 6 roll-calls in 2 or 3 or 4 parties. N = 29.

The following statistics are computed for the scale of the Left (4 parties):

Coefficient of Reproducibility = .96   *Minimum Marginal Reproducibility = .50*

Percent Improvement = .46   *Coefficient of Scalability = .92*

Δ erroneous vote   † erroneous roll-call

Table 2 provides, with few exceptions, the picture of a unidimensional proximity voting polity. How do roll-calls on resolutions and amendments relate to this? Table 3 presents for each resolution the number of runs of positive c.q. negative votes (ignoring missing data) and the number of errors calculated in two ways. The first column headed 'number of errors' produces the number of votes deviating from the most resembling proximity pattern; the other column lists the number of votes deviating from the most resembling pattern of proximity or strategic voting. One might as well say that the former column presents the number of changes one should make in the data to reduce the number of runs to a maximum of three; whereas the latter column reduces the number of runs to a maximum of five.

TABLE 3
Roll-calls on Resolutions, Cabinet-Marijnen (1963-1965).
Coalition of KVP, ARP, CHU and VVD

bill	date	PSP	CPN	PvdA	Gv	KVP	CHU	ARP	VVD	GPV	SGP	BP	NofR	NofE	StrE	N/S/E
Second Chamber:																
7400	631121	+	+	+	-	-	-	-	-	?	-	-	2	0	0	N
7400	631121	+	+	+	-	-	-	-	-	?	-	-	2	0	0	N
7533	640304	+	+	+	-	-	-	-	-	-	-	-	2	0	0	N
7800	641217	+	+	+	+	-	-	-	-	-	-	-	2	0	0	N
7800	650204	+	+	+	+	-	-	-	-	?	-	-	2	0	0	N
7800	650204	+	+	+	+	+	+	+	-	-	?	?	2	0	0	N
7605	650223	-	-	-	+	+	+	-	+	+	+	+	4	1	0	S
First Chamber:																
5380	641208	-	?	+	-	+	-	-	+	?	?	?	6	2	1	E

There are 3 errors in 2 roll-calls against the proximity pattern; 1 error in
1 roll-call against the proximity or strategic proximity patterns. N = 8.

NofR = number of runs

NofE = number of errors against the proximity pattern

StrE = number of errors against the proximity or strategic proximity patterns

N/S/E= nature of the pattern: normal proximity / strategic / error pattern

TABLE 4
Roll-calls on Amendments, Cabinet-Marijnen (1963-1965)

bill	date	PSP	CPN	PvdA	Gv	KVP	CHU	ARP	VVD	GPV	SGP	BP	NofR	NofE	StrE	N/S/E
7400	631112	-	+	-	+	-	-	-	-	-	+	+	6	2	1	E
7400	631121	+	+	+	-	-	-	-	-	?	-	-	2	0	0	N
7400	631121	+	+	+	-	-	-	-	-	?	-	-	2	0	0	N
7400	631212	+	+	+	-	-	-	-	-	-	-	?	2	0	0	N
7505	631213	+	+	+	-	-	-	-	-	?	-	-	2	0	0	N
6780	640128	+	-	+	-	+	+	+	-	+	+	+	7	2	1	E
6780	640128	+	?	+	-	+	-	+	-	?	-	+	7	2	1	E
6811	640129	+	+	+	-	-	+	-	-	+	+	-	6	2	1	E
6811	640129	-	+	+	-	-	-	-	+	?	-	+	6	2	1	E
6811	640129	-	-	-	+	+	-	-	+	-	-	+	6	2	1	E
7559	640304	?	-	-	+	+	+	+	+	+	+	-	3	0	0	N
4800	640318	+	+	+	-	-	-	-	-	-	+	+	3	0	0	N
7044	640428	-	-	-	-	+	+	+	-	+	+	+	4	1	0	S
5380	640527	-	-	-	+	+	+	-	+	+	+	+	4	1	0	S
5380	640527	-	-	-	+	+	+	-	+	+	+	+	4	1	0	S
5380	640527	+	+	+	-	-	-	-	+	-	-	+	5	1	0	S
5380	640527	-	-	-	-	+	-	-	-	?	-	-	3	0	0	N
5380	640527	-	-	-	-	-	-	-	+	-	-	+	6	2	1	E
5380	640527	+	+	+	-	-	-	-	-	-	-	-	2	0	0	N
5380	640527	+	+	+	-	-	-	-	-	-	-	+	3	0	0	N
5380	640527	-	-	-	+	+	-	-	+	?	-	-	5	1	0	S
5380	640527	+	+	+	-	-	-	-	-	-	-	+	3	0	0	N
5380	640527	-	-	-	+	+	+	+	+	+	+	-	3	0	0	N
6808	640616	+	+	+	-	-	+	-	+	-	+	+	7	2	1	E
7762	641110	+	+	+	-	-	-	-	-	-	-	-	2	0	0	N
7736	641117	+	+	+	-	-	+	-	-	-	-	-	4	1	0	S
7800	641124	+	+	+	-	-	-	-	-	?	-	+	3	0	0	N
7733	641201	-	+	-	+	+	+	+	+	+	+	+	4	1	0	S
7733	641201	+	+	+	-	-	-	-	-	-	-	+	3	0	0	N
7813	641202	-	-	-	+	+	+	+	+	+	-	-	3	0	0	N
7800	641221	+	+	+	-	-	-	-	-	-	-	-	2	0	0	N

See Table 3. N = 31; there are 16 normal proximity patterns, 7 strategic proximity patterns, and 8 errorpatterns.

It is not surprising, then, that the latter column adds up to a lower total number of errors than the former. The difference is not convincing, however, as only three errors against the proximity pattern have been found, of which two can be explained by strategic voting. The preliminary conclusion at this point can only be that strategic voting may have occurred at two out of eight resolutions, whereas one roll-call fits neither the models of sincere proximity voting nor those of strategic voting.

Table 4 presents the roll-calls on amendments discussed during the Marijnen period. It is fully comparable to Table 3; note that the First Chamber has not got the right to amend and is absent from the table.

The first, naïve, conclusion from Table 4 must be that in seventeen cases the unidimensional proximity model explains the data and in eight additional cases strategic voting may have occurred, whereas seven more roll-calls are error patterns under any model. Inspection of the data, however, tells that the number of strategic voting cases is being overestimated rather than underestimated. Some roll-calls, if not most of them, are simply improbable patterns of strategic voting. For example, it does not make sense for the small and extreme parties to vote strategic (i.e. against their sincere preferences) if the outcome of the vote among the main parties is completely unambiguous. Add these roll-calls to those which cannot be explained by strategic voting anyway, and it will be clear that little is to be gained by assuming the occurrence of strategic voting. Rather, a different explanation should be sought for the non-scale patterns among the roll-calls on amendments.

Table 5 presents a summary of comparable analyses of roll-calls on resolutions and amendments taken between 1965 and 1971. By and large, the conclusions must be similar: the concept of strategic voting is not a useful tool in explaining a substantive amount of roll-calls.

STRATEGIC VOTING
AND THE VOTERS' PARADOX

Arrow[11] and various writers after him[12] have shown that strategic

TABLE 5
Roll-calls on Resolutions and Amendements (1963-1971).
(Summary table)

period	Cabinet	coalition parties	NofE	NofP	NofS	NofEP	NofRC	nature
63-65	Marijnen	ARP, CHU, KVP, VVD	3	6	1	1	8	resol.
"	"	" " " "	23	16	7	8	31	amend.
65-66	Cals	ARP, KVP, PvdA	4	7	4	0	11	resol.
"	"	" " "	12	10	8	2	20	amend.
66-67	Zijlstra	ARP, KVP	4	6	2	1	9	r + a
70-71	De Jong	ARP, CHU, KVP, VVD	10	11	4	3	18	resol.
"	"	" " " "	119	78	51	34	163	amend.

NofE = number of errors against proximity pattern

NofP = number of correct proximity pattern roll-calls

NofS = number of correct strategic proximity pattern roll-calls

NofEP= number of error pattern roll-calls

NofRC= number of roll-calls = NofP + NofS + NofEP

nature = nature of the roll-calls (resolutions or amendments or both)

Note: As stated in the text, many of the roll-calls with strategic voting patterns are improbable instances of strategic voting.

voting is a wilful and calculated endeavour of legislators to create the Voters' Paradox. Does the conclusion, that strategic voting does not occur very often (and perhaps never), imply that paradoxical voting is infrequent or non-existent in the Dutch Parliament?

In its basic form, the Voters' Paradox is a cyclical and inconclusive sequence of roll-calls on three alternative proposals among three groups of legislators with different preferences. Legislator (or group of legislators) X prefers proposal a over b over c; legislator Y prefers b over c over a; and legislator Z prefers c over a over b. Subsequent roll-calls of a against b (a winning), a against c (c winning), c against b (b winning) and b against a (a winning) would produce an unending series of alternating majorities. In the real life of most parliamentary House Rules, however, taking votes on previously rejected proposals is precluded, so that the cycle stops at the arbitrary point in time of c beating a.

Strategic voting produces such a cyclical (and arbitrarily ending) series of roll-calls in situations when sincere voting would not lead to a paradox. Say, legislator X prefers a over b over c; Y prefers b over c over a; and Z prefers c over b over a (whereas c over a over b in the example above). Proposal b would beat a in the first roll-call, and would subsequently beat c in the second roll-call. Since a is the least preferred of both Y and Z, a has little chance of winning. Z has a chance to make c beat a and b by strategic voting, however. If Z votes for a rather than for b at the first roll-call, the second roll-call is between a and c rather than between b and c, and by consequence c wins. Subsequent roll-calls along this line would reveal, however, that b would beat c, which exposes the paradox. By changing its preference order from c over b over a to c over a over b, Z creates the paradox. At the first roll-call, the strong proponent of a, X, and the strong opponent Z combine forces against the moderate Y — to put it in McCrone's words. At the second and final roll-call, legislators vote sincerely.

When we try to substitute more substantial concepts for the proposals a, b and c, taking into account the rules that bills are introduced first, then amendments, whereas roll-calls are taken between amendments and proposed bills first, then between final (possibly amended) proposals and the status quo, a might be an amendment to bill b which proposes to change the status quo c. Thus, strategic voting at the roll-call over the amendment against the bill is an endeavour to create a paradox out of this roll-call and the subsequent one of the bill against the status quo. We have seen, though, that such a paradox does not, or infrequently, occur in Dutch politics, as there are few voting patterns that can be explained by strategic voting and not by sincere voting.

Moreover, the above analysis of strategic voting as aiming at a paradox points to a second indication that there is little strategic voting in the Dutch parliament. Under Dutch House Rules, the paradox can only occur in such a way that the proposed bill is defeated. This must be so, since under the paradox the alternative brought up fresh in the last roll-call is the winner, and this is the status quo (or, more exact, the state of affairs after the proposal has been defeated). In practice, very few bills are completely killed in the Dutch Parliament, either in the Second Chamber or in the First Chamber.[13] In the period under study (1963-1971) only 10 bills failed, whereas 172 were brought to the vote in one or both Chambers and many more (some 2000) passed without roll-calls. Thus, potential strategic voters should have very little hope of success. A different situation arises, of course, when the strategy is to kill an (sub-amended) amendment to a bill, rather than the bill itself. Unfortunately, the data necessary for investigating such situations are lacking.

PROXIMITY VOTING AND THE VOTERS' PARADOX

The fact that the voters' paradox does not seem to materialize as the result of strategic voting, does not preclude its appearance by chance, i.e. when parties vote sincerely. Although it has been held that in a unidimensional polity with single-peaked preferences the paradox cannot exist on logical grounds,[14] it can be shown that the very nature of proximity voting defines an exception.

The unidimensional polity is certainly what Black had in mind when he formulated his conditions for collective transitivity (intrasitivity is the occurrence of preferential cycles such as 'prefers a over b over c over a). Though later authors[15] have shown that his conditions are sufficient but not necessary, Black's analysis covers the Dutch case. Black's conclusion, then, is that in a unidimensional polity all legislators (c.q. parties) should have preference orders with only one peak or local maximum. Thus, at both sides of the maximum point the preference order should be a monotonously decreasing function, to the left and to the right, respectively. Preference orders in which extremes of left *and* right rank higher than any intermediate point are not allowed.

Under proximity voting, a legislator (party) compares the proposal at the vote to a personal reference point, whether political ideals or the party platform or the party line in general. The closer the proposal is to that reference point, the more the legislator will favor it; the farther away the proposal is, the more he/she will reject it. Thus, preference functions are monotonously decreasing at each side of the reference point, which, in turn, is identical to the single peak of the function. Black's conditions are fulfilled.

In the deterministic form of the model, all proposals farther away from the reference point than some critical distance[16] are rejected by the legislator; all proposals within that distance get his/her vote. The present paper does not deal with the probabilistic case.

A new element may now be introduced into the analysis: the status quo, or state of affairs that will arise after the proposal has been defeated. This is, according to the proximity model, completely disregarded by the legislator, but in real life it exists nevertheless. In the analysis, both the status quo and each individual reference point are of the same kind as and comparable to proposals: they could formally be proposed as amendments (or alternative proposals) to the motion at the vote. But, in a sense, the status quo is at the vote indeed: it will endure if the nays have it. By consequence, preference functions are not completely single-peaked: the status quo ranks higher than all rejected alternative proposals and therefore forms a local second peak.

Figure 4 provides an example of such a situation. Imagine a right-wing status quo, which for simplicity is the reference point of the legislator of the right, X, as well. Also imagine a moderate proposal p in the center, perhaps introduced by the moderate legislator Y, also in the center. Finally, imagine left-wing legislator Z and left-wing amendment a. Table 6 presents the sincere preference orders of the legislators, their vote patterns at the two roll-calls (a against p and p against sq, respectively), and the orders that can be deduced from the vote patterns. Legislator Z is the one creating the

FIGURE 4
Proximity voting and the Voters' Paradox. Explained in text.
X, Y, Z = legislators; a = amendment; p = proposal; s.q. =
status quo

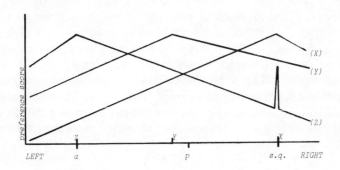

TABLE 6
Proximity Voting and the Voters' Paradox

leg.	sincere pref.	1st RC	2nd RC	deduced order (Paradox)
X	sq > p > a	p > a	sq > p	sq > p > a
Y	p > a > sq	p > a	p > sq	p > a > sq
Z	a > p > sq	a > p	sq > p	a > sq > p

X, Y, Z are legislators; *p* is a proposal brought to the vote in the second roll-call (2nd RC) against *sq*, the status quo that will continue if the proposal fails. In the first roll-call (1st RC), an amendment *a* is pitted against *p*.

The sincere preference orders of X, Y and Z do not constitute a Paradox: there is a majority for *p* over *a*, and a different majority for *p* over *sq*. Z, however, does not vote for *p* in the second roll-call, since it is too far from Z's reference point; thus, Z implicitly votes for *sq* over *p*. The orders deduced from both roll-calls do not form a paradox. There is a majority for *p* over *a*, a different majority for *sq* over *p*, and a third roll-call would reveal yet another majority for *a* over *sq*.

Cf. Figure 4 for a graphical illustration of the same case.

voters' paradox as can be seen from Z's preference curve in Figure 4.

Even if, in Figure 4, alternative *a* is not formally introduced as an amendment and brought to the vote against *p*, it serves as Z's reference point so that the paradox still holds. Thus, irrespective of the presence and number of amendments, any defeated proposal in a polity voting according to the proximity model may be the victim of the Voters' Paradox. And, what is more, any roll-call, irrespective whether the proposal is accepted or rejected, tends to be Paradoxical. This is not to say that the Paradox is at hand all the time. Rather, it exists as a threat in the background, and strong measures have been taken to keep it from popping up.

The paradoxical (or rather semi-Paradoxical) character of any roll-call under proximity voting is, of course, found in the unison of Left and Right against Center. The roll-call becomes a Paradox if and only if the numbers of seats of Left, Right and Center match the following inequalities:

Left + Center> Right;
Left + Right> Center;
Right + Center> Left.

Common coalition building practices preclude that all three of these inequalities become realities. The coalition partners, represented in Government, promise loyalty to the Government's proposals to make sure that at least one majority exists all the time. Only when the coalition falls apart (or is based on a minority in Parliament) does the Voters' Paradox get a chance to materialize.

All this points to a Paradox of the Voters' Paradox: It always looms in the background in a proximity voting polity, but exactly for that reason never crystallizes.

CONCLUSIONS

Polynomial regression techniques are useful tools to detect instances of strategic voting in polities characterized by proximity voting. Moreover, sign (runs) testing is an efficient shorthand for repeated regression when parties are homogeneous (and many). McCrone's suggestions in this area are fruitful outside the domain of Guttman scaling as well.

The empirical use of these techniques in order to highlight cases of strategic voting in the Dutch Parliament (1963-1971) shows that voting in The Netherlands is sincere or erroneous (in the sense of non-scale) rather than strategic in most cases. Insincere voting is not a popular strategy.

The analytical explanation for this finding may be that the Voters' Paradox (which is the aim of strategic voting) looms large in the background of a proximity voting polity such as the Dutch Parliament. This continuing threat has induced politicians to take strong measures against its materializing. One such measure is the formation of cabinets based on a stable majority. The result is the Paradox of the Voters' Paradox: just because the menace of its occurrence is so real, strong measures preclude the Voters' Paradox from crystallizing so that it is (almost) completely absent from Dutch roll-calls. By consequence, potential strategic voters must have very few hopes that their strategies will succeed.

NOTES

The author wishes to express gratitude to Dr Arend Lijphart and Dr Albert Verbeek for their useful comments on an earlier draft, which was presented at the ECPR Joint Sessions at Grenoble, 9 April 1978, to the workshop on formal Political Analysis.

1. K. J. Arrow: *Social Choice and Individual Values* (New York: Wiley, 1951).

2. D. J. McCrone, 'Identifying Voting Strategies from Roll Call Votes: A Method and an Application', *Legislative Studies Quarterly*, II, 1977.

3. J. A. Ferejohn and M. P. Fiorina, 'Purposive Models of Legislative Behavior', *American Economic Review*, 65, 1975.

4. R. Farquharson: *Theory of Voting* (New Haven: Yale University Press, 1969).

5. R. Niemi and W. Riker, 'The Choice of Voting Systems', *Scientific American*, 234, 1976.

6. M. Wolters, 'Models of Roll-Call Behavior', *Political Methodology*, 5, 1978.

7. M. Wolters, dissertation, Leiden: (forthcoming). The unidimensional Motion-Conditonal/Motion-Weighting Proximity Model is more parsimonious and convincing than any other Model of Roll-Call Behavior. The dissertation also

discusses 2-dimensional descriptions which cover almost all roll-calls. The present article assumes unidimensionality.

8. A. Verbeek has drawn my attention to the fact that a regression curve may have less maxima and minima than the degree of its polynomial. E.g., $y = x^3$ is a monotonously increasing function without any maxima or minima. Therefore, the correct procedure should include checking derivatives. This renders regression analysis a rather cumbersome technique.

9. A run of ayes corresponds to a maximum of the curve; a run of nays to a minimum. Note that the transfer from regression to runs is actually the transfer from probabilistic to deterministic models. This seems justified in a system with highly cohesive parties.

10. Participants to the ECPR Workshop on Formal Political Analysis (1978) have pointed out that certain logrolling contracts also lead to higher order polynomials. In particular, this is the case if non-adjacent parties cooperate (e.g. PvdA and VVD). In practice however, logrolling appears to always pertain to adjacent ranges of parties; it is mainly confined to standing coalitions, either the ruling cabinet coalition or the enduring coalition of progressive parties (D'66, PPR, PvdA).

11. K. J. Arrow, op. cit., note 1.

12. D. Black, *The Theory of Committees and Elections* (Cambridge: Cambridge University Press 1958); W. Riker, *The Theory of Coalitions* (New Haven: Yale University Press 1962); and J. Buchanan and G. Tullock, *The Calculus of Consent* (Ann Arbor: University of Michigan Press 1962).

13. M. Wolters, 'Is de Eerste Kamer Overbodig?', *Bestuurswetenschappen* 32, 1978.

14. D. Black, op. cit. note 11.

15. A. K. Sen, *Collective Choice and Social Welfare* (San Francisco, 1970); W. H. Riker and P. C. Ordeshook, *An Introduction to Positive Political Theory* (Englewood Cliffs: Prentice Hall, 1973).

16. The concept of critical distance is discussed and defined in my 'Models of Roll-Call Behavior' (note 6).

14 Economic Conditions and Conflict Processes

Dennis J. D. Sandole

University of Southern California, USA
United Kingdom Program in International Relations

THE PROBLEM

This is a study of the relationship between economic factors and conflict behaviour. By economic factors we mean level of economic development and economics-related deprivation. And by conflict we mean a dynamic phenomenon comprised of initiation, escalation, controlled maintenance, abatement, and termination/resolution of manifest conflict processes (MCPs). In this study we are concerned with initiation of MCPs.

An MCP is defined as a situation in which at least two actors, or their representatives, try to pursue their perceptions of mutually incompatible goals by undermining, directly or indirectly, the goal-seeking capability of one another. We are particularly concerned with aggressive manifest conflict processes (AMCPs) — i.e., situations in which at least two actors, or their representatives, try to pursue their perceptions of mutually incompatible goals by physically damaging or destroying the property and high-value symbols of one another; and/or psychologically or physically injuring, destroying, or otherwise forcibly eliminating one another.[1]

The reasons for studying aggressive conflict seem obvious enough. Whether expressed at the intra-psychic level as suicide, at the inter-personal level as homicide, at the intra-societal level as insurgency and counter-insurgency, or at the international level as war, AMCPs — or as Rapoport labels them, 'fights'[2] — involve irreparable costs to some or all the parties concerned and, depending upon the nature and scope of the process, to others as well. Yet, AMCPs continue to manifest themselves, to increase — or to threaten to increase — in frequency or intensity, thereby increasing, or threatening to increase, the costs involved. The general question posed in the project which subsumes the work reported here is, simply, 'Why?'.[3]

In this paper we are concerned with the relationships between, on the one hand, societies' economic development and economics-related deprivation and, on the other hand, their domestic and foreign conflict behaviour. The reasons for investigating the relationships between economic factors and conflict behaviour are both theoretical and practical.

On the theoretical side, Dougherty and Pfaltzgraff tell us that, in studies of conflict and cooperation, 'economic factors have held a position of considerable importance.'[4] This, of course, is not surprising, since all societies are always characterized by some level of economic development and tend to be characterized by some degree of economics-related deprivation. What may be surprising and, in any case, what is interesting here is that different scholars, for instance John Stuart Mill and Karl Marx, have formulated different propositions with regard to the relationships between economic factors and conflict. (The relevant ideas of Mill and Marx will be summarized below.)

By investigating the relationships between economic factors and conflict, we may not only make a contribution to the development of theory on the initiation of MCPs and AMCPs within and between societies but, on the practical side, we may increase our capability to cope creatively and functionally with ongoing AMCPs, if not to prevent their incidence in future.

For both theoretical and practical reasons, therefore, it is important not only to explore the relationships between economic factors and conflict behaviour but also to try to determine which of at least two competing conceptualizations of those relationships is more reflective of what Karl Popper calls verisimilitude or truthlikeness.[5] In this regard, although Thomas Kuhn has asserted that 'It makes a great deal of sense to ask which of two actual and competing theories fits the facts better',[6] such comparative assessments do not abound in the conflict literature. Michael Sullivan, for instance, in his comprehensive survey and ordering of theory and research in international relations, points out that 'At the present time...our study of international behavior deals primarily with the testing of single theories or hypotheses, rarely evaluating them against competing theories or hypotheses.'[7]

Although comparative assessments of competing theories or hypotheses have not been too common in the study of conflict, our comparative assessment of the ideas of Mill and Marx with respect to the relationships between economic factors and conflict processes is not the first such assessment. We have tracked down one other — Graeme Duncan's comparative study of Mill's and Marx's views on social conflict.[8] While Duncan was concerned primarily with what each was saying, and to what extent their views are compatible with each other, we will be concerned primarily with which view accords best with the empirical record — both in terms of the real world and simulation.

Before we get into our comparative assessment, two points on this empirical record are worth mentioning. First of all, while Mill's and Marx's theses have particular relevance to capitalist systems, the real-world findings we have located in various studies apply to noncapitalist as well as to capitalist systems. In terms of the relationships between economic factors and conflict behaviours, this difference between capitalist and noncapitalist systems may be more apparent than real — i.e., certain economic factors may stimulate conflict in any system. Still, we should be aware of this absence of strict comparability in our real-world assessment. Secondly, our selected simulation operation has not been designed to replicate any particular system and, indeed, does not replicate the economic dimension of society to any great extent. Hence, the connection between our simulate-worlds and the world about which Mill and Marx were writing may not be too secure. Still, on the assumption that simulation may tap aspects of human behaviour in general (an assumption to which we will return later in this paper), the simulation part of our study may be suggestive —

but certainly not demonstrative — of the nature of the relationships between economic factors and conflict processes as well as the relevance of the ideas of Mill and Marx to those processes.

THEORETICAL SETTING

John Stuart Mill's *Principles of Political Economy* and Karl Marx and Frederick Engel's *Manifesto of the Communist Party* were published in the same year and in the same country — 1848 in Great Britain. Beyond the date and place of publication, however, there is apparently not much similarity between the two works.

Mill put forward a positive-sum conceptualization of the relationship between economic factors and conflict. As the wealth of a society increased, everyone in the society would tend to be better off. Economics-related deprivation might persist but, with increasing economic growth and concomitant developments in other spheres, this would tend to be expressed nonviolently. Not only would increased economic growth stimulate individual and national prosperity, thereby leading to a diminution in the frequency or intensity of violent domestic conflict but, given that such prosperity would be due in part to unrestricted international trade, economic growth would also reduce war between states. Indeed, economic growth would ultimately render war obsolete.[9]

Marx and Engels, in contrast, put forward primarily a zero-sum (which tails off into a negative-sum) conceptualization of the relationships between economic factors and conflict processes. As the wealth of a society increased, the rich ruling class would get richer and the poor working class would get poorer. As the surplus value — i.e., the difference between what labour was paid for producing a given item and what the ruling class received from the sale of that item — increased, economics-related deprivations on the part of the workers would increase. Consequently, conflict between the working and ruling classes would also increase.

As fewer and fewer workers were able to purchase the fruits of their own labour, and as successful domestic and foreign competition necessitated access to larger and larger markets, the ruling class would be compelled to search for guaranteed markets abroad. And as successful competition necessitated the availability of cheaper and cheaper raw materials, the ruling class would be compelled to search for sources of these, also abroad. This would stimulate the development of economic rivalry between capitalist states as well as the development of imperialistic relationships with the sources of cheap raw materials as well as with the guaranteed markets. In addition to wars occurring between the capitalist states and potential sources of raw materials, wars would also occur between the capitalist states themselves because more and more of them would be competing for a diminishing supply of such sources. Without these cheap raw materials and guaranteed markets, economic development in the capitalist states would start to come to a grinding halt.

As more and more members of the ruling class would lose the competitive struggle, and themselves be thrown into the ranks of the working class, and as more and more members of the working class would be rendered unemployed, the contradictions inherent in capitalism would begin to lead to reductions rather than continued increases in economic development. At this point, the conflict between the capitalist states would be eclipsed by a more ferocious conflict between the expanding working class and diminishing ruling class, leading ultimately to the overthrow of the existing order by the working class in each capitalist state.[10]

According to Marx, therefore, what Kenneth Boulding calls the Duchess's law, after the Duchess in *Alice in Wonderland* — i.e., 'The more there is of yours, the less there is of mine'[11] — occurs both within and between societies as a concomitant of increases in economic growth. This, as well as the resulting intra- and intersocietal 'fights' is, for Marx, a deterministic consequence of economic conditions. In other words, in Marxism, economic conditions determine everything else: they are sufficient conditions of certain societal, economic, political, legal, and cognitive developments.[12] (Determinism is not a feature of Mill's thesis.)

Some general hypotheses which derive from the above are

(1) for Marx:
(a) There will be strong positive relationships between certain economic factors (economic development and economics-related deprivation) and aggressive conflict (domestic and foreign).

(b) The magnitude of those positive relationships may increase across successive stages of economic development.

(c) The positive relationship between economic development and aggressive conflict will tend to become nonlinear in advanced stages of economic development (i.e., in addition to increases in economic development stimulating aggressive conflict during early stages of development, decreases in economic growth will stimulate increases in aggressive conflict during late stages of development).

(d) There will be more aggressive conflict for societies in late stages of development than for societies in early stages of development.

(2) for Mill:

(a) There may be positive relationships between certain economic factors and aggressive conflict during early stages of economic development.

(b) The magnitudes of those positive relationships will tend to diminish across successive stages of economic development, perhaps with the positive relationships disappearing or being transformed into negative relationships during late stages of development.

(c) There will be less aggressive conflict for societies in late stages of development than for societies in early stages of development.

Some of the above hypotheses can be derived from other theoretical schema as well. For instance, the hypothesized positive relationship between economics-related deprivation and aggressive conflict can be derived from Ted Robert Gurr's relative deprivation theory,[13] from Johan Galtung's rank disequilibrium theory,[14] and from the frustration-aggression theory put forward by John Dollard and others.[15] And the positive relationships of decreasing magnitude over time, between economic factors in general and aggressive conflict, eventually becoming negative relationships, can be derived from various consensus/social pluralism theories.[16]

Before we assess these hypotheses against the empirical record to see how well each holds up, we will mention briefly what we mean by deterministic, primary, contributory, and chimerical relationships. As already mentioned, a factor which has a deterministic relationship with some behaviour would be a sufficient condition of that behaviour — i.e., the behaviour, or some change in the behaviour, would follow automatically or nearly automatically from that factor or some change in that factor. One operational test of determinism can be found in studies which have made use of product-moment correlations to assess the strength of the relationship between two variables. Another indicator would be partial correlations which have been computed to assess the strength of relationship between two variables while taking into account the impact of other factors on the behaviour that one wants to explain. In either of these cases, by squaring the value of the correlation coefficient, we can compute the coefficient of determination which tells us what proportion of the variation in the behaviour of one variable, the dependent variable (the variable we want to explain), is accounted for by the independent or explanatory variable. For our purposes, a correlation coefficient of 0.87, which means that an explanatory variable has accounted for 75 per cent of the variation in the behaviour of the dependent variable ($0.87 \times 0.87 = 0.75$), will be used as our minimum condition of determinism.

A primary relationship is one in which an explanatory factor, which does not have a deterministic relationship with some phenomenon, is nevertheless the most important source of influence on it. Operational indicators of primary relationships can be, for bivariate studies, product-moment correlations of less than 0.87 and, for multivariate studies, partial correlations of less than 0.87 whose corresponding standardized regression coefficients have the highest rankings (on these, see below).

A contributory relationship is one in which an explanatory variable, amongst a number of explanatory variables in a multivariate relational system, is the second, third, or fourth, etc., most important source of influence on some phenomenon. Operational indicators of contributory relationships can be found in studies which make use of standardized regression coefficients. These coefficients, which will be explained later when we discuss the methodology underlying the simulation section of our study, enable one to rank explanatory variables in terms of their relative degrees of influence on some phenomenon.

Finally, a chimerical relationship is one which, on the basis of some theory or conventional wisdom, is expected to obtain but does not occur. An operational indicator of a chimerical relationship would simply be the absence of an expected relationship — i.e., the absence of an expected explanatory variable — in a multivariate relational system. It could be argued that a low-magnitude product-moment (bivariate) correlation coefficient, something less than 0.10, would also constitute an index of a chimerical relationship. However, given the possibility that any relationship between two variables might actually increase in value only after other explanatory variables were brought into the relational system[17] — in other words, only after a bivariate relationship were transformed into a multivariate one — we will adhere to the multivariate criterion of a chimerical relationship.

Now on to an assessment of our hypotheses against the empirical record.

ASSESSMENT OF HYPOTHESES (I): REAL-WORLD DATA

On the relationship between economics-related deprivation, or anything similar to economics-related deprivation, and domestic conflict in the real world, Ted Robert Gurr found correlations of +0.34 on the relationships between economic deprivation and conspiracy, +0.31 between economic deprivation and internal war, +0.25 between economic deprivation and turmoil, and +0.44 between economic deprivation and total strife during 1961-65 for 114 polities. And in a multivariate analysis involving the regression of each of his four dependent variables on eight explanatory variables (including economic deprivation), his findings indicate that economic deprivation was the fourth most potent predictor of internal war and total strife and the sixth most potent predictor of conspiracy and turmoil.[18] Ivo and Rosalind Feierabend have investigated the relationship between systemic frustration during 1948-55 and political instability during 1955-61 for 84 nations and found a correlation of +0.50. The Feierabends also found a slightly nonlinear correlation of +0.67 on the relationship between modernity and political instability. In this regard, the Feierabends divided the 84 nations in their data-set into traditional, transitional, and modern countries and found that the transitional nations were more unstable than either the traditional or the modern nations and that the modern nations were more stable than either the transitional or the traditional countries.[19]

On the relationship between economic development and domestic conflict, Gurr and Duvall found positive relationships between economic development and four indicators of domestic conflict — turmoil, rebellion, extent of strife, and manifest political conflict — during 1961-65 for 86 nations. In each of these cases, economic development was, out of five explanatory variables, either the fourth or the fifth most potent predictor of the conflict variable.[20]

On the one hand, the above findings could be viewed as supportive of *either* Marx or Mill. For instance, in support of Marx, there seems to have been positive relationships between economic development/economics-related deprivation and domestic conflict in the real world — at least between 1948 and 1965. In support of Mill, however, none of the bivariate coefficients fulfilled our 0.87 criterion of determinism and, in the multivariate studies, economic factors were never more than relatively low-ranking contributory conditions of domestic conflict.

On the other hand, the findings are supportive of *both* Marx and Mill in that both may be right, but for different stages of economic development. In this regard, the fact that transitional societies were more unstable than traditional societies is partially supportive of the hypothesis derived from Marx that there will be more aggressive conflict for societies in late stages of development than for societies in early stages of economic development. And that modern societies were more stable than either transitional or traditional societies is supportive of the hypothesis derived from Mill that there will be less aggressive conflict for societies in late stages than for societies in early stages of development.

On the relationship between economic development and foreign conflict in the real world, Jack Vincent and his associates found an association between high levels of economic development and high levels of cooperation,[21] which is very supportive of Mill. Also supportive of Mill, Michael Skrein, in a study of 19 British Commonwealth nations, found that developed nations tended to have higher ratios of cooperative to non-cooperative behaviour than did less developed nations. And in another study, involving 69 nations, Skrein found that developed nations tended to have smaller ratios of physical violence to total behaviour than did less developed nations.[22]

David Moore studied the 1963 behaviour of up to 109 nations and found positive relationships between economic development and defense expenditures as a proportion of GNP, with values of coefficients ranging from $+0.16$ to $+0.38$. He also found positive relationships between economic development and foreign conflict, with values of coefficients ranging from $+0.01$ to $+0.20$. In his multivariate analysis, which involved the regression of these two conflict variables on nine explanatory variables, Moore found that economic development was the fourth best predictor of defense expenditures and the sixth best predictor of foreign conflict.

While Moore's findings may seem to have created the same kind of impasse we briefly encountered in our discussion of real-world findings on the relationship between economic factors and domestic conflict, i.e., where either Marx or Mill are supported, Moore did investigate the relationships between his selected variables for nations at different stages of economic development, which prevents this impasse from assuming a permanent character. In this regard, he found that the positive relationship between economic development and defense expenditures was greater for undeveloped ($+0.38$) than for developed nations ($+0.27$) and that the positive relationship between economic development and foreign conflict was also greater for undeveloped ($+0.17$) than for developed nations ($+0.02$).[23] These particular findings are supportive of the hypotheses derived from Mill that there may be a positive relationship between economic factors and foreign conflict, but that the magnitude of that relationship will tend to decrease across successive stages of economic development.

Steven Salmore and Charles Hermann, in a study of the 1966-67 foreign-conflict behaviour of 76 nations, found that less developed nations tended to engage in more offensive verbal conflict behaviour (accuse, demand, warn, and threaten) and more acts of conflict than did developed nations, whereas developed nations tended to engage in more defensive verbal conflict behaviour (rejections, protests, and denials) than did less developed nations.[24] The trend here of a diminution in the incidence of aggressive or offensive conflict across stages of economic development is clearly supportive of Mill. The trend of an increase in what Salmore and Hermann have called 'defensive' behaviour is also supportive of Mill because it suggests that, with increasing development, although conflict in general certainly does not, and should not disappear, it tends to find relatively nonviolent modes of expression.

While the findings of Vincent, et al., Skrein, Moore, and Salmore and Hermann are supportive of Mill, the Feierabends have done a study which is supportive of Marx. In this regard, using their 84 nation data for 1955-61, they found a negative relationship between economic development and foreign conflict for mid-modern nations and a positive relationship for high-modern nations.[25]

Amongst studies which could be viewed as supportive of either Marx or Mill, Maurice East and Charles Hermann, in a multivariate study of the foreign behaviour of 33 nations during 1959-68, found a positive relationship between economic development and percentage of foreign conflict events, a negative relationship between economic development and percentage of cooperative events, and, more in support of Mill than Marx, a negative relationship between economic development and percentage of military events. In only the second case was the relationship statistically significant at the 0.05 level.[26] We will discuss statistical significance and the 0.05 level when we get into the methodology underlying the simulation part of our study. For the present, we will say that, in the simulation part of our study, the 0.05 level constitutes the minimum criterion which explanatory variables had to fulfill in order to remain in a multivariate system. What this means is that, if an economic factor had a relationship with a conflict variable which did not fulfill this criterion, the relationship would be defined as chimerical. On this basis, then, we can define two of East and Hermann's relationships as chimerical. While the cancellation of one of these relationships, the positive one between development and percentage of foreign conflict events, seems to be supportive of Mill, the statistically significant negative relationship between development and percentage of cooperative events seems to be supportive of Marx.

Rudolph Rummel has also done a study which could be viewed as applicable to either Marx or Mill. In this regard, he analyzed the relationships between economic conditions during 1955 and foreign conflict during 1955-57 for between 39 and 72 nations and found a number of positive relationships whose values ranged from $+0.30$ to $+0.45$.[27]

Finally on the relationship between economic development and foreign conflict, Michael Haas has done a study which is supportive of both Marx and Mill, thereby suggesting, once again, that both may be right, but for different stages of economic development. Haas studied approximately 70 nations and found that the least and the most developed nations had the most foreign conflict, with urbanized and wealthy nations having slightly higher conflict.[28] This is supportive of the hypothesis derived from Mill that societies in early stages of development will have more conflict than societies in subsequent stages and supportive of the hypothesis derived from Marx that societies in late stages of development will have more conflict than societies in earlier stages.

On the foreign-conflict side of the real-world assessment of our hypotheses, we have looked thus far only at the relationship between economic development and foreign conflict. On the relationship between economics-related deprivation and foreign conflict, Rummel, in his aforementioned study, looked at the relationships between some indicators of these variables but, because only one of his resulting coefficients was equal to his threshold value of 0.30, he did not report the majority of his findings. The one reported finding was a correlation of -0.40 on the relationship between, on the one hand, percentage of population with 50 percent of the land and, on the other hand, ambassadors expelled or recalled.[29] This suggests that economics-related deprivation is associated with some form of foreign conflict, a proposition which could find comfort in the conceptual houses built by either Marx or Mill.

The only other foreign-conflict studies which involve an independent or explanatory variable bearing some similarity to economics-related deprivation appear to be those which have focussed on the relationship between status inconsistency/discrepancy and foreign conflict. One scholar in this regard, Michael Wallace, has made observations on these relationships in terms of different — albeit mostly overlapping — time periods which correspond, to some extent, to different stages of economic development. For instance, for the international system during 1820-1944, he reports coefficients of $+0.38$ on the relationship between status inconsistency (SI) and alliance aggregation; $+0.38$ on the relationship between SI and rate of change in military capability; and $+0.50/+0.53$ on the relationship between SI and battle fatalities. For the period

1850-1964, he reports coefficients of $+0.47/+0.66$ on the relationship between SI and alliance aggregation; $+0.37/+0.38$ on the relationship between SI and rate of change in military capability; and $+0.47$ on the relationship between SI and battle fatalities.[30]

Recalling the distinction made earlier by Salmore and Hermann between defensive and offensive foreign conflict behaviour, if we were to interpret Wallace's alliance aggregation as an example of defensive conflict and his battle fatalities as an example of offensive conflict, we might also be able to say, in view of his findings, that the relationship between SI and defensive foreign conflict increased, while the relationship between SI and offensive foreign conflict decreased, in magnitude across stages of economic development. Although we might be reading too much into Wallace's findings to make a point, it does seem that this overall interpretation supports the hypothesis derived from Mill that the magnitude of a positive relationship between economics-related deprivation and aggressive foreign conflict will tend to decrease across stages of economic development. It also supports a view which could be associated with Mill, a view which is not contained in the hypotheses already drawn from Mill, i.e., that the magnitude of a relationship between economics-related deprivation and less offensive forms of foreign conflict will tend to increase across stages.

Before moving on, one more point about Wallace's study is worth mentioning. In the multivariate part of it, SI apears to have emerged as a contributory condition of battle fatalities.[31]

In summary of the results of our real-world assessment of the hypotheses derived from Mill and Marx, most of the bivariate findings on domestic conflict suggest that either Mill or Marx may be right, while one set of findings suggests that they may both be right but at different stages of economic development — Marx for the interval tapped by the Feierabends' traditional and transitional stages and Mill for the interval tapped by the transitional and modern stages.

In relation to the two multivariate studies we consulted on domestic conflict, those by Gurr, alone and together with Duvall, we will mention now what we neglected to mention earlier — namely, that all but one of Gurr's four relationships (that between economic deprivation and total strife) and all but one of Gurr and

Duvall's four relationships (that between economic development and extent of strife) were below our 0.05 significance criterion. In terms of these particular studies, therefore, the relationships between economic factors and domestic conflict tended to be chimerical.

Most of the bivariate findings on foreign conflict also suggest that either Marx or Mill may be right. Among the remaining findings, quite a few suggest that Mill may be right, one set suggests that Marx may be right, and one set suggests that both may be right. The relatively large number of findings which are supportive of Mill are compatible with the findings of one of the few researchers who has compared the warlikeness of capitalist and non-capitalist societies — Quincy Wright. In this regard, Wright, who has done, perhaps, the most comprehensive study of war to date, says, 'States with economies based on agriculture, though less warlike than those based on animal pasturage, have generally been more warlike than those based on commerce or industry.'[32] He also argues that capitalist societies have been the most peaceful while state-socialist societies have been the most warlike.[33]

The one study which suggests that both Mill and Marx may be right, but for different stages of economic development, that by Haas, indicates that the least developed (the traditional) and the most developed (the modern) societies have the most foreign conflict. If we integrated Haas's findings with those of Salmore and Hermann, it could be that the least developed societies have the most offensive conflict while the most developed societies have the most defensive conflict. And if we include the findings of Wallace, it could be that, during early stages of development, economic factors lead to offensive foreign conflict, whereas during later stages of development, they lead to defensive foreign conflict.

In relation to the three multivariate studies we consulted on foreign conflict, two of them, those by Moore and Wallace, do not present significance levels, which means that, in these particular studies, economic factors emerged as qualified contributory conditions of foreign conflict. In the one study which did present significance levels, that by East and Hermann, two of the three reported relationships emerged as chimerical.

In general, the bivariate findings tempt us into inferring that, for both domestic and foreign conflict, the ideas of Marx apply to early stages of economic development, though by no means in a deterministic manner, whereas the ideas of Mill apply to late stages of development. The multivariate findings, however, tempt us to infer that, for both domestic and foreign conflict, economic factors play little or no role. This suggests that factors other than, or in addition to, economic ones are the significant sources of influence on the domestic and foreign conflict behaviour of societies.

We now move on to the simulation part of our study to determine to what extent the above observations hold up in another research context.

ASSESSMENT OF HYPOTHESES (II): SIMULATION DATA

Since the simulation component of our empirical record consists of findings which have been generated by a study which we have conducted, we will discuss some preliminaries before we get into this part of our assessment of the hypotheses — i.e., we will first discuss simulation in general, the particular simulation we selected for this study, how we operated it, theoretical and operational definitions of the variables we employed, and the methodology relevant to our analyses of the relationships between those variables.

Before moving on, we must mention, once again, that what applies to the simulate world may not apply to the real world. If we neglect to keep this caveat in our minds, we may make fallacious inferences about the real world on the basis of simulation data. On the other hand, if our real-world observations are supported by our simulation study, we will have 'killed two birds with one stone' — i.e., we will have strengthened our faith in the validity of our real-world findings as well as underscored the value of the use of simulation in the analysis of complex conflict processes.

Simulation

Simulation is similar to laboratory experiment in that both involve the creation of artificial settings and the generation of data within those settings. However, whereas laboratory experiment involves intervening *directly* into a subject-matter, albeit under almost unreal conditions, simulation involves intervening into a *model* of a subject-matter.[34]

As is perhaps implied, simulation has both static and dynamic properties. In relation to the static, simulation is a model of a corresponding referent, and a script for playing out that model. And in relation to the dynamic, simulation is the operation of the model in accordance with the script.

Obviously all scripts call for some degree of exogenous human operation, but not all scripts call for human players, even in cases where the simulation has been designed to replicate human processes. For instance, simulations in a strict sense, such as TEMPER and SIPER,[35] involve highly structured models which are played-out by computers in accordance with highly structured formats or scripts. 'Scenario-games', such as the PME (or PE),[36] on the other hand, involve relatively simple models and scripts as well as human players. Somewhere in between the model-script complexity of simulations and the model-script simplicity of scenario-games are 'gaming simulations', such as the INS, IPS, and WPS,[37] which involve human — or some combination of human and programmed — players.

It has been decided to use simulation in general because it permits total access to the systems which it generates, thereby enabling a researcher to make observations on a number of variables at various levels — e.g., the decision-making, societal, and trans-societal levels of analysis. And because these systems have beginning and terminating phases, with something in between, a researcher can make observations on multi-level variables at various levels of economic and general development.

The Prisoner's Dilemma Simulation

The particular simulation we have used is the 'Prisoner's Dilemma Simulation' (PDS). The PDS, a gaming-simulation, was selected primarily because it had already been employed by its designer Charles Powell to generate a raw data base to which we had access and upon which we could build.[38]

The PDS is so called because it incorporates a paradoxical situation known in game theory as the 'Prisoner's Dilemma' which involves a clash — with respect to each of the parties to a conflict situation — between individual and collective rationality, with collective loss the outcome of decisions based exclusively upon individual self-interest.[39]

The PDS incorporates this paradox in that it permits players to trade or to arm, but *not* to do both, with respect to the same target-group at the same time. Hence, players may frequently be confronted with conflicts of mixed motives — i.e., whether to trust the members of another group and trade with them or to distrust them and arm against them. In this regard, the members of one group may reason that they are better off arming, no matter what the members of another group do, because (1) if they do not arm and the others do, they stand to suffer a loss (e.g., make themselves liable to conventional or nuclear blackmail); or (2) if they do arm and the others do not, they will stand to gain and the others will lose. The paradox here is that the members of both groups may reason the same way, each ending up not only with the opportunity costs associated with forfeited trading opportunities, but also with confirmation of their suspicions that the others were out to get them. This may facilitate their locking-in to a conflict spiral, resulting in further opportunity costs and eventual war. If they trusted each other, on the other hand, each would end up with the material benefits of increased trade.

Even if the PDS had not already been used to generate a raw data base, it still has advantages, for us at least, over scenario-games or the most widely-used gaming-simulation in international relations, the INS. One reason is that scenario-games tend to involve the playing of specific personalities (e.g., Kaiser Wilhelm) while the INS involves the playing of specific roles (e.g., Central Decision-Maker, External Decision-Maker). In contrast, the PDS involves players being themselves, albeit with the grand title of Decision-Maker (and in the early runs, that of Validator as well). Whether one plays a specific personality or a specific role in a hierarchical system of differentiated roles, the effect of a player's personality on his/her behaviour might be distorted by systematic error.[40]

This is not to say that a study of the effects of certain role-types on behaviour within simulated or real-world settings would not be a proper research undertaking or that the PDS is wholly devoid of role-expectations.[41] But, given our intention, as part of our original undertaking, i.e., in the larger project which subsumes the present study, to investigate the relationships between certain personality variables and conflict, the PDS is more relevant to this purpose than are the other operations.

Another reason why the PDS is preferred to the INS in particular is because the INS and its derivatives appear to be the only gaming-simulations in the field of international relations whose outputs have been submitted to validity checks. Harold Guetzkow, the principal architect of the INS, has completed a comprehensive assessment of INS findings and has found that, in general, they compare rather favourably with findings from corresponding field and international studies.[42] On the one hand, one could argue that the wide-spread use of the INS and the relative success of Guetz-kow's assessment of its findings should have motivated us to prefer the INS to other operations — in order to build upon a validated data base. On the other hand, we would argue that, if part of one's overall research objective is to explore whether small-group systems in general, rather than only one particular operation, are capable of tapping real-world processes, then one should employ an operation other than the INS.

Operating the PDS

Each of five operations was conducted once each week for two hours during a 13-15 week period. PDS 1, 2, 3, 4 and 5 were laboratory supplements to undergraduate courses in American Foreign Policy and in International Politics at Temple University (Department of Political Science), Philadelphia, from Spring 1966 until Spring 1968. The players, therefore, were the students enroll-ed in those courses. They were neither paid cash for their participa-tion nor were they graded for their performance.

Powell and his co-workers operated PDS 1-3. The author was a player in PDS 1 and a co-worker in PDS 2-3. PDS 4-5 were operated by the author and his co-workers.

Prior to the first week of each operation, players were divided in-to two nation-groups, usually called Sumo and Ergo, each of which had decision-making and validation components. The determination of who went where was based upon players' responses to certain items on a personality questionnaire which had been administered to them earlier.[43] The Decision-Makers in each group were to decide whether to trade, arm, declare war or do nothing with regard to the other group and the Validators were to decide whether to approve or disapprove of these decisions.

Addenda to a Basic Simulation Manual were administered to the players on a weekly basis in order to increase progressively the complexity of the decision-making environment. According to one of the early addenda, the Validators in each group could stage coups, split off from their parent, and form a new group — a measure which facilitated the transformation of the system from a two-nation into a multi-group world (usually by the fourth week). Thereafter, all players occupied decision-making roles (the role of Validator having been assumed by structured routines) and made decisions with regard to the United Nations and alliances as well as about trading, arming (in nuclear or conventional terms) and declaring war.

The groups (and in the two-group system of the early runs, the decision-making and validation sub-groups) occupied separate rooms. Communication between them was conducted via written messages, which were carried by runners. Occasionally, communication was conducted by telephone. For each of the five operations a television studio was available, which is where the UN was located and its proceedings televised. Each group had a TV monitor with which it could observe the proceedings at the UN. The television medium was also employed by the operators — the 'Administration' — to issue general outcomes of decisions, news bulletins, and reminders to the players that they had to submit their decisions to 'The Computer' within the allotted time period, which varied between approximately 10 and 20 minutes, lest a 'do nothing' be recorded for them.

The Variables

The dependent or conflict variables in the simulation part of our study are DOMESTIC INSTABILITY, BELLICOSITY, ALLIANCES, MANIFEST DISTRUST, and AGGRESSIVE AT-

TACKS, and our two explanatory or economic variables are RELATIVE ECONOMIC STATUS and RELATIVE ECONOMIC DEPRIVATION.

Observations were made on these variables within each of the five PDS operations on the basis of actors' decisions, outcomes of decisions, and observations of actors which were made by members of the Administration based in each group.

The actor unit of analysis in terms of which observations were made is the group, and the temporal unit of analysis is the two-hour weekly simulation run. Consequently, the observations are of the longitudinal as well as of the cross-sectional kind. Moreover, as is indicated in the definitions which follow, observations on the independent variables were lagged with respect to observations on the dependent variables — i.e., most of the conflict variables were measured at current time (t) while both economic variables were measured at one run prior to current time ($t-1$).

Relative Economic Status (RES) refers to a political unit's level of economic development relative to the levels of other units. It has been measured in terms of each group's average GNP, as a proportion of the sum of all groups' average GNPs, at $t-1$.[44] RES was selected over absolute levels of economic development because it was felt that a unit's level of growth, not in a void, but in relation to the levels of other units is what influences its conflict behaviour most (though it could be argued that absolute levels would be more relevant to accounting for internal conflict). The other economic variable, Relative Economic Deprivation (RED), refers to the discrepancy between a political unit's desired economic status and its actual economic status, relative to other actors. It has been measured in terms of the ratio of each group's frequency of decisions to trade, as a proportion of the sum of all groups' trading frequencies, to its average GNP, as a proportion of the sum of all groups' average GNPs, at $t-1$; i.e.,

$$\text{RED} = \frac{\text{Group's Frequency of Trade}}{\text{Sum—All Groups' Freq. of Trade}} \Bigg/ \frac{\text{Group's Average GNP}}{\text{Sum—All Groups' Avge. GNPs}}$$

Domestic Instability (DI) refers to internal or domestic conflict. It has been measured for each group in terms of the number of actors, as a proportion of the total number, who staged coups or defected during the second half of t plus the first half of $t+1$ (future time).[45]

Among the foreign conflict variables, Manifest Distrust (MD) refers to a political unit's location in a conflict-cooperation space — i.e., to its ratio of conflictful-to-cooperative behaviours. It has been measured for each group in terms of the ratio of its incremental number of decisions to arm to its incremental number of decisions to trade, at t. Bellicosity (BEL) refers to a political unit's active capability to wage war. It has been measured for each group by the cumulative amount of funds it has invested in armaments as a proportion of its GNP, at t. Alliances (ALL) refers to a political unit's cooperative associations with other units for the purpose of common defense. It has been measured for each group in terms of the cumulative number of other groups with which it has entered into alliances, at t. The remaining foreign conflict variable, Aggressive Attacks (ATT), refers to the employment by a political unit of its active capability to wage war. It has been measured for each group in terms of the number of other groups against which it has declared war (excluding counter-declarations of war — i.e., those issued in self-defense against incoming attacks), at t.

Data Analysis

In order to explore the relationships between economic conditions and conflict at different stages of economic development, it was decided to combine PDS 1, 2, 3, 4 and 5 and then to divide the composite data-set into three sections. Finding breakpoints in the composite data-set which produced three sections which could appropriately be labelled early, intermediate, and late stages of economic and general development was facilitated both by the static and operational dimensions of the PDS. For instance, soon after each PDS operation began, the Decision-Makers and Validators in Ergo and Sumo received the first addendum to the Basic Simulation Manual which specified conditions under which coups and revolutions among the Validators could occur. It also specified conditions under which new nations could be formed. By the end of the third run, in most cases, at least one new nation had formed from each of the two original groups. Runs 1-3, therefore, tended to be characterized by the transition from a two- to a multi-group system — an interval which we have designated as the early stage of economic development.

During Runs 4-7 of each operation, the PDS world was a multi-group system, with each group, as already mentioned, tending to consist of human players in only one role, that of Decision-Maker. 'Live' domestic conflict during this interval (as well as during Runs 8-11), therefore, tended to occur only among the Decision-Makers in each group. Moreover, an addendum which was administered during this interval permitted the actors to become nuclear powers. Runs 4-7, therefore, were characterized primarily by nuclear-technology availability in a multi-group system. This interval was designated as the intermediate stage of economic development.

During Runs 8-11,[46] the flow of addenda to the actors ceased, and some of the actors, apparently with a need for environmental stimulation which had been previously satisfied to some extent by the complexity introduced by the various addenda, appear to have attempted to fill this 'stimulation-gap' by creating their own environmental complexity — e.g., by devising and implementing new 'world orders'. Runs 8-11, therefore, appear to have been characterized primarily by an increase in the scope of attempts of actors to intervene into, and to control their systemic environment. This interval was designated as the late stage of economic development.

Within each of these three intervals, observations on the selected variables were submitted to bivariate and multivariate analyses. At the bivariate level, product-moment correlation coefficients were computed on the relationships between the economic and conflict variables. In addition to being computed for the data as originally measured, coefficients were also computed for logarithmically-transformed data in order to facilitate assessing whether any relationship was nonlinear.

At the multivariate level, the data were submitted to ordinary least-squares regression in order to generate a model for each of the five conflict variables at each of the three intervals. A number of potential independent variables (including, of course, RES and RED) — which are operative at the decision-making, societal, and transsocietal levels — were involved in this model-building venture.[47] The particular procedure used for selecting variables for each model was stepwise regression. Stepwise regression selects variables which account for less and less of the variation in the behaviour of the dependent variable, until some cut-off point is reached. In addition to the cut-off point inherent in most stepwise programs, the researcher may also use another criterion, such as a certain statistical significance level, to determine which of the variables selected by the program should remain in the model. A model so developed, therefore, is comprised of one variable which accounts for the greatest proportion of the variation in the behaviour of the dependent variable and another variable which, taking into account the proportion of variation accounted for by the first variable, accounts for the second highest proportion of variation — assuming, of course, that the second variable has not reached the cut-off point inherent in the program or that established by the user.[48]

As mentioned earlier, the criterion of variable-selection used in the simulation part of our study is the significance level of 0.05. That is, the *minimum* condition that a variable had to satisfy in order to remain in a model generated by the stepwise procedure was that the probability that its relationship with the dependent variable was due to chance was only five per cent — that the relationship was incorrect in only one out of a minimum of twenty cases. The procedure used in determining whether any potential independent variable satisfied this condition was application of the t-test to the standardized regression coefficient on the relationship between each potential independent variable and the dependent variable.[49]

As implied above, the data on the variables were standardized prior to regression, thereby producing partial standardized regression coefficients or 'beta-weights' in the subsequent analysis. Standardization coupled with regression makes the regression coefficients comprising a model internally comparable and consequently enables us to rank the independent variables as to their relative capabilities to account for the behaviour of the dependent variable. This ranking is relevant to testing for primary and contributory relationships.

Partial correlation coefficients were also computed for the relationships in each model. Partial r's are similar to beta-weights in that they facilitate ranking the independent variables in a model, usually in the same order as the ranking provided by the beta-weights. They are dissimilar to beta-weights in the basis of the ranking facility — i.e., whereas beta-weights indicate how much change in a dependent variable is produced by a standardized change in an independent variable when the others are controlled, partial correlation coefficients, or their corresponding coefficients of determination (the partial squared), indicate the amount of variation in the dependent variable explained by each independent variable after the others have accounted for all they could.[50] Partial r's, therefore, are relevant to testing for deterministic as well as primary relationships.

Now on to our findings.

Simulation Findings

Table 1 contains bivariate findings which are relevant to testing our hypotheses on domestic conflict.

TABLE 1
Relationships Between Economic Conditions
and Domestic Conflict*

	Early Stage (N = 50)	Intermediate Stage (N = 130)	Late Stage (N = 147)	Composite PDS 1-5 (N = 342)**
RES-DI	+ 0.05	+ 0.19(a)	+ 0.07***	+ 0.14(b)
RED-DI	+ 0.28(a)	—0.06	+ 0.05***	—0.14***(b)

*The variables here are DI = Domestic Instability, RES = Relative Economic Status, and RED = Relative Economic Deprivation.

**The sum of the N's for the three intervals is less than the N for the composite data-set (342) because two runs of observations were removed from PDS 5 during the late stage to make its number of runs rqual to those of PDS 1, 2, 3, and 4 for that period.

***Nonlinear relationship — both the economic and conflict variables have been logarithmically transformed.

(a) Significant at the 0.05 level.

(b) Significant at the 0.01 level.

Given the results of bivariate analysis in Table 1, there are positive relationships between RES and DI across all three stages of development as well as for the composite data-set. While the relationship for the composite data-set may be viewed as supportive of either Mill or Marx, the relational trends across the three stages of development indicate that both are right, but for different stages. Given that the magnitude of the positive relationship between RES and DI increased between the early and intermediate stages, Marx is supported for earlier stages of development. And that the magnitude of the relationship decreased between the intermediate and late stages is supportive of Mill for later stages.

On the relationships between RED and DI, the negative relationship for the composite data-set may be viewed as more supportive of Mill than of Marx. On the relational trends, we have a reversal of what we had for the relationships between RES and DI. The transformation of the relationship between RED and DI from a positive to a negative one between the early and intermediate stages is supportive of Mill, whereas the transformation of the relationship from a negative to a positive one between the intermediate and late stages is supportive of Marx.

Hence, on the relationship between economic development and domestic conflict, Marx is supported for early stages of development and Mill is supported for later stages of development. And on the relationship between economics-related deprivation and domestic conflict, Mill is supported for early stages while Marx is supported for later stages of economic development.

If these particular findings are reflective of verisimilitude, not only are Marx and Mill right for the same economic factors at different stages, but they are right for different economic factors at the same stage.

It is interesting that, during the early stage, when RES was characterized by its minimum conflict-stimulating power, RED was characterized by its maximum conflict-stimulating power. Similarly, during the intermediate stage, when RES was characterized by its maximum conflict-stimulating power, RED was characterized by its minimum. That RED preceded RES in having its maximum conflict-stimulating impact suggests the proposition that economics-related deprivation will tend to stimulate domestic conflict before economic development does. Perhaps when economic development is in a primitive stage, economics-related deprivations will be acutely felt and lead to conflict, whereas when development in all spheres is a bit more advanced, factors other than economics-related deprivation, perhaps other kinds of deprivation, become operative as determinants of conflict.

One more point about the data in Table 1 is worth mentioning before we move on — in those cases where Marx has been supported, the relationships are very far from being deterministic.

Table 2 contains multivariate findings which are relevant to testing our hypotheses on domestic conflict.

TABLE 2
Models of Domestic Conflict*

Early Stage (N = 50)

$$DI^{**} = +0.32RED_{t-1} - 0.38SEC_t \qquad R = 0.47, R^2 = 0.22$$

t	+2.48	−2.93
signif.	0.02	0.01
partial r	+0.34	−0.39

Composite PDS 1-5 (N = 342)

$$DI^{**} = +0.16ACH_t + 0.10RED_{t-1} + 0.17MD_{t-1} - 0.31SEC_t \quad R = 0.44, R^2 = 0.19$$

t	+3.31	+2.09	+3.38	−6.14
signif.	0.001	0.05	0.001	0.001
partial r	+0.18	+0.11	+0.18	−0.32

*Only those models are presented here (as well as in Table 4) which contain either RES or RED (or both) as explanatory variables. On the variables contained in these models, DI = Domestic Instability, RED = Relative Economic Deprivation, SEC = Systemic Environmental Complexity (number of groups in the system), ACH = Need for Achievement, and MD = Manifest Distrust.

**DI was measured during the second half of current time plus the first half of future time.

Only one of our two economic factors, RED, appears in any of the DI models. And although RED appears in the composite model for DI, it appears in only one of our development models, that for the early stage. One interesting methodological observation we can make here is: to infer from the presence of RED in the composite model that RED must have also stimulated, to some extent, DI during the intermediate and late stages as well as during the early stage, is to commit what W. S. Robinson calls the 'ecological fallacy' — i.e., making inferences about disaggregated units from information on aggregated units.[51]

Although the presence of RED, as a contributory condition, in the early model for DI is compatible with our bivariate finding that RED had its greatest conflict-stimulating impact during the early stage, the nearly total absence of economic factors in the DI models suggests that, in the PDS, the relationships between economic development/economics-related deprivation and domestic conflict were largely chimerical. This, plus the fact that RED had a positive relationship with DI during the early stage, but a relationship which disappeared during the intermediate and late stages, tends to be supportive of Mill.

One more point — in harmony with the bivariate findings on DI, the multivariate findings suggest that economics-related deprivation may stimulate domestic conflict during early stages of economic development but, during later stages, factors other than economics-related deprivation will tend to stimulate domestic conflict.

Table 3 contains bivariate findings which are relevant to testing our hypotheses on foreign conflict.

The foreign-conflict hypotheses which we developed on Marx and Mill did not distinguish between offensive and defensive foreign conflict, but, instead, focussed on aggressive or what might be called offensive foreign conflict only. Our real-world assessment, however, suggested that we could also develop hypotheses from Marx and Mill on the relationships between economic factors and defensive foreign conflict. For instance, for Marx, across the stages of development, we could expect either positive relationships of decreasing magnitude or negative relationships of increasing magnitude between economic factors and defensive foreign conflict. And for Mill, we could expect either positive relationships of increasing magnitude or negative relationships of decreasing magnitude between economic factors and defensive foreign conflict. Given that our PDS conflict variables lend themselves to classification as offensive foreign-conflict variables (MD, BEL and

TABLE 3
Relationships Between Economic Conditions and Foreign Conflict*

(a) RES as Economic Conditions

	Early Stage (N = 50)	Intermediate Stage (N = 130)	Late Stage (N = 147)	Composite PDS 1-5 (N = 342)
RES-MD	—0.25	+0.25**(b)	+0.12	+0.05
RES-BEL	—0.18	+0.38(c)	+0.14	+0.11(a)
RES-ALL	+0.21**	—0.26(b)	+0.19**(a)	+0.17**(b)
RES-ATT	+0.29**(a)	+0.28(c)	—0.11	+0.16(b)

(b) RED as Economic Conditions

RED-MD	—0.04	+0.09**	—0.12	—0.08
RED-BEL	+0.18	—0.19(a)	—0.14	—0.11(a)
RED-ALL	+0.27**	+0.49(c)	—0.16(a)	+0.25**(c)
RED-ATT	+0.32**(a)	—0.19(a)	+0.05	—0.09

*The conflict variables here are MD = Manifest Distrust, BEL = Bellicosity, ALL = Alliances, and ATT = Aggressive Attacks. Our economic variables are RES = Relative Economic Status and RED = Relative Economic Deprivation.

**Nonlinear relationship — both the economic and conflict variables have been logarithmically transformed.

(a) Significant at the 0.05 level.

(b) Significant at the 0.01 level.

(c) Significant at the 0.001 level.

ATT) and as defensive foreign-conflict variables (ALL), we can assess, in terms of our simulation data in Table 3, Marx and Mill for defensive as well as offensive foreign conflict.

Accordingly, looking first at the relationships between economic development and offensive foreign conflict, the trends across economic stages indicate that, for the relationships between RES and MD and between RES and BEL, Marx is supported for early stages and Mill is supported for later stages of economic development. And for the relationships between RES and ATT, Mill is supported across all three stages. For the relationships between economic development and defensive foreign conflict (between RES and ALL), the trends indicate that Marx is supported for early stages while Mill is supported for later stages of economic development.

Looking next at the relationships between economics-related deprivation and offensive foreign conflict, the trends indicate that, for the relationships between RED and BEL and between RED and ATT, Mill is supported for early stages while Marx is supported for later stages of economic development. And for the relationships between RED and MD, Marx is supported for early stages and Mill is supported for later stages of economic development. For the relationships between economics-related deprivation and defensive foreign conflict (ALL), Mill is supported for early stages while Marx is supported for later stages of development.

On the assumption that later trends are more important than earlier trends in assessing theories, the relationships between economic development and offensive/defensive foreign conflict are more supportive of Mill whereas the relationships between economics-related deprivation and offensive/defensive foreign conflict are more supportive of Marx. (In no case supportive of Marx was the relationship deterministic.)

Table 4 contains multivariate findings which are relevant to testing our hypotheses on foreign conflict.

On the foreign-conflict models, the transformation of the relationship between RES and MD from a negative one during the early stage, in which RES was a contributory factor, to a positive one during the intermediate stage, in which RES was the primary factor, is supportive of Marx. And the absence of a relationship between RES and BEL during the early stage but the presence of a positive relationship between these two variables during the intermediate stage, in which RES was the primary factor, is also supportive of Marx.

The movement from positive relationships between RES and MD and between RES and BEL during the intermediate stage to no relationships between these variables during the late stage, plus the appearance of a negative relationship between RED and BEL during the late stage, is supportive of Mill.

As is obvious from the exclusion of certain models in Table 4, economic factors did not appear in the models for our defensive foreign-conflict variable, ALL. Nor did they appear in the models for our remaining offensive foreign-conflict variable, ATT. However, BEL, with which RES has a primary positive relationship

TABLE 4
Models of Foreign Conflict*

Early Stage (N = 50)

$$MD_t = -0.27RES_{t-1} - 0.48SEC_t \qquad\qquad R = 0.54, R^2 = 0.29$$

t	—2.17	—3.90
signif.	0.05	0.001
partial r	—0.30	—0.49

Intermediate Stage (N = 130)

$$MD_t = +0.22RES_{t-1} \qquad\qquad\qquad r = 0.22, r^2 = 0.05$$

t	+2.44
signif.	0.02

$$BEL_t = -0.21DOG_t - 0.27POLC_t - 0.23TO_t + 0.37RES_{t-} \qquad R_1 = 0.52,$$
$$R^2 = 0.27$$

t	—2.48	—3.22	—3.01	+4.68
signif.	0.02	0.01	0.01	0.001
partial r	—0.22	—0.28	—0.26	+0.39

Late Stage (N = 147)

$$BEL_t = -0.20SSEC_t + 0.12TO_t - 0.12RED_{t-1} + 0.65BEL_{t-} \qquad R_1 = 0.73,$$
$$R^2 = 0.53$$

t	—3.43	+2.07	—1.99	+11.09
signif.	0.001	0.05	0.05	0.001
partial r	—0.28	+0.17	—0.16	+0.68

*The conflict variables here are MD = Manifest Distrust and BEL = Bellicosity. The explanatory variables are RES = Relative Economic Status, SEC = Systemic Environmental Complexity (no. of groups in system), DOG = Dogmatism, POLC = Political Cynicism, TO = Temporal Overload, SSEC = Sub-Systemic Environmental Complexity (no. of decision-makers in a group), and RED = Relative Economic Deprivation.

during the intermediate stage, does appear, as a contributory factor, in the ATT model for that stage. (The ATT model is not shown here.) Hence, RES may be viewed as an *indirect* contributory condition of ATT during the intermediate stage.

In the PDS, therefore, the relationships between economic factors and defensive foreign conflict were chimerical, whereas the relationships between economic factors (particularly economic development) and offensive foreign conflict tended to be primary or (directly or indirectly) contributory ones. Moreover, relational trends on offensive foreign conflict indicate that Marx was supported for early stages while Mill was supported for later stages of economic development.

One further comment — although RES dominated the behaviour of MD and BEL during the intermediate stage, economic factors in general did not dominate in the remaining two models contained in Table 4 nor, obviously, did they dominate (or even appear at all) in the ALL and ATT models. The immediate implication here is that, in order to adequately account for (domestic as well as) foreign conflict, we have to go beyond economic factors. (We will come back to this in the conclusion to our paper).

Whereas the data in Tables 1-4 enabled us to assess hypotheses on the relationships between economic factors and domestic/foreign confict, the data in Table 5 are relevant to assessing our hypotheses on the amount of conflict occuring at each of the three stages of economic development.

TABLE 5
Average Group Domestic and Foreign Conflict*

| | Stages of Economic Development | | |
Conflict	Early	Intermediate	Late
DI	0.204	0.045	0.032
MD	0.072	0.030	0.014
BEL	0.198	0.171	0.223
ALL	0.600	1.540	1.690
ATT	1.160	2.090	0.800

*The conflict variables are DI = Domestic Instability, MD = Manifest Distrust, BEL = Bellicosity, ALL = Alliances, and ATT = Aggressive Attacks.

In terms of group averages, DI and MD decreased across the three successive stages, thereby providing support for Mill; BEL decreased between the early and intermediate stages, providing support for Mill, but increased between the intermediate and late stages, thereby providing support for Marx; ALL (the defensive foreign-conflict variable) increased across all three stages, providing support for Mill; and ATT increased between the early and intermediate stages, providing support for Marx, but decreased between the intermediate and late stages, providing support for Mill.

In general, therefore, our findings on the amount of domestic and foreign conflict per group across the three stages are far more supportive of Mill than they are of Marx.

In summary of the results of our simulation assessment of the hypotheses derived from Mill and Marx, the bivariate findings on the relationships between economic development (RES) and domestic conflict (DI), economic development and defensive foreign conflict (ALL), and economic development and offensive foreign conflict (MD, BEL, and ATT) suggest that Marx is right for early stages and that Mill is right for later stages of econmomic development. The bivariate findings on the relationships between economics-related deprivation (RED) and the conflict variables suggest the opposite — that Mill is right for early stages and that Marx is right for later stages. On the assumption that later trends are more important than earlier trends in assessing theories, it could be argued, as we implied earlier, that the relationships between economic development and conflict in general are more supportive of Mill whereas the relationships between economics-related deprivation and conflict in general are more supportive of Marx.

Some of the interesting aspects of the bivariate findings, e.g., when economic development was having its maximum conflict-stimulating impact, economics-related deprivation was having its minimum, never appeared in our multivariate findings. In this regard, each of the above domestic and foreign conflict models contained either RES or RED, but not both. Also, the neat split in the bivariate findings between support for Mill and support for Marx is not replicated in the multivariate findings. In this regard, the appearance of only one economic factor (RED) in only one of our domestic-conflict models (early stage) suggests that economic factors in general did not influence domestic conflict in the PDS, which is more supportive of Mill than Marx.

Although the trends in the relationships between economic development and MD/BEL between the early and intermediate stages are strongly supportive of Marx, the disappearance of these trends between the intermediate and late stages, coupled with the absence of economic factors in the ALL and especially the ATT models, tends also to be more supportive of Mill than Marx.

The above, coupled with the findings on the average amount of conflict per group in the PDS, suggests that, in terms of our simulation assessment, Mill and Marx are, under different circumstances, both right, but that Mill is more right than Marx.

THE REAL-WORLD AND SIMULATION ASSESSMENTS OF MARX AND MILL — COMPATIBLE OR INCOMPATIBLE RESULTS?

Given that the great majority of the studies which featured in our real-world assessment of the hypotheses were bivariate and about the relationships between economic development (rather than economics-related deprivation) and conflict, we will compare the general conclusion from that assessment with the results of the bivariate, economic-development part of our simulation assessment. In this regard, for both sets of findings, we have exactly the same observation — Marx is right for early stages and Mill is right for later stages of economic development.

The general finding of the multivariate part of our real-world assessment, i.e., that economic factors play little or no role in influencing domestic and foreign conflict, has also been replicated in our simulation assessment, particularly for domestic conflict, with the addition that the simulation multivariate findings, particularly for foreign conflict, have supported the general bivariate observation — that Marx is right for early stages while Mill is right for later stages of economic development. Once again, on the assumption that later trends are more important than earlier trends in theory-assessment, it seems that, in both the real-world and simulation assessments, Mill is more right than Marx. This is also the result of Graeme Duncan's effort to assess Mill and Marx empirically.[52] Our real-world and simulation assessments also suggest, however, that factors other than economic ones — or at least factors other than the economic ones which have featured in our assessments — tend to be the important sources of influence on domestic and foreign-conflict behaviour. In other words, to account adequately for the incidence of conflict in general, we have to go beyond economic factors.

CONCLUSION

This has been a study of the relationships between certain economic factors and domestic/foreign conflict. Given the relevance of the incompatible ideas of Mill and Marx to these relationships, we have attempted to assess these ideas against an empirical record compris-ed of real-world and simulation data. The results of our real-world and simulation assessments are strikingly similar — the ideas of Marx, though not his determinism, have been supported for early stages and the ideas of Mill have been supported for later stages of economic development. Moreover, Mill seems to be more right than Marx.

The similarity in the results of our real-world and simulation assessments is striking not only because of the methodological and epistemological differences between the real-world studies themselves, but also — and especially — because of the differences between them and our simulation study. In this regard, we seem to have succeeded in 'killing two birds with one stone' — we have strengthened our faith in the validity of the results of the real-world assessment and have demonstrated that simulation is a useful device for investigating complex conflict processes.

Again, this similarity between the results of the two assessments is not meant to imply that, for instance, our RES is the same as real-world levels of economic development or that our early stage of development is the same as some definition of the early stage of capitalism. What it does imply is that the PDS has been able to replicate aspects of the real world — to generate findings which correspond to comparable real-world findings.[53]

One aspect of the similarity between our two assessments was that factors other than economic ones seem to be the important determinants of conflict processes. In this regard, the aforementioned multivariate studies by Moore and by East and Hermann indicate that size and political accountability of nations were the most important sources of influence on foreign conflict behaviour.[54] The multivariate study by Wallace indicates that rate of change in armed forces levels was the most important source of influence on his war variable.[55] And on domestic conflict, the multivariate study by Gurr indicates that 'social and structural facilitation' of domestic conflict was the most important source of influence, and the study by Gurr and Duvall indicates that 'tension' (a multiplicative term comprised of strain, stress, and previous domestic conflict) was the most important source of influence.[56]

The simulation-generated models presented in this paper suggest that SEC, or the number of groups in the system, may be the most important source of influence on domestic- and some kind of foreign-conflict behaviour during an early stage; that economic development may be the most important source of influence on arming-related foreign-conflict behaviour during an intermediate stage; and that previous arming may be the most important source of influence on subsequent arming during a late stage of economic development.

This, coupled with the non-economic primary variables in the PDS models which are not shown here,[57] suggests that a comprehensive theory (or theories) of domestic and foreign conflict must certainly include economic factors, particularly for relational trends between early and intermediate stages of development, but it must also go beyond economic factors. In terms of accounting for increases in the incidence of aggressive or offensive conflict, this means that such a theory must go beyond Marx.

In saying this, we are aware that we may have looked at the wrong economic variables in this study or, if we looked at the right ones, we (and the researchers whose works we consulted) may have operationalized them incorrectly and treated their temporal relationships with the conflict variables incorrectly. Or we may have attempted to measure the unmeasurable because the economic determinants of structures and processes may be so deeply embedded in society that no measure of surface phenomena (e.g., GNP) can root them out. As Bertell Ollman points out, 'By treating these entities [i.e., capital, value, money, profit, etc.] as things rather than relations, followers as well as critics have cut themselves off from what Marx is saying.'[58] Doubts such as these can only be resolved through further research.

Although, in general, the real-world and simulation relationships which we have looked at make more sense in terms of Mill than Marx, the explanations which can be inferred from Mill, or which are implicit in the writings of contemporary consensus theorists, may not adequately account for those relationships. Hence, in terms of accounting for decreases in the incidence of aggressive or offensive conflict (and for concomitant increases in defensive conflict), a comprehensive theory might even have to go beyond Mill.[59]

On the directions for further research into the determinants in general of conflict, and on the relationships between economic factors and conflict in particular, our study reinforces a recommendation made in another context by Robert Burrowes and Bertram Spector:

> If relationships exist between [certain variables], they probably do so for certain types of nations, at certain times, and under certain circumstances. Further inquiry in this area will require that these and other conditions be identified and built into our theoretical frameworks and research designs.[60]

The larger project which subsumes the work reported here will continue to move in these and other directions.

NOTES

Thanks and gratitude are acknowledged to Fay Trager-Green and Ingrid Sandole-Staroste for typing this manuscript.

1. The definitions of conflict, MCP, and AMCP presented here derive from our attempts to synthesize definitions from a wide variety of works — too numerous, in fact, to justify being catalogued here. One point, however, should be made — namely, that this extensive literature lacks consensus on the meaning either of conflict or aggression.

2. On 'fights', as well as 'games' and 'debates', see Anatol Rapoport's appropriately titled *Fights, Games and Debates* (Ann Arbor: University of Michigan Press, 1960).

3. Other reports on this project are: D. J. D. Sandole, 'Mapping and Modelling of Complex Conflict Processes', presented to the Workshop on Formal Political Analysis during the Joint Sessions of Workshops, European Consortium for Political Research (ECPR), Grenoble, France, 6-12 April 1978; D. J. D. Sandole, 'A Mega-Concatenated Theory of Complex Conflict Processes', presented at the 15th European Conference of the Peace Science Society (International), Geneva, Switzerland, 3-5 September 1978; and D. J. D. Sandole, 'The Genesis of War: Mapping and Modelling of Complex Conflict Processes', Doctoral dissertation, University of Strathclyde, Glasgow, Scotland, 1979.

4. James E. Dougherty and Robert L. Pfaltzgraff, Jr., *Contending Theories of International Relations* (Philadelphia: Lippincott, 1971), 172.

5. See Karl R. Popper, *Objective Knowledge: An Evolutionary Approach* (London: Oxford University Press, 1972), 52-60.

6. Thomas S. Kuhn, *The Structure of Scientific Revolutions*, 2nd Edition (Chicago: University of Chicago Press, 1970), 147.

7. Michael P. Sullivan, *International Relations: Theories and Evidence* (Englewood Cliffs: Prentice-Hall, 1976), 9. Some of the reasons for the tendency of scholars to avoid making comparative assessments of competing theories may be found in Kuhn, op. cit., Chapter XII, and elsewhere in his volume.

8. Graeme Duncan, *Marx and Mill: Two Views of Social Conflict and Social Harmony* (London: Cambridge University Press, 1973).

9. See John Stuart Mill, *Principles of Political Economy*, Books Three and Four, edited by John M. Robson and V. W. Bladen (Toronto: University of Toronto Press, 1965).

10. See Karl Marx and Frederick Engels, *Manifesto of the Communist Party* (Moscow: Foreign Languages Publishing House, 1960) and Karl Marx, *Capital*, Vol. I (Moscow: Foreign Languages Publishing House, 1958). Although Marx saw that capitalism would lead to economic imperialism and that the latter would lead to war between capitalist states, he did not develop these ideas. Lenin responded to this gap in Marxist theory with his *Imperialism: The Highest Stage of Capitalism* (Moscow: Foreign Languages Publishing House, 1950).

11. Kenneth E. Boulding, *Conflict and Defense: A General Theory* (New York: Harper and Row, 1962), 190.

12. Marx's economic determinism is subject to more than one interpretation, even among Marxists themselves. See William Leon McBride, *The Philosophy of Marx* (London: Hutchinson, 1977), 15, 19, 113.

13. See Ted Robert Gurr, *Why Men Rebel* (Princeton: Princeton University Press, 1970).

14. See Johan Galtung, 'A Structural Theory of Aggression', *Journal of Peace Research*, Vol. I (1964), 95-119.

15. See John Dollard, et al., *Frustration and Aggression* (New Haven: Yale University Press, 1939).

16. For a survey and, within the context of our comparative assessment of Marx and Mill, a relevant critique of consensus/social pluralism theories, see Irving Louis Horowitz, 'Consensus, Conflict, and Cooperation: A Sociological Inventory', *Social Forces*, Vol. 41 (1962), 177-188.

17. See Mordecai Ezekiel and Karl A. Fox, *Methods of Correlation and Regression Analysis*, 3rd Edition (New York: Wiley, 1959), 195.

18. See Ted Robert Gurr, 'A Causal Model of Civil Strife: A Comparative Analysis Using New Indices', *American Political Science Review*, Vol. LXII (1968) and reprinted in J. V. Gillespie and B. A. Nesvold (eds.), *Macro-quantitative Analysis* (Beverly Hills & London: Sage, 1971), 234 and 236.

19. See Ivo K. Feierabend and Rosalind L. Feierabend, 'Aggressive Behaviors Within Polities, 1948-1962: A Cross-National Study', *Journal of Conflict Resolution*, Vol. 10 (1966) and reprinted in E. I. Megargee and J. E. Hokanson (eds.), *The Dynamics of Aggression* (New York: Harper and Row, 1970), 225.

20. See Ted Robert Gurr and Raymond Duvall, 'Civil Conflict in the 1960s: A Reciprocal Theoretical System with Parameter Estimates', *Comparative Political Studies*, Vol. 6 (1973), 157.

21. See Jack Vincent, et al., 'Empirical Tests of Attribute, Social Field, and Status Field Theories on International Relations Data', *International Studies Quarterly*, Vol. 17 (1973); cited in Sullivan, op. cit., 112.

22. See Michael Skrein, 'The Commonwealth: An Application of Event/Interaction Data', Support Study 2, mimeographed. University of Southern California, Los Angeles, 1969; cited in Sullivan, op. cit., 112-113.

23. See David W. Moore, 'National Attributes and Nation Typologies', in James N. Rosenau (ed.), *Comparing Foreign Policies* (New York: Wiley, 1974), 257, 262-263. See also Moore's 'Governmental and Societal Influences on Foreign Policy in Open and Closed Nations' in the same volume, 184-185.

24. See Steven A. Salmore and Charles F. Hermann, 'The Effect of Size, Development and Accountability on Foreign Policy', *Peace Research Society (International): Papers*, Vol. 14 (1970); cited in Sullivan, op. cit., 113.

25. See Ivo K. Feierabend and Rosalind L. Feierabend, 'Level of Development and Internation Behavior', in R. Butwell (ed.), *Foreign Policy and The Developing Nation* (Lexington: University of Kentucky Press, 1969); cited in P. J. McGowan and H. B. Shapiro, *The Comparative Study of Foreign Policy: A Survey of Scientific Findings* (Beverly Hills and London: Sage, 1973), 109.

26. See Maurice A. East and Charles F. Hermann, 'Do Nation-Types Account for Foreign Policy Behavior?', in Rosenau, op. cit., 296-297.

27. See Rudolph J. Rummel, 'The Relationship Between National Attributes and Foreign Conflict Behavior', in J. David Singer (ed.), *Quantitative International Politics* (New York: Free Press, 1968), 189.

28. See Michael Haas, 'Societal Approaches to the Study of War', *Journal of Peace Research*, Vol. 2 (1965); cited in Sullivan, op. cit., 113.

29. Rummel, op. cit., 189.

30. See Michael Wallace, 'Status, Formal Organization, and Arms Levels as Factors leading to the Onset of War, 1820-1964', in Bruce M. Russett (ed.), *Peace, War, and Numbers* (Beverly Hills and London: Sage, 1972), 60-61.

31. Ibid., 62-66.

32. See Quincy Wright, *A Study of War*, Abridged Edition (Chicago: University of Chicago Press, 1964), 165. Also see 303.

33. Ibid., 302 and 305.

34. See Abraham Kaplan, *The Conduct of Inquiry* (Scranton: Chandler, 1964), 150-151.

35. TEMPER is an acronym derived from Technological, Economic, Military, and Political Evaluation Routine and SIPER derives from Simulated International Processer. On these and the operations mentioned in notes 36-37, see Stuart A. Bremer, *Simulated Worlds: A Computer Model of National Decision-Making* (Princeton: Princeton University Press, 1977); Harold Guetzkow, et al., *Simulation in International Relations* (Englewood Cliffs: Prentice-Hall, 1963); Guetzkow, 'Simulations in International Relations', in W. D. Coplin (ed.), *Simulation in the Study of Politics* (Chicago: Markham, 1968); and Guetzkow, 'Substantive Developments from the Simulation of International Processes', delivered at the 10th World Congress of the International Political Science Association (IPSA), Edinburgh, Scotland, 16-21 August 1976.

36. PME stands for Political-Military Exercise (and PE for Political Exercise).

37. INS stands for Inter-Nation Simulation; IPS for International Processes Simulation; and WPS for World Politics Simulation.

38. Powell has discussed his use of the PDS in 'Simulation: The Anatomy of a Fad', *Acta Politica* (April 1969), 299-330.

39. See Anatol Rapoport, op. cit., 173-174.

40. See Kenneth W. Terhune, 'The Effects of Personality in Cooperation and Conflict', in Paul Swingle (ed.), *The Structure of Conflict* (New York and London: Academic Press, 1970), 222.

41. Other than an initial distinction between Decision-Maker and Validator, which disappears after a few runs, the PDS imposes no differentiated roles upon the players. Hence, whatever authority structures are manifested, either within or between groups, are generated by the players themselves.

42. See Harold Guetzkow, 'Some Correspondences Between Simulations and "Realities" in International Relations', in Morton Kaplan (ed.), *New Approaches to International Relations* (New York: St Martin's Press, 1968).

43. On the assumption that decision-makers tend to be high in need for power and/or achievement, players who scored relatively high on items suggestive of these needs were assigned the role of Decision-Maker and those who achieved relatively low scores were assigned the role of Validator. See Powell, op. cit., 321.

44. An average GNP was computed for each group by summing its GNP levels for all decision periods during a two-hour run, and then dividing that sum by the number of decision periods.

45. DI, as one of our conflict or dependent variables, was measured across temporal units because, in the larger project which subsumes this study, DI as a lagged explanatory variable was also measured across temporal units — for the second half of $t-1$ and the first half of t. In this regard, see Sandole, Grenoble, op. cit., 31 or Sandole, Geneva, op. cit., 53.

46. Runs 12 and beyond for the five PDS operations were not included in the analysis because most of these were subjected to experimental intervention and manipulation by students employing various research designs.

47. These variables are spelled out in Sandole, 1979, op. cit., Chapter 2.

48. This is not to suggest that, across stages of the stepwise procedure, explanatory or independent variables retain their original status as most potent, se-

cond most potent, etc. At each stage, the stepwise procedure examines each prior entry as if it were the most recent and each recent entry as if it came in earlier. In addition to some variables changing position within the potency line-up, others may drop out. See Norman Draper and Harry Smith, *Applied Regression Analysis* (New York: Wiley, 1966), 171-172.

49. According to Hubert Blalock, 'Significance tests tell us how likely a given set of results would be if certain assumptions were true.' [Blalock, *Social Statistics* (New York: McGraw-Hill, 1960), 125]. One of these assumptions is that the data to which significance tests have been applied comprise a random sample — i.e., that the selection of any one case for inclusion in the sample had no bearing on the selection of any other case. Clearly, since our data are longitudinal or time-series data, i.e., variables on the same cases have been measured at different points in time, this assumption has not been met. Indeed, our data are not even about samples at all, whether randomly or otherwise drawn, but about universes.

So, why employ significance tests if the assumptions underlying their use have not been fulfilled? Quite simply, as Fred Greenstein and Sidney Tarrow put it, 'as a rule of thumb for deciding which variations are worth discussing.' [Greenstein and Tarrow, 'The Study of French Political Socialization', *World Politics*, Vol. XXII (1969), 102.]

(Incidentally, the assumptions underlying the use of significance tests tend to be the same as those underlying the use of product-moment and partial correlational analysis as well as regression analysis — all of which we have used for this paper. Chapter 7 of Sandole, 1979, op. cit., contains a discussion of some of the problems we may have created — e.g., heteroscedasticity and autocorrelation — by the violation of some of these assumptions.)

In addition to the t-tests, which apply to the regression coefficients, we have also computed F-tests, which apply to the product-moment correlations in our study. If we were testing one set of hypotheses, either those derived from Marx or those from Mill, we could employ one-tailed versions of the t- and F-tests. Since, however, we are assessing two sets of hypotheses with essentially contrary predictions on the direction of relationship, particularly across stages of economic development, we have decided to use two-tailed versions of these tests.

50. See Blalock, op. cit., 345.

51. See William S. Robinson, 'Ecological Correlations and the Behavior of Individuals', *American Sociological Review*, Vol. 15 (1950), 351-357.

52. See Duncan, op. cit., 300-315.

53. We have conducted a number of validation assessments of the bivariate and multivariate findings generated by the PDS. In general, we have obtained a 75 per cent agreement between the PDS and comparable real-world and other findings. See Chapters 4 and 7 of Sandole, 1979, op. cit.

54. See Moore, op. cit., 257 and East and Hermann, op. cit., 296-297.

55. See Wallace, op. cit., 62-66.

56. See Gurr in Gillespie and Nesvold, op. cit., 236 and Gurr and Duvall, op. cit., 157.

57. On the models of DI, MD, BEL, ALL and ATT not presented in this paper see Sandole, 1979, op. cit., Chapters 5-6.

58. See Bertell Ollman, *Alienation: Marx's Conception of Man in Capitalist Society* (London: Cambridge University Press, 1971), 168.

59. In this regard, see Duncan, op. cit., 306-311.

60. See Robert Burrowes and Bertram Spector, 'The Strength and Direction of Relationships Between Domestic and External Conflict and Cooperation: Syria, 1961-67', in Jonathan Wilkenfeld (ed.), *Conflict Behavior and Linkage Politics* (New York: McKay, 1973), 317.

Notes on Contributors

James Alt is Associate Professor of Politics, Washington State University and was formerly a Lecturer in Government, University of Essex, and the Director of the Essex Summer School in Social Science Data Analysis. He is the author of *The Politics of Economic Decline* (Cambridge University Press, 1979) and numerous articles in leading journals.

John Burton was until recently a Principal Lecturer in Economics at Kingston Polytechnic. He is now a lecturer in the Department of Industrial Economics and Business Studies, University of Birmingham, UK. He has acted as consultant to the OECD and currently to the Institute of Economic Affairs. His publications include *Wage Inflation* (Macmillan, 1972) and articles in such journals as the *British Journal of Industrial Relations*, *Applied Economics*, *Research in Labor Economics*, and the *Scottish Journal of Political Economy*.

Bruno S. Frey is Professor of Economics, University of Zurich. Previously he has been Professor at the University of Konstanz and the University of Basel. He is the author of *Modern Political Economy* (Robertson, 1978) and is the editor of *Kyklos* (International Social Science Review).

Takashi Inoguchi is Associate Professor of Political Science at the University of Tokyo. He has published 'Negotiation as Quasi-Budgeting in *International Organization* (Spring 1979) and 'The Politics of Decrementalism', in *Behavioral Science* (November 1978).

Gareth Locksley is Senior Lecturer in Quantitative Methods and Economics, Polytechnic of Central London. He has contributed articles to such journals as *Political Quarterly* and *Cambridge Journal of Economics*.

Henrik Madsen is Assistant Professor, acting, University of Aarhus and since September 1978 has been a graduate student in the Department of Government, Harvard University. He has published several articles on political economy, as well as *Poetics*, a collection of political economic data covering 1920-1975.

Hannu Nurmi is Assistant Professor of Methodology of the Social Sciences at the University of Turku. He is the author of *Causality and Complexity* and *Rationality and Public Goods* as well as papers in the field of cybernetics, model building and game theory applications.

Jean-Jacques Rosa is Professor of Economics at the Institut d'Etudes Politiques, Paris. He is co-editor of the *Journal of Banking and Finance* and chairman of the Fondation pour la Nouvelle Economie Politique.

Dennis Sandole is Assistant Professor at the University of Southern California, United Kingdom Graduate Program in International Relations. He has previously taught at University College, London and obtained his PhD from the Department of Politics, University of Strathclyde, Glasgow.

Hans Schadee is a Lecturer in Politics at the University of Liverpool, UK.

Friedrich Schneider is a Lecturer at the University of Zurich, Switzerland.

Norman Schofield is Reader in Economics at the University of Essex and was formerly Associate Professor in the Department of Government, University of Texas at Austin. His research interests centre on formal political and economic theory and international political economy, and he has published articles in such journals as *Journal of Economic Theory*, *Review of Economic Studies*, *Public Choice*, and *Political Studies*.

Richard Wagner is Professor of Economics, Auburn University, USA. He was until very recently in the Department of Economics, Virginia Polytechnic Institute and State University, Blacksburg, USA. His recent publications include *The Consequences of Mr Keynes* (with James M. Buchanan and John Burton), 1978, and *The Tax Expenditure Budget: An Exercise in Fiscal Impressionism*, 1979, in addition to numerous articles in such journals as *Public Choice*, *Journal of Law and Economics*, *Kyklos*, and *Journal of Monetary Economics*. He has also edited *Perspectives on Tax Reform* (1974), *Fiscal Responsibility in Constitutional Democracy* (with James M. Buchanan, 1978), *Policy Analysis and Deductive Reasoning* (with Gordon Tullock, 1978), and *Government Aid to Private Schools: Is It a Trojan Horse?* (1979).

Paul Whiteley is a Lecturer in Politics at the University of Bristol. His research interests are in electoral behaviour, political methodology and statistics and political economy. His publications include articles in the *British Journal of Political Science, Political Studies,* and *Policy and Politics.* He is co-author of *Pressure for the Poor* (Routledge & Kegan Paul 1980).

Menno Wolters graduated in political science in 1972 at Leiden University and has since held research positions at the Universities of Iowa City, Leiden and, currently, at Utrecht. His research is concerned with Dutch local coalition building and Dutch roll-call voting. His forthcoming publication is entitled *Interspace Politics.*

DATE DUE

GAYLORD			PRINTED IN U.S.A.